# Alexander Alekhine

## Fourth World Chess Champion

by

Isaak and Vladimir Linder

Foreword by Andy Soltis

Game Annotations by Karsten Müller

*The World Chess Champion Series*

2016
Russell Enterprises, Inc.
Milford, CT USA

Alexander Alekhine
Fourth World Chess Champion

by Isaak and Vladimir Linder

© Copyright 2016

Isaak Linder and Vladimir Linder
Russell Enterprises, Inc.

ISBN: 978-1-936490-72-1

Published by:
Russell Enterprises, Inc.
PO Box 3131
Milford, CT 06460 USA

http://www.russell-enterprises.com
info@russell-enterprises.com

Translated from Russian by Oleg Zilbert
Editing and proofreading by Nick J. Luker
Cover design by Janel Lowrance

Printed in the United States of America

# Table of Contents

# Foreword

"War hero" isn't a phrase you expect to use in describing a chess grandmaster. Neither is "crime scene investigator."

Or "firing squad candidate." Or "scoundrel."

But all of these could be applied to that most complex of world champions, Alexander Alekhine.

So much has been written about the fourth world champion – and so much of it is fanciful, if not wrong. There have been various accounts of how Alekhine got out of German internment at the start of World War I, of whether he faced a firing squad during the Russian Revolution, and how he eventually fled his homeland, never to return. Reuben Fine, for example, said it was Alekhine's fluency in foreign languages that allowed him "to attach himself to a delegation sent abroad." Actually, he got out after marrying his second wife, a Swiss journalist who was 13 years older than he, and left her and their son not long after they settled in Paris.

This book clears up some of the mysteries of Alekhine and provides some wonderful details. To name a few:

- He had to give up chess for three youthful years because of encephalitis.
- As a boy he was nicknamed "the quiet one."
- He was a Red Cross volunteer during the Great War. He was twice wounded and, indeed, was a hero, who received battlefield medals and awards.
- He tried to become a Russian movie actor.
- When that failed he served as a criminal investigator whose job it was to study the scene of a crime and analyze it.
- He was absent-minded and superstitious, being particularly fond of the number 13.
- He nearly killed himself by falling asleep while smoking in bed.
- Six of his teeth had to be removed during the 1927 world championship match.
- He met the popular author S. S. Van Dine in New York and planned to accept the role of playing a chess master in a movie based on one of Van Dine's detective stories.
- He was 46 when he joined the French army, as an interpreter, at the start of World War II, and he was over 50 when he survived scarlet fever.
- He composed his first problem without sight of the board.
- He attended Carlsbad 1929 to report on it for the *New York Times*.
- And there's a planet named for him.

There are so many intriguing aspects to Alekhine's life that it's easy to forget how much he dominated the chess world. His career scores against the older generation is impressive: Six wins, seven draws, no losses against Frank Marshall; seven wins, five draws, no losses with Géza Maróczy; Siegbert Tarrasch and Akiba Rubinstein did only slightly better against him.

But against contemporaries Alekhine was also deadly – nine wins, three losses and nine draws with Aron Nimzovich. Salo Flohr managed five losses and seven draws in their games. And Paul Keres – who was reaching his peak while Alekhine was well past his when they played – lost five times and won once out of 14 games.

The Linders capture quite well the drama of Alekhine's world championship matches with José Capablanca and Max Euwe. Even the blowouts against Efim Bogoljubow are well described. Alekhine was the most peripatetic of champions, and this book details many of his travels on simul tours.

As usual with the Linders' books, we get a welcome series of mini-biographies of the champion's contemporaries. In this case, they are Euwe, Capablanca, and Bogoljubow, as well as Fine, Nimzovich, Ossip Bernstein, Flohr, Beniamin Blumenfeld, Evgeny Znosko-Borovsky, Boris Verlinsky, Nikolai Grigoriev, Stepan Levitzky, and the unfortunate Alexander Evenson, among others. This book is more enjoyable than the original from which it was excerpted because of the addition of the excellent game annotations.

The authors refrain from value judgments. A lot could be said about Alekhine's double-dealing with his world championship match challengers, his shameful treatment of Capablanca, and his participation in tournaments in Nazi-occupied Europe. The Linders stick to the facts. There are certainly enough amazing ones about Alexander Alexandrovich Alekhine to go around.

Andy Soltis
New York
January 2013

## Signs and Symbols

| | | | |
|---|---|---|---|
| 1-0 | White wins | !? | a move worth consideration |
| 0-1 | Black wins | = | an equal position |
| ½-½ | Draw agreed | ± | White stands slightly better |
| + | check | ± | White has a clear advantage |
| # | mate | +− | White has a winning position |
| ! | a strong move | ∓ | Black stands slightly better |
| !! | a brilliant/unobvious move | ∓ | Black has a clear advantage |
| ? | a weak move, an error | −+ | Black has a winning position |
| ?? | a grave error | (D) | see the next diagram |

## Publisher's Note

This book originally appeared in Russian, part of the massive historical tome published in 2001, *Korolyi Shakhmatnovo Mira* (*Kings of the Chess World*). By the time we had the pleasure of meeting with Isaak Linder and his son Vladimir in Moscow in March 2008, the original single-volume work of almost one thousand triple-column, small-font, large-format pages had been split into individual books, one for each world champion. We quickly reached an agreement with the Linders to bring out these books in what would become in English *The World Chess Champion Series*.

The first in the series was about José Raúl Capablanca, the great Cuban world champion; the book on Lasker was the second in the series.

With the permission and encouragement of the authors, we made some changes to the original Russian edition. The original contained a fine selection of Alekhine's games. We brought in German grandmaster Karsten Müller to provide refreshing new notes to these classic games. Finally, we created indexes of the players, games and openings, and included more complete information in the headers of each game and game fragment.

There is a tendency for modern-day chessplayers either to ignore or fail to appreciate the great masters of the past. We hope this series helps to change that.

# A Word about the Authors

The creative union of the Linders, father and son, came about in the late 1980s, when together they created a trilogy about three world champions, Capablanca, Lasker, and Alekhine (in that order) as part of the *Geniuses of Chess* series by the Sportverlag publishing house of Berlin (1988-1992). Since that time, their "trophy wall" has grown to include a number of other co-authored projects. There is the unusual documentary/artistic book, *The Two Lives of Grandmaster Alatortsev* (1994), and also the creation of a popular chess encyclopedia, printed both in Germany (1996) and in Russia (2003), as well as the fundamental work *Korolyi Shakhmatnovo Mira* [*Kings of the Chess World*], published by Bolshaya Rossyiskaya Entsiklopedia and Terra-Sport (2001).

I can boldly state that the formation of this union took place right before my eyes, for I have known the senior Linder, Isaak Maksovich, for nearly 70 years! We began playing together in the Young Pioneers' Stadium in the mid-30s. I met Volodya when we prepared the *Chess* encyclopedia for the BCE, which would be 20 years ago.

At the authors' request, I have edited a few of their recent voluminous works, and I must admit to being bowled over by the breadth of their conceptions! Very few people would be capable of taking such large swaths of chess history and recasting them into such an unusual literary form. How have they been able to put their ideas into concrete form?! Above all, because they have a system for dividing up the work. The elder takes charge of the historical approach, and the analytical duties; the son handles the literary decorations and the statistical basis of their works. As a reader, I can say that the results are a delectation for chess gourmets.

Shortcomings? Well, you know the old saying: The only man who never makes mistakes is the man who never does anything. This new series of books by Isaak and Vladimir, *The World Chess Champion Series*, is a reworked, corrected and filled-out edition of *Kings of the Chess World*, broken up into 14 separate volumes, from Steinitz to Kramnik. It is a panoramic, epic-length mural of the chess struggle on the topmost level from the end of the 19th through the beginning of the 21st centuries.

> Yuri Averbakh
> Moscow
> April 2010

## Prologue

Among the greatest players of all time, Alexander Alekhine stands out because of the magnitude of his creative heritage and the aesthetic attractiveness of his games. From 1908 to his last years, he participated in 94 tournaments, winning 64 and finishing second in 12. He played 26 matches, including five world championship matches, and was the only champion in chess history who died while still wearing the crown.

He influenced the chess life of dozens of countries and peoples owing to his brilliant performances in tournaments, matches, exhibition tours, as well as his literary works. Thinking about the most important tendencies in his creative work, we have come to the conclusion that the greatness of his chess lies primarily not in his combinative talent, as is universally contended, but in deeply penetrating the strategic secrets of a position's struggle, resulting in the apotheosis of Alekhine's combinations that the world admires.

Admittedly, Alexander Alekhine developed as a chessplayer in the best traditions of the Russian Chess School, assimilating many of his predecessor's, Mikhail Chigorin, sound principles. But, the phenomenon of Alekhine lies in the fact that he also naturally imbibed everything that was new (and sometimes truly revolutionary) in the contemporary chess milieu. Specifically, he was tremendously influenced by Emanuel Lasker. Alekhine, seven years after becoming world champion, admitted that "[w]ithout him, I could never have become what I have become." Only with this approach to the study of his creative heritage can one understand how he succeeded in synthesizing the scientific and artistic treatments of the game, thus raising his style to an universal one, and in systemically preparing for competitions, which enabled him to defeat the other incomparable geniuses and triumphantly ascend chess Olympus. The epic struggle of his match with Capablanca and the sudden reversals of situations in their "correspondence match" that lasted many years, as well as the story of his two duels with Bogoljubow and the other two with Euwe, constitute full-blooded, drama-saturated pages of the struggle for the world championship. Without their knowledge and objective coverage, one cannot understand the regularities governing the more than one-hundred-year long history of rivalry at the top nor its modern stage of development.

Alekhine's activities directed toward raising the ancient game to the level of high art, his rivalry with the other outstanding masters of the game in the struggle for the world championship proceeded under the conditions of a highly complex (and acute in its collisions) societal process. The two world wars, the October Revolution, and the other political repercussions were a heavy trial for Alekhine – with his unusually complicated and contradictory personality.

Endowed with enormous will power and strength of character, Alekhine was able, under these exceptionally difficult conditions, to achieve ever new sporting successes, including the highest of them, winning the title of world chess champion. Today, there are also a number of issues in the theory and practice of chess art, which, in solving, we check against Alekhine for the truth of chess positions and views. Chessplayers are attracted by his credo expressed in his aphoristic saying: "For me, chess is not a game, but an art. Yes, I regard chess as an art and accept all obligations which it imposes on its followers." His predecessors, Lasker and Capablanca, made statements in the same spirit. Subsequently, his great successors have repeatedly stressed their commitment to chess as an art.

There are several lines of research in chess in which the authoritative views and practice of the first four world champions are very helpful, namely, correspondence play, blindfold play, and issues of work in chess literature. Alekhine was an outstanding chess writer, analyst, and annotator. His books of his best games of 1908-1923 and 1924-1937, as well as the international tournaments in New York (1924 and 1927) and Nottingham (1936) "should be closely studied by everyone who is seriously interested in chess art" (Mikhail Botvinnik).

The most important thing in the creative heritage of a great master is his games. The depth of strategy and the brilliance of combinative ideas represent the eternal value of the chess genius Alexander Alekhine.

Isaak Linder
Vladimir Linder
Moscow 2012

## Chapter 1: Life and Destiny

**Childhood and Adolescence**

Alexander Alexandrovich Alekhine was born on October 31, 1892 in Moscow, a city that, at the turn of the century, had become one of the centers of Russian and international chess life. Here, the return match Lasker-Steinitz was held. Here, the tours of the famous chess masters Harry Pillsbury, Jacques Mieses, Georg Marco, and Oldrich Duras took place. In Moscow, the first (1899) and second (1900-1901) All-Russia tournaments were held, which were won by Mikhail Chigorin – the first Russian player to contend for the world championship.

It was in this "chess climate" that the young Alekhine was initiated into this wise game. He was strongly impressed, for example, by the performance of American master Harry Nelson Pillsbury, who, during his Moscow tour, played a simultaneous blindfold exhibition against twenty-two opponents. "I perceived Pillsbury's exhibition as a wonder," recalled Alekhine in later years. This is especially interesting to note because three years prior José Raúl Capablanca had been equally astounded by the abilities of the American master. So, Pillsbury's influence on the development of these two future world champions proved to be surprisingly similar.

At that time Alekhine also attended other events organized by the Moscow Circle (the chess club on Bolshaya Dmitrovka Street). Among the common and noble intelligentsia, there were enthusiasts who arranged chess evenings at their homes. The house of the high-ranking official and hereditary nobleman Alexander Ivanovich Alekhine (1856-1917) located on Nikolsky Lane, near the Arbat, had become such a salon where Moscow chessplayers would gather. He had three children: the eldest son, Alexei (1888-1939), a daughter, Varvara (1889-1944), and the younger son, Alexander.

They all were captivated by chess. Their parents were their first teachers and supported their interest in chess by all possible means. True, they used to spend much time living abroad, which only very well-off people could then afford. Alekhine's father had graduated from the Department of History and Philosophy of Moscow University. In 1904, he was elected a Marshall of Nobility of the Voronezh Governorship and later became a member of State Duma (Russian Parliament). He was also a landowner in the Zemlyansky district. Alekhine's mother, Anisia Ivanovna Prokhorova (1861-1915), came from the family of a textile manufacturer, who owned the Trekhgornaya (Three Mountains) manufacturing firm, which was well known in Moscow and throughout Russia.

In the late 1980s, new evidence emerged about Alekhine's parents and earlier ancestors. The historian Igor Lazebnik, who examined these documents, came to the conclusion that "good memory, aptitude for abstract thinking, observation, initiative, inherent in Alekhine, were also noted in his ancestors." In 1901, Alexander was sent to one of the best private gymnasia of Moscow – Polivanov's, where, in a

*Alekhine's parents Alexander Ivanovich and Anisia Ivanovna.*

mansion on Prechistenka Street, the children of the writers Leo Tolstoy and Alexander Ostrovsky (a famous playwright) studied, as well as Valery Bryusov and Andrei Belyi, who, in later years, became famous Russia poets.

The Polivanov gymnasium became popular because of its methods of instruction, which were far from formal drill. These methods cultivated the ability of the students to think independently and fostered their interest in history and poetry. Alexander was a good student; however, he took greater interest in the humanities, though, even then, he preferred chess to all other disciplines. Having started to play chess

*The Alekhines – Prokhorovs*
*On the right – mother Anisia Ivanovna Alekhine (Prokhorova); in the center –the grandmother Anna Alexandrovna Prokhorova with the grandchildren: Alexander (embracing her), Alexei, and Varvara.*

at the age of seven, he soon felt its ir-resistible attraction. And, only a seri-ous illness (encephalitis) could result in a three-year break in his chess stud-ies. When the doctor's ban was re-moved, he started playing in correspon-dence tournaments organized by the Moscow magazine *Shakhmatnoe obozrenye*.

Alexander's brother and sister were not the only ones among his first teachers and opponents. Their home was visited by strong Moscow chessplayers who subsequently became chess masters – Fyodor Duz-Khotimirsky, Vladimir Nenarokov, and Beniamin Blumenfeld.

They also performed the function of chess teachers. As Duz-Khotimirsky recalled, the Alekhines even paid him for chess lessons. Nevertheless, Alexander realized early that the best method of improving one's game was to do original work. So, he tirelessly analyzed games of outstanding players, which became embedded in his uncom-mon memory for his entire life. And, of course, he carefully analyzed his own games.

If anyone happened to drop by his room, that person would notice how the youth's eyes were burning while he was absorbed in the officiating of chess pieces on the board. His own people nicknamed him "Tisha" (the quiet one) or "Tishaishyi" (the very quiet one), and Alexander got used to it. Accordingly, in his chess correspondence he soon started signing his name as "T. Alekhine."

From 1902 to 1904, Alexander partici-pated in correspondence battles against

*Alexander Alekhine, a scholar of the Polivanov Gymnasium in Moscow*

his elder brother, Alexei, playing for the most part unsuccessfully. But his apti-tude for analysis and persistent study of chess theory were bearing fruit. In a brief biographical reference to him, the magazine *Shakhmatnoe obozrenye* (1909) mentioned that "A.A. Alekhine had made his first appearance in our 16th (gambit) correspondence tourna-ment, played in 1905-1906, and took first prize in it." This must have been what Alekhine was referring to when he recalled that he has "played since [he] was seven years old, but ... started to play seriously when [he] was twelve."

A copy of young Alekhine's scorebook was preserved, with cuttings from Chigorin's chess column, in the St. Petersburg magazine *Niva* and with it the records of his correspondence games played during 1902-1907. Here is one of them, played against Manko from the town of Kamyshin in the tour-nament of 1906-1907, sponsored by Prince F. Shakhovskoi. It shows that, even at this young age, the feel of the position was not alien to Alekhine, who correctly evaluated the advantages of exchanging the queens, to wit, the lead in development, possession of an open file, and the threat of an effective rook invasion to the seventh rank...

**(1) Alekhine – Manko,V.M.**
corr Russia 1906
Scotch Game [C45]

**1.e4 e5 2.♘f3 ♘c6 3.d4 e×d4 4.♘×d4 ♘f6 5.♘×c6 b×c6 6.♗d3 d5 7.e×d5 c×d5 8.0-0 ♗e7 9.♘c3 0-0 10.♗g5 c6 11.♕f3 ♘g4?!** The main line is 11...♖b8. **12.♗×e7 ♕×e7 13.♖ae1 ♕d6 14.♕g3 ♕f6?!** 14...♕×g3 15.f×g3 ♗e6 16.♘a4 ♖ae8 17.h3 ♘f6 18.♘c5 ♖e7 was the lesser evil, especially against the attacking genius Alekhine. **15.h3 ♘h6 16.♖e5 g6 17.♘e2?!** Slightly slow. 17.♖fe1!? ♘f5 18.♕f4 ♔g7 19.♘a4 applies even more pressure. **17...♗f5 18.f4 ♖fe8?!** It is more natural to address the problem of the h6-knight immediately with 18...♗×d3 19.♕×d3 ♘f5. **19.♕e3 ♖×e5?** This exchange plays into White's hands because he can use the resulting e-pawn as a battering ram. 19...♕d8 is called for, to meet 20.♘d4 ♗d7 21.c4 with 21...♕b6. **20.f×e5 ♕h4?! 21.♘d4 ♗×d3 22.♖f4?** Unneccessarily sophisticated. The direct 22.c×d3 c5 23.♘f3 ♘f5 24.♕×c5± is fully sufficient for a comfortable advantage. **22...♕e7?** This retreat is too passive. 22...♕g5 23.c×d3 c5 24.♘f3 (24.♘e6? ♕e7 25.♘×c5 ♘f5 26.♕f2 ♕×e5=) 24...♕e7 is only slightly better for White. **23.c×d3 ♖c8?! 24.♖f6 c5** 24...♔g7? runs into 25.♕×h6+ ♔×h6 26.♘f5+. **25.♘c6 ♕e8** (D)

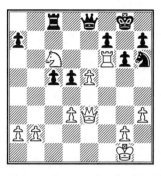

**26.e6** Alekhine opens the floodgates. **26...♘f5** 26...f×e6 27.♖×e6 ♕d7 28.♘e7+ +– **27.e×f7+** 27.♖×f5? is met by 27...f×e6!=. **27...♕×f7 28.♖×f5!** **1-0** Black resigns, because, after 28...g×f5, White wins a piece: 29.♘e7+ ♔f8 30.♘×c8 ♕c7 31.♕e6.

Correspondence play was instrumental for the rapid progress of the young talent. Already, by age 14, he had surpassed many of his opponents in the assessment of a position, the length of analysis, and tactical complications. And Alexander started playing in over-the-board competitions – tournaments organized by the Moscow Chess Circle. It should be noted that in the first round of such a tournament, Alekhine adopted, as in the game with Manko, the Scotch Game. Later, he justified his decision by saying that "[i]t was a line that [he] learned by heart. It was based on the Maroczy-Janowsky game from the London tournament of 1899... [he] decided to follow the book line not because [he had] hoped to get some (even slight) advantage as a result of the opening. [He] could, in this case, just be sure that [he] would not find [himself] in a lost position after only a few moves." Curiously enough, five years later, meeting world champion Emanuel Lasker over the board for the first time in his life, Alekhine again adopted the same opening.

**(2) Alekhine – Rozanov**
Moscow 1907
Scotch Game [C45]

**1.e4 e5 2.♘f3 ♘c6 3.d4 e×d4 4.♘×d4 ♘f6 5.♘×c6 b×c6 6.♗d3 d5 7.e×d5 c×d5 8.0-0 ♗e7 9.♘c3 0-0 10.♗g5 c6 11.♕f3 ♗g4 12.♕g3 ♗h5 13.♕e5?** This hands Black the initiative. After 13.♖fe1, White is slightly better. **13...♗g6 14.♗×g6 h×g6 15.♖ad1 ♗d6 16.♕d4 ♕c7 17.♕h4 ♘h7 18.♗e3 f5 19.f4 ♔f7 20.♗d4 ♖h8 21.♖de1?** White's queen should leave its exposed position with 21.♕f2. **21...♘f6 22.♕g5 ♘g4?** (D) Running into a powerful blow. The knight should go to h5, when Black is clearly on top.

**23.♖e6!! ♔×e6?** This brings Black to the brink of disaster. He had to play 23...♖h6 24.♖fe1 ♖b8, which seems to lead to a draw: 25.h3 (25.h4 ♕d7 26.♗×g7 ♗c5+ 27.♔h1 ♔×g7 28.♖e7+ ♕×e7 29.♖×e7+ ♔f8 30.♖e5 ♖e8 31.g3 ♔f7 32.♔g2 ♗d4 33.♘e2 ♗e3 34.♖×e8 ♔×e8 35.h5 ♗b6 36.h×g6 ♖h2+ 37.♔f1 ♖h1+ 38.♔g2 ♖h2+=) 25...♖b4 26.h×g4 ♖×d4 27.g×f5 ♖×f4 28.f×g6+ ♔g8

29.♕×f4 ♗c5+ 30.♔e3 ♗×e3+ 31.♖1×e3 ♕h2+ 32.♔f2 ♕f4+ 33.♗f3 ♕d4+ 34.♖fe3 ♕f4+=. **24.♕×g6+ ♔d7 25.♕×f5+ ♔d8 26.♕×g4 ♗f8?!** (D) 26...♖e8 27.♗×g7 ♕e7 is slightly more harmonious.

**27.♖e1?** The first step in the wrong direction that will lead to Black's king escaping to the a8-corner. 27.h3 ♖b8 28.♘e2 ♕d7 29.f5 ♗d6 30.♘f4 ♗×f4 31.♖×f4 ♕d7±. **27...♕d7 28.♕g5+?!** 28.♕g3!? **28...♔c7 29.♖e3 ♔b7 30.♘a4 ♖e8 31.♖b3+ ♔a8 32.♕g3 ♖h6** 32...♗d6!?= is more precise. **33.♕d3 ♖he6?!** Again, not the best defense because 33...♕c8, in order to meet 34.♗e5 with 34...♗d6, is called for. **34.♗e5 c5 35.♖b5** (D)

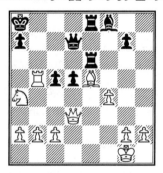

**35...♖c8?** Black does not have time for this. He should exchange queens with 35...c4!? 36.♕×d5+ ♕×d5 37.♖×d5 g5, placing his hopes on his rooks. 35...♕c6?! is less precise in view

16

of 36.♖b6! c4 37.♖×c6 c×d3 38.♖×e6 ♖×e6 39.c×d3 g5 40.g4 g×f4 41.♗×f4±. **36.c4! a6?** Losing directly, but 36...♖a6 37.♘c3 d4 38.♘d5 is also hopeless in the long run. **37.♘b6+ ♖×b6 38.♖×b6 ♔a7 39.♕g6 ♕a4 40.♖b3 ♕c6 41.♕f7+ ♔a8 42.c×d5 1-0**

This game became memorable for Alekhine not only because it was his first tournament game. The game reflects both the merits and shortcomings of the fourteen-year-old's play. It testifies to the deficiencies in his knowledge of opening theory, as well as the lack of strategic depth. At the same time, it clearly shows his acute apprehension of danger, maximum concentration of thought in searching for counter-chances, ability to see combinations, and accurate calculation of variations. The import of this game was great for Alekhine because he saw it molding his style. He recalled that:

*This game had a profound influence on my play and development in the years to come. Evidently, it aroused my ambition and desire for perfection. On the other hand, the game generated in me a peculiar psychological weakness which, for a long time and with much effort, I had to expunge, namely, the impression that I, having got in a tight spot, shall always or almost always be able to think up some unexpected combination and with its help extricate myself from all the difficulties. A dangerous delusion!*

The first over-the-board competitions had not yet brought him any marked success. Thus, in the 1907 autumn tournament held by the Moscow Circle, he found himself in the lower half of the field. Nevertheless, even then, the public had noticed the talented youth. His chess strength was progressing very rapidly, spurred on by his insatiable ambition, single-mindedness, capacity for work, and without a doubt, the natural talent of the "young gymnasium scholar."

As early as 1908, the youth who was dreaming of gaining a master title went to Düsseldorf to participate in the 16th Congress of the German Chess Union, at that time one of the most prestigious European competitions. The program of the congress included a number of tournaments: "international," where only masters could play, "main" (or two "main" tournaments, as was the case, for example, in Düsseldorf), and "side" events. To gain the title of master, one had to win a "main" tournament.

Although Alekhine's result was not all bad for his first international appearance – he won eight games, lost three, and drew two – he did not succeed in overcoming the master barrier, sharing 4th and 5th places, two points behind the winner. There might have been some consolation for Alekhine in that he scored as well against the first eight finishers as did the tournament winner F. Köhnlein (+4 -1 =2) and that his game against the winner himself was won on move 16 by a spectacular shot.

**(3) Alekhine – Köhnlein**
Düsseldorf 1908 (D)

**16.♕×d6!!** A thunderbolt. The prosaic 16.♘f7+? ♖×f7 17.♗×f7 ♗d7 18.♗e6 wins as well, but is not as clear of course. There follows a last desperate attempt: **16...♕×g2+** 16...c×d6 17.♘f7+ ♖×f7 18.♖e8+ ♖f8 19.♖×f8# **17.♔×g2 1-0**

After the end of the congress, Alekhine did not make haste to return to Moscow. He tried his hand in two small training matches, defeating the well-known German master Curt von Bardeleben (1861-1924) and drawing his match with Swiss champion Hans Fahrni (1874-1939). It is interesting to note that just then, August 17, the world championship match between Emanuel Lasker and Siegbert Tarrasch had started, and the young Alekhine had the opportunity to witness the historic contest for the world chess crown.

On his return home, Alekhine played one more match against a master, defeating Beniamin Blumenfeld (1884-1947) by the same score (4½ -½) that he had beaten Bardeleben. *Shakhmatnoe obozrenye* magazine reported that "[t]he match was won by Alekhine in excellent style."

*Young Alekhine – A drawing by the painter A. Kiprianovich.*

More surprising was his failure in the next match against the 1908 Moscow champion, and one of the strongest Russian masters of the time, Vladimir Nenarokov (1880-1953). The same magazine mentioned that "[t]his match, which had promised to be very exciting, ended unexpectedly quickly. Nenarokov's young opponent, having lost the first three games, resigned the match. The resignation was undoubtedly premature, which was pointed out in the chess media."

The same year (1908), in the autumn tournament held by the Moscow Chess Circle, Alekhine finished first, gaining the right to play in the All-Russia Amateur tournament. Winning that event brought him the title of master. Previously, that title could only be earned by playing in tournaments abroad. During the tournament Alekhine also showed himself to be an excellent game commentator. *Shakhmatnoe obozrenye* magazine, and later the book, *The International Chess Congress in Memory of M.I. Chigorin* (also known as St. Petersburg 1909), had lent him their pages to analyze a number of games between Russian players. In his annotations, the young master showed a good knowledge of games played in the current competitions, searching for the truth in critical positions, doing his best to evaluate chances of both opponents objectively. By the way, a book in which all games of this international tournament were annotated by world champion Lasker was very carefully studied by Alekhine, as he himself admitted, and this was very helpful in improving his game. In later years, he used to say that already at that time, in his creative searches, he began to feel Lasker's influence on him.

At about that time, Alekhine's first simultaneous exhibitions in Moscow took place. He was also invited to make tours. Thus, he gave simultaneous exhibitions in the town of the Russian gunsmiths, Tula, played a demonstration game against Tula's strongest player Konstantin Vasilevsky, and played three games against seven to ten consultants. Such resounding successes and boundless passion for chess could have given rise to a natural desire to devote himself, after graduation from the gymnasium, to his beloved art. But, his faculties and knowledge were so versatile that his parents did not seem to have much trouble directing their younger son to acquire a prestigious civil profession that would enable him to take a suitable place in the hierarchy of society.

The profile of classical education that Alekhine had received was quite suitable for further study at the Law Department of Moscow State University, where he studied for one and a half semesters (September 1910 to February 1911) and at St. Petersburg Imperial School of Law, which he entered in the autumn of 1911.

**Family**

His first love had already visited him when he came to St. Petersburg. The chosen one of the student and already well-known chess master was the Russian painter, baroness Anna von Severgin. On December 15, 1913, their daughter Valentina was born. In 1921, Anna left for Austria with her daughter; Alekhine and Anna were destined to see each other again only one more time, during the Vienna international tournament of 1922.

Alekhine's first marriage to Alexandra Lazarevna Batayev, a widow and a clerk (as was indicated in the archival document found by Yu. Shaburov), occurred in Moscow on March 5, 1920. A year later the marriage was dissolved.

Alekhine soon joined his future with another woman. The new marriage proved fateful for his chess career. In the summer of 1920, Alekhine, who spoke the principal European languages (French, German, and English) very well, started working as an interpreter in the Comintern. There he met the journalist Anneliese Ruegg, an active figure in the Swiss Social Democratic Party. On coming to Moscow, she was soon granted an interview with Lenin. In Russia, she addressed audiences with reports, Alekhine interpreting for her. He also accompanied her on trips to other Russian cities. Thus, early in 1921 he went with her to the Urals.

*Anneliese Rueg*

On February 13, 1921, he left his work in the Comintern and a month later married Ruegg (curiously, the same day the world championship match between Lasker and Capablanca started in Havana, Cuba). In the marriage certificate, one finds the following information: the bridegroom: born in 1892; profession; interpreter; civil status: divorced from first wife and is getting married a second time; the bride: born in 1879; delegate, unmarried, getting married for the first time. The spouses expressed the wish to bear the common surname – Alekhine. They rented room #164 at the Luxe Hotel on Tverskaya Street. And, six weeks later, Alekhine obtained permission to leave Russia. It read: "The People's Commissariat of Foreign Affairs sees no obstacles for citizen Alexander Alexandrovich Alekhine going to Latvia via Sebezh, which is testified to by the signature and application of the hand. Deputy People's Commissar Karakhan, No. 01139, April 29, 1921"

It should be noted that late in April, the match in Havana had ended, and the telegraph brought the news: José Raúl

Capablanca had become the third world chess champion. For Alekhine, this news sounded like a call to action, as the necessity to subordinate all his life to the motto "Excelsior" – forward to the very top!

When abroad, Alekhine went from Latvia to Berlin, where his battles with German players began. Then, there was a series of brilliant tournament performances. In 1922, he permanently settled in Paris. Anneliese Alekhine went from Berlin to Switzerland, where she gave birth to a son, named Alexander, on November 2, 1921. She was raising the child herself, while continuing her political and literary activities.

Alekhine visited the son infrequently: a picture taken in Zürich shows them together. Anneliese died May 2, 1934, and the son was taken to live on a pension. At present, the only son of the fourth world chess champion lives near Basel. He was twice invited to Moscow, where he attended the Alekhine Memorial Tournaments. During the celebration of Alekhine's centennial, the authors of the present book met him and gave him their book dedicated to the chess genius. He shared with them his reminiscences of his father and told us about his father's two last wives, whom he happened to meet in different circumstances. Already, in the middle of the 1920s, Alekhine had found a new spouse, the kind-hearted and thoughtful Nadin, as he used to call her. Nadezhda Semyonovna Vasiliev (née Fabritsky), the widow of a Russian general, was born in Odessa March 19, 1884. Alekhine met her at a ball in Paris in 1924.

20

*Alekhine with his son Alexander, Zürich, 1926.*

Their life together lasted less than a decade. But those were the most difficult and important years in Alekhine's chess career – the period of preparation for storming chess Olympus and the days of great jubilation – winning the world champion's crown in his struggle against Capablanca. There were also months of strenuous work on his main chess books, and years of great tournament successes. And Nadin was always at his side. The reason for their parting is still unclear.

On March 24, 1934, Alekhine was married for the last time: his American-born wife Grace Wishart was the widow of the British captain Archibald Freeman. This took place in the French Riviera. He was not yet forty-two, and his "bride" was fifty-four-years old. Adolf Pavelchak, one of the first biographers of Alekhine, finds that

*[t]he distinguishing feature of Alekhine's nature was that he always chose spouses who were considerably older than himself. From this, it follows that he did not seek in marriage a realization of amorous feelings, that he was incapable of the true great sacrificial love in weal and in woe, for his nature, focused on his ego, nipped such sprouts in the bud. He sought in a woman not an ideal of beauty but a mother caretaker.*

21

Still one could say that Alekhine finally had found the one he was looking for! "She is the only one who understands me," he would say. Grace freed him from daily cares, managed his affairs, looked after his correspondence, and advised him on some matters. And, last but not least, she was the only woman in his life who was not alien to chess. She even played by correspondence and participated in household blitz tournaments. Moreover, Grace was well-off, for her late husband had left her a substantial sum, as well as a castle in the north of France, near Dieppe.

The Second World War had destroyed the idyllic life of this Alekhine's family, too. The Nazis had commandeered part of their property and were putting pressure on Wishart to subdue the world champion. After the death of her husband, Mrs. Wishart made a will in which she forbade the opening of the family archives until fifty years after her death. In 1956, the grave joined them forever. In Montparnasse cemetery, their bodies are buried under the same tombstone.

**Personality**

"The purpose of a human life and the meaning of happiness," Alekhine used to say, "is to do the maximum a person is capable of." Saviely Tartakower's memoirs *Meetings with Giants* poignantly captures Alekhine's other two credos. Alekhine once told Tartakower that "[o]ne should not be surprised if nothing at all comes from the Nothing Principle," and that "[o]ur fate does not chase us. It is we who ought to chase our fate." For Tartakower, "[t]hese two phrases contain his contemplation of life and his attitude to matters of life."

Alekhine was above all a single-minded man with a boundless love for chess, ready to give himself unreservedly to the glorification of this ancient game, raising it to a level of high art. Generated by the collision and rivalry with other outstanding masters, the art of chess also required other qualities: ambition, great will power and strength of character, colossal memory and capacity for work. All these qualities Alekhine possessed in excess, allowing him persistently, day after day, to achieve ever new sporting successes and finally the highest of them all: winning the world chess championship.

Alekhine impressed his contemporaries greatly, as a man remembered because of his unusual appearance, phenomenal memory, analytical skill, fantasy of combinative revelations, and broad cultural demands. The third world champion, Capablanca, just before his match with Alekhine, gave a flattering description of Alekhine. He is

> ...a representative of the Slavic nation, over six feet tall, about 200 pounds in weight, fair-haired and blue-eyed, he catches the eye of the public because of his appearance when he enters the tournament hall. He fluently speaks six languages, and holds the academic rank of a Doctor of Law. And his intellect is much above that of the average man. It appears that Alekhine has the most remarkable chess memory that has ever existed. He is said to remember by heart all the games played by the chess masters in the last 15-20 years.

Alekhine's remarkable memory was mentioned by many of his contemporaries. In his younger years, he astounded his friends and acquaintances. Sergei Shishko recalls that

*[i]n St. Petersburg, on Znamenskaya Street, in the apartment of Professor P. Tsitovich, the young Alekhine was among the guests. Someone suggested that it would be good to verify the rumors of the unusual memory of Alekhine – a future lawyer, an advocate who hopes to deliver flaming speeches and conduct complex processes in the court of law without consulting the files. So the host took at random a book from the bookshelf, opened it to page 277, and handed it over to Alekhine. It turned out to be a translation of a novel by a little known Spanish author. Alekhine sat down in an armchair and immersed himself in viewing the text. Three or four minutes later he returned the open book to the host, stood up and, with half-closed eyes, confidently and quickly repeated in a loud whisper word for word the text of one and a half pages without making a single mistake.*

But, as Saviely Tartakower wrote that while Alekhine "possess[ed] an amazing memory for chess, [he] was very absent-minded in everyday life. He often left behind his wallet in Montparnasse cafés. Once, during his chess tours of Yugoslavia, he fell asleep while holding a burning cigarette between his teeth, and nearly perished."

Kharlampy Baranov, who encountered Alekhine in Moscow tournaments of 1918-1919, paid attention to the following trait of Alekhine's character, also mentioned by many other contemporaries. Alekhine "treated any opponent with equal attention and correctness, always ready to explain patiently the mistakes that had been made, and to show long variations to players of any strength. We never perceived in him either arrogance or carelessness and always got from him exhaustive answers to any questions."

Two more traits of Alekhine deserve mentioning – exceptional self-restraint and will power. Lev Lyubimov remembers that "[d]uring the world championship match with Capablanca, Alekhine badly suffered from a toothache; while he was fighting Capablanca, six of his teeth were removed. Sometimes it was done at night, and the following day, with a swollen cheek, he again took a seat at the chessboard. Now talking to Paris chessplayers he recalled this with a smile." He had to exercise his will power to rid himself of his addiction to alcohol and smoking. And, among the numerous congratulations and gifts he received on his victory in his rematch with Euwe (1937), a fruit basket from the Dutch Anti-Alcohol Society perhaps gave him special pleasure.

His contemporaries also noted his versatility and high culture. It would be curious to know some of the answers to the questionnaire he filled out when studying at the Gardin film studio. To the question about the Russian painters he liked most, he named Surikov, Levitan, and Vrubel, and to that about

*Grace Wishart-Alekhine and Alexander Alekhine during an analysis of the game with the Austrian master Josef Lokventz, Prague, 1943.*

his three favorite operas he mentioned *Carmen*, *Tristan*, and *The Queen of Spades*.

Alekhine's complex and contradictory character had regularly shown itself both in the life and games of the great chess master. As Pyotr Romanovsky noted, the study of Alekhine's games allows one to discover the contradiction caused by the inner struggle between the romanticist in the chess artist he used to be from his younger years, on the one hand, and a deep thinker, one may say a scientist who penetrated the secrets of positional play in his mature years, on the other. Alekhine himself once admitted in an interview (1926) that "[a] strange struggle takes place in [him] when [he] play[s] chess, a struggle between fantasy, on the one hand, and sober prudence, on the other. You see, an excess of fantasy is as harmful as an excess of prudence ... However, with me it is fantasy that dominates."

Alekhine was not free from some weaknesses and shortcomings, which became particularly evident in the years of the world cataclysms. The two world wars, the great social revolutions and other political upheavals had become a hard trial for him. And his deeds often were not in harmony with all his preceding activities. Now, he accepts the revolution, helps to organize the first chess competitions in the young Soviet state, applies to join the Bolshevik party, and works in the Comintern. Then, he leaves his motherland and, in spite of the famine and devastation, denounces the authorities for their lack of attention to chess.

Now, he feels the pangs of conscience because his motherland has achieved tremendous successes without him and declares that he "is sorry for his mistakes" (See, Russia), and, then, he plays into the hand of the Nazi propaganda in disseminating their racist ideas... (See, Journalist). And only death freed him from the hard feelings. Therefore, modern chessplayers, understanding the enormous psychic burden that he had to bear, put aside his fallacies and focus on what constitutes his greatness as an artist of chess and a sportsman who ascended the highest pedestal and exerted a tremendous influence upon the progress of the chess art.

## The First World War

Alexander Alekhine directly participated in World War I. On returning to the motherland from imprisonment in Germany, where a group of Russian chessplayers who were playing in the Mannheim tournament of 1914 found themselves, Alekhine gave several charity exhibitions; the first was in Moscow on November 5 (+9 -9 =5), and the second was in Petrograd on December 7 (+20 -1 =0). The money thus collected being sent to the endowment for the Russian chessplayers detained in Germany. And the money collected from the exhibition given on December 8, 1914 at the Chess Circle of Petrograd Polytechnic Institute (+22 - 6 =6) was sent to a student of that institute, the future two-time Soviet Champion Pyotr Romanovsky, who was then imprisoned in Germany.

After the tours of Odessa and Kiev in the spring of 1916, Alekhine decided to go to the front as a volunteer. At that time, his grandfather Ivan Alekhine and his first cousin Anna, both awarded the bravery badge of the Red Cross, were in the army. Alexander Alekhine was appointed chief of a detachment of the Red Cross for the Galician front. And, it is precisely at that front that the Russian army launched an offensive in August 1916. For bravery and resolution

*Alekhine: "In my case, fantasy dominates"*

in rescuing the wounded from the battlefield, Alekhine was awarded two St. George medals and the Order of St. Stanislaus with swords. He was twice wounded, the second time seriously, whereupon he was taken to a Tarnopol (now Ternopol) hospital. "Entire months I was in bed in the hospital in Tarnopol, unable to move," he recalled. "Blindfold play proved then a real savior for me. At my request I was often visited by the local players, and I had the opportunity to give them a series of small blindfold exhibitions. It is in one of such exhibitions that my best known blindfold game ,namely the one against Feldt, was played."

By the way, the surname Feldt – from other sources von Feldt – became one of the mysteries of Alekhine's chess biography. It is known that in 1915-1916 in one of the hospitals of

Tarnopol there worked, as a member of the medical personnel, 20-year-old Leon Stolzenberg, subsequently a chess master in Detroit (USA). He regularly played Alekhine, and it cannot be excluded that he was exactly that mysterious von Feldt, the more so because (in Russian) the abbreviation Feldt can mean a surgeon's assistant from Tarnopol. Although, thirty-five years after that game was played, Stolzenberg disavowed the honor of having participated in the creation of this masterpiece, suggesting that Alekhine's opponent in that game was one "Doctor Fischer." A. Buschke published this fact in "Alekhine's Early Chess Career" in the American magazine *Chess Life* (October 20, 1951). The game which Alekhine recalls was played in a simultaneous exhibition against five opponents, the score being 5-0 in favor of Alekhine (See, Combinations).

Having undergone treatment, Alekhine returned to Moscow. At the opening of the "chess season," he gave a simultaneous exhibition against thirty-seven opponents (+28 -3 =6) in the new rooms of the Moscow Chess Circle. Then, he again went on a tour of Odessa where he gave a number of charitable exhibitions. One of them, the blindfold simultaneous exhibition given in the hall of the City Duma on 4 October 1916, was reported the following day by the *Odessa News*: "This time the master played on nine and not eight boards, playing very fast: the simul was finished in three hours and fifty minutes. In all the games, over 300 total moves were made, that is, Alekhine was making 80 moves an hour, playing blindfold. However, he won eight games; his ninth opponent, a Mr. List, who also played blindfold, stopped playing on move 17 in an inferior position."

*Officer of the Russian Army Alexander Alekhine.*

Prokofiev requested his friends and close acquaintances express their thoughts about the sun. Here is what Alexander Alekhine wrote in Petrograd on April 28, 1917: "On gray cloudy days I miss Him, dream of Him. When I see Him, I look for dark spots. With excruciating pleasure I had experienced the days of eclipse, and I again was waiting for Him to appear so that I would not think of Him anymore." For comparison, José Raúl Capablanca, in the same album a year and a half later in New York, said that "[t]he Sun is life. When we see it, we are happy. When it is hidden from us by clouds, gloom settles in our hearts."

How similar and at the same time how

*Alekhine's autograph in Prokofiev's album.*

different are the thoughts of these two brilliant players about the sun! One exudes optimism, the enjoyment of life, whereas the other reflects anxiety and mental confusion caused by the cataclysms of the epoch. It is interesting that, like Alekhine, Potemkin and Prokofiev lived in Paris in the 1920s. In 1929, Alekhine and his wife were among the guests of the composer who celebrated the housewarming of his new apartment in Paris. These facts have been made available to the present authors by collector Sergei Karestalin, who, in the archives of S.S. Prokofiev, found previously unknown documents concerning his friendly contacts with the third and fourth world champions.

### In Gardin's Film Studio

After the dramatic episode in Odessa – where, late in 1918, Alekhine, accused of anti-Soviet activities, found himself under the threat of execution by firing squad – he decided to give up playing chess and on return to Moscow to engage in other activities. Under the influence of his stage-struck sister Varvara, Alexander decided to try his hand at an artistic career in the then new field of cinema. In August 1919, he passed the examination with honors and entered the recently opened State Studio of Cinematic Art, directed by Vladimir Rostislavovich Gardin. As Alekhine explained to his friend and a passionate lover of chess Sergei Fyodorovich Shishko, by taking up the career of a cinema actor he hoped to achieve universal acceptance.

At first, Alekhine carefully attended the classes, and was filmed in screen tests, but soon felt that regardless of what he did, the world of chess was again attracting him. He had not become a cinema actor and, in the autumn of 1920, left the studio. Shishko's story of his last meeting with Alekhine has a cinematic *mise en scène*: "One October night of that year, I met him near the Moscow Soviet (Mossovet) building. A fine rain was lashing in our faces, it was cloudy and windy. Alekhine was shivering in his old shabby coat. We both felt ill at ease. We did not know what to talk about. After a few meaningless phrases, there came awkward

27

silence. Alekhine half raised his felt hat and extended his hand. Our eyes met. I sensed embarrassment on his face. He told me: "Of course, it's a pity... A great pity... The art of a cinema actor excites and moves me... I hoped it would replace the art of chess for me... But that was not to happen...."

And still, Alekhine had acting abilities. They were appreciated not only by the "Cinema Grandmaster" Gardin who accepted him in his studio in Moscow. It is not accidental then that many years later, in 1928, Alekhine was invited to star in Hollywood. He agreed to play the role of a foreign chess master in a sound film to be shot in the spring of the following year. But that idea remained only a project.

### Investigator, 1920-21

Accustomed to being comfortably well off, Alekhine, after the October Revolution and the "expropriation of the expropriators" that took place in the country as a result of it, found himself in the poverty line. He had already started looking for a more reliable source of income when he was still at Gardin's Film Studio. In May 1920, he applied for a job at Moscow Criminal Detection Department. In the Central State Archive of the USSR, there remained, among other documents, also his application, written in a sprawling handwriting on a sheet of paper torn from a copybook: "Please enroll me in the currently vacant position in the Department entrusted to you. Signed: Alexander Alekhine. Moscow, 13 April 1919."

For nine months, from May 13, 1920 to February 13, 1921, Alekhine worked

*Actress Renee Adere and film director Fred Niblo at a game of chess with the world champion during his visit to Hollywood, 1929.*

as a criminal investigator at the Central Investigation and Detection Department of the Main Directorate of Militia, his salary being 4,800 rubles a month. His duty at the Detection Department was to investigate the scene of a crime and analyze the circumstances under which the crime had been committed. The employees of that department subsequently recalled the professional mastery of his analysis, his amazing memory and, of course, his frequent chess battles with his chief, director of the Central Registration Bureau of Criminal Detection, Doctor Pyotr Sergeyevich Semyonovsky. The latter was in the habit of recounting not his games with the famous chessplayer, but rather what an interesting interlocutor Alekhine was, about his extensive knowledge in jurisprudence, history, and literature.

### Dissertation

In his 1925 letter to chess master and the Chief Arbiter of the Moscow International Tournament of 1925, Nikolai Grigoriev, Alekhine informed him that "[u]ntil the beginning of the next year, [he had] no intention at all to

*Alekhine the investigator –
a break in work.*

participate in chess competitions, because [he is] wholly absorbed in the preparation for the examinations for the degree of Doctor of Law, to be taken at the end of November this year. This takes a lot of time. The main difficulty is to adapt to the French law terminology." Quite unexpected was the subject of his dissertation – "The Penitentiary System in China." The famous Sorbonne University in Paris honored him with the degree of Doctor of Law in 1925.

It appeared outwardly that nothing changed in his life. In fact, the prefix "Doctor" meant a great deal to him.

The Russian man of letters Lev Lyubimov, who was then on friendly terms with him, recalls that "Alekhine considered himself not only the best chessplayer in the world, which was entirely justifiable, but also, in general, a man of a great all-embracing mind, a man for whom it befits to rise above the others" (*In a Strange Land*).

Phrases like "Such man as I am" and "with my accomplishments," etc., could frequently be heard from him. Having achieved world chess glory already as a youth, Alekhine came to believe in his star.

The revolution destroyed the world in which he rose. Having settled in France, he conceived of making a public career there. Now that was rather naïve. To the French, he remained a foreigner who only recently had taken French citizenship and who had impressed very few persons of influence – for the simple reason that very few people in France were captivated by chess at all. So, the "King of Chess" never enjoyed any special glory and lived as an ordinary man in the street, having no access to the "whole Paris." But, now the status of the Russian grandmaster in French society could change because he had become the respected Doctor Alekhine! Now, he was "equal" to the one so respected by him, Doctor of Mathematics and Philosophy, Emanuel Lasker. His self-esteem was satisfied.

### Circumnavigation (August 3, 1932-May 11, 1933)

Alekhine craved to see as many peoples, countries, and continents as possible. He celebrated his 40th birthday on the other side of the ocean. Leaving Paris in early August, Alekhine, in the following five months, won a small tournament in Pasadena (USA), gave simultaneous exhibitions in Mexico, and paid a visit to Cuba. Then, he again returned to the United States, visited New York, paid a brief visit to Canada, and went to Hollywood and Los Angeles, both in California.

He kept warm memories of his visit to Cuba. Alekhine "saw Havana, a city of unusual beauty, elegant, lush, and rich... The Havana players treat [him] without any hostility at all, extremely well in fact. Of course, in the case of a new match their sympathies would be with Capablanca, but they are not in the least infected by chauvinism so that, from this side, there would not be any obstacles to playing (the match) in Havana."

On December 22, 1932, on the ship *President Garfield*, Alekhine and his Siamese cat with the unique name "Chess" continued their circumnavigation, which lasted almost a half-year. The journalists were joking, calling the world champion a "Chess Magellan." Indeed, he visited Hawaii, Japan, Shanghai, Hong Kong, the Philippines, Singapore, Sumatra, Java, New Zealand, Ceylon, Alexandria, Jerusalem, and Genoa. He returned to Paris in May 1933.

Along with chess, Alekhine took interest in virtually everything: local attrac-

*His talisman – the Siamese cat – Alekhine named "Chess."*

tions, customs, national games, etc. In all countries he visited, he purchased souvenirs. When visiting Bali, he bought a national costume, and, after appearing in it at a carnival arranged aboard the ship, he was unexpectedly awarded the first prize for the most original garment. During his travels, he became acquainted with the Japanese version of chess (shoghi), opened a football match in Shanghai, where, by the way, he was given a grand reception by the Russian immigrant community, and, as he himself admitted, "relatively failed in a blindfold exhibition." All in all, during his wanderings all over the world, Alekhine played 1,320 games (+1,161 -65 =94), a fantastic percentage of 91.5%! Here is one of the games played in these exhibitions. It took place in the capital of Indonesia, Batavia (now Jakarta) on March 1, 1933. Alekhine playing against fifty opponents (+46, -2, =2). In this particular game, his opponent was Maurice Wertheim (1880-1950), subsequently one of the prominent chess organizers in the United States. Curiously, the game appeared on November 12 of that year in the chess column of the newspaper *Football* published in Rio de Janeiro. It was mentioned that the variations in the annotations had been indicated by Alekhine himself, whose friendly relationship with Brazilian chessplayers had already been established during his 1926 tour of Brazil.

**(4) Alekhine – Wertheim, Maurice**
Jakarta 1933
Queen's Gambit Declined [D31]

**1.d4 d5 2.c4 e6 3.♘c3 h6?! 4.e4 d×e4 5.♘×e4 ♗b4+ 6.♘c3 c5 7.a3 ♗×c3+ 8.b×c3 ♘f6 9.♘f3**

*After a simultaneous exhibition in Shanghai, 1933.*

♘c6 10.♗e2 0-0 11.0-0 ♕a5
12.♕b3 ♘e4 13.♗b2 ♕b6
14.♕c2 ♘f6 15.a4 ♖d8 16.♖fd1
♗d7 17.♗a3 c×d4 18.c×d4 ♗e8
19.♗b2 ♖ac8 20.♗c3 ♕c7 21.a5
♕f4 22.♖ab1 (D)

**22...♖c7?** Playing with fire. The retreat 22...♕c7 is called for. **23.♗d2**
**♕e4?** The queen should still leave the
danger zone with 23...♕d6. **24.♗d3**

♕g4 25.h3 ♕h5 26.♗f4 ♖cd7?!
A better try is 26...♖cc8 in order to
answer 27.♖b5 with 27...♘d5 28.c×d5?
♘×d4, but White remains on top after
28.♗d2!. **27.♖b5 ♘×d4!?** The last
chance to confuse the issue. **28.♘×d4
♕×d1+ 29.♕×d1 ♖×d4** (D)

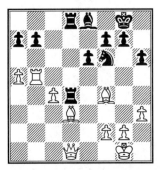

**30.♖d5?** 30.♖×b7 ♖×d3 31.♕e2+–
leaves more winning potential on the
board. **30...♖8×d5?** 30...e×d5
31.♗h7+ ♘×h7 32.♕×d4 ♘f8 gives
Black more hope to survive because his
minor pieces can come quickly to the
posts on c6 and e6. **31.c×d5 ♖×f4
32.d×e6 f×e6 33.♕b3 ♗c6?**
33...♖d4 was the last chance, but White
should win in the long run after
34.♕×e6+ ♔f8 35.♗c2±. **34.♕×e6+
♔h8 35.a6 ♘h5 1-0**

**Curiosities**

Alexander Alekhine's life abounded in
the most unusual events. Some of them
could end tragically as, for example, the
death sentence he received in Odessa
in 1918, when he was accused of coun-
terrevolutionary activities. Others, on
the contrary, are more whimsical. Here
some of them.

An optimistic tragedy. During a simultaneous exhibition, one of Alekhine's
opponents joyfully announced to the
world champion: "You are checkmated
in three moves!" "Why in three?"
Alekhine was surprised, "You are
checkmated in two!"

A joke of the genius. Once, in Paris,
Alekhine dropped into a café, where
visitors were playing chess games for
a stake. One of them proposed that he
and Alekhine play a game. "Sorry, I am
very bad at chess" the grandmaster tried
to refuse. "Oh, it's nothing, I'll give you
the odds of a queen," the man said.
Alekhine agreed and, to make fun, lost
the game. "Yes, indeed, you are not too
good," the winner said condescend-
ingly. "It seems to me that I lost because this unnecessary piece" Alekhine
pointed to the queen "was always in the
way." The stranger laughed and proposed another game in which he would
be given the odds of a queen. Imagine
how he was surprised when he lost several games in a row. "So you see now,"
whispered Alekhine mysteriously, "as
I told you, this piece only interferes
with your play."

Unique in history. On the cover of the
third issue of the Moscow magazine
*Shakhmatny Vestnik* (Chess Messenger) for 1916, a chess position was
published that could have arisen in the
course of some amazing analysis made
by Alekhine of the game he played with
Black against Nikolai Grigoriev in the
autumn tournament of the Moscow
Chess Circle. In this position, there
were five queens on the board: three
white and two black! Eleven years later,
the world champion published, by the
right of the first discoverer, a new edition of the game. In it, Alekhine had the
white pieces, and an unknown opponent,
the black ones…

**(5) Alekhine – NN**
Moscow 1915
French Defense [C12]

**1.e4 e6 2.d4 d5 3.♘c3 ♘f6
4.♗g5 ♗b4 5.e5 h6 6.e×f6 h×g5
7.f×g7 ♖g8 8.h4 g×h4 9.♕g4 ♗e7**
9...♕f6 is the main line. **10.g3?!**
10.♘f3 is more critical. **10...c5
11.g×h4 c×d4** Extremely risky but
probably not bad. 11...♗f6 represents
the safety first approach. **12.h5 d×c3
13.h6 c×b2 14.♖b1 ♕a5+
15.♔e2** (D)

**15...♕×a2?** The real mistake, as
Kasparov has found the amazing resource 15...♗f8!! when Black is not
worse after 16.g×f8♕+ ♖×f8 17.♘f3
b6. **16.h7 ♕×b1 17.h×g8♕+ ♔d7
18.♕×f7** 18.♕×c8+ ♔×c8 19.g8♕+
wins as well. **18...♕×c2+ 19.♔f3
♘c6** (D)

**20.♕g×e6+?!** This should win but
greatly complicates matters. Both
20.♕ff4 b1♕ 21.♕×e6+ ♔×e6
22.g8♕+ ♔d7 23.♕×d5+ ♗d6
24.♕f×d6+ ♔e8 25.♖h8# and
Kasparov's 20.g8♕ win much more
easily. **20...♔c7 21.♕f4+ ♔b6** (D)

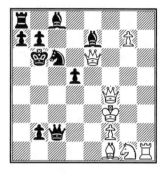

**22.♕ee3+?!** Again, Alekhine misses
the best continuation: 22.♗d3 ♕b3
(22...♕×d3+? 23.♕ee3+ ♕×e3+
24.♕×e3+ ♔c7 25.♘e2 ♗f5
26.♕f4++−) 23.♕ee3+ d4
24.♕f×d4+ ♘×d4+ 25.♕×d4++−.
**22...♗c5** 22...d4? 23.♗d3 (Kotov)
23...♕b3 24.♕f×d4+ ♘×d4+
25.♕×d4+ ♔c7 26.g8♕ ♕×g8
27.♕c3+ ♔d6 28.♖h6+ ♗e6
29.♕b4+ ♔d7 30.♕×b7+ ♔d6
31.♗f5+− **23.g8♕ b1♕** (D)

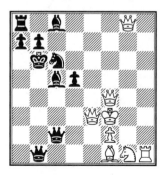

A really amazing position as five queens
are an extremely rare occurance on the
chessboard! **24.♖h6** and Alekhine
won later. Later, Timman found the only

defense, 24...♗g4+!! 25.♕g×g4 ♗×e3, but it seems that White has very good winning chances after 26.♕×e3+ ♔c5 27.♕×c5+ ♔×c5 28.♔g2 ♕e4+ 29.♕×e4 d×e4 30.♖h5+ ♔d6 31.♘e2±.

In the annotation made to this position, Alekhine wrote that "[i]n this mind-boggling position, White wins with the quiet move 24.♖h6!! (the threat is 25.♕d8#). The position that occurred in the game after move 23 is probably unique in the history of chess!" Thus, the once fantastic variation became a "real" game, and, in it, White beautifully finishes the struggle, announcing checkmate in several moves.

*The cover of Moscow magazine "Chess Messenger" with the diagram of the position taken from the Grigoriev – Alekhine game.*

Moreover, this "game," starting from Black's 15th move, became the subject of analysis by Andor Lilienthal, Jan Timman and other expert analysts. The 13th world chess champion, Garry Kasparov, computer-analyzed it in the first volume of the series *My Great Predecessors*, which he co-authored with Dmitry Plisetsky.

**England**

It is not without trepidation that Alekhine first stepped onto English soil in the summer of 1922, when he arrived in London to participate in the "Tournament of Winners." For it is from England that Paul Morphy, Adolf Anderssen, Wilhelm Steinitz, and Emanuel Lasker had begun their ascent to the very top of world glory. And they clearly did not suffer Hamlet's torments with answering the question of "to be or not to be."

Alekhine was also sure of himself. It was in London where he put his signature on the London Agreement proposed by Capablanca, listing twelve main clauses regulating future world championship matches. And subsequently, he especially insisted on taking a principled stand precisely in his negotiations with the Cuban, when the latter, already a former world champion, attempted to waive one or more clauses of these largely onerous conditions. As Charles tells Oliver, "There is no news at the court, sir, save the old news" (*As You Like It* I.i.99). It unambiguously resonated when Alekhine chided Capablanca after he "complied with the terms [Capablanca had] laid down and won six games from [him]. Do you believe that in the return match I [i.e., Alekhine] will allow conditions that reduce chess to a game of chance, like baccarat?" Therefore, after the gentlemen's agreement they reached on the soil of the foggy Albion, Monsieur Alekhine and Señor Capablanca could never more agree – not once and in no other place.

Alekhine played in fourteen tournaments in England; the first time at London 1922 and the last time at Plymouth 1938. Capablanca played in ten; the first time at Hastings 1918 and the last time at Margate 1939. Remarkably, their roads crossed only twice, in the famous tournaments at London (1922) and Nottingham (1936). The first of these games was a rapid draw, but, in the second, a Dutch Defense (perhaps as a token of respect for the then world champion Max Euwe of Amsterdam) ex-champion Capablanca defeated Alekhine on move 38. It is surprising that Alekhine played at Hastings four times (1922, 1925-26, 1933-34, and 1936-37) and at Margate three times (1923, 1937, 1938), which is exactly as often as his "old pal" Capablanca did in other years: Hastings (1919, 1929-30, 30-31, 1934-35) and Margate (1935, 1936, and 1939). In England, Alekhine won seven tournaments and tied for first/second places twice. The Cuban won first only three times and once shared first/second places, but, in the events where they both competed, he confidently surpassed his rival.

Then, Alekhine had an exceptionally successful year in England in 1926. He then won three tournaments in a row: first the New Year's tournament at Hastings, then the tournaments at Scarborough and Birmingham, having played in these competitions altogether

twenty-two games, of which he won twenty and drew only two. In *On the Road to the Highest Chess Achievements*, Alekhine reveals his own road to chess improvement:

*Since none of these tournaments had major sporting significance, I predominantly focused on perfecting the style of my play. It was necessary to uncover and then remove the deficiencies still inherent in it, as compared to Capablanca's play. In the games with Yates, Znosko-Borovsky, and Janowsky, I paid special attention to the moment of transition from opening to middlegame.*

*The last of the above-mentioned games, just as my game against Colle at Scarborough, gave me a chance to study the queen and rook struggle against queen and rook. The knowledge I thus gained, subsequently proved useful in my match with Capablanca. Also, at Hastings, fate reminded me that I had insufficient experience as a sportsman. I had already outplayed my chief rival Vidmar in the opening but then agreed to a draw he offered, hoping to outstrip him in the following rounds more easily. For this, I was punished by fate: like me, Vidmar won all the remaining games, and I had to share first place with him.*

Apart from the individual tournaments, Alekhine took part in a team event – "Tournament of Nations" – in Folkston (1933, +8 -1 =3). The world championship match between Alekhine and Botvinnik would have taken place in London, but the sudden death of the fourth world chess champion in Estoril (Portugal) prevented it.

## Germany

Alexander Alekhine was not yet 16-years old when he first came to an international tournament, the 16th Congress of the German Chess Union held in Düsseldorf. On the eve of his 50th birthday, in September 1942, he played in the 12th and his last tournament on German soil, the so-called European Championship in Munich. If we add the Tournament of Nations in Hamburg (1930), four training matches (with Fahrni, von Bardeleben, Teichmann, and Sämisch) and two world championship matches with Bogoljubow, we have a total of nineteen events played in thirty-four years.

Their results are quite impressive: four times he took first prizes (Mannheim 1914; Baden-Baden 1925; Dresden 1936; and Munich 1942), twice he tied for first place (Carlsbad 1923; Bad-Nauheim 1936), and twice he came second (Semmering and Dresden, 1926) and twice he shared second and third places (Bad-Nauheim 1937 and Munich 1941). Of special significant are his fantastic result (nine wins in nine games) at the Tournament of Nations (Hamburg 1930) and two convincing victories in the world championship matches of 1929 and 1934.

In other matches, he won twice and drew twice. The French writer Jules Renard once remarked that "[t]he danger of success lies in that it makes us forget the monstrous injustice of this world," and it was in Germany that this "monstrous injustice" quickly reared its ugly head. It would be enough to recall his remarkable performance at the 19th Congress of the German Chess Union in the summer of 1914 when, with six rounds to play before the end of the tournament, World War I broke out and all the Russian participants became prisoners of war in Germany. There he successively tasted the "delights" of the guardhouse in Mannheim, then the military prison of Ludwigshoven, where, because of his picture in the uniform of a graduate of the School of Law that was found on him, he was considered a Russian officer.

Then there was the prison in Rastatt, where he played blindfold games with Bogoljubow in the presence of his cellmates – A.Rabinovich and S. Veinstein. (I. Lazebnik, Alexander Alekhine: July 1914-February 1917; *Shakhmaty v SSSR*, 3/1990). His excellent tour of Latin America, which began after the 1939 Tournament of Nations in Buenos Aires, also proved ominous in many respects. During the tour, he won the tournaments in Montevideo and Caracas, but, unlike many of his comrades in chess arms, he decided to return to a Europe enveloped in the fire of the Second World War, and soon was taken into Nazi political bondage...

It seemed to him that the world was collapsing – the German armies were already near his native Moscow. In despair he agreed to do anything to survive and save his wife. You want me to write some articles as you order them? All right, just leave me and Grace alone.

You need a playing champion? All right, I will be playing. You want me to give an exhibition for officers of the Wehrmacht? I have no objections… You want me to edit the chess column in *Novoe slovo* published in Berlin? I agree, only without politics (from August 4, 1943 to January 30, 1944, there were twenty five issues of the journal published with the chess column edited by "World and European Champion A.A. Alekhine").

From 1921 to 1932, Alexander Alekhine published six books in Germany (in Berlin and Leipzig). On the front page of the first of them, *Chess Life in Soviet Russia*, also published in German, Alekhine significantly prefixed his surname with "von," thus reminding the world of his aristocratic origins…

## Spain

In the great sequence of the countries that Alekhine visited, where he struggled and felt veneration, the two hubs of Iberia, Spain and Portugal, became his last refuges during the stormy years of the Second World War. Spain, a country of centuries-old chess traditions had already attracted Alekhine in the very first years of his immigration from Russia. He first visited Spain as early as May-June 1922, giving simultaneous exhibitions in five cities (+185 -9 =13). He also greatly impressed the Spaniards with his simultaneous blindfold exhibitions in Madrid, Barcelona, Seville, Murcia, and Gijon, where he played a total of sixty blindfold games (+49 -2 =9). The Russian champion was given so rousing a welcome that he was pleased to return to Spain at the close of the same

year to give exhibitions (also with clocks and blindfold) in Madrid, Barcelona, and Saragossa in December and January (+78 - 6 =10).

The next time he arrived in Spain was as the world champion, returning to Europe after his victory over Capablanca. That was in January 1928. He came with his wife Nadezhda at the invitation of the chess club of Barcelona, where, on January 24th, he gave a simultaneous exhibition in "Iris Park," with a number of losses that was rare for him (+21 -7 =2). Perhaps that resulted from too warm a welcome that the new champion was given. Seven years later, in January, the chess king paid another visit to Barcelona. This time, he came with his new wife Grace Wishart, and the tours lasted three months. After Barcelona, he continued to give exhibitions in Palma de Mallorca, Valencia, Alcoa, Alicante, Cartagena, Murcia, Madrid, Seville, La Corunna, Santander, Bilbao, Logrono, Saragossa, and San Sebastian. His score in the exhibitions given between January 24 and March 25 proved quite impressive (+640 -32 =58).

His subsequent visits to Spain occurred during World War II, in the autumn and winter of 1941. In September, he arrived from Lisbon in Madrid, where he gave two exhibitions, and in late November and early December he played in a small tournament in Madrid with five Spanish players; he won all the games. Then, he gave exhibitions in Malaga, Seville, Cordova, Vitoria, and San Sebastian (+133 -8 =12).

His last visit to Spain was the longest: October 1943 until the end of 1945.

*An exhibition in Barcelona, 1935.*

Already ill and morally devastated, he had decided to leave the Nazi Germany for the country where his chess genius (Alas! No longer shining as brightly as before) was worshipped. Writer and journalist Pablo Moran, who also authored the book about the last period of Alexander Alekhine life, *The Agony of a Genius* (published in Madrid in 1972 and in the USA in 1989), presents the July 1944 interview the champion gave to the Spanish correspondent Juan Ferdinand Rua in Gijon. In it, we see an Alekhine devoid of his tenacious fighting spirit that made him world champion. He lamented: "What plans can I have? The best part of my life passed between two world wars, which covered Europe with ruins and crosses, which hemmed in my will accustomed to victories. Both have devastated me, but in different ways: when the first of them ended I was 26-years old, I was then full of enthusiasm and of inordinate ambition. Now I have neither."

Still, the Spanish period of his life had not become a "blank sheet." He travelled all over the county, gave exhibitions, played in, and won, tournaments and small matches, annotated games, gave consultations to the magazine *Spanish Chess*, and gave lessons to the gifted young player Arturo Pomar, who would become Spanish champion and later, an international grandmaster (See, Alekhine's pupil in the section "Chess creations: Games and Discoveries"). The Spanish Chess Federation invited Alekhine to participate in the international tournament in Madrid, October 4-20, 1943. Among the participants were Keres, Sämisch, Brinckmann, and the strongest Spanish players. Alas! All his efforts to come there with his wife were in vain: Grace Wishart had been refused a visa, and Alekhine was only able to arrive on October 15 when the tenth round was played! So, he had to be content with the blitz tournament that was held afterwards and the exhibitions given on October 19 and 23.

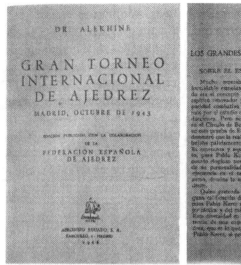

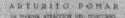

*Alekhine's book about
the international
tournament in Madrid
(1944) and two pages
from it, devoted to Keres
and Pomar, respectively.*

At the request of the Spanish Chess Federation, Alekhine agreed to annotate the games of the Madrid tournament and compose a course of lectures for Arturo Pomar, subsequently published in book form, *Legado* (Legacy). In 1944, Alekhine also played a small match in Saragossa against one of the strongest Spanish players, many-time Spanish champion Ray Ardid (1903-1988). It was held in April, and ended with the score of +1 -0 =3 in favor of Alekhine. From July 14 to 23, he was first in the tournament at Gijon, where eight very strong Spanish players took part (+7 -0 =1). The only player who managed to draw (on move 71) was the 13-year-old Pomar.

The following year, provided richer battles in which Alekhine took part. It started with an impressive victory in Madrid (February 26-March 6), where he conceded only one draw in ten games, winning nine and coming two points ahead of the second-prize winner. The only opponent who succeeded in drawing their game (on move 40) was master Juan Manuel Fuentes, who finished third. Alekhine failed to place first in the tournament at Gijon (held from June 12-21), where he lost two games, one to Medina, who shared second and third places with him, and the other to Bone, who ended in the middle of the field. The latter played the endgame excellently and was, according to some contemporaries, much praised and complimented by "El Colosso," as the Spanish nicknamed the Russian world champion. It is in this tournament, however, that Alekhine won, according to Pablo Moran, the best of all his games played in Spain:

**(6) Alekhine – Pomar,Arturo**
Gijon 1945
Catalan Opening [E09]

**1.d4 d5 2.c4 e6 3.♘f3 ♘f6 4.g3 ♗e7 5.♗g2 0-0 6.0-0 c6 7.♘bd2 ♘bd7 8.♕c2 ♖e8** 8...b6 is the main line. **9.♖d1 ♕c7?! 10.b3 d×c4?** Playing into White's hands. But Black's position is already uncomfortable in any case. **11.♘×c4!** Alekhine develops quickly and forcefully. **11...♘f8 12.♗f4 ♕d8 13.e4 ♘g6 14.♗g5 h6 15.♗e3 ♕c7 16.♘fe5 ♘×e5 17.d×e5 ♘d7 18.f4 ♘b6 19.♘d6 ♖d8 20.♘b5 ♕b8 21.♖×d8+ ♗×d8 22.♘d6 ♕c7 23.a4 ♗e7 24.♖d1 ♘d7 25.b4 b6 26.♕d2 ♘f8 27.f5 f6 28.e×f6 ♗×f6**

**29.♘e8 ♕e7 30.♘×f6+ ♕×f6 (D)**

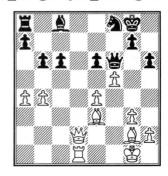

Now the time has come for the final onslaught: **31.e5! ♕f7** 31...♕×e5 32.♗×c6 ♖b8 33.♗f4+– **32.f6!** Alekhine rips open the king's cover. **32...♗b7 33.f×g7 ♕×g7 34.b5 c×b5 35.♗×h6 ♕h7 36.♕g5+ ♔h8 37.♕f6+ ♔g8 38.♗×b7 ♕×b7 39.♖d4 ♔h7 40.♗×f8 1-0**

But, in the subsequent three tournaments Alekhine made up for the Gijon failure by winning: in August, the events at Sabadell (+6 -0 =3); Almeria (first and second with Nunes, +4 -1 =3); in September at Melilla (first with the score +5 -0 =1), which is in Morocco, but was then ruled by Spain. It was only in the Christmas tournament in Caceres, with six participants, that he yielded the first prize to the Portuguese champion Francisco Lupi, losing to him in their game and finishing a half-point behind him (+2 -1 =1).

**Portugal**
Alekhine spent the last three months of his life in the other Iberian country. He also knew this country well. Moreover, it brought back pleasant memories. He had spent two weeks there in early 1940 and visited Lisbon when returning from South America to Paris. At that time, "Alekhine," as Lupi wrote

later, "impressed one as a king at the zenith of his glory. He was tall and stout, of noble bearing and very affable. The Portuguese players were just charmed by his kindness when he taught them or gave them bits of advice, and he also played his brilliant demonstration games." In those days, Alekhine gave four exhibitions in Portugal, two in Estoril (blindfold on January 24 and a regular simul on January 27), and two in Lisbon (February 1 and 10). The world champion's fourth exhibition was against eight opponents and with clocks. It lasted 3 hours 45 minutes, and Alekhine won every game.

After France had capitulated to the Germans, he wrote to Lupi in June 1940 that he would like to return to Portugal, to sail to America from there. But this dream never came true. In April 1941, he managed to visit Lisbon briefly. But how he had changed! Now, Lupi drew a different picture of the champion. Alekhine "looked quite aged, and he no longer had his former majestic appearance and piercing eyes. Alekhine again took to smoking, which he had not done during his previous visit." Lupi also noticed his passion for wine. Needless to say, there were sufficient reasons for Alekhine's anxieties. In those days, he especially felt his loneliness. Grace had not followed him. She was staying in her castle in Dieppe, and she lived under the constant threat of repression from the Nazis. To rescue his wife, Alekhine had to return to France and start playing in chess tournaments. He visited Portugal that summer and played the famous blindfold game against Supico, which finished with a spectacular queen sac-

rifice that placed it in the treasury of chess art.

## (7) Alekhine – Supico,A.
Lisbon 1941
Danish Gambit [C21]

**1.e4 e5 2.d4 e×d4 3.c3 d×c3 4.♘×c3 ♗b4 5.♗c4 ♕e7?!** Too provocative. **6.♘ge2 ♘f6 7.0-0 0-0 8.♗g5 ♕e5?!** This is asking for trouble, but good advice is already hard to give. **9.♗×f6 ♕×f6 10.♘d5 ♕d6 11.e5 ♕c5 12.♖c1 ♕a5?** Losing a piece. The last chance to fight was 12...c6, but Black's cause is almost hopeless in any case: 13.♗b3 (13.♘c7? ♕×e5 14.♘×a8 d5 is not so clear.) 13...♕a5 14.♘×b4 ♕×b4 15.♕g3 ♘a6 16.♖c3 with a strong initiative. **13.a3 ♗×a3 14.b×a3 c6 15.♘e7+ ♔h8 16.♕d6 ♕d8 17.♘d4 b6 18.♖c3** The rook joins the attack with devasting effect. **18...c5 19.♘df5 ♗a6** (D)

**20.♕g6!!** A very beautiful shot that forced immediate resignation in view of 20...f×g6 21.♘×g6+ h×g6 22.♖h3+ ♕h4 23.♖×h4#. **1-0**

This game is also remarkable because the mortal blow delivered by the white queen on g6 happened to become the most beautiful variation of such sacrifices to occur in the sequence of preceding and subsequent events. The best known of them are Levitzky-Marshall (Breslau, 1912), Rossolimo-Reissmann (San Juan, 1967), and Kasparov-Ljubojevic (Brussels, 1987).

Early in 1946, Alekhine had to move to Portugal because of the unfavorable political situation for him in Spain. Just a week after Caceres, he played a match with Lupi that ended with the score +2 -1 =1 in Alekhine's favor. The following game is from that match, which proved to be his last official competition. His opening choice was peculiar, the Petroff Defense (or the Russian Game as it is referred to in Russian chess literature).

**(8) Lupi,Francesco – Alekhine**
Estorial m(4) 1946
Petroff's Defense [C42]

**1.e4 e5 2.♘f3 ♘f6 3.♘c3 ♗b4 4.♘×e5 0-0 5.d3?** Giving Black a dangerous initiative, which develops rapidly in Alekhine's hands. The main lines are 5.♗e2 and 5.♘d3. **5...d5! 6.a3 ♗×c3+ 7.b×c3 ♖e8 8.f4 d×e4 9.d4 ♘d5 10.c4?** White does not have time for this. He should develop rapidly with 10.♗c4. **10...♘e7 11.♗e2?** This runs into a devasting double attack. 11.d5 ♘f5 12.g3 is the lesser evil. **11...♘f5! 12.c3 ♕h4+ 13.♔f1 e3 14.♕e1** 14.♘d3 ♘g3+ 15.♔g1 ♘×h1 16.♔×h1 ♘c6 17.d5 ♘a5 18.♕a4 ♗g4-+ **14...♕×f4+ 15.♔g1** (D)

**15...♘×d4!** Alekhine destroys White's proud pawn center with one stroke. **16.c×d4 ♕×d4 17.♖b1 ♕×e5 18.♗b2 ♕f5 19.♖d1 ♘c6**

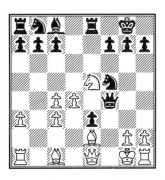

**20.♖d5 ♕c2 21.♗a1 ♗f5 22.♗d1 ♕b1 0-1**

In his memoirs, Francisco Lupi (d. 1954), who was in those days the closest friend of the chess genius, recounted Alekhine's fall. Alekhine was stressed by the troubles caused by the serious, though doubtful, accusations of Nazi collaboration, his ever increasing loneliness, enhanced by his estrangement from the chess world, and, lastly, by his dire poverty. During the last days of Alekhine's life, poverty, misery and illness finally overwhelmed him. Several Portuguese chessplayers and Lupi decided to appeal to Alekhine's wife. "Since the time your husband arrived here," he wrote, "he has been in an unbearable situation, ill and without any means of support. He lives on the charity of the pension administration."

Days passed but there was no reply to the letter. Alekhine passed his time staying in bed or pacing his room like a lion in a cage. And, when a ray of light at last penetrated his dark abode – there came glad news that Botvinnik had challenged him to a world championship match – he again plunged into despair when he heard that Winston Churchill made a speech in Fulton (United States) that sharply attacked the USSR. Alekhine called Lupi, asking him to come immediately. He was very agitated, exclaiming: "Look how unlucky I am! The whole world has gone mad and goes to a new war. I am convinced that my match with Botvinnik will never take place."

Lupi tried to reassure and console Alekhine. Though it started well, it ended abruptly and tragically:

*We again started to work on the games of the Hastings tournament. Once, when we had a break for a cup of coffee, I [i.e., Lupi] asked Alekhine about his plans for opening strategy against Botvinnik. He at once forgot the game we had just analyzed and whispered that the chess world would be astounded by his tactics. He said with a sly twinkle in his eye that he had prepared a small surprise for Botvinnik. "I am going," he said, "to play open games, trying all the time to make Botvinnik play the Ruy Lopez." "But Botvinnik will never play the Ruy Lopez," I objected. Alekhine replied that he has recently studied some lines of the French Defense. When I asked him to show me the variations, he made a gesture as if he had wanted to say, "Why should I reveal my secret weapons?"*

*On the last day of his life, Alekhine felt a new burst of energy. That was the old Alekhine. He even expressed his wish to go somewhere in the evening to have fun, but even there he never* *stopped talking about his forthcoming match with Botvinnik.*

But his illness and hard experiences took their toll: on March 24, 1946, in the Park Hotel of Estoril, near Lisbon, Alexander Alekhine passed away. In the morning he was found dead at the table on which his evening meal and a chess set stood (See, Epilogue).

## Russia

Alekhine was born in Moscow, and he was educated in the best traditions of the domestic chess school. In Russia, his mastery matured, and he achieved fame as one of the strongest players on the planet. But, World War I and two revolutions interfered with his dream of ascending Chess Olympus. The years of post-revolutionary transformations also brought many troubles to Alekhine, a son of a wealthy, noble family. Thus, having come to Odessa to play chess, he became embroiled amongst the military action and struggle for power. There followed his arrest by the Odessa Gubcheka, and he was faced with the threat of being shot. A happy coincidence preserved Alekhine for the chess world; his fate had been decided by a revolutionary boss, still unknown, but a chess lover.

Eighteen months later, a new case was filed against him, this time in Moscow, where he was kept under secret surveillance. The hearing of February 21, 1921 made clear the falsehood of the accusation and the case was dropped. Having gone abroad two months later, Alekhine never returned to his motherland, but threads, visible and invisible, tied him to Russia. His publications appeared on the pages of the

43

Moscow journal *Shakhmaty*. The Soviet media extensively covered his sporting and creative achievements; winning the world title in 1927 received a broad response. The articles and books of Romanovsky, Levenfish, Ilyin-Genevsky, and other Soviet chess masters emphasized that Alekhine's victory had been the realization of the old dream that had existed in Russia ever since the battles between Chigorin and Steinitz for the world championship.

*The estate formerly owned by the Prokhorov family.*

During the celebration of his victory in Paris, Alekhine inadvertently made a careless remark about what was going on in Soviet Russia. There followed an angry rebuff. The leading article in the sixth issue of the journal *Shakhmatny listok* for 1928 was titled "On the new white-guard statement by Alekhine." The author, a public prosecutor of the RSFSR and simultaneously the Chairman of the All-Union Chess Section, Nikolai Krylenko, wrote that "[i]f, after his victory over Capablanca, there were rumors that he would not mind returning to the USSR, now the absurdity and groundlessness of these suppositions have become evident. We now are finished with the citizen Alekhine…He is our political enemy. Talent is talent, and politics is politics, and with renegades, be it Alekhine or Bogoljubow, no relationship should be maintained."

Subsequently, the world champion would seek ways of reconciling, regretting that some of his public utterances had been interpreted as having been directed against his motherland. His moods are well reflected in Lyubimov's book *In a Strange Land*:

*Chunky and short-necked, Alekhine produced the impression of a powerful and strong-willed man. He knew how to speak intelligently, with weight, but one could discern in his talking some involuntary irritation. Yes, undoubtedly something in his fate continually irritated him. He was really inspired only when talking about chess, and, if his interlocutor happened to be a foreigner, he always stressed that the highest chess culture was in the Soviet Union."*

*Alekhine was, of course, a man of great passions, but living in a foreign land, with the realization that he was not at home, that only "in his own home," for which Bunin so anguished, could he be really acclaimed and, at the same time, a kind of pusillanimity that prevented him from the resolute recognition of his fallacy in being separated from home – all this has broken him, deprived him of inner support.*

Beginning in 1933, Alekhine no longer concealed his aspirations of returning to the USSR. The world champion was then at the zenith of his chess glory, and he was looking for a chance to really prove that he had radically changed his attitude toward the Soviet country. Such an open turn became clear when, on October 29, 1935, he sent a letter, from Amsterdam where his world championship match with Euwe was taking place, to the editorial office of the newspaper *64*. "Not only as a chess worker for many years," Alekhine wrote, "but also as a man who had realized the tremendous significance of what has been achieved in the USSR in all fields of cultural life, I am sending my sincere greetings to the chessplayers of the USSR on the occasion of the 18th anniversary of the October Revolution." The text of this letter was published in the newspaper *Izvestiya*, and, on November 20, 1935, *64* published a facsimile of it. It was reproduced at the bottom of the second page, alongside of a lengthy article by Salo Flohr "On the Match Alekhine-Euwe." The Moscow press was exceptionally attentive to this contest, publishing all the games with detailed annotations by Soviet and foreign chessplayers.The loss of the match prevented Alekhine from realizing his desire to return to the motherland. He wanted to return as world champion. During the major 1936 international tournament at Podebrady (Czechoslovakia), he sent two letters to the editorial office of *64*, in which he expressed his desire to be actively involved in Soviet chess life.

*To the Editors of* 64
*July 27, 1936*

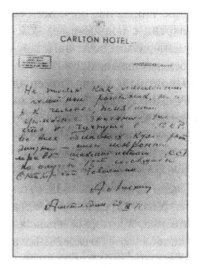

*The congratulatory letter of Alekhine to Soviet chessplayers on the occasion of the 18th anniversary of the October Revolution. It was sent from Amsterdam during the 1935 world championship match.*

*I would be very glad indeed if, by collaborating with your journal, I could, after so many long years, again become moderately involved in the chess development in the USSR. I am availing myself of the opportunity to send my very cordial regards to the new Russia of steel.*

*A. Alekhine*

He sent one more letter from London right after the end of the 1936 Nottingham tournament, where Alekhine first met the leader of the Soviet chessplayers, Mikhail Botvinnik. This letter, like the previous one, did not appear in the press during Alekhine's life. It was first published three decades later by one of the present authors (*Shakhmaty v SSSR 9/ 1969*), who had received them from the daughter of R.G. Golts, an active participant of Soviet chess in the pre-war years.

*To the Editors of 64*
*London, 1 September 1936*

*Concerning my possible collaboration with your journal I consider it my duty to make the following statement:*

*1. For me, it would be a great joy to make my modest contribution to the development of chess in the USSR.*

*2. I hope that my past mistakes, now entirely realized by me, will not turn out to be an insurmountable barrier to the said participation.*

*These mistakes consisted in the following:*

*(a) The unforgivably passive attitude to the coverage of my political face by the international anti-Soviet press, which for many years has appended to me the label it has invented of a White Guard Russian.*

*(b) The wrong and biased (mainly because of the absence of direct evidence) interpretation of facts of chess development and chess public manifestations in the USSR in (my) articles and partially oral addresses.*

*I am the more sorry about these mistakes because in recent years my indifferent attitude to the giant growth of Soviet achievements changed to that of admiration. To prove this attitude in practice would be, I repeat, my greatest satisfaction.*

*A. Alekhine*

World War II prevented the realization of Alekhine's dream. Not long before his death, Alekhine, who denied the accusations of collaborating with the Nazi occupational regime, also touched upon the painful question of his alleged anti-Sovietism: "Unfortunately, all my life, especially after I won the world chess title, people attributed to me entirely absurd political views. Thus, for almost twenty years I was called a White Russian, which was especially painful because this made it impossible for me to have any contact with the country where I was born, the country which I never stopped loving and never stopped admiring."

**The United States and Canada**
Three appearances in tournaments, several hundred games played in exhibitions during his tours of the United States and Canada, a number of world records in simultaneous blindfold exhibitions plus the conquered heart of American lady millionaire Grace Wishart – such is a brief list of feats performed by the Russian chess Hercules in these countries.

In 1923, Alekhine first sailed across the ocean when he was 31-years old, which is somewhere between the age of Wilhelm Steinitz, who did it when

46

he was 47-years old in 1883, and Emanuel Lasker, who saw the land discovered by Columbus at age 24 in 1893. Alekhine started conquering the New World in Montreal, which was widely known for its chess traditions. As early as 1894, it had hosted several world championship games between Steinitz and Lasker. Alekhine realized that he could only arouse the interest of the Americans in his performances by setting records or by surprising them with novel forms of competition.

On December 1, 1923, in Montreal, he gave a simultaneous blindfold exhibition against twenty-one opponents, winning twelve games, drawing five, and losing four. At the time, this was a new world record. During the American tours, he gave three kinds of exhibitions: blindfold, ordinary, and mixed. From November to April, he played, altogether, in the United States and Canada 993 games, the total score being 846 wins, 55 losses, and 92 draws. His blindfold exhibitions against the ten strongest players of Baltimore created special excitement because he won seven games without losing a single one. Against the same number of players from the renowned Manhattan Chess Club, he won eight games and drew two.

Newspapers published sensational reports of the performances of the "European Champion," making a big fuss about the necessity of a match between Alekhine and Capablanca. It is not surprising that prominent U.S. chess organizer Norbert Lederer reported that "interest in chess on this side of the ocean has reached a very high level, owing especially to Alekhine's stay and

his remarkable achievements." It appeared that Alekhine achieved his objective "to conquer America." Yet, he still had a feeling of dissatisfaction, associated, as before, with the uncertain prospects of arranging a match with Capablanca. Late in 1923, many newspapers of the New World published Alekhine's open letter to Capablanca. *Shakhmatny Listok* (2/1924) also published it, though in a slightly shortened version:

> *Montreal, 28 November 1923*
> *Dear master Capablanca:*
>
> *On the basis of the article that appeared in the chess column of the Times Weekly (London) I dare to address you with this letter, deeming it necessary to indicate that the above article was published with my consent. It presents the opinion of one Havana correspondent who, while emphasizing that he is well informed about myself, nevertheless believes that the arguments I would be able to advance to challenge you to a world championship match are hardly undisputable. He also mentions the conditions upon which I allegedly insisted. I am taking advantage of this occasion to disown this statement: no conditions have ever been mentioned. The only statement I have made reduces to the fact that I consider myself sufficiently strong to compete with you successfully. Had he been in the know of all the details of such negotiations, he would, of course, have known, as I do, that you are*

47

*bound by your word to Rubinstein, because my challenge got into your hands later than Rubinstein's. Also, during the London tournament of 1922 this subject had been discussed in the presence of many masters and you had confirmed that I was to wait, but not until after 1 January 1924, i.e., the time allowed Rubinstein to arrange everything. That I am the next candidate to challenge also corresponds with the views held by the press of the entire chess world. Since I am strongly convinced that Rubinstein will not succeed in organizing the match, I undertook the voyage to America somewhat earlier than expected in order to discuss all the issues having to do with organization of the match. Please, forgive my verbosity and also that I gave the permission to publish this letter in the press, but unfortunately I saw no other ways of avoiding the wrong interpretations.*

*Please, accept the assurances of my highest consideration*
*A. Alekhine*

By crossing the ocean Alekhine started "paving the road" to his match with Capablanca. On April 27, 1924, in the Japanese Hall of the Alamac Hotel in New York, he gave a record blindfold exhibition against twenty-six opponents. Following suit of the idol of his youth, Harry Nelson Pillsbury (a brilliant blindfold player!), Alekhine divides his opponents into four groups: on boards 1 through 8 he opens with 1.e2-e4; on boards 9 through 13, with

1.d2-d4; 14 through 21, again with 1.e2-e4; and on boards 22 through 26, again with 1.d2-d4. The exhibition continued for twelve hours and ended in Alekhine's favor (+16 -5 =5). Here is one of the games from this exhibition. His opponent was 19-years-old Herman Steiner, a future U.S. Champion.

**(9) Alekhine – Steiner,Herman**
New York 1924
Sicilian Defense [B38]

**1.e4 c5 2.♘f3 g6 3.d4 c×d4 4.♘×d4 ♗g7 5.c4 ♘c6 6.♗e3 ♘f6 7.♘c3 d6 8.♗e2 ♗d7 9.f3 0-0 10.♖c1 ♖c8 11.0-0 a6 12.♘d5?!** This is too early. The main line is 12.♕d2. **12...♘×d5 13.e×d5 ♘b8?** 13...♘×d4 14.♗×d4 ♗f6 is more in the spirit of the position. **14.♕d2 a5 15.♖fe1 ♘a6 16.b3 ♘c5 17.♖cd1 ♕c7 18.♗h6 ♗×h6 19.♕×h6 e5 20.d×e6 f×e6 (D)**

**21.♘b5?** This hands Black the initiative and gives him a mobile center. After 21.♕e3, White has a very pleasant position. **21...♗×b5 22.c×b5 d5 23.♗f1 ♖f5 24.♕e3 ♕d6 25.a3 ♖e8 26.b4?!** Alekhine plays on the wrong flank. 26.g3 ♘d7 27.f4= **26...a×b4 27.a×b4 ♘d7 28.♕c3 ♖h5?!** The wrong plan. Playing in the center with 28...♖f4 29.♖c1 e5 is called for. **29.g3 ♕b6+?! 30.♔g2 ♖f8?** Steiner improves the wrong rook. 30...♖f5 is only slightly better for White. **31.♕d4?** Alekhine would not have played this in a real game I am sure. He should heat up the pressure with 31.♖c1± to invade on the c-file. **31...♕×d4 32.♖×d4** (D)

**32...♘e5?** Playing for a trick, which will work in the game. But, if White reacts carefully, Black's h5-rook will be stranded. So activation with 32...♖e5!= is the order of the day. **33.f4??** A terrible miscalculation, which can only be explained by the fact that it was a game from a simul. 33.♖e3 gives White very good winning chances. **33...♖×h2+ 34.♔×h2 ♘f3+ 35.♔g2 ♘×d4 36.♖c1 ♖f7 37.b6 ♘c6?** (D) This runs into a mighty undermining shot. After 37...♔g7, Black should win in the long run, but matters are not completely clear.

**38.♗a6!! ♘×b4?** Only the passive retreat 38...♘d8! defends, e.g., 39.♖c8 ♖f8 40.b5 d4 41.♖c7 (41.♖c4 d3 42.♖d4 ♔f7 43.♖×d3 ♔e7 44.♖c3 ♖f7 45.♖c7+ ♔e8 46.g4 ♖d7 47.g5 ♔e7 48.♔f3 ♔d6=; 41.♖b8 d3 42.♔f2 e5 43.♗×b7 ♘×b7 44.♖×b7 e×f4 45.g×f4 ♖f6 46.♔e3 ♖d6 47.♔d2 h5=)

41...♖f7 42.♔f3 e5 43.♖c8 ♖f8 44.♔e4 e×f4 45.g×f4 h5 46.♖c7 ♖f7 47.♖c8 ♖f8=. **39.♗×b7!** Alekhine's point. **39...♖e7** After 39...♖×b7 40.♖c8+ ♔f7 41.♖c7+ ♖×c7 42.b×c7, White's c-pawn will queen. **40.♗c8 ♔f7 41.b7?!** This advance violates the endgame principle "do not rush." 41.♔f3!? **41...♘a6 42.♖a1 ♘b8 43.♖a8 ♘c6** (D)

**44.b8♕?!** Alekhine cashes in too early and underestimates the difficulty of the coming technical task – a typical mistake. The quiet 44.♔f2 +– is better technique. **44...♘×b8 45.♖×b8 ♔f6 46.♔f3?** White must avoid the pin prophylactically with 46.♖b6±. **46...h6?** The pinning 46...♖e8! leads to a theoretical draw, e.g., 47.g4 g5 48.f5 e×f5 49.♖b6+ ♔e5 50.♗×f5 h5. Alekhine can of course continue to apply pressure with his extra bishop.

**47.♖b6 g5?!** 47...h5 is at least a better practical try to close the inroads. **48.f×g5+ h×g5 49.♔g4 ♖e8?** This makes it easy because the rook is now dominated. 49...♔e5 50.♔×g5 ♖e8 51.♗a6 ♖g8+ 52.♔h4 ♖h8+ 53.♔g4 ♖f8 is more tenacious because Black's rook breathes freely, but it should also lose in the long run. **50.♗d7 ♖e7 51.♗c6 d4** 51...♔e5 52.♖b7+− **52.♗e4** Exchanging rooks with 52.♖b7!? wins directly. **52...♔e5 53.♗d3 ♖c7 54.♖b5+ ♔f6** (D)

**55.♔f3!** Alekhine is alert. 55.♖×g5?? runs into 55...♖c3 56.♗b1 ♖×g3∓. **55...♖c1 56.♖b1 ♖c3 57.♖d1** 57.♔e4 is easier. **57...♔e5 58.♔g4 ♔d5** 58...♔f6 59.♖f1+ ♔e7 60.♖f3 ♖c5 61.♗h7 ♖d5 62.♖d3+− **59.♔×g5 e5 60.♔f5 ♖×d3** A last, desperate try, but Black should be lost in any case, e.g., 60...♖c8 61.♗e4+ ♔d6 62.g4 ♖f8+ 63.♔g6 ♖f4 64.♗f5 ♔d5 65.♔f6 e4 66.g5 e3 67.g6 e2 68.♖e1 d3 69.g7 d2 70.g8♕++−. **61.♖×d3 e4 62.♖d1 d3** (D)

**63.♖a1 d2** 63...e3 64.♔f4 e2 65.♔e3+− **64.♔f4** and Black resigned in view of 64...♔d4 65.♖a8 ♔d3 66.♖d8+ ♔e2 67.♔×e4+−. **1-0**

This exhibition was given after the New York Tournament 1924, in which the roads of Emanuel Lasker, Jose Raul Capablanca and Alexander Alekhine again crossed after a decade's interval. Surprisingly, just as ten years previously in St. Petersburg, they came to the finish exactly in the same order. Three years later, in the absence of Lasker, Alekhine came second after Capablanca in the New York Tournament of 1927.

From March to June 1929, Alekhine, now the world champion, made his second triumphant tour of U.S. cities, playing (from March 21 to June 16) 451 games, winning 373, losing 36, and drawing 42, a winning percentage of over 87%! The exhibition given on May 2 in Denver is exceptionally noteworthy because Alekhine won all forty games!

The world champion shared his American impressions with journalist Lev Lyubimov. On seeing Alekhine having grown so thin, the journalist asked him how he managed to do it.

*For three months I have eaten nothing but vegetables, lettuce and fruit, not once tasted wine and I have never drunk anything at all during meals. I've worked off 12 kilos of weight..."* Alekhine shared his *"secret"* and added, *"It's the first time I've come to America after my match with Capablanca. I'm highly satisfied with the trip. I gave a number of exhibitions there, played in a tournament and won easily, in general. I visited New York, Chicago, Cincinnati and Milwaukee, where the Americans of German descent predominantly live. Chicago is preparing for the international exhibition of 1933. They want this exhibition to surpass all the previous exhibitions. I just could not recognize the city. Lake Michigan is receding from Chicago with every month. There is the tremendous job of moving the lake water away to allow the city to expand.*

*In New York, I made the acquaintance of S.S. van Dyne, the author of the novel* The Crime of a Black Officer *that was published in the* Renaissance [a Parisian newspaper] *From my observation, the fascination with depicting crime, both in literature and in cinematograph, has reached its apogee in America. And the writers who want to earn big money must willy-nilly adapt to this taste. Van Dyne formerly used to write serious books and even now he tries to maintain the standard of good literature and substantiate scientifically his arguments. He has created the type of a snob detective, and this type is now known almost all over America.*

*Marshall and Alekhine are playing an exhibition game, New York, 1929.*

*For his last four books, Van Dyne got a total of about $200,000. By the way, I have been offered a role in the movie* The Crime of a Black Officer *to be filmed next spring. I have already agreed, and I will play the role of a chess master. It will be a sound film. As the chessplayer in Van Dyne's novel is a foreigner, I will have no difficulty with the language.* (Shakhmaty v SSSR, 10/1990).

Alekhine paid a new visit to the United States and Canada in 1932. He celebrated his 40th birthday and won a tournament in Pasadena. From 3 November to 22 November, he gave exhibitions in Baltimore, Bridgeport, New York (two), Toronto, Buffalo, and Chicago (+233 - 21 =21). In early December, the modest Russian actor Alexander Alekhine – remember that in 1919 Alekhine joined the State Studio of Cinematic Art in Moscow, but withdrew a year later, preferring again to serve chess art – gave a blindfold exhibition against five Hollywood stars (the result of the exhibition is unknown) and then set out on his famous circumnavigation. It was during this visit that he

51

made the acquaintance of Grace Wishart and, two years later, married her in the French Riviera.

In January, 1933, he stopped at Honolulu on the island of Oahu, the administrative center of the then territory of Hawaii and beat the local amateurs in an exhibition by the score of 20-0. In July, 1933, he paid a brief visit to Winnipeg and Chicago, which he could not visit during the International Exhibition. In August, he played a consultation game in Washington, and on September 6, another in New York. And this was his last visit to North America.

## Switzerland
This neutral Alpine country (where he first found himself on September 1, 1914, when returning to Russia from the German imprisonment via Basel) more than once emerged on the "life horizon" of the Russian chess genius. Thanks to his marriage to the Swiss journalist Anneliese Ruegg, the Soviet champion was able to go abroad in 1921. His son, Alexander, later lived in Zürich, where Alekhine infrequently visited him. Alekhine altogether played in four tournaments held in Switzerland; three times in Bern (in 1925 and twice in 1932) and once in Zürich (1934) and was invariably successful, taking three first prizes and sharing first-third places once. It is in a tournament in Switzerland (Zürich 1934) that he was finally able to defeat for the first (and only) time his teacher, former world champion Emanuel Lasker, who played there after a nine-year hiatus!

It should be noted that Alekhine played his first international match against the 34-year-old Swiss champion Hans Fahrni (1½-1½), and, fourteen years later, Fahrni would dedicated a book that he published in Bern (1922) to the creative chess of the young challenger from Russia. The death of his mother in Basel (December, 1915) is also associated with Switzerland. She was very seriously ill and stayed there for treatment.

## France
In 1913, a 21-year-old Alekhine had the good fortune to visit the Café de la Régence in Paris, where, in 1742, Philidor had taken his first lessons in chess and, a century later, where Morphy and Anderssen had fought each other. Alekhine gave a simultaneous exhibition there against sixteen opponents, winning fifteen games and losing one. There, he also began his exhibition match with Edward Lasker, consisting of three games. The second and the third games of the match were played in the Café Continental in Paris and in the City Chess Club in London, respectively. All three games were won by the Russian player.

Emigrating from Russia in 1921, he stayed for a short while in Berlin and played quite successfully in the international tournaments in Triberg, Budapest, and The Hague. Then, he settled in Paris. It is in Paris that, on the last day of October 1922, he celebrated his 30th birthday. He soon married the widow of a Russian general, Nadezhda Vasiliev. The new family unit proved helpful in meeting the challenges set by the ambitious chessplayer. He successfully defended his doctoral dissertation in law at the Sorbonne in 1925. While living in

Paris, he produced a number of books of excellently annotated games, included those of his own played during 1908-1923 as well as those of the two legendary New York tournaments (1924 and 1927).

France, too, soon experienced the beneficial effect upon its chess climate as a result of Alekhine's presence on its soil. In 1923, he played a small match (winning both games) with the 23-year-old French master André Muffang in Paris. For him and other young players, meeting Alekhine over the board was a good education. The same year Muffang placed second in the French championship and also shared second-fifth places with Alekhine, Bogoljubow, and Mitchell in the international tournament at Margate (England). Chess tournaments again started to be organized in France. And, it is there that the Fédération Internationale des Echecs (FIDE) was founded in 1924. In Paris, Alekhine had given many simultaneous exhibitions and also set a world record in blindfold simultaneous play in 1925. Five times he led the French team in the world team chess championships, the "Tournaments of Nations."

Alekhine, playing under the French flag, defeated Capablanca in their world championship match. Early in 1928, Alekhine returned to Paris from Buenos Aires. He performed in all the chess centers of Paris, Palais Royale, Rotonda, Café de la Régence, and received a warm welcome everywhere. He was hailed by the famous chessplayers who then lived in France: grandmaster Ossip Bernstein and master Evgeny Znosko-Borovsky. Essays by the fa-

*Alexander Alekhine –*
*an interpreter with the French Army.*

mous Russian writers Alexander Kuprin and Boris Zaitsev, dedicated to Alekhine, appeared in the Paris newspaper *Renaissance* on December 1 and 3, 1927. "Now the world chess champion is a Russian," proudly exclaimed Zaitsev, "and this gloomy morning has been brightened up for us by your victory. Hurray!" Kuprin added that "great is it to be the king who reigns not because of the law of succession and not by the accident of a plebiscite, but because of the sharpness of his mind."

It is possible that Alekhine's fate and character to some extent inspired Vladimir Nabokov to write his *Luzhin's Defense*, where one can find the profound thoughts of the writer on the essence of the ancient game and a romantic essay on the tragic fate of a Russian grandmaster who is screened off from the hustle and bustle of everyday life by the world of spectral chess symbolism.

Recently, based on Yu. Shaburov's archival findings (See his publication "The Mystery of Astrea's Lie" in *Shakhmatny vestnik* , Moscow, 4/1994), it has been established that Alekhine, together with the other Russian grandmaster Ossip Bernstein, joined the Masonic lodge "Astrea," the fraternity of "freemasons." He remained a member for almost a decade, until June 12, 1937, when he was excluded from the lodge because he had no time to carry out the assignments of the Russian freemasons. Answering the question of what motivated him to apply for membership in the lodge, Bernstein said that he "desires to communicate with the cultured and well-educated Russians who are above the party differences," whereas Alekhine, as the lodge master Prince Vyazemsky wrote, "explains his desire to join our society by his quest for spiritual interests." The other member of the lodge (Teslenko) was more specific in disclosing the reasons for Alekhine's wish to join the mason lodge of Paris: "he came to this decision under the heavy burden of his spiritual loneliness."

Like a quarter century previously in Russia, this time Alekhine found himself captured in a whirlwind of tragic events in France caused by the new world war. On returning to Paris after the chess Olympiad in Argentina (1939), he joined the French Army as an interpreter. When France capitulated in June, 1940, he intended to leave France for a while and went to Portugal. However, his wife, Grace Wishart, who lived in France and owned a castle near Dieppe, was not allowed to follow him. To rescue the wife, Alekhine returned to occupied France and started playing in tournaments held in the Third Reich. He also wrote for the Nazi press. "At that time, I was a prisoner of the Nazis... Those years undermined my health and nerves," wrote Alekhine shortly before his death.

His ashes rest now in Paris, in Montparnasse cemetery. On his tombstone of black marble is engraved "Alexander Alekhine. Genie des echecs de Russie et de France [Chess genius of Russia and France]."

**Inevitable Parallel**

The fate of the brilliant Russian chessplayer Alexander Alekhine surprisingly resembles certain events in the life of the great French general Napoléon Bonaparte. Precisely one hundred years after the death of Napoleon, in the spring of 1921, the Russian master Alexander Alekhine, full of Napoleonic plans to conquer the chess world, comes to Paris. A splendid memory, hyper-ambition, strong character, awareness of his mission, readiness to go all the way and, at the same time, spiritual loneliness, suspiciousness, a sense of offended dignity – is not that a picture of the great general Napoléon Bonaparte?

In Alekhine's life, there had been his own Ajaccio (his father's house in an Arbat side-street), his own Brienne (the Imperial School of Law in St. Petersburg), his own Marie-Louise (Anneliese Ruegg, a figure of the Swiss Social Democratic, mother of his son, Alexander). How was he dreaming of his own Austerlitz! And his hour had come. During the autumn of 1927, the battle of the giants in Buenos Aires lasted two and a half months, resulting

*Alekhine's reburial in Montparnasse in Paris, 1956.*

in Alekhine's victory and ascension to the chess throne.

The round-the-world tours of Alekhine can be compared to Napoléon's campaign in Egypt. And his battle with Max Euwe perhaps had not brought him laurels in the same way as Borodino had not brought laurels to Napoléon. The Second World War was a real moral Waterloo for the world champion. In order to survive, Alekhine found himself in zugwang; he had to compromise with his morals. His final months were passed in quiet Estoril, which was a little unlike St. Helen.

And there are two more facts, making the rebellious souls of the General and the chessplayer kindred spirits. Their ashes had not at once found their resting places but were reburied in Paris several years after their deaths. The film *White Snows of Russia* was dedicated to Alexander Alekhine, but nobody would be surprised if a film of this title were to be dedicated to Napoléon. Ultimately, both men seem to embody Napoléon's decree that "[t]he only reward of a genius is glory and immortality."

## Chapter 2: Matches, Tournaments, Rivals

### Tournaments

Alexander Alekhine was a phenomenal tournament fighter: of 94 tournaments in which he played, he won 64 and was runner up in 12. His tournament results in the early 1930s draw particular attention; he achieved record results in a number of the strongest tournaments: San Remo 1930 (+13 -0 =2), Bled 1931 (+15 -0 =11), finishing first an astonishing 5½ points ahead of the runner up.

Between 1909 and 1939, Alekhine participated in most of the major national and international events, including the All-Russia tournaments in St. Petersburg in 1909 and 1913/1914 and the All-Russia Olympiad in Moscow (1920), where he became the first champion of Soviet Russia. In international events, his most significant achievements, apart from San Remo and Bled, were at St. Petersburg and Mannheim (1914), London (1922), New York (1924 and 1927), the victories at Budapest and The Hague (1921), Carlsbad (1923), Baden-Baden (1925), Kecskemet (1926), London and Berne (1932), Zürich (1934), Margate (1938), etc. In the difficult times of the 1940s, Alekhine participated in sixteen tournaments, winning nine and sharing 1st-2nd places in four. Between 1941 and 1943, several major tournaments were held in Germany and Nazi-occupied territories. In Munich, Krakow, Prague, and Salzburg, Alekhine came ahead of such renown players as Keres, Bogoljubow, Sämisch, Stoltz, Lundin, Barcza, and others. As he wrote in December 1945, "I played chess in Ger-

many and the occupied countries for the sole reason that it was our only means of subsistence and moreover, the price I had to pay for the freedom of my wife."

Geographically, Alekhine regularly participated in an unusually wide set of tournaments. He played in England the most (13), then Germany second (8), Spain and Portugal (8 together), Holland (6), and finally Czechoslovakia (5). He played in international tournaments in the USA, France, Austria, Switzerland (4 times each), Hungary (3), Italy and Poland (2 times each). As world champion, he played several times in Latin and South American: Argentina, Uruguay, and Mexico. And everywhere his appearance caused great interest of the chess public because of the brilliant uncompromising play he demonstrated as the challenger and then as the world champion.

### Matches

Between 1908 and 1946, Alekhine played five world championship matches and twenty-one short matches: two of ten games (with Levitzky and Euwe), the others not exceeding six games. Alekhine drew four minimatches: with Fahrni (Düsseldorf 1908, +1 -1 =1), Nimzowitsch (St. Petersburg 1914, +1 -1 =0), Teichmann (Berlin 1921, +2 -2 =2), and Bernstein (Paris 1933, +1 -1 =2). He lost twice: to Nenarokov (Moscow 1908, when he stopped playing after losing three games) and to Capablanca (St. Petersburg 1913; when he lost both games). Alekhine won, by a significant margin, a number of mini-matches: against Bardeleben (Düsseldorf 1908, +4 -0 =1), Blumenfeld (Moscow 1908, +4 -0 =1), Grigoriev (Moscow 1921, +2 -0 =5), Sämisch (Berlin 1921, +2 - 0 =0), and Muffang (Paris 1923, +2 -0 =0). He narrowly won a couple: against Evenson (Kiev 1916, +2 -1 =0) and Lupi (Estoril 1946, +2 -1 =1).

Thus in match-play Alekhine demonstrated his best qualities as a fighter, having won the overwhelming number of such contests. Incidentally, Alekhine won his rematch against Max Euwe in the 1937 world championship; he was the first, and Botvinnik would follow suit.

## Bardeleben-Alekhine Match, August 1908

This match took place soon after the end of the 16th German Chess Union Congress in which the 15-year- old Alekhine shared fourth and fifth places (+8 -3 =2) in a side tournament, being just a little short of being able to surmount the master "hurdle." Alekhine was not in a hurry to leave this beautiful city on the Rhine and not only because he wanted to admire its many old castles and churches. The world championship match between Emanuel Lasker and Siegbert Tarrasch had recently begun on August 17. The first four games of the match were played there; none of them were drawn and Lasker took the lead with 3-1. In any case, it was at that time that the young Alekhine was able to follow personally the games of a world championship contest, and it is just possible that he perceived the strength and philosophic depth of Lasker's play.

Interestingly, almost twenty years earlier the native Berliner Curt von Bardeleben (1861-1924) had played a small match with his young compatriot Emanuel Lasker and, after stout resistance, lost (+1 -2 =1). Since then, master Bardeleben had several major successes, including a tie for first and second places at Kiel (1893), and sharing first-third places at Coburg (1904). In 1895, he won a match against Richard Teichmann, (+3 -1 =6), and drew a match against the strongest English master Joseph Blackburne (+3 -3 =3).

He also became known to the chess world as a theorist and writer who published, *inter alia*, a book on the Ruy Lopez, as well as a chess manual (1906). However, as the match with the talented youth from Russia had shown, the peak of the chess form of the German Baron Curt von Bardeleben lagged far behind and, as Alekhine subsequently wrote, "My opponent showed neither due will to win nor his former master strength." In that match, Alekhine won his first international victory, and a rather convincing victory at that (+4 -0 =1). The following game "has some significance from the viewpoint of chess history and is of some interest by itself," wrote Alekhine, whose own notes appears in brackets.

**(10) Von Bardeleben, Curt – Alekhine**
Düsseldorf 1908
Philidor's Defense [C41]

**1.e4 e5 2.♘f3 d6 3.d4 ♘d7 4.♗c4 c6 5.d×e5 d×e5 6.♗e3** [White wants to prevent 6...♗c5.] The main line runs 6.♘g5 ♘h6 7.0-0. White wants to prevent ♗c5. **6...♗e7**

**7.♘c3 ♛c7** [At this time, this move is not needed. To continue development by 7...♘gf6 and 8...0-0 would be more logical.] **8.a4 ♘c5** [Now, the move 8...♘gf6 would also look more natural and be better.] **9.b4?** White is not ready for action yet. 9.0-0 is more natural. [This is a mistake on two counts. First, White weakens his queenside pawns without any compensation, and, second, he lets the opportunity to obtain an advantage by 9.♘g5 ♘h6 10.h3! slip.] **9...♘e6 10.♖b1 ♘f6 11.0-0 0-0 12.♘e1?** White does not have time for this regrouping. 12.♛c1 is more prudent. [Apparently, the idea behind this move is to counter 12...♖d8 with 13.♘d3. However, if White had foreseen the opponent's reply, he would have prevented the following thrust by playing either 12.♗d3 or 12.♗e2, though even then Black, by playing 12...♖fd8 and 13...♘d4, would have the better position.] **12...b5?** 12...a5 hits the Achilles' Heel directly. [In connection with the next move, this is the best way of utilizing White's mistake on move 9, as well as the unlucky placement of his queen's knight. It is clear that on 13.a×b5 c×b5 White would be a piece down.] **13.♗d3?** This runs into a mighty shot; 13.a×b5 c×b5 14.♘d5 ♘×d5 15.♗×d5 ♗b7 is more or less equal. **13...a5!** Destroying White's queenside. **14.a×b5** [White has in fact no choice because after 14.b×a5 b4 15.♘e2 ♛a5, the a4-pawn can hardly be defended.] **14...a×b4 15.b6** [A forced move. Otherwise, White would lose the pawn.] **15...♛b7 16.♘e2 c5** [It is this position that I had in mind when making my 12th move, and I supposed that it would secure for Black a decisive advantage. However, White has at his disposal a

hidden defensive resource.] **17.c3** [White now not only rids himself of the weak c-pawn, but he also indirectly parries the threat to his e4-pawn because 17...♘×e4 would be met by 18.c×b4 c×b4 19.♘c2 with fairly decent counter-chances for White.] **17...♗d7?!** 17...♖d8 18.♛c2 ♘g4 creates even more pressure. [This is the strongest continuation. Black intends to counter 18.f3 with 18...♗a4 19.♘c2 ♖ad8, retaining the advantage. Accordingly, White decides to protect his pawn on e4 with the knight, thus agreeing to the preliminary pawn exchange on the queenside, which is unfavorable for him.] **18.c×b4 c×b4 19.♘g3 ♘c5** (D)

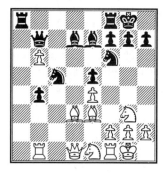

[With this move Black actually attacks two pawns at once. White, quite justifiably, decides to preserve his passed pawn.] **20.♗c4?** White must capture his main enemy immediately: 20.♖×b4 ♘×d3 21.♘×d3 ♗×b4 22.♘×b4, and his b-pawn gives him some compensation. **20...♘c×e4** It would be bad to play 20...♛×b6 because 21. ♘d3! gives White sufficient positional compensation. **21.♘×e4 ♘×e4** [This is stronger than 21...♛e4, which White can answer with 22.♛d3!.] **22.♗d5** 22.♛d5 ♛×d5 23.♗×d5 ♘c3 24.♗×a8 ♘×b1 –+ [The simplification caused by this move is only beneficial for Black.

He ought to have played 22.♕d5 after which the outcome of the struggle would still be unclear. For example, 22...♗c6 23.♕×e5 ♗d6 24.♕f5 ♖ae8 or 22...♕×d5 23.♗×d5 ♘c3 24.♗×a8 ♘×b1 25.♗e4.] **22...♗c6 23.♗×c6 ♕×c6 24.♕h5?!** 24.♕c2 ♘c3 25.♘d3 ♕c4−+ [This quickly leads to the loss of the game. But even after the best move, 24.♕f3, Black, by playing 24...♕c4, would get an overwhelming position.] **24...♘c3 25.♖b2** [On 25.♖c1, Black would push the white queen back with g7-g6 and f7-f5, and, then, there would follow ♘e2+.] **25...♕b5** [Black is preparing for the upcoming combination, winning the exchange. If White attempted to prevent it by playing 26.g3, then Black could continue 26...♖a1, followed by the triumphant march of the passed pawn.] **26.♘f3 ♘e2+ 27.♖×e2** 27.♔h1? ♘f4−+ [This is forced, because 27. ♔h1 would be met by 27...♘g3+.] **27...♕×e2 28.♕×e5 ♗f6 29.♕c5 b3 30.♗f4?!** 30.b7 is more tenacious but insufficient in the long run: 30...b2 31.b×a8♕ ♕×f1+ 32.♔×f1 b1♕+ 33.♔e2 ♖×a8−+ [White's last hope is to push his passed pawn.] **30...♖fe8** [The threat contained in this move was overlooked by White.] **31.b7** (D)

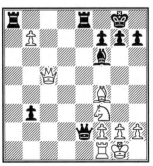

**31...♕×f1+! 32.♔×f1 ♖a1+ 33.♗c1 b2 0-1**

**Nenarokov, Vladimir Ivanovich** (January 4, 1880, Moscow-December 13, 1953, Ashkhabad)
Russian player, International Master (1950), author of a number of manuals on chess and openings treatises. He became one of the strongest Moscow players as early as age 18. In 1899, he participated in the first All-Russia tournament, where he shared 6th-7th places, while his attack in the game with A. Abaza became the jewel of the tournament.

**(11) Nenarokov – Abaza**
Moscow 1899

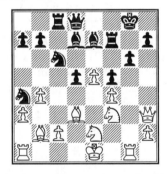

White opens the roads to the king's castle with **18.e6! ♗×e6?** This loses by force. 18...♘×b2 19.e×f7+ ♔g7 was the only way to continue to resist, but White is on top after 20.♗×f5 +− . **19.♖×g6+! ♔f8** 19...h×g6? 20.♕h8 ♯ **20.♕h6+ ♔e8 21.♖g8+ ♖f8 22.♖×f8+ ♗×f8 23.♕×e6+ ♘e7 24.♗b5+ ♖c6 25.♗×a4 ♕b6 26.♘e5 1-0**

In the 2nd All-Russia tournament, Nenarokov finished fifth. In 1900 and 1908, he became Moscow champion. He also successfully played in matches. Thus, in 1905, he drew a match with Saviely Tartakower (+2 -2); in 1907 he won a match with Feodor Duz-Khotimirsky (+5 -3 =1); and in 1908 he defeated the 16-year-old Alekhine (+3 -0 =0). For Alekhine, Nenarokov became one of his most inconvenient opponents, and the negative score in their encounters remained a part of history because after Alekhine's emigration to the West, they never met again.

**(12) Nenarokov – Alekhine**
Moscow m(1) 1908
Philidor's Defense [C41]

**1.e4 e5 2.♘c3 ♘f6 3.♘f3 d6 4.d4 ♘bd7 5.♗c4 ♗e7 6.0-0 0-0 7.♕e2 c6 8.♗b3 ♕c7 9.♗g5?!** 9.a4!? **9...b5 10.d5 b4! 11.d×c6 b×c3 12.c×d7 ♗×d7 13.b×c3 ♕×c3 14.♖ad1 ♖ab8 15.♖fe1 a5 16.a4 ♕b4?** (D) This allows a tactical shot. 16...♖fc8 is more or less equal.

**17.♘×e5! ♗×a4 18.♘g4 ♗×b3 19.♗×f6?** Nenarokov wants too much. He should simply recapture, 19.c×b3 ♕×b3 20.♘×f6+ ♗×f6 21.♗×f6 g×f6 22.♕g4+ ♔h8 23.♕f5, with a slight advantage. **19...♗c4 20.♘h6+** After 20.♕f3!? g×f6 21.♘×f6+ ♗×f6 22.♕×f6 ♖fe8 23.♕g5+, Black's king escapes to the queenside: 23...♔f8 24.♕h6+ ♔e7 25.e5 ♔d7 26.♖×d6+ ♔c7.

**20...♔h8** 20...g×h6?? 21.♕g4# **21.♗×g7+ ♔×g7 22.♘f5+** 22.♕g4+ is met by 22...♔h8-+. **22...♔h8 23.♕h5** (D)

**23...♖be8??** 23...♕b7 24.♕h6 ♖g8 parries White's attack. **24.♕h6 ♖g8 25.♘×e7 ♖g7** 25...♖×e7? 26.♕f6+ ♖g7 27.♕×e7+- **26.♕f6 ♗e6 27.♖e3 ♕b5 28.e5 ♗g4** (D)

**29.♖de1?** Nenarokov misses 29.e×d6, which decides matters directly: 29...♗×d1 30.♘f5 ♖eg8 31.♘×g7 ♖×g7 32.♖e5 ♕d7 33.♖g5+-. **29...d5 30.h3?!** 30.h4!? h5 31.♕h6+ ♖h7 32.♕d6 ♗e6 33.♖b3 is even stronger. **30...♕d7 31.h×g4** 31.♘d5!? ♕×d5 32.h×g4± **31...♖×e7?** (D) 31...♕×e7 is absolutely forced, and Black keeps practical drawing chances.

**32.e6!** The sting of the scorpion. **32...♖×e6** 32...f×e6 33.♖×e6 ♖×e6

34.♖×e6 a4 35.♖d6+–; 32...♕d6
33.♖e5 a4 34.♖g5+– **33.♖×e6 f×e6
34.♖×e6 h5 35.g×h5 ♔h7
36.♕f5+ ♔h8 37.♖h6+**, and
Alekhine resigned in view of 37...♔g8
38.♕×d7 ♖×d7 39.♖a6+–. **1-0**

Nenarokov became Moscow champion
twice more by defeating Nikolai
Grigoriev in matches (+6 -3 =2) in
1922 and in 1924 (+6 -4 =4). In those
years, the winner of the Moscow championship tournaments (Grigoriev) voluntarily agreed to decide the title in
matches with Nenarokov, two of which
he lost, with one drawn (in 1923).
Nenarokov also played with success in
three USSR championships (1923,
shared 3rd-5th places; 1924, shared
6th-8th places; 1927, 7th). He also won
prizes in other Soviet competitions.

His contributions as a chess theoretician, methodologist, and author were
noted in the *Shakhmatny Slovar*
(Chess Dictionary 1963): "His hand-
book of openings has for many years
served as the main source of information for Soviet players."

Selected works:
*ABC of the Game of Chess*. 1924.
*Chess Manual*. 1925.

*Chess ABC*. 1926.
*Ruy Lopez Opening*. 1932.
*A Course of Openings*. Vol. 1-3. 2 ed.
1933.

### Nenarokov-Alekhine match, October 1908

Having convincingly defeated two
skilled tacticians (Bardeleben and
Blumenfeld), and hoping to build on his
success, Alekhine challenged the 1908
Moscow champion, Vladimir
Nenarokov, to a match. The latter, however, understood very well the style of
his young opponent, with whom he had
played many skittles games when he
was a guest at the Alekhine's home.
They had also met in the autumn 1907-
1908 tournament of the Moscow Chess
Circle. There, Nenarokov, playing
Black, won in forty-four moves.

The match was held at Nenarokov's
apartment. The scoresheets from two
of the three games were preserved. In
both, Nenarokov played White and
opened with 1.e2-e4. In the first, a
Three Knights Game occurred. After a
number of exchanges, Alekhine obtained a queenside initiative, but, in so
doing, he underestimated his
opponent's counterplay on the
kingside. Alekhine's experienced opponent sacrificed a piece, and his threats
started to multiply. Tired of the preceding battles, Alekhine failed to find a
satisfactory defense and lost (See the
game under Nenarokov). In the third
game, Alekhine decided to adopt the
French Defense, but this time White's
queenside attack proved more dangerous than the pawn advance that Black
launched on the kingside.

**(13) Nenarokov – Alekhine**
Moscow m(3) 1908
French Defense [C10]

1.e4 e6 2.d4 d5 3.♘c3 ♘c6 4.♘f3 ♗b4?! 5.e5 f6 6.♗b5 ♗d7 7.♗×c6 ♗×c6 8.0-0 ♕d7 9.♘e2 0-0-0 10.c3 ♗e7 11.a4 ♖f8 12.b4 ♕d8 13.♘f4 ♗d7 14.♕e2 f5 15.♘d3 g5 16.♘c5 g4 17.♘d2 ♗×c5 18.d×c5 f4 19.f3 h5 20.♘b3 g3 21.h3 White's king is safe, but the same cannot be said about Black's of course. 21...♘e7 22.b5 c6 23.♘d4 ♕c7 24.a5 c×b5 25.a6 b×a6? Black should try to exchange attacking potential with 25...♘f5, but White's attack goes on after 26.a×b7+ ♔b8 27.♕d2 ♘×d4 28.♕×d4 ♗c6 29.♗×f4. **26.♖×a6 ♔b7?** (D) This meets with a powerful blow. But, 26...♕b7 does not solve the problems either, e.g., 27.♕a2 ♔b8 28.♗d2 ♘c6 29.♖a1 +– .

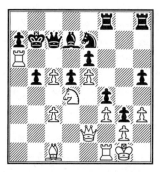

**27.c6+!!** ♗×c6 27...♘×c6 28.♕×b5+ ♔a8 29.♘×c6 ♖c8 30.♘×a7 +– **28.♕a2 ♖a8 29.♘×e6 ♕×e5 30.♘c5+ ♔b8 31.♖×c6 ♖d8** 31...♘×c6 32.♘d7+ +– **32.♕a6 1-0**

Having lost three games in a row, Alekhine was discouraged and resigned the match. Many years later, one of the students of Alekhine's creative heri-tage, grandmaster Alexander Konstantinopolsky (1910-1990) wrote that the games of that contest had shown that Alekhine then "still needed to attain the true harmony between his thirst for attack and positional under-standing."

**Blumenfeld, Beniamin Markovich** (June 5, 1884, Vilkavishkis, Lithuania-March 5, 1947, Moscow)
A Russian chess master, theoretician and author, lawyer, Candidate of Peda-gogical Sciences. Beniamin Blumenfeld may be called one of the first teachers of young Alexander. For he, together with Moscow masters Fyodor Duz-Khotimirsky and Vladimir Nenarokov, frequently visited the Alekhine's home on Nikolsky Street where he played friendly games and analyzed moot positions. Erudite and well-educated, prone to sharp gambit play, with characteristic Jewish humor, Blumenfeld, consciously or uncon-sciously, exerted no small influence on the introverted youth. Alekhine, like his older friend, decided to obtain a degree in law. Like his older friend, Sasha Alekhine preferred combinational com-plications on the chessboard. Blumenfeld gained the title of a mas-ter at the Fourth All-Russia Tournament (1905/1906, St. Petersburg), having shared 2nd-3rd places with Akiba Rubinstein. He also played success-fully in the first Soviet Russia Cham-pionship (the All-Russia Chess Olym-piad 1920), where he took eighth place but showed an excellent result against the first seven players (+2 -0 =5).

After Alekhine returned from Düsseldorf in 1908, he played a small match with Blumenfeld, which ended in a convincing victory of the pupil over his teacher (+4 -0 =1). *Shakhmatnoe obozrenye* reported to its readers that "[t]he match was won by Alekhine in excellent style." Interestingly, when Blumenfeld invented his gambit (1.d4 ♘f6 2.c4 e6 3.♘f3 c5 4.d5 b5) in the early 1920s, it was soon tested by Alekhine (who was then already living abroad) in his game against Siegbert Tarrasch in the Piestany tournament (1922), which garnered Alekhine a brilliancy prize.

Blumenfeld continued to follow the chess career of Alexander Alekhine closely. Thus, he edited the book *Alekhine-Bogoljubow World Championship Match* (Moscow, 1931). He also participated in several tournaments in Moscow, specifically, the Moscow Championship of 1925, in which he shared 2nd-3rd places. There are quite a few interesting lines first analyzed by Blumenfeld in the Queen's Gambit Declined, Semi-Slav: Meran Variation, Scotch Game, Volga (Benko) Gambit, and other openings. He was one of the first in the USSR to pay attention to psychological preparation and the psychology of the chess struggle. On this subject, he wrote a number of articles and also defended his candidate dissertation, "Problems of Visually Effective Thinking on the Basis of Chess Material" (1945). His other books include *The Role of the Endgame in the Game of Chess* (Leningrad, 1929) and *Combination in the Game of Chess* (Moscow, 1938).

## All-Russia Amateur Tournament, February 2-27, 1909

This event was held simultaneously with the international one and was in-

cluded in the program of the 1909 St. Petersburg Chess Congress, dedicated to the memory of Mikhail Chigorin. To make the event possible, the St. Petersburg Chess Assembly organized fund-raising among the patrons of the arts. The donations amounted to almost ten thousand rubles, one thousand of which having been donated by the Russian Tsar Nikolas II. He also established a special prize, a magnificent artistically-designed porcelain vase for the winner.

Before the start of the contest, an appeals tribunal, consisting of the most respected participants, was elected to settle disputes. Among the three members was the 16-year old Alexander Alekhine on whom, even then, the Russian chess community pinned great hopes. And these expectations were justified. Through the entire competition, Alekhine was in the lead group, together with the 24-year old Bernhard Gregory of Revel (now Tallinn) and 20-year old Grigory Rotlewi of Lodz. Alekhine managed to defeat both of them and, having scored 13 points in 16 games, he won the main trophy, the porcelain vase of "Their Imperial Majesties," and a money prize of 300 rubles.

On the creative side, the tournament showed Alekhine's ability to obtain a noticeable positional advantage in the transition from the opening phase (in those relatively few openings he then adopted) to the middlegame. He was then able to force matters rather quickly. Of the twelve games he won, seven were won in less than thirty moves. Playing Black, Alekhine, as a rule, replied to 1.e4 or 1.d4 with 1...e6. As White, he only once abandoned his

*The participants of the All-Russia Amateur Tournament. Alekhine is sitting down third from the right. St. Petersburg, 1909.*

favorite move 1.e4, having adopted a Queen's Pawn Opening. The following game is one of his best achievements in the tournament.

**(14) Alekhine – Gregory,Bernhard**
St. Petersburg 1909
Vienna Game [C28]

**1.e4 e5 2.♘c3 ♘f6 3.♗c4 ♘c6** 3...♘xe4!? is critical. **4.d3 ♗b4 5.♗g5 ♘d4?!** 5...h6 is the main line. **6.a3 ♗xc3+ 7.bxc3 ♘e6 8.h4?!** Capablanca's choice, 8.♗xe6 fxe6 9.f4 from his game against Munoz Ximenez, Montevideo 1911, is more natural. **8...h6 9.♗d2 d6 10.♕f3 ♗d7 11.g4?! ♕e7?!** 11...♘f4!?, with the idea 12.♗xf4 ♗xg4 13.♕g2 exf4 14.f3 d5!, gives Black good play. **12.g5 ♘g8 13.♖b1 ♗c6 14.♘h3 ♔d7?** The king had to be evacuated directly with 14...0-0-0. **15.♕g4 ♖f8 16.f4 f5?** 16...♔c8 17.f5 h5 18.♕e2 ♘c5 also does not inspire confidence for Black but avoids the direct desaster in the game. **17.exf5 ♗xh1 18.fxe6+**

♔c8 18...♔e8 19.fxe5 dxe5 20.♕g1 ♗c6 21.♕xa7 +– **19.♕g1!** A killing retreat. **19...c6** (D)

**20.♕xa7** Typical Alekhine! He prefers the attack over the materialistic 20.♕xh1, which wins as well. **20...c5** 20...b5 21.♕a8+ ♔c7 22.♕a5+ ♔c8 23.a4 +– **21.d4 ♕c7 22.d5 ♘e7** 22...♕b8 23.♖xb7 ♕xa7 24.♖xa7 ♔b8 25.♖f7 +– **23.♖xb7! ♕xb7 24.♗a6 ♗xd5** (D)

**25.c4!** Alekhine opens the path of his second bishop with deadly effect. **25...♕xa6 26.♕xa6+ ♗b7 27.♕xd6 ♘c6 28.gxh6 gxh6 29.f5 ♖xf5 30.♕d7+ ♔b8 31.e7**

**All-Russia Amateur Tournament 1909**

| | | 1 | 2 | 3 | 4 | 5 | 6 | 7 | 8 | 9 | 10 | 11 | 12 | 13 | 14 | 15 | 16 | 17 | Total |
|---|---|---|---|---|---|---|---|---|---|---|---|---|---|---|---|---|---|---|---|
| **1** | **Alekhine** | X | 1 | 1 | 0 | 1 | 1 | ½ | 1 | 1 | 0 | 1 | 1 | 1 | ½ | 1 | 1 | 1 | **13** |
| **2** | **Rotlewi** | 0 | X | 1 | ½ | ½ | 1 | 0 | 1 | 0 | 1 | 1 | 1 | 1 | 1 | 1 | 1 | 1 | **12** |
| **3** | **Gregory** | 0 | 0 | X | 1 | 0 | 1 | ½ | 1 | 0 | 1 | 1 | 1 | 1 | 1 | 1 | 1 | 1 | **11½** |
| **4** | **Daniuszewski** | 1 | ½ | 0 | X | 1 | ½ | ½ | 1 | ½ | 1 | 1 | 1 | ½ | 0 | 0 | ½ | ½ | **9½** |
| **5** | **Eljaschoff** | 0 | ½ | 1 | 0 | X | 1 | 1 | ½ | 1 | ½ | 1 | ½ | 0 | 0 | ½ | 1 | 1 | **9½** |
| **6** | **Maliutin** | 0 | 0 | 0 | ½ | 0 | X | 1 | 1 | 1 | 0 | 1 | ½ | 1 | 1 | 1 | ½ | 1 | **9½** |
| **7** | **Lebedev** | ½ | 1 | ½ | ½ | 0 | 0 | X | ½ | 0 | 1 | ½ | 1 | ½ | 1 | 1 | 0 | 1 | **9** |
| **8** | **Rosenkrantz** | 0 | 0 | 0 | 0 | ½ | 0 | ½ | X | 1 | 1 | 1 | 1 | 1 | 1 | 0 | 1 | 1 | **9** |
| **9** | **Tereshchenko** | 0 | 1 | 1 | ½ | 0 | 0 | 1 | 0 | X | 0 | ½ | ½ | 1 | 1 | 0 | ½ | ½ | **7½** |
| **10** | **Romanovsky** | 1 | 0 | 0 | 0 | ½ | 1 | 0 | 0 | 1 | X | 0 | 1 | 0 | 0 | 1 | ½ | 1 | **7** |
| **11** | **Verlinsky** | 0 | 0 | 0 | 0 | 0 | 0 | ½ | 0 | ½ | 1 | X | 0 | 1 | 1 | 1 | 1 | 1 | **7** |
| **12** | **Evtifeev** | 0 | 0 | 0 | 0 | ½ | ½ | 0 | 0 | ½ | 0 | 1 | X | 1 | 1 | 1 | 0 | 1 | **6½** |
| **13** | **Izbinsky** | 0 | 0 | 0 | ½ | 1 | 0 | ½ | 0 | 0 | 1 | 0 | 0 | X | 1 | 0 | 1 | 1 | **6** |
| **14** | **Tschepurnoff** | ½ | 0 | 0 | 1 | 1 | 0 | 0 | 0 | 0 | 1 | 0 | 0 | 0 | X | 1 | 1 | 0 | **5½** |
| **15** | **Viakhirev** | 0 | 0 | 0 | 1 | ½ | 0 | 0 | 1 | 1 | 0 | 0 | 0 | 1 | 0 | X | ½ | 0 | **5** |
| **16** | **Helbach** | 0 | 0 | 0 | ½ | 0 | ½ | 1 | 0 | ½ | ½ | 0 | 1 | 0 | 0 | ½ | X | ½ | **5** |
| **17** | **Nikolaev** | 0 | 0 | 0 | ½ | 0 | 0 | 0 | 0 | ½ | 0 | 0 | 0 | 0 | 1 | 1 | ½ | X | **3½** |

♘×e7 32.♕×e7 ♖hf8 33.♕d6+
♔a8 34.♗×h6 ♖8f6 35.♕d8+
♔a7 36.♗e3 ♖f3 37.♗×c5+ ♔a6
38.♕b8 1-0

**(15) Verlinsky,Boris – Alekhine**
St. Petersburg 1909
Ruy Lopez [C68]

**1.e4 e5 2.♘f3 ♘c6 3.♗b5 a6
4.♗×c6 d×c6 5.d4 e×d4 6.♕×d4
♕×d4 7.♘×d4 c5 8.♘e2 ♗d7
9.b3?!** 9.♘bc3 is the main line.
**9...c4?!** This atempt to punish b3 immediately rushes matters too much.
9...0-0-0 is called for. **10.b×c4 ♗a4?**
This just goes too far. 10...0-0-0 is again
the order of the day. **11.c3?** 11.♘bc3!
♗b4 (11...♗×c2?? 12.♔d2 +−)
12.♗d2± refutes Black's concept.
**11...0-0-0 12.♘d2 ♗c2?!** 12...♘f6
and 12...♘e7 are more logical. **13.f3
♗c5 14.a4** 14.♘d4? is too early in
view of 14...♖×d4! 15.c×d4 ♗×d4
16.♖b1 ♗×b1 17.♘×b1 ♘e7, when
Black's pawn structure is superior. But,
14.♗b2!? was a serious alternative.
**14...♘f6 15.♗a3?!** From now on, the
centralization of the knight with
15.♘d4! is right, e.g., 15...♗×d4
16.c×d4 ♖×d4 17.♖a2 ♗d3 18.♗b2
and White is better. **15...♗e3
16.♘f1?!** 16.♘d4 ♖he8 17.♔e2
♗×d2 18.♔×d2 ♗×e4 19.f×e4 c5=

16...♗a7 17.a5?! 17.♘d4 is still advisable and leads after 17...♗×e4
18.f×e4 ♘×e4 19.♘g3 ♘×c3 20.♘de2
to a more or less dynamically balanced
position. **17...♖d3 18.c5?!** 18.♗e7
is called for. **18...♖hd8** (D)

**19.♔f2?** The king jumps from the frying pan into the fire. 19.♖c1 ♗a4
20.♘fg3 keeps Black's advantage
within bounds. **19...♘d7! 20.♘e3
♘×c5 21.♘d4** 21.♘×c2? runs into
21...♘×e4+ 22.♔e1 ♖d1+ 23.♖×d1
♗f2+ 24.♔f1 ♖×d1+ 25.♘e1 ♖×e1 #.
**21...♗b3 22.♔e2?** 22.♗×c5 ♗×c5
23.♖ac1 was forced. **22...♖×c3
23.♗b2 ♖×e3+ 24.♔×e3 ♘e6
25.♖a3 ♘×d4 26.♔f4 ♗c5
27.♖ha1 ♘e2+ 28.♔g4 ♗e6+ 0-1**

Since he won the tournament, Alekhine
was granted the title of chess master.

**Carlsbad Tournaments**
Alekhine happened to play twice at this
health resort (now Karlovy Vary).

**August 20-September 24, 1911**
In this tournament of twenty-six players, Alekhine finished eighth, scoring
13½ points and appearing to the world
as a rising star. The Russian master defeated such strong players as Vidmar,
Duras, Tartakower, and Kostic.

**April 27-May 22, 1923**

The tournament gathered eighteen players, among whom there were two prize-winners of the very first Carlsbad tournament of 1907, Rubinstein and Maróczy, as well as the winner of the 1911 tournament, Teichmann. With the exception of the world champion and the former world champion, the field boasted of many leading grandmasters. Alekhine shared 1st-3rd places with Bogoljubow and Maróczy, scoring 11½ points, a full point ahead of Grünfeld and Réti. Of the nine wins he scored in the tournament, three were over his nearest competitors Maróczy, Bogoljubow, and Grünfeld. He also received two brilliancy prizes.

**(16) Grünfeld,Ernst – Alekhine**
Carlsbad 1923
Queen's Gambit Declined [D64]

**1.d4 ♘f6 2.c4 e6 3.♘c3 d5 4.♗g5 ♗e7 5.♘f3 ♘bd7 6.e3 0-0 7.♖c1 c6 8.♕c2 a6 9.a3 h6 10.♗h4 ♖e8 11.♗d3 d×c4 12.♗×c4 b5 13.♗a2 c5 14.♖d1?! c×d4 15.♘×d4 ♕b6 16.♗b1 ♗b7 17.0-0 ♖ac8 18.♕d2?! ♘e5 19.♗×f6?!** This relinquished the bishop pair for an attack, which does not really materialize. 19.♕e2 is called for. **19...♗×f6 20.♕c2 g6 21.♕e2 ♘c4 22.♗e4 ♗g7 23.♗×b7 ♕×b7 24.♖c1 e5 25.♘b3 e4 26.♘d4 ♖ed8 27.♖fd1 ♘e5 28.♘a2 ♘d3 29.♖×c8 ♕×c8 30.f3?** (D) Allowing Alekhine to deliver a mighty blow. 30.♘c3 was forced, but Black's initiative remains dangerous after 30...f5 31.f3 ♗×d4 (31...♖×d4? 32.e×d4 ♗×d4+ 33.♔f1!=) 32.e×d4 ♕c4! 33.d5 ♕c5+ 34.♔f1 (Kasparov) 34...♖f8.

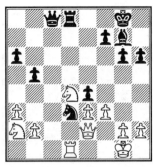

**30...♖×d4! 31.f×e4** 31.e×d4 ♗×d4+ 32.♔f1 ♘f4 33.♕×e4 (33.♕d2 ♕c4+ 34.♔e1 e3! 35.♕×d4 ♘×g2#) 33...♕c4+ 34.♔e1 ♘×g2+ 35.♔d2 ♗e3+ –+ (Kasparov) **31...♘f4!! 32.e×f4 ♕c4!** The sting of the scorpion. **33.♕×c4** 33.♘c3 ♕×e2 34.♘×e2 ♖×d1+ –+; 33.♔e1 ♕×a2 –+ **33...♖×d1+ 34.♕f1 ♗d4+ 0-1**

**(17) Alekhine – Rubinstein,Akiba**
Carlsbad 1923
Queen's Gambit Declined [D64]

**1.d4 d5 2.c4 e6 3.♘f3 ♘f6 4.♘c3 ♗e7 5.♗g5 ♘bd7 6.e3 0-0 7.♖c1 c6 8.♕c2 a6 9.a4 ♖e8 10.♗d3 d×c4 11.♗×c4 ♘d5 12.♗f4** 12.♗×e7 is the main line. **12...♘×f4 13.e×f4 c5 14.d×c5 ♕c7 15.0-0 ♕×f4 16.♘e4 ♘×c5 17.♘×c5 ♗×c5 18.♗d3 b6?** Allowing White to gain too much time, and, later, Alekhine's queen can invade via c6. After 18...♗e7, White still has a dangerous initiative, but Black's position cannot be overrun easily. **19.♗×h7+ ♔h8 20.♗e4 ♖a7 21.b4! ♗f8** 21...♗×b4? 22.♕×c8+– **22.♕c6** 22.g3!? **22...♖d7 23.g3 ♕b8?** (D)

Putting the queen out of play. 23...♕d6 24.♖fd1 ♕e7 (24...♕×d1+? 25.♖×d1 ♖×d1+ 26.♔g2 ♗d7 [26...♖ed8 27.♘e5 ♔g8 28.♕c7 f5 29.♗d3+–]

27.♕c2 ♖a1 28.♕c3 ♖×a4 29.♘e5 ♖e7 30.♘×d7 ♖×d7 31.♕c8+–) 25.b5± was the lesser evil.

"With very energetic play, White has pushed his opponents pieces to the edge. But Black's position still looks solid; only his king is a bit exposed" (Kasparov). Alekhine exploits this Achilles' heel vigorously. **24.♘g5!** **♖ed8** 24...g6 25.♘×f7+ ♔g7 26.♘g5+–; 24...♗×b4 25.♘×f7+ ♔g8 26.♗g6+– **25.♗g6!!** ♕e5 25...f×g6 26.♕g2 ♔g8 27.♕h3 ♗d6 28.♕h7+ ♔f8 29.♕h8+ ♔e7 30.♕×g7+ ♔e8 31.♕g8+ ♗f8 32.♕×g6+ ♔e7 33.♕×e6#; 25...♔g8 26.♕c4 ♗b7 27.♕h4+– **26.♘×f7+** **♖×f7** **27.♗×f7 ♕f5 28.♖fd1 ♖×d1+** **29.♖×d1 ♕×f7 30.♕×c8 ♔h7** **31.♕×a6 ♕f3 32.♕d3+ 1-0**

**(18) Alekhine – Chajes,Oscar**
Carlsbad 1923
Queen's Gambit Declined [D64]

**1.d4 ♘f6 2.c4 e6 3.♘f3 d5 4.♘c3** **♘bd7 5.♗g5 ♗e7 6.e3 0-0 7.♖c1** **c6 8.♕c2 a6 9.a3 ♖e8 10.h3 b5** **11.c5 ♘h5 12.♗f4 ♘×f4 13.e×f4** **a5 14.♗d3 g6 15.h4 ♗f6 16.h5** **♘f8 17.g3 ♖a7 18.♘d1 ♗g7** **19.♘e3** (D)

**19...f5?!** The first step in the wrong direction. 19...b4 gives more counterplay. **20.♕e2 a4?** Now, Black has absolutely no play and can only wait for the coming invasion. **21.♘c2** **♖ae7 22.♔f1 ♗f6 23.♘e5 ♗×e5** **24.♕×e5 ♕c7 25.♕f6 ♖f7** **26.♕h4 ♕e7 27.h×g6 ♘×g6** **28.♕h5 ♕f6 29.♗e2 ♖g7 30.♕f3** **♘f8 31.♕e3 ♖ee7 32.♘b4 ♗d7** **33.♗h5 ♘g6 34.♘d3 ♗e8** **35.♔e2 ♔f8 36.♔d2 ♖b7** **37.♗f3 ♔e7 38.♖he1 ♘f8** **39.♘b4 ♔d8 40.♔d3 ♖ge7** **41.♕d2 ♖a7 42.♖h1 ♖ec7** **43.♖h2 ♗g6 44.♕e3 ♔c8** **45.♖ch1 ♔b7 46.♔d2 ♖e7** **47.♘d3 ♘d7** (D)

**48.♗h5!** Alekhine opens the gates by exchanging the guard. **48...♖a8** **49.♗×g6 h×g6?!** It is better to keep the h-file closed with 49...♕×g6 50.♖h6 ♕g8, but White should win in

**Carlsbad 1923**

| | | 1 | 2 | 3 | 4 | 5 | 6 | 7 | 8 | 9 | 10 | 11 | 12 | 13 | 14 | 15 | 16 | 17 | 18 | Total |
|---|---|---|---|---|---|---|---|---|---|---|---|---|---|---|---|---|---|---|---|---|
| 1 | **Alekhine** | X | 1 | 1 | ½ | 1 | ½ | 0 | 0 | ½ | ½ | 1 | 1 | 1 | 1 | ½ | 1 | 0 | 1 | **11½** |
| 2 | **Bogoljubow** | 0 | X | ½ | 0 | ½ | 1 | 1 | ½ | ½ | 1 | 1 | 1 | 0 | ½ | 1 | 1 | 1 | 1 | **11½** |
| 3 | **Maróczy** | 0 | ½ | X | ½ | 1 | ½ | ½ | 1 | ½ | ½ | ½ | ½ | ½ | 1 | 1 | 1 | 1 | 1 | **11½** |
| 4 | **Réti** | ½ | 1 | ½ | X | ½ | ½ | ½ | 1 | 1 | 1 | ½ | 1 | 1 | 0 | ½ | 1 | 0 | 0 | **10½** |
| 5 | **Grünfeld** | 0 | ½ | 0 | ½ | X | 1 | 1 | ½ | ½ | 1 | ½ | ½ | 1 | ½ | ½ | ½ | 1 | 1 | **10½** |
| 6 | **Nimzowitsch** | ½ | 0 | ½ | ½ | 0 | X | 0 | 1 | ½ | 1 | 1 | 1 | 1 | 1 | 1 | 0 | 1 | 0 | **10** |
| 7 | **Treybal** | 1 | 0 | ½ | ½ | 0 | 1 | X | 0 | ½ | ½ | ½ | ½ | 1 | ½ | ½ | 1 | 1 | 1 | **10** |
| 8 | **Yates** | 1 | ½ | 0 | 0 | ½ | 0 | 1 | X | ½ | ½ | 1 | ½ | 0 | 1 | 1 | ½ | 1 | ½ | **9½** |
| 9 | **Teichmann** | ½ | ½ | ½ | 0 | ½ | ½ | ½ | ½ | X | ½ | 0 | ½ | ½ | ½ | ½ | 1 | 1 | 1 | **9** |
| 10 | **Tartakower** | ½ | 0 | ½ | 0 | 0 | 0 | ½ | ½ | ½ | X | ½ | ½ | ½ | ½ | 1 | 1 | 1 | 1 | **8½** |
| 11 | **Tarrasch** | 0 | 0 | ½ | ½ | ½ | 0 | ½ | 0 | 1 | ½ | X | 0 | 1 | 1 | ½ | 1 | 0 | 1 | **8** |
| 12 | **Rubinstein** | 0 | 0 | ½ | 0 | ½ | 0 | ½ | ½ | ½ | ½ | 1 | X | 0 | 0 | 1 | 1 | 1 | ½ | **7½** |
| 13 | **Bernstein** | 0 | 1 | ½ | 0 | 0 | 0 | 0 | 1 | ½ | ½ | 0 | 1 | X | ½ | 0 | 1 | 0 | 1 | **7** |
| 14 | **Wolf** | 0 | ½ | 0 | 1 | ½ | 0 | ½ | 0 | ½ | ½ | 0 | 1 | ½ | X | 0 | ½ | 1 | 0 | **6½** |
| 15 | **Sämisch** | ½ | 0 | 0 | ½ | ½ | 0 | ½ | 0 | ½ | 0 | ½ | 0 | 1 | 1 | X | 0 | 0 | 1 | **6** |
| 16 | **Thomas,** | 0 | 0 | 0 | 0 | ½ | 1 | 0 | ½ | 0 | 0 | 0 | 0 | 0 | ½ | 1 | X | 1 | 1 | **5½** |
| 17 | **Spielmann** | 1 | 0 | 0 | 1 | 0 | 0 | 0 | 0 | 0 | 0 | 1 | 0 | 1 | 0 | 1 | 0 | X | 0 | **5** |
| 18 | **Chajes** | 0 | 0 | 0 | 1 | 0 | 1 | 0 | ½ | 0 | 0 | 0 | ½ | 0 | 1 | 0 | 0 | 1 | X | **5** |

the long run. **50.♖h7 ♖ae8 51.♘e5! ♘f8** 51...♘xe5? 52.fxe5 ♕f8 53.♕g5+– **52.♖h8 ♖g7 53.♘f3 ♖b8 54.♘g5** (D)

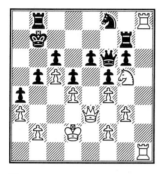

**54...♖e7?** This allows Alekhine, first, to exchange Black's main defender, his queen, and, then, to invade on the kingside. 54...♖c8, in order to meet 55.♕e5 with 55...♘d7 56.♕xf6 ♘xf6 57.♖xc8 ♔xc8 58.♖h8+ ♖g8, is much more tenacious. **55.♕e5! ♕xe5 56.fxe5 ♖a8 57.♖g8 b4 58.♖hh8 ♖ee8 59.axb4 ♔a7 60.♔c3 ♔a6 61.♘f7 ♖ec8 62.♘d6 ♖d8 63.♖h1 ♖d7 64.♖a1 1-0**

**Znosko-Borovsky, Evgeny Alexandrovich** (August 28, 1884, Pavlovsk-December 30, 1954, Paris) A Russian chess master, theoretician, and author. His first teacher was his elder brother Sergey, a member of the St. Petersburg Chess Assembly. Evgeny won several tournaments in which the strongest players of St. Petersburg participated (1903, 1906-1907, and 1911). He also successfully played in several All-Russia tournaments: 1903, 6th-7th places; 1905-1906, 4th place; 1907, 3rd-4th places. In 1906, he made his debut in the international tournament at Nuremberg (the 15th Congress of the German Chess Union), where he shared 9th-10th places (+5 -6 =6) with

Vidmar. He drew his games with the first three prize-winners, Marshall, Duras, and Forgacs. He also won against Spielmann and Janowsky. As a result of this success, he earned the title of master.

The following year, he shared 12th-14th places at Ostend (with thirty participants), defeating such luminaries as Rubinstein, Teichmann, Duras, and Blackburne. When, in 1928, Russian émigré chessplayers celebrated the 25th anniversary of Znosko-Borovsky's chess activities, world champion Alexander Alekhine dedicated an article to his friend and teacher, in which he referred to the above-mentioned appearances as "a great take-off in chess." Znosko-Borovsky "appeared in them, above all, as an artist and creator who was in love with chess." Alekhine also emphasized his important role in organizing the 1909 Chess Congress in St. Petersburg dedicated to the memory of M.I.Chigorin. The program of the congress included an international tournament and a tournament of the strongest amateurs who had not obtained the master title.

*The organizers were faced, among other things, with the question of which of the two tournaments I (a 16-year-old student of gymnasium and without a formal title) should be entered in. Most members of the committee stood for my participation in the international tournament and only one – or almost one – Znosko-Borovsky understood how dangerous, in the sense of the further development of the talent of such an inexperienced*

*player as I then was, the conse-
quences would be of the almost
inevitable failure in the international masters tournament. Because of Evgeny Alexandrovich's
insistence I was only admitted to
the amateur tournament, where I
succeeded in coming out the winner – with new confidence gained,
new ambitions and new thirst for
self-improvement. That was the
first time that Znosko-Borovsky,
whom I then had not yet met personally, had done me a very
good turn in chess.*

Alekhine also discussed the sudden
decision of Evgeny Znosko-Borovsky
to give up active practical play and be
predominantly engaged in chess writing activity.

*Apart from his special study of
the Muzio Gambit, testifying to
his extraordinary analytical talent, he put out his* Ways of Development of the Game of Chess, *
in which he gives a brilliant de-
piction of the outstanding contemporary masters. He was then
one of the first to discover
Capablanca, with a special
monograph dedicated to the Cuban who had only just started his
victorious career... It is already
from these few works that
chessplayers – and not only Russian players – understood that
they could expect much from
Znosko-Borovsky as a peda-
gogue and thinker – and their
expectations have not been de-
ceived.*

Znosko-Borovsky's book on
Capablanca that Alekhine mentions was
the first work published on the creativity of the Cuban master and contained
a number of interesting observations
and original deductions concerning
Capablanca's play and the tendencies of
the development of his style. He observed much elegance, passion, as well
as many combinations and ideas in the
Cuban's games. He rejected the comparison that Lasker's play appears as if
it were crystal clear water containing a
drop of venom, whereas Capablanca's
play resembles the water even more
transparent, but entirely without poi-
son. According to Znosko-Borovsky,
one sees "play which is simple but not
straightforward; even but not impas-
sioned; clear but not without venom"
in Capablanca's games.

His other observations were also interesting. He noted the universality of
Capablanca's style: "Capablanca treats
intricate positions as excellently as the
simple." He also draws attention to
Capablanca's exceptional tenacity in
defending difficult positions: "Any danger greatly enhances Capablanca's resourcefulness." And, of course, he
singles out his skill in handling
endgames: "Capablanca is an unquestionable master of the endgame."

Having thoroughly studied the games
of the Cuban, Znosko-Borovsky proved
to be the only Russian master who defeated Capablanca during his triumphal
tours of Russia in 1913. And, a year
earlier, in the chess match Moscow-St.
Petersburg, Znosko-Borovsky (St. Petersburg) and Alekhine (Moscow) drew
their game on first board. Here is this

*Evgeny Znosko-Borovsky*

game, with notes in brackets by the master from St. Petersburg.

**(19) Znosko-Borovsky – Alekhine**
Moscow 1912
Ruy Lopez [C61]

**1.e4 e5 2.♘f3 ♘c6 3.♗b5 ♘d4 4.♘×d4** [4.♗a4 is played more often. The exchange leads to some simplification of the game and an absolute definiteness of the plan.] **4...e×d4 5.d3 c6 6.♗c4** [This is better than the retreat to a4 because it hampers d5 and retains the attack on this square.] **6...♘e7** 6...♘f6 and 6...d5 are the main lines. [Theory recommends 6...♘f6 because 7.e5 is then unplayable because of 7...♕a5+.] **7.0-0 d5 8.♗b3** [Although the bishop will long be inactive here, White does not dare dissolve Black's doubled pawns on the d-file, for his game is entirely based on their presence on the board.] **8...♗e6 9.♘d2** [9.f4 would be met by 9...g6 or even 9...f5) **9...g6 10.Nf3 Bg7 11.Bg5 0-0** [Black can get rid of his doubled pawns by 11...d×e4, however, White would then have an excellent chance to attack with his pawns along the e- and f- files.] **12.♖e1 ♖e8** [Now 12...d×e4 is no longer playable because of 13.♗×e6

e×f3 14.♗b3 ♖e8 15.♕×f3, winning. With the text, White regains this possibility, which becomes threatening to White, as he moved his rook from f1.] **13.♕d2 ♕d7 14.♗×e7 14.♕f4!? 14...♖×e7 15.e×d5** [Not only to prevent the above threat, but also to win a pawn almost by force.] **15...c×d5 16.♕f4 a5 17.a4 ♖ae8** [Black defends very ingeniously.] **18.♘×d4 ♗g4** [This is much better than 18...♗f5.] **19.♖×e7 ♕×e7 20.h3** 20.♕×g4?? ♕e1+ 21.♖×e1 ♖×e1# **20...♗d7 21.♘f3** [The double threat cannot otherwise be parried.] **21...♗×b2 22.♖b1 ♗e5 23.♕d2 b6 24.♗×d5 ♗×a4 25.♖e1?!** 25.♖×b6 ♕c5 26.♘×e5 ♖×e5 27.♖b8+ ♖e8 28.♖×e8+ ♗×e8 29.c4 a4 30.d4 is a better try. [Playing all along for the win of the pawn, White fails to do so just when he could. In chess jargon, this is explained by psychological interference. In my calculations, I saw that Black could not capture a4 because of ♖×b6, but when my opponent made his 24th move, I believed him that it was I, and not he, who had erred, and I saw my mistake in the possibility of him replying with ♕c5, forgetting the variations I had calculated. Alekhine, however, had calculated further. And, I was so impressed that I at once made the move which, I could see, enabled me to draw.] **25...♕f6?** (D)

25...♛c5 26.♞×e5 ♛×d5 27.♞g4 ♛d4= is called for. **26.d4?** White misses the moment to exploit the lack of harmony in Black's camp with 26.♜e4!, when Black cannot fight on after 26...♝c3 (26...♛d6 27.♞×e5 ♜×e5 28.♝×f7+ ♚×f7 29.♜×a4 ♜e7) 27.♜f4 ♝×d2 28.♜×f6 ♜d8 29.♝a2 ♝c1 30.♜×f7 ♚h8, but it will be uphill struggle in both cases. **26...♝f4 27.♜×e8+ ♝×e8 28.♛e2 ♝d7?!** 28...♚f8 makes it more difficult for White to challenge Black's bishop pair. **29.♞e5** Now, it is Black who, having the bishop pair and two connected passed pawns, stands better] **29...♝×e5 30.d×e5 ♛e7** The last series of moves was made quickly in time pressure. **31.c4** Strange as it may appear, this is the only move that saves the game, for otherwise Black will advance his b-pawn – b6-b5-b4. **31...a4 32.♛e3 a3** If 32...♛c5, then 33.♛f3 and 34.e6 would cause great difficulties for Black. **33.♛×b6 ♛×e5** With 33...a2, 34.♛b8+ and ♛b2, it would still be possible to win the game. **34.♛d8+?** (D) 34.♛a7 is more prudent and should hold the position.

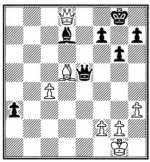

**34...♛e8?** Now White's counterplay with the c-pawn will be just in time. After the surprising king maneuver 34...♝e8 35.c5 (35.♝c6? a2-+) 35...♚g7 36.♛a8 ♚f8, Black is winning in the long run because his a-pawn will cost White's bishop sooner or later. **35.♛a5! a4 36.c5 ♛b5 37.♛a8+ ♚g7 38.c6 ♛×d5 39.♛×a4 ♛c5 40.g3 ♛c1+** ½-½

Znosko-Borovsky had lived in Paris since 1917. He played in several tournaments in Paris, finishing third, behind Alekhine and Tartakower in 1925, sharing 2nd-4th places in 1929, and taking the first prize in 1930. He also played successfully at Scarborough (3rd-4th places in 1926) and Nice (3rd place in 1930). He authored several books and published his articles in the newspaper *Poslednye novosti* on a regular basis.

**Bibliography**

Znosko-Borovsky, Evgeny. *Ways of Development of the Game of Chess*. St. Petersburg, 1910.

–. *J.R. Capablanca. An Experiment in Character*. St. Petersburg, 1911.

–. *Chess Code*. St. Petersburg, 1913.

–.*Chess and Its Champions*. Leningrad, 1925.

–. *Muzio-Gambit*. Leipzig, 1911.

–. *How not to Play Chess*. L., 1931.

–. *Traps on the Chessboard or Dangers in the Openings*. London, 1938.

–. *How to Play the Chess Endings*. 6 ed. New York,1953.

**Stockholm Tournament, June 25-July 7, 1912**

This traditional competition was the championship of the north countries and was held as an open international round-robin tournament of eleven players. It was won by the young Russian master Alexander Alekhine who scored 8½ points out of 10 (+8 -1 =1), 1½ points ahead of the second-prize winner.

**Consultation Games**

Having just reached the playing strength of master and gaining publicity owing to his resounding victories in tournaments, Alexander Alekhine started giving simultaneous exhibitions or playing against several players in consultation with one another. As a rule, those who played against him in consultation were strong players, sometimes even masters. For example, during his tour of Kazan, his opponents were Ado and Kopotansky who worked at Kazan University. Playing Black, Alekhine developed a rapid attack and finished the game with a spectacular mate.

**(20) Consultants – Alekhine**
Kazan 1912
Queen's Gambit Declined [D40]

**1.d4 ♘f6 2.♘f3 c5 3.e3 e6 4.c4 d5 5.♘c3 ♘c6 6.a3 ♗d6 7.d×c5 ♗×c5 8.b4 ♗d6 9.♗b2 a5 10.b5 ♘e5 11.c×d5 e×d5 12.♗e2 ♗e6 13.♕d4 ♘g6 14.♖d1 ♕e7 15.e4?** White is not ready to open the position yet. 15.0-0 is called for because 15...♗×a3? 16.♗×a3 ♕×a3 17.♖a1 ♕d6 18.b6 0-0 19.♘b5 ♕d8 20.♘c7 plays into White's hands. **15...♗c5 16.♕a4 ♘f4 17.♖d2** 17.0-0 is answered by 17...♘×e4 18.♗d3 f5. **17...♘×g2+ 18.♔f1 ♗h3 19.♘g5 ♘e3+ 20.♔e1** (D)

**20...♗g2?** Alekhine seeks tactical complications as usual. 20...d4 21.♘×h3 d×c3 22.♗×c3 ♕×e4 23.♕×e4+ ♘×e4 gives Black a safe advantage. **21.♖g1 ♘d7** A very difficult decision because 21...♕e5!?

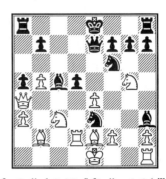

22.f×e3 ♕×h2 23.♗f1 ♕×g1 24.♖×g2 ♕e3+ 25.♗e2 ♗d6 26.b6+ ♔f8 is also hard to assess. **22.f×e3 ♕×g5 23.♖×d5?** The alternative, 23.♘×d5 ♕h4+ 24.♔d1 ♕×h2 25.♖×g2 ♕×g2 26.b6, gives White the initiative. **23...♕h4+ 24.♔d2 ♘b6** After the alternative 24...♕×h2!?, an interesting ending arises almost by force: 25.♖×g2 ♕×g2 26.♖×d7 ♔×d7 27.♕c4 ♕g3 28.♕×c5 ♕d6+ 29.♕×d6+ ♔×d6 30.e5+ and White can still fight. **25.♖e5+ ♔f8 26.♕b3?** The wrong retreat. After 26.♕c2, White is by no means worse. **26...♖d8+ 27.♔c2?** (D) 27.♘d5 ♕f2 28.♖×g2 ♕×g2 29.♕c3 offers more resistance.

**27...a4!** The straw that breaks the camel's back. **28.♕a2 ♗×e3 29.♖d1 ♖×d1 30.♘×d1 ♗×e4+ 31.♔c3 ♕e1# 0-1**

Alekhine played the following, in Alekhine's words "lively," game against two Moscow players, Isakov and Tselikov. It was published with his annotations in *Shakhmatny vestnik* (13-14/1916).

**(21) Alekhine – Consultants**
Moscow 1915
King's Gambit Declined [C30]

**1.e4 e5 2.f4 ♗c5 3.♘f3 d6 4.♗c4 ♘c6 5.b4?!** This combination of an Evans and King's Gambit looks highly dubious. The main lines are 5.c3, 5.♘c3, and 5.d3. **5...♗b6 6.a4 a6 7.♘c3 ♗g4** 7...♘f6!? **8.♘d5 ♗a7 9.♘e3 ♘f6** 9...♗xe3!? 10.dxe3 ♘f6 is even more critical. **10.♗b2?** Too stereotypical. The position demands a quicker tactical solution: 10.♗xf7+ ♔xf7 11.♘xg4=. **10...0-0** 10...exf4!? 11.♗xf6 ♗xf3 12.♗xd8 ♗xd1 13.♔xd1 fxe3 14.♗g5 ♔d7 is also very promising for Black. **11.b5 ♗xf3 12.gxf3 exf4 13.bxc6 fxe3 14.dxe3 ♗xe3?!** Removing White's options on the queenside with 14...bxc6 is more natural. **15.cxb7 ♖b8 16.♗d4?** (D)

This runs into a mighty shot. 16.♗xa6 ♘xe4 17.fxe4 ♕h4+ 18.♔e2 ♖fe8 seems to be dynamically balanced, e.g., 19.♔xe3 ♕xe4+ 20.♔f2 ♕e3+ 21.♔g2 ♕g5+=. **16...♘g4!! 17.♗xe3** 17.fxg4 ♕h4+ 18.♔e2

♕f2+ 19.♔d3 ♗xd4 20.♕e1 ♕f3+ 21.♔xd4 c5+ 22.♔d5 ♕xg4 23.♗xa6 ♕e6+ 24.♔c6 d5+ 25.♔b5 ♕d7+ 26.♔b6 ♕d6+ 27.♔b5 ♖xb7+ 28.♗xb7 ♖b8 29.exd5 ♖xb7+ 30.♔c4 ♕f4+ 31.♔d3 ♕d4+ 32.♔e2 ♖e7+ 33.♔f3 ♕xd5+ also gives Black winning chances. 17.♗xg7? ♕h4+ 18.♔e2 ♕f2+ 19.♔d3 ♗c5-+ **17...♘xe3 18.♕d3 ♕g5?!** 18...♕h4+ 19.♔e2 ♘xc4 20.♕xc4 ♖xb7 is more precise. **19.♔e2?** (D) 19.♔f2 forces the exchange, e.g., 19...♘xc4 20.♕xc4 ♕d2+ 21.♔g3 ♖xb7 22.♖ab1 with some compensation.

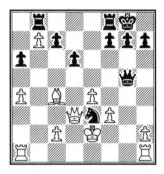

**19...♘xc4?** Exchanging an important attacker. After 19...♘g2 20.♕d2 ♘f4+ 21.♔f1 ♖xb7 22.♖g1 ♕e5-+, Black's powerplay on the dark squares will prevail. **20.♕xc4 ♕g2+ 21.♔e3 d5?** 21...♖xb7 is more natural, e.g., 22.♕d5 ♖fb8 23.♖ab1 ♖xb1 24.♖xb1 ♖f8, and Black is preferable. **22.♕xd5 ♖fd8 23.♖ag1 ♕xc2** (D)

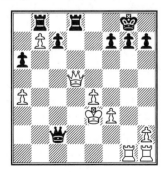

**24.♖×g7+!** Alekhine takes the last exit. **24...♔×g7 25.♕e5+ ♔f8 26.♕h8+ ♔e7 27.♕e5+ ♔d7 28.♕d5+ ½-½**

Little known is the following game, played by Alekhine against consultants in Berlin in November 1921; it was published in the journal *Echo* (12/1923).

**(22) Consultants – Alekhine**
Berlin 1921
Sicilian Defense [B44]

**1.e4 c5 2.♘f3 e6 3.d4 c×d4 4.♘×d4 ♘f6 5.♗d3** The main line is 5.♘c3. **5...♘c6 6.♗e3 d5 7.♘d2 e5 8.♘4f3?!** 8.♘×c6 b×c6 9.0-0= **8...h6 9.c3 ♗e7 10.0-0 0-0 11.♕e2 ♗e6 12.♖fd1 ♕c7 13.e×d5 ♘×d5 14.♘e4 ♘a5?!** It is more natural to take the bishop pair with 14...♘×e3 15.♕×e3 ♖ad8. **15.♗d2 ♖ae8!?** Alekhine prepares the advance of his kingside pawns because the direct 15...f5 16.♘g3 e4? runs into a powerful counterattack (16...♘c6 is called for, e.g., 17.♘d4 ♘×d4 18.c×d4 e4 19.f3=), 17.♘×e4 f×e4 18.♕×e4 ♖f6 19.♘d4 ♕d7 20.c4 ♘b4 21.♕h7+ ♔f7 22.♘×e6 ♕×e6 23.♗e4+-. **16.♘g3 ♗d6 17.♘f5?** This runs into a strong attack. After 17.♘e4 ♗e7 18.♘g3, the position is more or less equal. **17...♗×f5 18.♗×f5 e4! 19.♘d4** 19.♗×e4? ♘f6-+ **19...♗×h2+ 20.♔h1 ♗f4 21.c4?** 21.♗e1 e3 22.♕f3 is more tenacious. **21...♘×c4 22.♖ac1 b5!** **23.b3** (D) 23.♘×b5 ♕e5 24.♖×c4 ♕×f5 25.♘c3 e3 26.♘×d5 e×d2-+

**23...e3!** The battering ram smashes open the king's position. **24.f×e3**

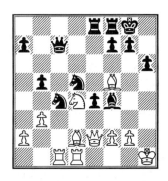

**♘d×e3 25.♗×e3 ♗×e3 26.♘×b5 ♕g3!** The queen enters the attack with decisive effect. **27.♕×c4 ♗f4 28.♔g1 ♖e5! 29.♘d6 g6 30.♗h3 ♗e3+ 31.♔h1 ♖h5 0-1** and White resigned in view of 32.♕f1 ♗f4 33.♔g1 ♕h2+ 34.♔f2 ♖×h3-+.

**Levitzky, Stepan Mikhailovich** (April 13, 1876, Zadonsk-March 21, 1924, Nizhneturinsk)
A Russian chessplayer. He spent his childhood in Serpukhov (a small town about 100 km from Moscow), where he graduated from the gymnasium. He studied chess on his own and successfully played against first-category players. After graduating from the gymnasium, Levitzky entered Moscow University, but in 1897 he suddenly left it to go to the Greco-Turkish War. He fought on the side of the Greeks, fell ill with typhus, was evacuated to Odessa and, after having recovered, returned to Moscow.

It is then that Levitzky achieved his first major success. In 1899, participating in the first All-Russia chess tournament in Moscow, he finished third after Chigorin and Schiffers. After the tournament, he moved to the Urals, where he started working as a mining engineer in the mines near the Nizhneturinsk mills.

His play was distinguished by great originality. It was Levitzky whom Chigorin called "the chess hope of Russia." But, living far away from the country's centers of chess life hampered his progress. He played with varying success in the third and fourth All-Russia tournaments (7th-8th and 11th places, respectively). However, he later had a great success in the All-Russia tournament of the strongest amateurs held in St. Petersburg in the autumn of 1911. There he scored 16½ points in 21 games and finished first, two points ahead of Flamberg. Behind him were Rosental, Verlinsky, Bogoljubow, L. Kubbel, Romanovsky, and other players who were soon to become very well-known. For this success, Levitzky was awarded the title of master and earned the right to participate in the 18th Congress of the German Chess Union in Breslau, which gathered one of the most representative fields in its history.

Although not among the top six (Duras, Rubinstein, Teichmann, Tarrasch, Schlechter, and Marshall), Stepan Levitzky proved himself worthy of the select company by drawing against Schlechter and Marshall, and defeating Mieses, Przepiorka, Lovtsky, and Treybal. All in all, he scored 7 points out of 17 (+5 -8 =4). In 1912, he finished third in the All-Russia Masters Tournament in Vilno, behind Rubinstein and Bernstein. He also twice defeated the sixth prize winner Alexander Alekhine, whereupon he was challenged by the younger master to a match.

Evaluating the play of his rival, Alekhine wrote: "Both [Levitzky's] predominantly combinative style and, most of all, his entirely original and hard-to-define understanding of position are extremely interesting. It is in this originality, in our opinion, that his strength and his chance of success lies." Their match proceeded in the spirit of 19th century games – without draws! Alekhine won decisively with seven wins and three losses (See, *Levitzky-Alekhine match*, 1913).

**(23) Levitzky – Alekhine**
St.Petersburg m(5) 1913
Center Game [C22]

**1.e4 e5 2.d4 e×d4 3.♕×d4 ♘c6 4.♕e3 ♗e7 5.♘c3 ♘f6 6.♗d2 0-0 7.♗d3** 7.0-0-0 is the main line. **7...d5!? 8.e×d5 ♘b4 9.♘ge2 ♖e8 10.0-0 ♗d6 11.♕d4 ♘f×d5 12.♘×d5 c5 13.♘f6+ g×f6?!** (D) This runs into a dangerous attack. 13...♕×f6!? 14.♕×f6 g×f6 was safer.

**14.♗×h7+!? ♔×h7 15.♕h4+ ♔g8 16.♖ad1?** This is too optimistic. The knight should be rescued with 16.♘g3! when one sample line runs 16...♘×c2 (16...♗e5?! 17.♖ad1; 16...f5?! 17.♗g5 ♗e7 18.♖ad1 ♗×g5 19.♖×d8 ♗×d8 20.♕h6; 16...♗×g3? 17.♕×g3+ ♔h7 18.♖ad1) 17.♖ad1 ♘d4 18.♘h5 ♖e6

19.♖fe1 ♔f8 20.♗h6+ ♔e7 21.♘xf6 ♖xe1+ 22.♖xe1+ ♗e6 23.♗g5 with compensation. **16...♘d5?** Alekhine wants to bring back defenders, but White's sacrifice can only be refuted by taking more material with 16...♖xe2 17.♗f4 ♗f5 18.♖xd6 (18.♗xd6 ♕e8) 18...♕e7 19.c3 ♘c6 20.♖xf6 ♗g6 21.♗g5 ♕e5. **17.♘c3 ♗e5** 17...f5 18.♕h5+−; 17...♗c7 18.♗e1 f5 19.♕h5 ♗e6 20.♘xd5 ♗xd5 21.f4 ♖e6 22.c4 ♗xc4 23.♖xd8+ ♖xd8 24.♗c3 ♔f8 25.♖e1+−; 17...♘e7 18.♘e4 ♘d5 19.c4 ♗f5 20.f3+− **18.♗h6 (D)**

**18...♗e6?** Black must sacrifice his queen to stop the direct attack, but it will not help in the long run: 18...♘xc3 19.♖xd8 ♘e2+ 20.♔h1 ♖xd8 21.c3 ♗e6 22.f4 ♘xf4 23.♗xf4 ♗xf4 24.♕xf4±; 18...♕d7 19.f3 ♘xc3 20.♖xd7 ♘e2+ 21.♔h1 ♗xd7 22.f4 ♘xf4 23.♗xf4 ♗f5 24.♗xe5 ♖xe5 25.♕xf6 ♖ae8 26.h4±. **19.♘xd5** 19.♖xd5!? **19...f5** 19...♗xd5? 20.♕g4+ ♔h7 21.♕g7# **20.♗g5** ♕xd5 **21.♖xd5 ♗xd5 22.♗e7 f6?! 23.♗xf6 ♔f7 24.♗xe5 ♖xe5 25.♖d1 ♖ae8?** and Black resigned in view of 26.f4+−. **1-0**

After the relatively short period of successful performances, Levitzky again gave up practical playing. Levitzky attempted a comeback in 1923, when he

came to Petrograd to participate in the second championship of the Russian Federation, but it failed because of illness. Levitzky developed his own system of play in the Queen's Pawn Opening (1.d4 d5 2.♗g5), which is named after him. Among those who have adopted this system, one can name grandmasters Michael Adams, Viswanathan Anand, Boris Gelfand, Anthony Miles, Eric Lobron and others.

References:
Obukhov, G. "Levitzky's Jump. The Russian Master and His Opening."*Opening Almanac* (1, 2005)[See *Shakmatnaya Nedelya*(8, 2005)].
Pavlov, D.S. "S.M. Levitzky (1876-1924)." *Shakhmaty v SSSR* (7, 1939).

**Levitzky-Alekhine Match, March 1-16, 1914**

Alekhine sought to play this match because he wanted to take revenge for his failure against ten of the strongest Russian masters in a double round-robin tournament that was held in Vilno during August and September, 1912. He shared 5th-6th places with Levenfish. He lost both games not only to the winner of the tournament Rubinstein but also to Levitzky, who finished third.

On February 15, 1913 *Shakhmatny vestnik* reported that "[t]he match between master Alexander Alekhine and S.M. Levitzky for seven games up, draws not counting, should without a doubt be considered the most interesting phenomenon of St. Petersburg chess life." The patron who had donated one thousand rubles for the match imposed a condition that the games of the match should be opened with the king's pawn moves (1.e4 e5), excluding the Ruy Lopez and Four Knights Opening.

The match was an uncompromising struggle and ended with Alekhine's convincing victory (+7 -3 =0). At the start of the match, he won three consecutive games. It is curious that in the first game Levitzky as White came up with a novelty on move 6 in the King's Bishop Gambit, but his young opponent turned out to be familiar with the latest analyses and, parrying all threats, gained the advantage. The fourth and fifth games were lost by Alekhine. The sixth game was exceptionally hard fought, lasting ninety-one moves, and was won by Alekhine. He, however, yielded in the seventh game, and his lead in the match became minimal, 4-3. The eighth game, recognized as the best in the match, turned out to be decisive. Alekhine won it in great style.

**(24) Alekhine – Levitsky**
St.Petersburg m(8) 1913
Vienna Game [C27]

**1.e4 e5 2.♘c3 ♘f6 3.♗c4 ♘xe4 4.♕h5 ♘d6 5.♗b3 ♗e7!?** The safe option. 5...♘c6 6.♘b5 is the so-called Frankenstein-Dracula variation, which is very risky, e.g., 6...g6 7.♕f3 f5 8.♕d5 ♕e7 (8...♕f6!?) 9.♘xc7+ ♔d8 10.♘xa8 with wild complications. **6.♘f3 ♘c6 7.d3?** Too ambitious. 7.♘xe5= is the main line. **7...g6! 8.♕h3 ♘f5 9.g4 ♘fd4 10.♗h6 ♘xb3 11.axb3 f5?** This slow move opens the position for Alekhine's attack. Therefore, 11...d6 is called for in order to meet 12.♗g7? with 12...♖g8 13.♕xh7 ♖xg7 14.♕xg7 ♗xg4.

**12.♗g7 fxg4 13.♕h6 ♗f8** It is by no means easy for Black to deal with the threats. The alternatives are 13...gxf3 14.♗xh8 d6 15.♕xh7; and 13...♘d4 14.♗xh8 (14.♘xd4 is met by 14...♗g5) 14...♘xf3+ 15.♔e2, but Black is still uncomfortable in both cases. **14.♗xf8 ♖xf8 15.♘g5** (D)

**15...♘d4?** 15...♖f5? does not solve Black's problems either: 16.♘xh7 ♔f7 17.h4 ♕g8 18.♘d5 ♘d4 19.h5 g5 20.♘hf6 ♕g7 21.♕xg7+ ♔xg7 22.♘e8+ ♔h6 23.♘e3 ♖f4 24.♘xc7 ♖b8 25.♖xa7±. However, Black's best option is 15...d5! 16.♘xh7 ♔f7 17.♘g5 ♖f6, which is not easy to crack. **16.♘xh7 ♖g8 17.♘d5!** 17.0-0-0? is met by 17...♘f5. **17...♘xc2+?** This loses by force. 17...d6 18.0-0-0 ♗f5 is more tenacious. **18.♔d2?** The wrong square because White's king is exposed to checks. 18.♔d1! wins directly: 18...♘xa1 19.♘g5 d6 20.♕h7 ♕xg5 21.♕xg8+ ♔d7 22.♕f7+ ♔d8 (22...♘c6 23.♕xc7+ ♔xd5 24.♕c4#) 23.f4 gxf3 24.h4+–. **18...♘xa1 19.♖xa1** (D) 19.♘g5?? now runs into 19...c6–+.

**19...c6?** Black should develop his queenside with 19...d6 20.♘hf6+ ♔f7 21.♘xg8 ♕xg8 22.♘xc7 (22.♕g5 ♔g7 23.♕f6+ ♔h7 24.♘xc7 is met by 24...♗f5!) 22...♖b8 23.♘b5 ♗f5, when he has good drawing chances, e.g.,

24.♘×d6+ ♔e7 25.♘×f5+ g×f5 26.♖a5 ♕h8. **20.♘hf6+ ♔f7 21.♘×g8 ♕×g8** 21...c×d5? 22.♕h7+ ♔f8 23.♕h8 ♕g5+ 24.♔c2+−, and White's rook will enter the attack decisively. **22.♘b6 ♖b8 23.♘c4!** 23.♖×a7? d5 plays into Black's hands. **23...d6** 23...♔e6? 24.♘×e5 ♔×e5 25.♕g5+ ♔d6 26.♕f4++−; 23...♕f8 24.♘×e5+ ♔e8 25.♕e3 ♔d8 26.♖a4 ♔c7 27.♖f4 ♕e7 28.♖f7±. **24.♘×d6+ ♔e7** (D)

**25.♘c4?** Alekhine puts his knight on the wrong track. With 25.♘e4, he can more forcefully continue his strategy of pressurizing the dark squares, e.g., 25...♕f8 26.♕g5+ ♔e6 27.♔c3 ♔d5 28.♖a5+ b5 29.♖×a7±. **25...♗f5** 25...♕f8!? 26.♕×f8+ ♔×f8 27.♘×e5 ♔g7 28.♖×a7 ♔f6=. **26.♕g5+ ♔e6 27.♕e3 ♕h8 28.♖e1** (D)

**28...♖d8?** The king must leave the danger zone immediately with 28...♔f7

29.♘×e5+ (29.♕×a7 ♕f8 30.♘×e5+ ♔g8) 29...♔g8 30.♕×a7 ♖f8 31.♕×b7 ♕×h2 32.♖e2 ♕h6+, and Black has good chances to hold. **29.♘×e5 ♔f6?!** 29...♔d5 30.b4 ♕f8 31.♘f7 ♕×b4+ 32.♔c1+− **30.♘×g4+ ♗×g4 31.♕e5+ 1−0**

Having won the next two games, Alekhine won the match. "We sincerely congratulate the young Russian master," wrote *Shakhmatny vestnik*, "upon so brilliant a victory over such a strong opponent as S.M. Levitzky."

### Scheveningen Tournament, July 28-August 8, 1913

Alekhine performed splendidly, losing only one game and drawing one, but winning the remaining eleven games, thus scoring 11½ points out of 13. Second, a half-point behind, was another representative of Russia, David Janowsky, followed by third Adolf Oland, fourth Frederick Yates, and fifth Edward Lasker. The following game from the tournament is interesting because of the daring queen sacrifice made as early as move 11. Before presenting the following game, Kasparov mentions that "[g]radually Alekhine began to conquer the chess world with his magical combinations, which have already charmed many generations of chess enthusiasts" (*On My Great Predecessors* vol. 1).

### (25) Mieses,Jacques – Alekhine
Scheveningen 1913
Center Game [C22]

**1.e4 e5 2.d4 e×d4 3.♕×d4 ♘c6 4.♕e3 ♗e7 5.♗d2 ♘f6 6.♘c3 0-0 7.0-0-0 d5 8.e×d5 ♘×d5 9.♕g3 ♗h4 10.♕f3 ♗e6** Alekhine gives the alternative 10...♘×c3!? 11.♗×c3 ♕g5+ 12.♗d2 ♕c5 13.♗e3 ♕a5 with pressure. Hübner defends with 14.♕d5 ♕×d5 15.♖×d5, but Black still keeps the initiative with 15...♗e6. **11.♗e3 ♘×c3!** Alekhine executes his plan to play for an attack even without his queen. **12.♖×d8 ♘×a2+ 13.♔b1 ♖a×d8 14.♗e2 ♘ab4 15.♘h3 ♖fe8** Hübner's suggestion 15...♗f6!? might be a bit more precise. **16.♘f4 ♗f5 17.♖c1 g6 18.g4 ♗e4 19.♕h3** (D)

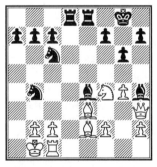

**19...♗f6** Alekhine believes in the long-term nature of his attack on the queenside. 19...g5!? was a very interesting try to win White's queen back, e.g., 20.♘h5 ♖e6 21.♗c4 ♘c2 22.♗×e6 ♘e1+ 23.♔a2 ♗g2 24.♗×g5 ♗×h3 25.♗×h4 ♖d6 26.♘f6+ ♔h8 27.♗×f7 ♘f3 28.♘e4 ♘×h4 29.♘×d6 c×d6 30.♗e6 ♘f3, and only Black can play for a win. 19...♘×c2 is met by 20.f3! (20.♖×c2? runs into 20...♗×f2 21.♗×f2 ♘b4) 20...♘a3+ 21.♔a1 ♘c2+ 22.♔b1=. **20.♗f3!** White must reduce the pressure through exchanges. **20...♗×f3 21.♕×f3 ♘e5 22.♕e2** The risky 22.♕×b7!? also seems to be playable, e.g., 22...♖b8 23.♕g2 ♘c4 24.c3 ♘a2 25.♔×a2 ♖×b2+ 26.♔a1 ♘×e3 27.♕c6 ♖eb8 28.f×e3 (Hübner) 28...♖2b3 29.♔a2 ♗e7 30.♕a4 ♖b2∓. **22...c5 23.♖g1** 23.♗×c5?! is met by 23...♘ed3 24.♕×e8+ ♖×e8 25.♘×d3 ♘c6; but 23.♖d1!? is a real option to reduce the pressure through exchanges. **23...c4 24.h4?!** This advance has no real point. Hübner's suggestion, 24.g5 ♗g7 25.♖d1, is more logical. **24...♘d5 25.♘×d5 ♖×d5 26.f4?!** 26.g5 ♗g7 27.♖d1 ♖b5 28.♗d4 ♖e6 29.♕f1 (Kasparov), and White is certainly not worse. **26...♘d3! 27.♕f3?!** 27.c×d3 is easier: 27...♖×d3 28.♖g3 ♗d4 29.♕c2!= (Hübner). **27...♖b5 28.c×d3** 28.b3? is refuted by 28...♖a5 29.c×d3 c×d3 30.♔c1 ♗c3 31.♔d1 ♖a1+ 32.♗c1 ♖e1+ 33.♖×e1 ♖×c1+ 34.♔×c1 d2+ 35.♔c2 d×e1♘−+ (Nunn). **28...♖×b2+ 29.♔c1 c×d3 30.♔d1 ♖c8** (D) Against 30...♗e7!?, White defends with 31.♗c1 ♖b1 32.♕d5 d2 33.♔c2!! d×c1♕+ 34.♖×c1 ♖b4 35.♕d7 with good drawing chances.

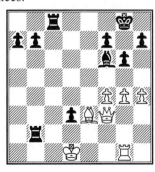

**31.g5?** Mieses does nothing to stop Black's attack. 31.♖g2? is also wrong because of 31...♖b1+ 32.♔d2 ♖b3 33.♔d1 ♗c3 34.♗c1 ♗b4 35.♗b2 ♖e8 36.♕f1 d2–+ (Hübner). But, after 31.♕e4!, Black has nothing better than a perpetual check with 31...♖b1+ 32.♔d2 ♖b2=. **31...♖cc2 32.♔e1 ♖b1+ 33.♕d1 ♗c3+ 0-1**

**Evenson, Alexander Moiseyevich** (1892-1919, Kiev)

Russian player and journalist. The contemporary and namesake of the fourth world champion became one of the leading Russian chessplayers in 1913, having won the All-Russia Amateur Tournament at St. Petersburg with the score of 6½ points out of 7 games. For this achievement, he was awarded the title of a master. "Evenson's victory is impressive not only because of the number of points he scored but also because of the quality of his games, distinguishing a true master. We can expect much of his talent" (*Shakhmatny Vestnik* 24).

In the All-Russia Masters Tournament (1913/14), which was also held in St. Petersburg, he finished ninth with 9 points out of 17 games. He then took part in the international blitz tournament held immediately after the famous grandmaster tournament at St. Petersburg, where he was present as the correspondent for the newspaper *Kievskaya Mysl*. He finished second behind Capablanca but ahead of Lasker, Alekhine, and others. In 1914, he won the quadruple round-robin tournament of Kiev's four strongest players. Evenson won all his matches: 2½-1½ against Bogoljubow, and 3½-½ against both Bogatyrchuk and Grekov. In 1916,

he played a mini-match with Alekhine (+1 -2). Recalling the game he lost, Alekhine said that Evenson outplayed him like a kid. Subsequently, in his book *Chess Life in Russia*, Alekhine eulogizes the 27-year-old master: "In 1919, they learned in Moscow about the death of the young and very promising chess master Alexander Moiseyevich Evenson, who had been shot by the detachments of General Denikin who were retreating from Kiev. He was shot because, on the one hand, he was a responsible Soviet official and, on the other hand, he had the misfortune to be born a Jew."

Alekhine also recalls the success achieved by the Kiev master in the 1914 masters tournament and especially noted his game against Levitzky (published in the Russian and world media) as a sample of his original and elegant style. Expressing his sorrow over the loss of Evenson, Alekhine notes that "[s]ince his talent was still in the stage of maturing, it cannot be doubted that had he been destined for a happier fate, he would have been one of the first on the Russian Chess Parnassus. May he rest in peace!"

In those troubled times of the World War I and civil war in Russia, it was difficult to know who was on which side and the merciless millstones of history were grinding human lives away one after another, Alexander's younger brother Semyon Evenson, who was in the Russian Army, perished in 1915 on the German front, while Alexander himself, as the well-known Russian player Bogatyrchuk asserted (in contrast to what Alekhine wrote), joined Denikin's Volunteer Army, which was, considering his nationality, rather naïve. According to Bogatyrchuk, Evenson most likely died at the hands of his fellow soldiers.

**(26) Evenson – Levitzky**
St. Petersburg 1913
Sicilian Defense [B46]

**1.e4 c5 2.♘f3 ♘c6 3.d4 c×d4 4.♘×d4 a6 5.♘c3 e6 6.♗e2 ♗b4 7.0-0 ♕c7 8.♘×c6 ♗×c3?** Ceding the bishop pair for no good reason. The main line is 8...b×c6. **9.b×c3 b×c6 10.♕d4 e5 11.♕d3 ♘f6 12.♗g5 ♗b7?! 13.♖ab1 d5 14.♗×f6 g×f6 15.f4 e×f4?** Opening the position for White, but good advice is hard to give. **16.e×d5 c×d5 17.♕d4 ♖g8 18.♗d3 0-0-0 19.♕a7 ♖d6 20.♗f5+ ♖e6 (D)**

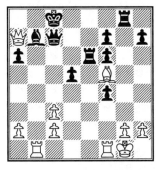

**21.♖×f4!** 21.♗×e6+?! f×e6 22.♖×f4 d4 is much less precise. **21...d4** 21...♕×f4 22.♗×e6+ f×e6 23.♕×b7+ ♔d8 24.♕b8++– **22.♖g4 ♖×g4 23.♗×g4 f5 24.♗×f5 d×c3 25.♗×e6+ f×e6 26.♕b6 ♕g7 27.♕×e6+ ♔b8 28.♕d5 a5 29.♕d8+ 1-0**

References
Averbakh, Yuri and Leonid Verkhovsky. *Meteors*. Moscow, 2005.

**All-Russia Masters Tournament, December 23, 1913 - January 17,1914**

In this event, eighteen players contested for the right to play in the forthcoming "Tournament of the Champions." In the first round, Alekhine lost to Moses Lovtsky because of time trouble, but the unlucky start did not shatter his confidence for eventual success. In a letter to his brother, Alexei, who then lived in Moscow, he referred to the game with Lovtsky as "fairly interesting" and later sent it to the *Shakhmatny vestnik* to be published with his annotations. In the next ten rounds, he scored 9½ points, winning seven games in a row and defeating his main competitors: multiple-time Warsaw Champion Alexander Flamberg and Grigory Levenfish, to whom he earlier lost in the St. Petersburg Quadrangular Tournament. He also defeated, in excellent style, his other main competitor, Aron Nimzowitsch of Riga.

**(27) Alekhine – Nimzowitsch**
St. Petersburg 1914
Ruy Lopez [C82]

**1.e4 e5 2.♘f3 ♘c6 3.♗b5 a6 4.♗a4 ♘f6 5.0-0 ♘×e4 6.d4 b5 7.♗b3 d5 8.d×e5 ♗e6 9.c3 ♗e7 10.♘bd2 ♘c5 11.♗c2 ♗g4 12.♖e1 0-0 13.♘b3 ♘e4** The main line is 13...♘e6. **14.♗f4 f5 15.e×f6 ♘×f6 16.♕d3 (D)**

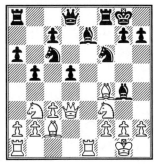

**16...♘e4?** This runs into a small combination. 16...♕d7 was Kortschnoi's choice against Almasi in Linz 1997. But, it seems that White is also better in this case. **17.♗×c7! ♕d7** 17...♕×c7 18.♕×d5+ ♔h8 19.♕×e4 ♗f5 20.♕e2± **18.♘e5 ♘×e5 19.♗×e5 ♗h4 20.♗g3 ♗×g3 21.h×g3 ♗f5 22.♕d4 ♖fd8?!** A strange move, but Black's cause is already hopeless. **23.♖ad1 ♕c7 24.♘d2 ♘×f2 25.♗×f5 ♘×d1 26.♖×d1 ♕×g3 27.♗e6+ ♔h8 28.♗×d5 ♖ac8 29.♘e4 ♕h4 30.b3 ♖c6 31.♕f2 ♕h5 32.♕f3 ♕×f3 33.g×f3 g6 34.♖d2 ♖b6 35.c4 b×c4 36.b×c4 ♖b1+ 37.♔f2 a5 38.c5 ♖c1 39.c6 ♔g7** (D)

**40.♗c4!** A nice final touch. **40...♖×c4** 40...♖×d2+ 41.♘×d2 ♖d1 42.♔e2 +− **41.♖×d8 ♖×c6 42.♖d7+ ♔h6 43.♔g3 ♖c4 44.♘f2 ♔g5 45.♖d5+ ♔f6 46.♖×a5 1-0**

**(28) Znosko-Borovsky,Eugene – Alekhine**
St.Petersburg 1913 (D)

Alekhine quickly seals the fate of White's king with the amazing **42...g5+! 43.h×g6 h5!!** and there is no escape: **44.♘e3** 44.g×h5 ♕g5♯; 44.♔×h5 ♕h1+ 45.♕h2 ♕×h2♯;

44.♕×c3 ♕h2♯ **44...♕×e3 45.♕a4 ♕f2+ 46.♔h3 h4 47.♕e8+ ♔g7 48.♕e7+ ♔×g6 49.♕e8+** 49.♕×e6 ♕g3♯ **49...♗f7 0-1**

In the twelfth round, Alekhine lost to Gregory, and the bitter struggle resumed. After all the dramatic turns, two players, Alekhine and Nimzowitsch, tied for first and second places, scoring 12½ points each. Immediately a tie-break of two games was played, which failed to determine the winner (1-1). Accordingly, it was decided to acknowledge both as the winners to the international tournament.

**St. Petersburg Tournament, April 21-May 22, 1914**
With his successes achieved in 1910-1913, Alekhine showed that he was approaching the strength of the world's best players. But how real were his chances; was he ready to struggle against Lasker, Capablanca, and Rubinstein?

It did not seem like it at first. In November 1913, when the challenger (Capablanca) first came to St. Petersburg, Alekhine played two training games with him. His admiration of the Cuban genius prevented him from playing with all his strength; Alekhine lost both games. It is true that the 21-year-old Russian master did not look too upset. Moreover, the young players – Capablanca was only four years older than Alekhine – very soon became friends. They could often be seen together visiting someone, in museums, theaters, or playing blitz games. Many years later, when Capablanca was no longer alive, Alekhine reminisced of those days and spoke about his sympathies and admiration for the Cuban chess phenomenon.

Four months later, it seemed that he could struggle against top-level masters. On March 28, 1914, Alekhine played an exhibition game against Lasker at the Moscow Chess Circle, as the club was then called. As White, Alekhine essayed the Scotch Game and probably was content that, by move 16, after a combination in which he sacrificed a rook, he was able to draw the game. The strong Moscow player and subsequently a well-known professor, Kharlampy Baranov, who was present at the game, recalled that

*...comparing the opponents, one could say – ice and flame – the older Lasker with his eternal cigar, cool and restrained, was diametrically opposite to his young opponent who incessantly twisted a strand of his hair and not infrequently jumped up after making a move. We did not need a commentator: his expressive face reflected all the emotions he was experiencing. He was in good humor, and the spectators were sure that he had a good game. When the game ended, Alekhine's thin arms started flick-*

*ering over the board, demonstrating innumerable variations.*

**(29) Alekhine – Lasker**
Moscow 1914 (Exhibition)
Scotch Game [C47]

**1.e4 e5 2.♘f3 ♘c6 3.d4 e×d4 4.♘×d4 ♘f6 5.♘c3 ♗b4 6.♘×c6 b×c6 7.♗d3 d5 8.e×d5 c×d5 9.0-0 0-0 10.♗g5 ♗e6 11.♕f3 ♗e7 12.♖fe1 h6** (D)

Now Alekhine forces a draw against the world champion: **13.♗×h6!? g×h6 14.♖×e6! f×e6 15.♕g3+ ♔h8** 15...♔f7?? 16.♕g6# **16.♕g6**, and in view of 16...♕e8 17.♕×h6+ ♔g8 18.♕g5+ ♔h8 19.♕h6+ a draw was agreed. ½-½

In an article published in the newspaper *Rech*, just before the tournament began, Lasker described Alekhine as "a Muscovite by birth, 21-years old. He is about to graduate from the school of law; a slender, handsome young man. He is highly intelligent and has a strong will. He will undoubtedly make a career. As a master, he is still developing, but, despite of his young age, he will perhaps fight with honor." The tournament was organized in two stages, a preliminary and a final.

The first stage was the all-play-all tour-

*Alekhine's first tournament game against Capablanca, St. Petersburg, 1914. Alekhine is in a Imperial School of Law student uniform.*

nament of eleven players, and the second stage was a double round-robin tournament of the five qualifiers from the first stage. The points scored in these two stages were cumulative. Alekhine went through the first stage in great style. He defeated the veterans Gunsberg, Blackburn, and Marshall. In the fifth round, he won his game against Rubinstein, in which both sides were playing for a win. Alekhine was eager to avenge his loss at Carlsbad three years earlier, whereas Rubinstein, who had lost to Lasker in the previous round and had fallen noticeably behind, hoped to come closer to the leaders.

**(30) Rubinstein – Alekhine**
St Petersburg 1914 (Preliminary)
Nimzo-Indian Defense [E43]

**1.d4 ♘f6 2.c4 e6 3.♘c3 ♗b4 4.e3 b6 5.♗d3 ♗b7 6.f3 c5 7.a3 ♗×c3+ 8.b×c3 d5 9.♘e2 0-0 10.0-0 ♘bd7 11.♘g3 ♕c7 12.c×d5 e×d5** (D)

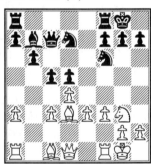

**13.e4?** White is not yet ready to open the position. 13.♖a2 and 13.♕e2 are possible options that prepare the central advance. **13...c×d4 14.c×d4 ♕c3! 15.♗e3 d×e4 16.f×e4 ♗a6!** The sting of the scorpion. **17.♗×a6 ♕×e3+ 18.♔h1 ♘×e4 19.♘f5 ♘f2+ 20.♖×f2 ♕×f2 21.♕g4 g6 22.♖f1 ♕b2 23.♘h6+?** 23.♘e7+

## St. Petersburg 1914, Preliminary

| | | 1 | 2 | 3 | 4 | 5 | 6 | 7 | 8 | 9 | 10 | 11 | Total |
|---|---|---|---|---|---|---|---|---|---|---|---|---|---|
| 1 | Capablanca | X | ½ | ½ | ½ | 1 | ½ | 1 | 1 | 1 | 1 | 1 | 8 |
| 2 | Tarrasch | ½ | X | ½ | ½ | ½ | ½ | 1 | 1 | 0 | 1 | 1 | 6½ |
| 3 | Lasker,Em | ½ | ½ | X | ½ | ½ | 1 | 0 | ½ | 1 | 1 | 1 | 6½ |
| 4 | Marshall | ½ | ½ | ½ | X | 0 | ½ | 1 | ½ | 1 | 1 | ½ | 6 |
| 5 | Alekhine | 0 | ½ | ½ | 1 | X | 1 | ½ | ½ | ½ | ½ | 1 | 6 |
| 6 | Rubinstein | ½ | ½ | 0 | ½ | 0 | X | ½ | ½ | 1 | ½ | 1 | 5 |
| 7 | Bernstein | 0 | 0 | 1 | 0 | ½ | ½ | X | ½ | 1 | ½ | 1 | 5 |
| 8 | Nimzowitsch | 0 | 0 | ½ | ½ | ½ | ½ | ½ | X | ½ | 0 | 1 | 4 |
| 9 | Janowski | 0 | 1 | 0 | 0 | ½ | 0 | 0 | ½ | X | 1 | ½ | 3½ |
| 10 | Blackburne | 0 | 0 | 0 | 0 | ½ | ½ | ½ | 1 | 0 | X | 1 | 3½ |
| 11 | Gunsberg | 0 | 0 | 0 | ½ | 0 | 0 | 0 | 0 | ½ | 0 | X | 1 |

## St. Petersburg 1914, Final

| | | 1 | 2 | 3 | 4 | 5 | Total |
|---|---|---|---|---|---|---|---|
| 1 | Lasker | X | ½1 | 11 | 1½ | 11 | 7 |
| 2 | Capablanca | ½0 | X | ½1 | 10 | 11 | 5 |
| 3 | Alekhine | 00 | ½0 | X | 11 | 1½ | 4 |
| 4 | Tarrasch | 0½ | 01 | 00 | X | 0½ | 2 |
| 5 | Marshall | 00 | 00 | 0½ | 1½ | X | 2 |

♔g7 24.♕×d7 offers better practical chances, but Black is on top after 24...♕×a3 25.♗c8 ♕d3. **23...♔g7 24.♘×f7** 24.♕×d7 is calmly met by 24...♖×h6–+. **24...♕b3 25.d5** (D) 25.♘g5 ♖×f1+ 26.♗×f1 ♕d5–+

**25...♘f6!** By far the easiest defense. White's attack has run completely out of steam. Black could have also won with 25...♕×d5?! 26.♗c4 ♕d2 27.♕h4 ♖ae8, but not 25...♖×f7? 26.♖×f7+

♔×f7 27.♕×d7+, which gives White a draw by perpetual check. **26.♕d4** 26.♖×f6 is calmly answered by 26...♔×f6 27.♕f4+ ♔g7 28.♕h6+ ♔g8–+. **26...♖×f7 27.♗c4 ♕a4 28.g4 ♖c8 0-1**

With this loss, Rubinstein had, for all intents and purposes, lost all chance to reach the final stage, which became one of the sensations of the tournament. With this win, Alekhine took the lead with four points out of five! No one had expected such a start. True, there were hard trials ahead, for in the sixth round he would play Capablanca, and in the seventh, Lasker. He adopted the wrong plan against Capablanca and came under attack, resigning on move 36. With Lasker, he played more spontaneously and even took a greater risk.

**(31) Lasker – Alekhine**
St Petersburg 1914 (Final)
Albin Countergambit [D08]

**1.d4 d5 2.c4 e5** A bold and very risky choice, which backfires in this game. **3.d×e5 d4 4.♘f3** Lasker does of course not fall into the famous trap 4.e3? ♗b4+ 5.♗d2 d×e3 6.♗×b4? e×f2+ 7.♔e2 f×g1♘+ –+ . **4...♘c6 5.a3 ♗g4 6.♘bd2 ♕e7 7.h3 ♗×f3 8.♘×f3 0-0-0 9.♕d3 h6 10.g3 g6?! 11.♗g2 ♗g7 12.0-0 ♘×e5 13.♘×e5 ♗×e5 14.b4 f5 15.c5 ♕e6 16.c6!** Driving a wedge in Black's queenside. **16...♘e7** 16...b×c6 17.♗b2 ♘e7 18.e3 ♖d6 19.♖fe1 ♗f6 20.♗×d4 is also very promising for White. **17.c×b7+ ♔b8 18.♗b2 ♖d6 19.♖ac1 ♖hd8 20.♖c2 f4 21.g×f4 ♗×f4 22.♖d1 ♘f5 23.♗c1?** White should just avoid the coming shot with 23.♕c4!± . **23...♘e3!! 24.♖c5** 24.f×e3? is not as good of a choice because, after 24...d×e3 25.♖c6 ♖×d3 26.♖×d3, Black has at least 26...♖×d3 27.♖×e6 ♖d1+ 28.♗f1 ♖×c1 with a slight plus. It is likely that he can even keep his queen. **24...♕f6 25.♕e4 ♘×d1 26.♗×f4 (D)**

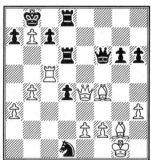

**26...♘c3?** Alekhine most probably miscalculates and misses 26...♘×f2! 27.♗×d6 (27.♔×f2? is met by 27...d3)

27...♖×d6 28.♕e8+ ♖d8 29.♘c6 ♕f4=. **27.♗×d6! ♕×d6** 27...♘e4? runs into 28.♗×c7+ ♔×b7 29.♗×e4++– . **28.♕e5 ♕b6?** Alekhine avoids the exchange of queens, but this plays into White's hands. He should opt for 28...♖f8±. **29.♕e7?** Lasker misses the immediately decisive 29.♖c6, when one sample line runs 29...♕×b7 30.h4 ♘a4 31.♕e4 ♘c3 32.♖d6+– . **29...♕d6 30.♖e5 d3?** 30...♕×e7 31.♖×e7 g5 offered more resistance. **31.e×d3 ♕×d3?! 32.♖e3 ♕d1+ 33.♔h2 ♘b5 34.♖e6 ♘×a3 35.♖f6 1-0**

In his second game against Lasker, Alekhine played the Ruy Lopez. He again lost (on move 90) after a fine tactical fight in the ending. His duel with Capablanca in the last round ended in Alekhine's defeat in the endgame, but this time in only 45 moves. The remaining three games were drawn, and Alekhine, having scored 6 points, shared 4th-5th places with Marshall. The preliminary stage was won by Capablanca, who had scored 7 points. In the finals, Alekhine scored well (+3 -3 =1).

At the same time, the sporting and creative results achieved in his games with Tarrasch, undoubtedly one of the greatest players of his time, were revealing. It was in these games that Alekhine demonstrated a high class of play, characterized by a natural fusion of positional maneuvering and combinative attacks. In other words, he showed how close he was to attaining a universal style.

**(32) Alekhine – Tarrasch**
St. Petersburg 1914 (Final)

*Participants and organizers of St. Petersburg 1914.*

Faulkbeer Countergambit [C32]

**1.f4 e5 2.e4 d5 3.e×d5 e4 4.d3 ♘f6 5.d×e4 ♘×e4 6.♘f3 ♗f5?!** The main lines are 6...♗c5 and 6...c6. **7.♗e3 c6 8.♗c4 b5 9.♗b3 c5?!** Very optimistic. 9...♗b4+ 10.c3 ♗c5 11.♗×c5 ♘×c5 12.0-0 0-0 gives Black more compensation. **10.d6 c4 11.♕d5 ♘d7 12.♕×f5** 12.♘d4!? **12...♘×d6 13.♕d5 ♗e7 14.0-0 0-0 15.♘c3 ♘f6 16.♕d2 c×b3 17.a×b3 b4 18.♘d5 ♘f5 19.♘×e7+ ♕×e7 20.♖fe1 ♖fd8 21.♗d4 ♘×d4 22.♘×d4 ♕c5 23.♖ad1 ♖d5?!** 23...♖e8!? **24.h3 ♖ad8 25.c3 h6 26.♕d3 ♕d6 27.♕f3 ♘h5 28.♖e4 ♘f6 29.♖e3 ♘h5 30.♖f1 ♘f6 31.♖fe1 ♕c5 32.♔h2 ♖c8 33.♖1e2** (D)

**33...♔f8?** Prophylaxis is good, but the king should leave the eighth rank with 33...♔h7 in order to meet 34.♖e5? with 34...b×c3 35.b×c3 ♕×c3 36.♖×d5 ♕×f3 37.♘×f3 ♘×d5=. **34.♖e5!** ♖cd8 34...b×c3 35.b×c3 ♕×c3?? runs into 36.♖c2+−. **35.♘f5 ♕b6?! 36.♕g3 ♘h5 37.♕h4 ♖×e5?!** A last desperate try, which backfires immediately. 37...♘f6 was forced, but White will win in any case, e.g., 38.c4 ♖d2 39.♖2e3 ♘g8 40.c5 ♕c6 41.♕g3 g6 42.♘d6+−. **38.f×e5 ♖d1 39.♖e3 ♕g6 40.♕×b4+ 1-0**

The style of play Alekhine demonstrated in the St. Petersburg tournament and his third place result, behind Lasker and Capablanca, became a sensation in the chess world. "A star has risen in the Russian sky," was how the success of the young master was acclaimed in the foreign press.

**Mannheim, July 19-August 2, 1914**
Over a hundred of world's best players came to the 19th traditional Congress of the German Chess Union dedicated to the 30th anniversary of its founding and also to the 50th anniversary of the Mannheim Chess Club. Four tournaments were held within the framework

of the congress. Among the participants there were fifteen Russian players, five of whom played in the masters: Alexander Alekhine, David Janowsky, Efim Bogoljubow, Alexander Flamberg, and Saviely Tartakower.

Of the world's top players, only Lasker and Rubinstein (who were preparing for the world championship match to be held in the autumn), and Capablanca failed to appear. Instead, the other stars of the chess world arrived, including Siegbert Tarrasch, Oldrich Duras, Frank Marshall, Rudolf Spielmann, Milan Vidmar, Richard Réti, Gyula Breyer, and Jacques Mieses, to name a few. The guest of honor at the tournament was world champion Emanuel Lasker.

In many speeches made at the opening ceremony, the thought that had been so vividly expressed by the founder of the modern Olympic movement, Pierre de Coubertin, was expressed: "Sport! You are the world!" The chairman of the Berlin Chess Union, Dr. Gebhard, proclaimed that "[c]hess is the spiritual struggle which presupposes unquestionable peace." Mayor Ritter of Mannheim called the assembled masters "envoys of peace." Dr. Tarrasch proposed a toast to the world brotherhood of chess. This dream of the chessplayers only came true a decade later when the World Chess Federation (FIDE) was founded in Paris.

Alas! Nothing hinted at the premonition of a war, soon to break out, as the so clearly expressed unanimity of the speakers in their desire for peace. But, the time of peace was only to last until the 12th round, and not for 17. World

*Alekhine during the Mannheim tournament.*

War I erupted on August 1, and the chess competition was stopped. Meanwhile, Alekhine was leading with 9½ points, a point ahead of Milan Vidmar.

Considering the strong field of the Mannheim tournament, Alekhine's sporting result was very good. He suffered only one defeat, again, like the previous year in Scheveningen, by Janowsky who had White. In that game, Alekhine, having adopted the Nimzowitsch line in the Queen's Pawn Opening, easily equalized. But, he then started playing for a win, thus showing, as *Deutsche Shahbletter* wrote, that "the young lion wishes to take revenge for Scheveningen." However, violent treatment of a position seldom leads to success. Janowsky sorted out the complications very well and brought the result of their encounters to +2 =1 in his favor. Alekhine evened the score a decade later when playing in the double round-robin tournament in New York 1924.

However, this failure, just as the unexpected draw with Kruger, did not affect the victorious progress of Alekhine who

90

made Breyer, Bogoljubow, Tarrasch, Fahrni, Duras, Flamberg, Carls, Post, and Mieses stop the clock. Among Alekhine's victories in the only major tournament in chess history that remained unfinished were both quite positional and sharply attacking games.

**(33) Alekhine – Tarrasch**
Mannheim 1914
Giuoco Piano [C53]

**1.e4 e5 2.♘f3 ♘c6 3.♗c4 ♗c5 4.c3 ♕e7 5.d4 ♗b6 6.0-0 d6 7.a4 a6 8.♗e3** 8.h3 is the main line. **8...♗g4 9.d5 ♘b8 10.a5?!** 10.♗×b6 c×b6 11.♘bd2 is more flexible. **10...♗×e3 11.f×e3 ♘f6 12.♘bd2 ♘bd7 13.♕e1 ♘c5 14.♕b1 ♗c8?** Too ambitious. The natural 14...0-0 was the order of the day. **15.b4 ♘cd7 16.♘h4 g6 17.♕e1 c6 18.♘hf3 c×d5 19.e×d5 e4 20.♘g5?!** The positional 20.♘d4 is more solid. **20...h6 21.♘h3 ♕e5?** Pseudo-active. After the normal options of 21...♘e5 or 21...0-0, Black is not worse. **22.♖c1 ♘g4?! 23.♘f4 g5?** Black cannot afford this and should try to defend with the retreat 23...♕e7. **24.h3 ♘gf6 25.♘e2 ♘×d5?!** Prudent, but not good. Since Black's king has no really safe home anymore, Black is in a bad spot in any case. **26.♗×d5 ♕×d5 27.♘d4** 27.♘g3!? **27...♕e5?** Running directly into the White's knights' attack. Tarrasch must try to regroup with 27...♘b8, but this will, of course, not really save him in view of 28.♕f2 ♖h7 29.♕f6. **28.♘c4 ♕d5** (D)

**29.♘f5!     ♕f8**     29...♕×c4?? 30.♘×d6++– **30.♘f×d6     ♖h7 31.♖d1 ♕c6 32.♖d4 b6 33.a×b6 ♗b7 34.♘a5 1-0**

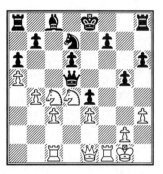

**(34) Duras,Oldrich – Alekhine**
Mannheim 1914
Ruy Lopez [C68]

**1.e4 e5 2.♘f3 ♘c6 3.♗b5 a6 4.♗×c6 b×c6 5.d4 e×d4 6.♕×d4 ♕f6 7.0-0** 7.e5 is more critical. **7...♕×d4 8.♘×d4 ♖b8 9.♘b3 ♘e7 10.♗d2 ♘g6 11.♗c3 ♘f4 12.♖e1 ♗e7 13.♘1d2 0-0 14.♘c4 ♖e8 15.♘ca5 ♗f8 16.♖ad1 c5 17.e5 ♘e6 18.♘c4 h6 19.h4 ♗e7 20.g3 g5 21.h×g5 h×g5 22.♘ba5 ♔h7 23.♔g2 ♔g6 24.♖h1 ♘d4 25.♗×d4 c×d4 26.♖×d4 ♗b4 27.♘b3 d5 28.♘e3** Surprisingly, 28.e×d6 seems to be playable as well, e.g., 28...♗b7+ 29.f3 ♖e2+ 30.♔f1 ♖be8 31.♖d1 ♗×f3 32.♘d4 ♗g2+ 33.♔g1 ♗c5 34.d7 ♖d8 35.♖h2 ♗f3 36.b4, and White defends. **28...c5 29.♖×d5 ♗b7 30.c4 ♖×e5 31.a3 ♗×a3 32.♘a5 ♗×d5+ 33.c×d5 ♖×e3** White also keeps drawing chances after the alternatives of 33...♗×b2 34.♘c6 ♖ee8 35.d6 or 33...♖×b2 34.♘ac4 ♖×e3 35.♘×e3 ♗b4 36.♖a1. **34.f×e3 ♖×b2+ 35.♔f3 f5 36.g4! f×g4+ 37.♔e4?** A miscalculation. 37.♔×g4 is forced: 37...♖b4+ 38.♔f3 g4+ 39.♔g3 ♗b2 40.♘c6 ♖e4 41.d6=. **37...♖b4+ 38.♔d3 ♗b2 39.d6 ♗f6 40.♖f1 g3 41.d7?!** (D) 41.♖g1!?

Now an instructive maneuver by Alekhine's rook follows: **41...♖b8!** First backward. **42.♖d1** 42.♘c6 g2 43.♖g1 ♖b6–+ **42...g2 43.♔e2 ♖b2+** Then forward again. **44.♔f3 ♖d2 45.♖g1 ♖×d7 46.♖×g2 ♖d3 47.♖c2?! ♖c3! 48.♖×c3 ♗×c3 49.♘c4 a5 50.♘b6 ♔f5 51.e4+ ♔e5 52.♘c4+ ♔d4 53.♘d6 ♔d3 54.♘b7 ♗b4 55.e5 c4 56.e6 c3 57.♘×a5 c2 58.♘b3 ♔c3 59.♘c1 ♔d2** and Duras resigned in view of 60.♘b3+ ♔d3 61.♔f2 ♔c3 62.♘c1 ♔d2 63.♘b3+ ♔d1 64.♔e3 c1♕+ 65.♘×c1 ♔×c1 66.♔e4 ♔d2 67.♔f5 ♗e7–+. **0-1**

**(35) Alekhine – Fahrni,Hans**
Mannheim 1914
French Defense [C14]

**1.e4 e6 2.d4 d5 3.♘c3 ♘f6 4.♗g5 ♗e7 5.e5 ♘fd7 6.h4 ♗×g5 7.h×g5 ♕×g5 8.♘h3 ♕e7 9.♘f4 ♘f8?** The main line is 9...♘c6, but Black has tried many moves here. **10.♕g4!** With the deadly double threat ♕×g7 and ♘f×d5. **10...f5 11.e×f6 g×f6 12.0-0-0 c6 13.♖e1 ♔d8 14.♖h6 e5?! 15.♕h4 ♘bd7 16.♗d3 e4 17.♕g3 ♕f7** (D) 17...♕d6 18.♘×e4 d×e4 19.♖×e4 b6 20.♕g7 +–

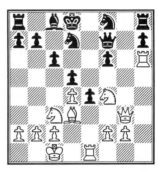

**18.♗×e4!** Alekhine just destroys Black's proud pawn wall. **18...d×e4** 18...♖g8 19.♗×d5 c×d5 20.♕e3 +– **19.♘×e4 ♖g8** 19...♕a2 20.♘×f6 ♘×f6 21.♕g5 ♘8d7 22.♘e6+ ♔e7 23.♕g7+ ♔d6 24.♕×h8 +– **20.♕a3 ♕g7** 20...♕e7 can be met by the technical 21.♕×e7+ (or the attacking 21.♕a5+ b6 22.♕c3 ♗b7 23.♘×f6+– which is more in Alekhine's style) 21...♔×e7 22.♘×f6+ ♔f7 23.♘×g8 ♔×g8 24.♖e7+–. **21.♘d6 ♘b6** (D)

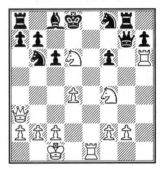

As *Shakhmatny vestnik* reported in August 1914, after war was declared "all Russian players were arrested as prisoners of war... Of the masters, Alekhine, Bogoljubow, Flamberg, and Janowsky remained in Mannheim."

Foreign publications also reported the imprisonment of the Russians. Thus, the Dutch newspaper *de Telegraaf* related an intriguing story about Mr. Elyashov, a well-known chessplayer and journalist, who was first arrested for taking a swim near "an important strategic object," a railroad bridge (August 17, 1914). After two days in custody, he was released, and his Dutch colleague took him to the railroad station. On the way to the border, he was again suspected to have been involved in espionage, arrested, and taken to Baden-Baden. He was mistaken for a Russian general disguised as a correspondent. These suspicions being based on his chess "coded communications."

In Baden-Baden, there already were other interned Russian players. The newspaper further reported that the young and brilliant grandmaster Alekhine, with his car and a French chauffeur, was for a while mistaken for Elyashov's aide-de-camp. According to another version, Alekhine was detained because of a picture found on him in which he was wearing his uniform of a graduate of the Imperial School of Law – he was mistaken for an officer! – but soon escaped to Switzerland, allegedly on a false passport.

A refutation of these rumors was published in *Shveytsarishe Shah Zeitung* when the newspaper received a letter from Boris Malyutin, a participant in the Mannheim side tournament (April, 1915).

*Being a witness to the events at Mannheim, I would like to somewhat clarify (the reports). The assumption that Mr. Elyashov was mistaken for a general seems implausible to me, but the misunderstanding involving Alekhine did indeed take place and cost him a night in the barracks. It should be mentioned that Alekhine had no car and also that he did not go to Switzerland on a false passport. Having been found unfit for military service by a medical board, Alekhine departed (from Germany) quite legally on 14 September.*

In later years, Alekhine more than once recalled the days in the German prison where he was together with Efim Bogoljubow, Samuel Weinstein, and the winner of one of the Mannheim tournaments, Ilya Rabinovich. "We had nothing else to do but to kill our spare time playing chess. However, since we had no chessboards at our disposal, we had to resort to blindfold play. I played in this manner a multitude of games with Bogoljubow and others."

How bizarre are the twists of fate! Who could then have foretold that, fifteen years later, two "cellmates" (Alekhine and Bogoljubow) having left Russia forever, would be fiercely fighting for the world title, while the other two cellmates – Rabinovich and Weinstein – would become notable Soviet players and chess authors, the latter translating Alekhine's books into Russian!

**Blindfold Chess**

As a 9-year-old boy, Alekhine first witnessed a simultaneous blindfold exhibition given by Harry Nelson Pillsbury while he was then touring Moscow. This exhibition, Alekhine related in later years, "[h]ad had an overwhelming impression on me... At the age of 12, I myself tried to play without sight of the board. And when I was 16, playing simultaneously against 4 or 5 opponents presented no difficulty for me at all." When playing blindfold, Alekhine sometimes produced very beautiful combinations, e.g., the blindfold exhibition games with Feldt (Tarnopol 1916), Gonsiorovsky (Odessa 1918), Potemkin (Paris 1925), to name just a few.

**(36) Gonsiorovsky – Alekhine**
Odessa 1915 (D)

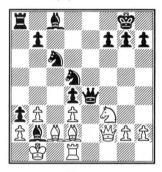

White's king will perish because of the attack on the dark squares: **1...♛e3!** Alekhine attacks the main defenders of the dark squares. **2.♖e1** 2.♗xe3? ♘c3# **2...♗f5 3.♖xe3 dxe3 4.♕f1** And here Alekhine announced mate in three: 24...exd2 25.♗d1 ♘cb4 and 26...♘c3# **0-1**

In the early 1920s, Alekhine gave blindfold simuls rather often, seeking, in some cases, to enhance interest in his exhibitions and, in others, to set new records surpassing those of Pillsbury (twenty-two boards) and the Hungarian master Breyer (twenty-five boards). As early as December 1, 1923, during his tour of North America, he gave a blindfold simultaneous exhibition against twenty-one opponents in Montreal. The score (+12 -4 =5) was then a new world record. In his tours, Alekhine gave three kinds of simultaneous exhibitions, blindfold, ordinary and mixed (some games were played over the board and some blindfold). There was special enthusiasm for his blindfold exhibitions in Baltimore, where he played against the ten strongest players and won seven games without losing any, and in New York, against the same number of Manhattan Club players (+8 -0 =2).

After the 1924 international tournament in New York, Alekhine "gave" Americans another blindfold record: on April 28 in New York he played twenty-six games in twelve hours (+16 -5 =5). Even Alekhine admitted that "[t]he organization of the exhibition was excellent. However, quite unexpectedly [he] found that [his] opponents were much above the average in strength. Suffice it to say that on the first eleven boards there were first-rate amateurs of the Manhattan and Marshall Clubs." Of course, three of them became known internationally: Kashdan, Herman Steiner, and Kevitz.

On his return to Europe, Alekhine decided to surpass that record, too. On Sunday February 1, 1925, at the Petit Parisian Hall in Paris, he gave, a blindfold exhibition against twenty-eight opponents (+23 -3 =2); according to Alekhine's book *On the Road to Highest Achievements in Chess*, it was a new world record. As the French press noted, Alekhine was in excellent form, playing with ease and rapidity. There were numerous spectators watching the exhibition who "reverently observed the required silence." Based on the foreign press publications, *Shakhmatny listok* described the atmosphere of this spectacle:

> *Alekhine was sitting in an armchair opposite the window that faced the street. During the day he had been offered, for breakfast and lunch, several hot meals, but he touched none of them. Several cups of coffee and 29 cigarettes were his only refreshment in 13 hours of play. Twenty eight boards were arranged behind his back in a horseshoe. The usual walk from board to board was performed by a "speaker" who announced the moves made by the participants of the exhibition. Alekhine responded almost instantaneously.*

> *Sometimes, when the opponent replied at once, there followed two or three moves in a row. Alekhine played positional chess, but with great vigor and, as one can easily see, almost always opened the games in the best way. After 6 hours, 18 minutes, the first game was finished, then with intervals of 19-20 minutes other games were ended. The exhibition ended at 11p.m. As one of those present expressed it, Alekhine was "fresh as a daisy." The audience gave him a big hand, but he quickly left the hall.*

Here is one of those fresh-as-a-daisy games.

**(37) Alekhine – NN**
Paris 1925
Alekhine's Defense [B02]

**1.e4 ♘f6 2.♘c3 d5 3.e×d5 ♘×d5 4.♗c4 ♘b6 5.♗b3 c5 6.d3** 6.♕h5 c4 7.♗×c4 ♘×c4 8.♕b5+ ♘c6 9.♕×c4 e5 gives Black compensation. **6...♘c6 7.♘f3 ♘a5?! 8.♘e5 ♘×b3** If 8...e6, then 9.♕h5 ♕c7? 10.♘b5 ♕e7 11.♗g5 (Alekhine). **9.a×b3 ♘d7?** Possibly better was 9...♗e6 followed by ...g6 and ...♗g7 (Alekhine). **10.♘c4 ♘b6 11.♗f4 ♘d5 12.♘×d5 ♕×d5 13.0-0 b5 14.♘e3 ♕c6 15.d4 e6?** 15...c×d4 16.♕×d4 f6 is more critical. **16.d5 e×d5?** Inviting White's pieces into the attack. Black had to try to keep the lines as closed as possible, e.g., 16...♕b7. **17.♘×d5 ♗d6 18.♖e1+ ♗e6 19.♗×d6** 19.♕f3 is even stronger. **19...♕×d6** (D)

**20.♖a6!** 20.♘f6+? is met by 20...♔e7. **20...♕d8** On 20...♕d7, White wins after 21.♖ax×e6+ f×e6 22.♖×e6+ ♔d8 23.♖e7 ♕d6 24.♕d2 a5 25.♖×g7 h6 26.♖g6 ♕d7 27.♕f4 (Alekhine). **21.♖a×e6+** 21.♖e×e6+ is the alternative: 21...f×e6 22.♕h5+ g6 23.♖×e6+ ♔f7 24.♕e5 ♖e8 25.♖×e8 ♕×e8 26.♕f6+ ♔g8 27.♘e7++−. **21...f×e6 22.♖×e6+** 22.♕f3!? is even stronger. **22...♔f7 23.♖e7+ ♕×e7** 23...♔g8? 24.♕f3 ♕f8 25.♘f6+ ♕×f6 26.♕×a8+ ♕f8 27.♕d5+ ♕f7 28.♕×f7#. **24.♘×e7 ♔×e7**

**25.♕e2+ ♔f7 26.♕h5+ ♔f6 27.♕×c5 ♖he8 28.g4 1-0**

Alekhine was often asked how he managed to remember so many positions at the same time. "[It is] very simple," he once explained. "First, I divide all boards into groups of openings. For example, on the first six, I open with the d-pawn, on the next six, with the e-pawn, then again d-pawn and so on. When a specific board number is called, you only need to recall in the course of play which opening was played and you are thus able to remember the specific plans, threats and defenses. The position comes back to your mind, then the previous move and you can proceed making combinations."

In 1931, the world champion published a long article about blindfold chess and let out the secret of memorizing such a large number of games, which "lies in the inborn sharpness of memory, which becomes properly developed as a result of sound knowledge of the chessboard and a deep penetration into the essence of the game of chess. Furthermore, the so-called opening and endgame technique plays a big part." With all that, Alekhine was not an adherent of this kind of competition, for, he believed, such games "are not free from typical mistakes," and that "the exploitation of an advantage already gained is far from faultless. I myself," wrote Alekhine, "despite the fact that I am the holder of the world record, cannot say that I am an enthusiastic follower of this kind of chess sport, and I merely value blindfold chess as a means of propaganda."

## Moscow Tournaments, 1915, 1918, 1919-20

Alekhine participated in tournaments of the Moscow Chess Circle (as the chess club was called early in the 20th century) as early as 1907 and 1908. In the first of them, he failed, but in the second, he finished first and, therefore, was entitled to participate in the All-Russia Amateur tournament in St. Petersburg in 1909.

### October-November, 1915

On returning from his imprisonment in Germany, Alekhine took part in the tournament of the Moscow Chess Circle, finishing first (+10 -0 =1). He won a brilliancy prize for the game he won against 21-year old Nikolai Zubarev. The Moscow newspaper *Utro Rossii* reported that "this game is worthy of the attention of chess lovers because of both its middle part and its spectacular finale" (January 3, 1916).

**(38) Alekhine – Zubarev**
Moscow 1915
Nimzo-Indian Defense [E32]

**1.d4 ♘f6 2.c4 e6 3.♘c3 ♗b4 4.♕c2 b6?!** This allows White to seize the center almost for free. **5.e4 ♗b7 6.♗d3 ♗×c3+ 7.b×c3 d6 8.♘e2 ♘bd7 9.0-0 0-0 10.f4 h6 11.♘g3 ♕e7 12.♕e2 ♖ae8 13.♗a3 c5 14.♖ae1 ♔h8 15.d5?** 15.e5 applies much more pressure because Black does not have a dark-square bishop. **15...♘g8 16.e5?** White is not prepared for this advance right now. 16.♗c2 ♗a6 17.♕d3, to prepare e5, is more prudent. **16...g6?** 16...d×e5 has to be played because 17.f×e5 can be answered by 17...e×d5

18.♘f5 ♕×e5. **17.♕d2** 17.♘e4!?
**17...e×d5?** Opening too many roads for White's attack. 17...d×e5 18.f×e5 e×d5 19.e6 f×e6 20.c×d5 ♗×d5 21.c4 ♗c6 22.♗×g6± is the lesser evil.
**18.c×d5 d×e5** 18...♗×d5 19.♗b5 ♗b7 20.e×d6 ♕d8 21.c4+− **19.c4 ♔h7 20.♗b2 ♘gf6 21.f×e5 ♘g4** (D)

**22.e6!** Destroying the integrity of Black's defensive pawn barricade.
**22...♕h4 23.♖×f7+ ♖×f7 24.♗×g6+!** Blow after blow!
**24...♔×g6 25.♕d3+ ♔g5 26.♗c1+ 1-0**

### May-June, 1918

This was a three-master match-tournament, in which Alexander Alekhine, Vladimir Nenarokov, and Abram Rabinovich participated. At last, Alekhine managed to take revenge on his old foe Vladimir Nenarokov, winning two games against him and drawing one. He also scored two points in his three games with Rabinovich.

### 1919-1920

This was the first Moscow championship after the revolution; thirteen players participated. Alekhine, who was in a class by himself, won all his games, taking first place three points ahead of Grekov.

**Verlinsky, Boris Markovich** (December 27, 1887, Bakhmut [now Artemovsk]-November 30, 1950, Moscow) Russian chessplayer, 1929 USSR Champion.

*Boris Verlinsky*

Verlinsky lived in Odessa and achieved his first successes in local tournaments. Since 1909, he participated in All-Russia Amateur Tournaments, each time improving on his previous result: 1909 (10th-11th), 1911 (6th-8th), 1913 (3rd). In 1910, he won the South Russia tournament in Odessa. In 1916 and 1917, he played a series of games with Alexander Alekhine. In 1916, he managed to draw their two-game match, whereas two years later, the future world champion had already "found the keys" to his manner of playing, defeating the Odessa player by a score of 6-0! Surprisingly, the opponents adopted a different opening in each game. For example, Alekhine as White opened with the Scotch Gambit, Scotch Game, and Ruy Lopez, and as Black he even adopted the Caro-Kann Defense. Verlinsky, as White, was true to 1.e2-e4. Once, he even could not deny himself the pleasure of opening with the King's Gambit.

Here is one game that Verlinsky won.

**(39) Verlinsky – Alekhine**
Odessa 1916
Scotch Game [C45]

1.e4 e5 2.d4 e×d4 3.♘f3 ♘c6
4.♘×d4 ♗c5 5.♗e3 ♗b6 6.♘c3
♘ge7 7.♗e2 0–0 8.0–0 d6 9.♕d2
f5 10.e×f5 ♗×d4 11.♗×d4 ♘×f5
12.♗e3 ♗e6 13.♘e4 d5 14.♘g5
♕f6 15.♗c5 ♖fe8 16.♗f3 ♖ad8
17.♘×e6 ♕×e6 18.♖ae1 ♘e5
19.♗h5 g6 20.f4 ♘c4 21.♕f2
♘ce3 22.g4 d4 23.g×f5 ♕×f5
24.♗×d4 ♘×f1 25.♖×e8+ ♖×e8
26.♗f3 c5 27.♗e5 1-0

After the revolution of 1917, Verlinsky moved to Moscow. Having finished second in the "Tournament of Cities" in 1923, he was entitled to participate in the 1924 USSR Championship, and he shared 10th-11th places, gaining the title of a master. In 1925, he participated in the first Moscow International Tournament, sharing 12th-14th places but winning a number of impressive victories over, for instance, Capablanca, Rubinstein, Spielmann, and Sämisch. The day the following game was played, Capablanca had just returned from Leningrad (now St. Petersburg), where he had given a simultaneous exhibition; naturally, this was not conducive for playing against Verlinsky.

**(40) Capablanca – Verlinsky**
Moscow 1925 (D)

Verlinsky managed to dominate Capablanca's rook: **54...♗c2!** Verlinsky preserves his pair of powerful bishops and makes the life of the rook difficult. **55.♖a2 f5 56.♔e3** 56.♖×c2? ♘d4+ –+ **56...♗e4 57.♖a5?! ♗d4+ 58.♔d2?** This runs into a deadly double attack. But 58.♔e2 ♗c5 59.♘c8 ♔g6 is also lost in the long run. **58...♗c5! 59.♖×c5 59.♘c8 ♗b4+ –+ 59...♘×c5 60.♔e3 ♔f6 0-1**

In later years Verlinsky achieved a number of major successes in domestic competitions: 1st-2nd in the 1926 Ukrainian Championship, and Moscow Champion 1928. For his victory in the 1929 USSR Championship, he was awarded the title of grandmaster of the USSR. In 1931, he shared 3rd-6th places in the national championship. Thereafter, he was unable to achieve good results because of illness.

## All-Russia Chess Olympiad, October 2-24, 1920

The initiator/promoter of the tournament was chess master Alexander Ilyin-Genevsky who was, in those years, Commissar of the Main Department of the Vsevobuch (The Military Education for All Organizations). Also actively involved in the organization of the first chess championship of Soviet Russia were Moscow players Alexander Alekhine, Nikolai Grigoriev, and Nikolai Grekov. They had succeeded in quickly bringing almost all the strongest Russian players to Moscow, which was very difficult in those hard times of the civil war, which brought complete devastation and famine to the country.

In the main tournament of the Olympiad, sixteen players from eight cities (Moscow, Petrograd, Nizhny Novgorod, Saratov, Vilno, Lodz, Mogilev, and Yamburg (now Kinghisepp) participated. Five of them already held the title of chess master: Alexander Alekhine, Beniamin Blumenfeld, Grigory Levenfish, Abram Rabinovich, and Ilya Rabinovich. A two-stage side tournament was held simultaneously with the main event, and, in it, Alekhine's elder brother, Alexei, played.

The Olympiad lasted twenty-one days. The playing conditions were unfavorable; the rooms were not heated and were poorly illuminated; the interruptions in the supply of the already very scant food rations almost resulted in a strike by the players. In the middle of the tournament, seven participants submitted an ultimatum to the organizing committee, threatening to withdraw unless their demands were satisfied. They demanded an advance payment of 15,000 rubles to each participant, the handout of all the remaining cheese, an increase in the bread ration, and the immediate handout of cigarettes.

The ultimatum was signed by Romanovsky, Kubbel, Rabinovich, Golubev, Danyushevsky, Mund, and Levenfish. Alekhine supported the ultimatum, declaring that he also would refuse to play further because he considered it impossible to play against "hungry opponents." These demands

were for the most part met, and it made it possible to play all the rounds.

Alekhine came first, scoring 12 points in 15 games (+9 -0 =6). He was persistently pursued throughout the tournament by Pyotr Romanovsky (2nd with 11 points) and Grigory Levenfish (3rd with 10 points). In some of the games, Alekhine escaped defeat only because of his exceptional skill in defending difficult positions. He especially often recalled in later years the following study-like draw.

**(41) Ilyin Zhenevsky, Alexander – Alekhine**
Moscow 1920 (D)

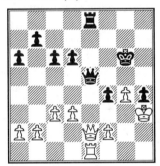

White should exchange queens but not rooks, so **35.♕e4+?** is wrong as 35.♕xe5 dxe5 36.♖e4 gives White good practical winning chances because of Black's weak pawns. (Of course not 36.♔xh4?? ♖h8#. **35...♕xe4 36.♖xe4**
This position arose after White's 36th move, after the main session had ended and a break was announced. Ilyin-Genevsky recalls:

*The bell rang, signaling the beginning of the break. At first, I wanted to wait until Alekhine sealed his move, but he was think-*

*ing so long and so hard that I left alone. I was in an excellent mood, having no doubts that I had a won position. Indeed, if Alekhine exchanges rooks, I would have a clearly won pawn ending. If, however, he plays 36...♖f8, I will check at e6 with my rook, and capture the pawn on d6. It looks like there is no escape for him.*

*So what did Alekhine do in my absence? I relate it as Grigoriev told me. Alekhine pondered over the game for about an hour, then he sealed his move and left. Not long before the end of the break he reappeared in the club, his face beaming. Having encountered Grigoriev, he handed over to him a whole book of variations, written at home, and said, "I dedicate this ending to you as a connoisseur of pawn endings."*

*And indeed, it turned out that Alekhine had taken the risk of transferring the game into a pawn ending, having finely calculated "only" moves to bring the game to a draw.*

**36...♖xe4 37.dxe4 ♔g5 38.f3 a5!** The only way to win the fight for extra tempi on the queenside. **39.c4 b5 40.cxb5 cxb5 ½-½**

Of the games Alekhine won in this tournament attention is given to his encounter with Ilya Rabinovich, which abounds in interesting combinative concepts on both sides.

**(42) Rabinovich,Ilya – Alekhine**
Moscow 1920
Nimzo-Indian Defense [E43]

**1.d4 ♘f6 2.♘f3 b6 3.c4 e6 4.♘c3 ♗b7 5.e3 ♗b4 6.♕c2 ♘e4 7.♗d3 f5 8.0-0 ♗xc3 9.bxc3 0-0 10.♘d2 ♕h4 11.f3 ♘xd2 12.♗xd2 ♘c6 13.e4?!** This opens the position too early. 13.♖ab1 and 13.♗e1 are the main lines. **13...fxe4 14.♗xe4** 14.fxe4 d6 is also not bad for Black. **14...♘a5 15.♖ae1?** A move based on a miscalculation. 15.♗d3 ♗a6 16.♗e1 ♕h6 17.♕e2=, Portisch-Nikolic, Niksic 1983. **15...♗xe4 16.♖xe4 ♕h5** (D)

**17.♕a4?** A tactical oversight. After 17.c5 ♘c4, Black is of course better because of the weaknesses on White's light squares, but White should be able to defend. **17...♘xc4! 18.♖e2** 18.♕xc4? d5–+ **18...b5 19.♕b3 ♕f5 20.♖fe1 ♖ab8 21.♗c1 a5 22.♖e4 a4 23.♕d1 ♖be8 24.♕e2 c5 25.♗e3 cxd4 26.♗xd4 e5 27.f4 d6** Alekhine decides to stay in the middlegame in accordance with his style. He could also choose 27...d5 28.♖xe5 ♘xe5 29.fxe5 ♕e4, with good winning chances. **28.h3 ♖e6 29.fxe5 dxe5 30.♗c5 ♖f7 31.♖b1** (D)

**31...h6!** Alekhine first secures his own king, the hallmark of a strong player. The direct 31...♘d2?? runs into 32.♕xd2 ♕xe4 33.♕d8+ ♖e8

34.♕×e8+ ♖f8 35.♕×f8#. **32.♖×b5?**
This greedy capture allows Alekhine to
exploit White's weak back rank.
32.♖d1 and 32.g4 offered more resistance. **32...♘d2! 33.♖×a4?! ♕c2!
34.♖b8+ ♔h7 35.♔h1 ♖f1+
36.♗g1 ♖×g1+ 37.♔×g1 ♕c1+
38.♔f2 ♖f6+ 39.♔e3** 39.♔g3
♘f1+−+ **39...♘b1+** White resigned
because he either loses the queen or is
checkmated. **0-1**

The Olympiad was the last tournament
in Russia in which Alekhine ever participated. During the tempestuous years
of the war and revolutions (1915-
1920), he had played a total of forty-
three tournament games there (+33 -0
=10).

**Budapest International Tournament,
September 5-19, 1921**
This was the second international tournament (after Triberg, July 1921) in
which Alekhine participated after leaving Soviet Russia. In the field of twelve
well-known European players (including himself), he scored 8½ points (+6
-0 =5), a half-point ahead of Grünfeld
and a full point ahead of Kostic and
Tartakower. Also, for his game with
Sterk (See, Middlegame), he was
awarded a brilliancy prize. Alekhine

introduced is namesake opening in his
game against Endre Steiner (See, Discoveries in the Opening).

**Grigoriev, Nikolai Dmitrievich** (August 14, 1895, Moscow-October 10,
1938, Moscow)
He was a Russian player, master, and
organizer of the domestic chess movement, as well as chess author and composer. Grigoriev was three years
younger than Alekhine and, it can be
said, learned from him. Of invaluable
benefit to him was their match held in
the spring of 1921, even though he
yielded to the strongest Russian player,
losing two games and drawing five.

A Chinese sage once said: "To make a
mistake and realize it – it is in this that
wisdom lies." And what about
Grigoriev? Endowed with great analytical gifts, he also knew how to learn from
his mistakes. From 1922 to 1924, he
won the Moscow championship three
times, and, in 1929, he repeated the
success, initially tying for first with
Panov and then winning their match (+6
-3 =3). During these years, he participated in six USSR championships
(1920-1929), finishing in 5th-7th
place in 1920. He defeated in matches
masters Makogonov (1928; +5 -1 =2)
and Goglidze (1929; +5 -4 =1) and
drew uncompromising contests with
Nenarokov (1923; +5 -5 =0) and
Zubarev (1923; +5 -5 =0). Simultaneous with his chess praxis, he engaged
in a great of amount of organizing activities (chairing the organizing com-
mittees of all three historic chess
events at Moscow – the international
tournaments of 1925, 1935, and 1936)
and was also active as a chess author.

For over a decade (1922-1933), he edited the popular chess column in the newspaper *Izvestiya*, covering all the major events of those years. Only Grigoriev could arrange to have Capablanca send his commentaries on the world title match in Buenos Aires to *Izvestiya*. Grigoriev was one of the founders and a member of the editorial board of the journal/newspaper *64*, and assistant editor-in-chief of *Shakhmaty v SSSR* in 1938. He composed over 150 studies, most of which are considered classics. For example, in 1936, he submitted ten of his studies to the prestigious international competition organized by the French chess magazine *La Stratégie*, and all of them received some kind of award. (D)

1.♔g3! 1.♔g2? ♚e4 2.♔f1 ♚f5! 3.♔f2 ♚f4; 1.♔h2? ♚d4! 2.♔g1 ♚e5! 3.♔g2 ♚e4! 4.♔f1 ♚f5 **1...♚e4** **2.♔g2!** 2.♔f2? ♚f4 **2...♚e3** 2...♚f4 3.♔f2 **3.♔f1 ♚e4! 4.♔e1 ♚e3 5.♔d1 ♚f4 6.♔d2 ♚e4** 6...♚g4 7.♔e3 **7.e3 ♚f3 8.♔d3 ♚g3 9.♔e4! ♚g4 10.♔e5! ♚×h4 11.♔f4 ♚h3 12.e4** 12.♔f3? h4! **12...♚g2 13.e5!** 13.♔g5? ♚g3! **13...h4 14.e6 h3 15.e7 h2 16.e8♕ h1♕ 17.♕e2+ 1-0**

In 1954, the Soviet publishers Fizkultura i Sport (Physical Culture and

*Nikolai Grigoriev*

Sports) brought out the book *The Chess Art of N.D.Grigoriev*. Then world champion Mikhail Botvinnik wrote the preface. Here are some fragments of his preface:

*Master N.D. Grigoriev was a representative of the pre-revolutionary Russian intelligentsia who brought their knowledge, their creative work to the people, thereby assisting the great cultural revolution in our country. Among such representatives there was a relatively small group of chessplayers who were handing down the experience accumulated by the Russian Chigorin Chess School to the young generation of Soviet chessplayers.*

*One should especially emphasize that Grigoriev was a great master in the field of analysis of chess endings. In this field, there were very few who were equal to him. He always shared the results of his analyses in the numerous lectures he gave. He used to read lectures in his peculiar manner – unhurriedly and with restraint. Gradually, he went deeper and deeper into the analysis, and the audience was able to perceive the beauty, logic, and ingenuity of his neat analytical search!*

*Needless to say, Grigoriev achieved such results by very hard work. But with what obvious satisfaction did he hurry to demonstrate to his friends the results of his work, peeking infrequently at the little sheets of paper scrawled all over in his minute handwriting...*

*In the field of endgame analysis, he achieved striking results, and his name will go down in the history of the endgame, together with the names of Philidor, Troitzky and other great analysts. Without a doubt the larger masses of our readers, by studying the analyses collected in the present book, will be in no small measure benefited as far as their qualification is concerned and will highly appreciate the ingenuity and depth of N.D. Grigoriev's work.*

**Grigoriev-Alekhine Match, 1921**

This was Alekhine's last contest before he emigrated. His opponent, Moscovite Nikolai Grigoriev, was well known to him. In August 1919, they had played a short match of four games, all won by Alekhine (See, A.A.Kotov, *The Chess Heritage of Alekhine* 2.147). "Afterward," writes Kotov, "these two talented players became friends and played many training games." They also met over the board in official tournaments – the All-Russia Chess Olympiad (1920) and Moscow Championship (1920/1921), Alekhine winning in

both these cases. And now – their next, and last, confrontation. It took place in the first half of March. Aside from playing their match game on March 15th, Alekhine also married the Swiss journalist Anneliese Ruegg. In that game, Alekhine played the white side of a Ruy Lopez and drew the game after thirty-nine move. So, it seems, the grandmaster was not in a hurry to go to his wedding party...

Altogether, there were seven games in this match (+2 -0 =5) in Alekhine's favor. The draws were long struggles, and his two victories were swift, twenty-two and eighteen moves, respectively. Here is one of these quick victories:

**(43) Grigoriev,N.D. – Alekhine**
Moscow 1921
Ruy Lopez [C67]

**1.e4 e5 2.♘f3 ♘c6 3.♗b5 ♘f6 4.0-0 ♘×e4 5.♕e2 ♘d6 6.♗×c6 d×c6 7.♕×e5+ ♗e7** Very risky, but typical of Alekhine's style. The main line is 7...♕e7. **8.♕×g7 ♗f6 9.♕h6 ♗e6 10.d3 ♖g8 11.♖e1 ♕e7 12.♘bd2** 12.♘c3!? **12...♖g6?!** 12...0-0-0 is more flexible. **13.♕f4 0-0-0 14.♘b3 ♘f5 15.g3 h5 16.♘e5 ♗×e5 17.♖×e5 ♘h4 18.♘c5?** The cause of the following problems. White should fight for the light squares with 18.h3. **18...♖d5 19.♖×d5 ♗×d5** (D)

**20.♘e4?** This runs into a devasting attack. The only way to fight on is 20.♕e3, but Black's initiative remains dangerous after 20...♕d8 21.c4 ♗xc4 22.♔f1 ♘f5 23.♕e4 ♘d6 24.♕e5 ♗d5; 20.♗e3? b6 21.♘b3 ♘f3+ 22.♔f1 ♖f6−+. **20...♖g4 21.♕h6** 21.♕e3 ♘f5 22.♕e1 (22.♕xa7 ♖xe4 23.dxe4 ♕xe4−+) 22...♘d4 23.♗g5 ♘f3+−+ **21...♖xe4 0-1**

**Teichmann, Richard** (December 24,1868, Lenich, Saxony-June 12, 1925, Berlin)
German player, one of the world's strongest in the early 1900s, chess composer and columnist.

By a surprising coincidence, Teichmann was born on the same day that Emanuel Lasker was and, also like the second world champion, started his chess career in Berlin, where he spent his years as a student. A year earlier than his great compatriot, he moved to London, where he improved his chess under the guidance of the already famous English masters Joseph Blackburn and Henry Bird and where he was awarded new titles. He made his first (and successful) appearance in an international tournament at Leipzig. In the 9th Congress of the German Chess Union, he finished third, behind Tarrasch and Lipke. The following year, he took part in the famous tournament at Hastings 1895. He performed quite decently there, scoring 11½ points out of 21 and sharing 7th-8th prizes with Curt von Bardeleben.

Unfortunately, the progressing disease of his right eye, damaged in his early years, prevented him from further participation in competitions for a while.

However, when he came back, with a truly pirate-like black patch over his eye, he proved that he indeed was one of the world's best players by performing well at Monte Carlo (1903), Ostend (1905 and 1906), Vienna and Prague (1908), Hamburg (1910), Piestany (1922). From 1894 to 1924, Teichmann took part in thirty-two tournaments, coming first in five of them and fifth in nine of them, earning him the nickname "Richard the Fifth." While being a great lover of exciting sports such as French wrestling, at the chessboard, he often behaved quite peacefully, never objecting to a draw. In the well-known book *On Chess and Chessplayers* by Rudolf Spielmann, he describes Teichmann as "[c]apable of amazingly and accurately grasping a position on the chessboard. He was distinguished by an unprecedented lack of emotion, bordering on laziness. How he nevertheless had been able to become an outstanding master is almost a mystery."

Incidentally, the first tournament game between Teichmann and Alekhine, which took place at the Hamburg tournament on July 19, 1910, ended in a draw on move 32 but only after an uncompromising struggle. The 17-year-old Muscovite, playing White, opened the game with the Ruy Lopez. Right in the opening, Teichmann sacrificed a pawn for a queenside initiative, but, having exchanged too many pieces, the opponents agreed to a draw. The Ruy Lopez turned out to be the most frequently adopted opening in the games between Teichmann and Alekhine. Both of them always adopted it when playing White. At Carlsbad 1911, Alekhine also tried to subject Teichmann to the

Spanish torture, but the tournament leader confidently cut short his attempts at a kingside attack, and, when the smoke of the battle had cleared, he simply exploited his advantage of two extra pawns.

**(44) Alekhine – Teichmann**
Carlsbad 1911
Ruy Lopez [C84]

**1.e4 e5 2.♘f3 ♘c6 3.♗b5 a6 4.♗a4 ♘f6 5.d4 e×d4 6.0-0 ♗e7 7.e5 ♘e4 8.♘×d4 0-0 9.c4?!** The main line is 9.♘f5. **9...♘c5 10.♗c2 ♘×e5 11.♕h5 ♘g6 12.f4 d6 13.f5?!** Too optimistic. **13...♗f6! 14.♗e3 ♘e5 15.♘d2 ♖e8 16.♔h1 ♘ed3 17.♘e6?** Alekhine's idea is good, but the execution is wrong. After 17.♗g1 ♘×b2 (17...d5!?) 18.♖f3 ♗d7?!, White can play 19.♘e6! f×e6 20.f×e6 ♘bd3 21.e×d7 ♕×d7 22.♖×f6 g×f6 23.♗×d3 ♘×d3 24.♕d5+. **17...♗×e6?!** 17...f×e6 is even stronger: 18.♗×c5 d×c5 19.♗×d3 (19.♘e4 ♘b4 20.♖ad1 ♕e7 21.♘×f6+ g×f6−+) 19...e×f5 20.♖ae1 g6−+. **18.f×e6 ♖×e6 19.♗×c5 g6!** 19...d×c5? is met by 20.♕h3. **20.♕f3 ♘×c5 21.♖ad1 c6 22.b4 ♘d7 23.♘e4 ♕e7 24.♕f4?!** In the end, this just improves Black's pieces, but good advice is already hard to give. **24...♗e5 25.♕h6 ♗g7 26.♕f4 ♘e5 27.♗b3 ♖f8 28.♖fe1 ♖e8 29.♖f1 ♖f8 30.♖fe1 ♖e8 31.♖f1 h6** Teichmann continues to play on of course. **32.h3 ♔h8** 32...♘d3!? 33.♖×d3 ♖×e4 34.♕×d6 ♖e1 35.♕f4 ♖×f1+ 36.♕×f1 ♕×b4−+ **33.g4?** 33.c5 d5 34.♘d6 ♖f8 and 33.♕d2 ♗f8 34.c5 d5 35.♘d6 ♖b8 are better, but Black will win in the long run in both cases as well. **33...♘×c4?!**

33...♘×g4!? is even stronger: 34.♘×d6 ♘e3 35.♘×e8 ♕×e8 36.♕h4 ♘×d1 37.♖×d1 ♔h7−+. **34.♘×d6 ♖×d6 35.♕×c4 ♖×d1 36.♖×d1 ♕e3** 36...♕e5!? is more precise because 37.♕×f7? loses directly to 37...♕e4+ 38.♔g1 ♖f8 39.♕e6 ♗d4−+. **37.♔g2** (D)

**37...♕e2+?!** This gives away one major advantage of Black: the better pawn shield of his king. As the endgame is not easy to win because of White's activity, Teichmann should keep the queens on the board with 37...♖e7 38.♕d3 ♕g5 39.♖f1 ♗f6 40.♕c4 ♗g7 41.♕f4 ♖e2+ 42.♔h1 ♕h4 43.♕f3 ♖e5 44.♔g2 h5−+. **38.♕×e2 ♖×e2+ 39.♔f3 ♖e7 40.♖d8+ ♔h7 41.♖d3 ♗b2 42.♗c4 ♔g7 43.a4 ♖c7 44.♔e4 ♖e7+ 45.♔f3 ♖c7 46.♔e4 b5 47.a×b5?!** Clearing the way for Black's rook. 47.♗b3 offers more resistance. **47...c×b5 48.♗d5 ♗c3 49.♗b7 ♖e7+ 50.♔d5 ♖d7+ 51.♔e4 ♖e7+ 52.♔d5 ♖d7+ 53.♔e4 ♖×b7 54.♖×c3 ♖d7 55.♔e5 ♖d1 56.♖b3 ♖c1 57.♔d6 ♖c4 58.♔e5 ♖c1 59.♔d6 ♖c2 60.♔d5 ♖c4 0-1**

The twenty-six-player, round-robin tournament at Carlsbad was the apex of Richard Teichmann's sporting career: of the twenty-five games he played there, he won thirteen and lost only two, thus finishing first, a full point ahead of Rubinstein and Schlechter. However, Alekhine shared 8th-11th places in that tournament. In an historical twist, twelve years later, again at Carlsbad, these opponents would virtually have a reversed standing; Alekhine shared 1st-3rd prizes with Bogoljubow and Maróczy, whereas Teichmann, for whom that event at the famous health resort was to become the last in his life, finishing only ninth.

Along with his tournament achievements, Teichmann had more than a few successes in matches. Thus he defeated his compatriot Curt von Bardeleben twice, in 1909, 4-2 (+3 -1 =2) and in 1910, 7-3 (+5 -1 =4). He also won matches against Spielmann (5-1 in 1914), Marshall (1½-½, also in 1914), and Mieses (5-1 in 1920). In 1921, in Berlin, he drew a match with Alekhine, 3-3 (+2 -2 =2) (See: Alekhine-Teichmann Match).The second world champion, Emanuel Lasker, had a high regard for Teichmann's play. In the concluding lecture of his celebrated *Common Sense in Chess*, in which he listed the outstanding chessplayers of the early 1900s, "each of whom was a true gift for the chess world," Lasker also mentioned the "precision thinking" of Richard Teichmann.

**Alekhine-Teichmann Match, June 1921**

The six-game match with the 53-year-old German master became a kind of "émigré début" for Alexander Alekhine. Consequently, he decided to avail himself of the opportunity just to play for his own pleasure and to test some new opening ideas and schemes, e.g.,

Queen's Indian Defense configurations as Black and the Vienna Game as White. No, it was not an accident that the hypermodernists would soon claim his presence in their ranks.

The result of the match was even (+2 - 2 =2). Peculiarly, all the games in which Alekhine played White ended decisively (2-1). Especially spectacular was the fourth game of the match, in which both players succeeded in finding the best moves for a long time. However, Alekhine played more precisely and consistently in the endgame.

**(45) Alekhine – Teichmann**
Berlin m(4) 1921
Ruy Lopez [C83]

**1.e4 e5 2.♘f3 ♘c6 3.♗b5 a6 4.♗a4 ♘f6 5.0-0 ♘xe4 6.d4 b5 7.♗b3 d5 8.dxe5 ♗e6 9.c3 ♗e7 10.♗e3 0-0 11.♘bd2 ♗g4 12.♘xe4 dxe4 13.♕d5 ♕xd5?!** This gives White a strong initiative. 13...exf3 is the main line. **14.♗xd5 exf3 15.♗xc6 fxg2 16.♔xg2 ♖ad8 17.a4 f6?! 18.axb5 axb5 19.♗xb5?!** 19.♖a7!? fxe5 20.♖xc7 ♖d6 21.♗e4 creates even more pressure. **19...fxe5 20.♗c4+ ♔h8 21.f3 ♗h5 22.♖a5 ♖d1 23.♗d5** A difficult choice since the alternative, 23.♖xd1!? ♗xf3+ 24.♔g3 ♗xd1 25.♗c5, also gives White more than enough compensation for the pawn. **23...♖xf1 24.♔xf1 ♗xf3 25.♗xf3 ♖xf3+ 26.♔e2 ♖f8 27.♔d3 ♔g8 28.♔e4 (D)**

**28...♖b8?** The source of the coming problems because White can activate his queenside majority easily against this defensive set-up. After 28...♖f1,

Black's active rook secures the draw. **29.b4 ♔f7** 29...♗xb4 30.c×b4 ♖×b4+ 31.♔xe5 ♖h4 32.♖a2± **30.b5 ♔e6 31.c4 ♔d7?!** 31...♗d6 32.♖a6 ♔d7 33.h3± **32.♖a7 ♗d6?!** Allowing a direct invasion, but nor does 32...♔d6 stop the king in view of 33.♖a6+ ♔d7 34.♔d5±. **33.♔d5 e4 34.b6 ♖f8** 34...♗×h2 35.c5 h5 36.c6+ ♔e7 37.b7+- **35.c5 ♖f5+** (D)

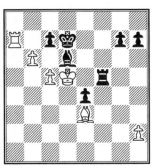

**36.♔c4!** and Teichmann resigned in light of 36...♗×h2 37.b7 ♖f8 (37...c6 38.b8♕++-) 38.♖a8+- but not 36.♔×e4? ♖e5+ 37.♔f3 ♖×e3+ 38.♔×e3 ♗×c5±. **1-0**

**(46) Alekhine – Teichmann**
Berlin m(6) 1921
Ruy Lopez [C68]

**1.e4 e5 2.♘f3 ♘c6 3.♗b5 a6 4.♗×c6 d×c6 5.♘c3 f6 6.d4 e×d4 7.♕×d4 ♕×d4 8.♘×d4 ♗d6**

**9.♘de2 ♘e7 10.♗f4 ♗e6 11.♗×d6 c×d6 12.0-0-0 0-0-0 13.♖he1 ♗f7 14.♘d4 ♖he8 15.f3 ♔c7 16.a4 b5 17.a×b5 a×b5 18.b4 ♘c8 19.♘f5 g6 20.♘e3 ♘b6** (D)

**21.♔b2?** The king is not really safe here, far away from the forthcoming action on the kingside. It should head in the other direction with 21.♘g4 ♘d7 22.♔d2=. **21...d5?!** (D) 21...f5! is the more powerful lever because 22.e×f5? runs into 22...♖×e3-+.

**22.♖d4?** 22.♘g4 ♘c4+ 23.♔b1 f5 24.♘f6 ♖e6 25.♘×h7 d×e4 26.f×e4 ♖×d1+ 27.♖×d1 f×e4 28.♘g5 ♖e7 29.♘g×e4= **22...f5! 23.♖a1?!** Since Black wants to reposition his knight, the prophylactic 23.g3 was better. 23.e×f5? is answered by 23...♘c4+ 24.♘×c4 ♖×e1 25.f×g6 ♗×g6-+. **23...♘c8! 24.g4?! d×e4 25.♖×d8 ♔×d8?!** 25...♖×d8 26.f×e4 f4 is even stronger. **26.f×e4 f4!** This dynamic solution is correct because White's kingside pawns remain very weak. The static 26...f×e4? 27.♘e2 plays into White's hands. **27.♖d1+?** The *zwischenschach* helps only Black. Therefore, 27.♘f1 ♘d6 28.♘d2 is a better way to fight against the passed f-pawn. **27...♔c7 28.♖f1?** 28.♘f1 g5 29.♘d2 is still called for. **28...g5 29.♘f5 ♘d6 30.♖a1 ♘c4+ 31.♔c1 ♔b7** 31...♔b6!? **32.♘d4 h5** 32...♘e5!? is even stronger: 33.h3 ♖d8 34.♘f5 h5–+. **33.g×h5 ♗×h5 34.♘b3 f3** (D)

**35.♘d2?** Now the passed f-pawn decides matters immediately. It must be blockaded by 35.♘d1, but this does not stop Black's initiative of course, e.g., 35...♗g6 36.♘c5+ ♔c7 37.♘f2 (37.♖a7+ ♔b8 38.♖b7+ ♔a8 39.♖g7 ♗×e4 40.♘a6 ♖e5) 37...♖h8 38.h3 g4 39.h×g4 ♖h2 40.♘cd3 ♗×e4, with good winning chances in both cases. **35...♘e3 36.♖a3 f2 37.♘a4 b×a4 38.♖×e3 ♖d8**, and White resigned in view of 39.♖d3 ♖×d3 40.c×d3 ♗e2–+. **0-1**

**The Hague International Tournament, October 25-November 5, 1921**
Having left Russia, the grandmaster of Moscow, as Alekhine was called by Tartakower in those years, was like an awakened volcano. Triberg, Budapest,

and The Hague become the witnesses of his brilliant successes. In these three tournaments, he played a total of twenty-eight games (+19 -0 =9). In Triberg, he finished two points ahead of Bogoljubow (2nd) and four points (!) ahead of Sämisch (3rd). At The Hague, he was a full point ahead of Tartakower and a point and a half ahead of Rubinstein. This result was of a special significance for Alekhine because immediately after Capablanca won the world title, Rubinstein challenged the Cuban grandmaster to a title match. And, although the world chess community treated the very possibility of organizing such a match with a fair dose of skepticism because of the financial difficulties involved, it was obvious that Rubinstein was the first in the line of the challengers.

Among the compeitors at the Hague were such well-known grandmasters as Saviely Tartakower (born in Rostov-on-Don), Yugoslav Bora Kostic (who had played successfully in a number of tournaments in New York), Hungarian Geza Maróczy (who by that time had won a dozen of first prizes in major international events and was future world champion Max Euwe's mentor), chess veterans Georg Marco of Austria and Jacques Mieses of Germany, Max Euwe (the 20-year-old Dutch champion), and Frederick Yates (the experienced champion of England).

Julius Caesar's immortal words "Veni, vidi, vici" ("I came, I saw, I conquered") is exactly what Alekhine's results at The Hague impressed on the chess world. The tournament was his third successive victory. He scored eight points in nine games (+7 -0 =2) in a tournament that brought together almost all the cream of European chess.

### (47) Alekhine – Rubinstein,Akiba
The Hague 1921 (D)

Alekhine chooses the technical win with **37.♕c4** The direct return of the extra exchange with 37.♖×c3!? wins as well: 37...♗×c3 38.♕×c3 ♖a8 (after 38...♖a2+ 39.♔f1 ♖a8 40.♔g1 +–, White's king is safe, something which cannot be said for Black's of course.) 39.d5 e5 40.♕c6 ♕×c6 41.d×c6 ♖c8 42.♖b6 ♔f7 43.♔d3 ♔e6 44.♔c4 ♔d6 45.♔b5 ♖c7 46.♖b7 ♖×c6 47.♖×h7 ♖c1 48.♖h8+–. **37...♔f7 38.♕c8 ♕a6+ 39.♕×a6 ♖×a6 40.e4 g5 41.♔d3 ♔g6 42.d5 f×e4+ 43.f×e4 e×d5 44.e×d5 ♖a4?!** But 44...♔×h6 loses as well, e.g., 45.♖e1 ♔h5 46.♖e7 h6 47.♖e6+–. **45.♖d1! ♔×h6 46.d6 ♔h5?!** (D)

This allows Alekhine to construct a mating net: **47.d7 ♖a8 48.♔e4 ♖d8 49.♔f5 ♔h4 50.♖h1+ 1-0** and Rubinstein resigned as 50...♔g3 51.♖h3# is game over.

The convincing victory at The Hague prompted Alekhine to send a challenge to Capablanca. There had even been some reports in the press (in particular, in *Shakhmaty*, 1/1922) that the world championship match between Capablanca and Alekhine would be held at the end of the year in America. However, Alekhine himself had then little faith in such a possibility, and, besides, he was not yet ready for such a battle. He admitted this several years later (after the match had taken place):

*Although I had already sent a challenge to Capablanca, I did not yet perceive myself mature, as far as chess was concerned. In many fields, especially in technique, Capablanca was then undoubtedly stronger than I, while among his rivals, Lasker still was in first place. The idea of holding a return match between them, in which the chess world took great interest, was an obstacle to my plans. Therefore, my challenge had the only objective of securing my candidacy for the future.*

**Bernstein, Ossip Samoilovich** (September 20, 1882, Zhitomir-November 30, 1962, near Paris)
An international grandmaster, Doctor of Law, advocate. In his life, there is something that resembles the fate of Steinitz. At 19-years old, he came to

*The Hague, 1921. Sitting at the board are Alekhine and Rubinstein.*
*Looking on (standing) are (from left to right): Tartakower, Kostic, Euwe,*
*Maroczy and Yates. Sitting at the center is Mieses.*

Berlin to study at the university, but instead spent all his free time at the local chess club, where he soon achieved success. A year later, he took part in the 13th Congress of the German Chess Union dedicated to the 25th anniversary of its founding, where he finished second in the second "main" tournament (or "main tournament" B). He drew a match with the Austrian master Heinrich Wolf (+1 -1 =5) in 1902 and gained the master's title as a result. He played magnificently in the 3rd All-Russia tournament in 1903, where he finished second and defeated Chigorin (the winner of the tournament) and Rubinstein. He played successfully in a number of German tournaments (e.g., at Coburg 1904, Barmen 1905), won tournaments in Ostend (1907, 1st-2nd with Rubinstein) and Stockholm (1906, 1st-2nd with Schlechter). He participated in the major international tournaments in San Sebastian (1911, shared 8th-9th places) and St. Petersburg (5th place in 1909 and 6th-7th places in 1914).

Interestingly, on the eve of the 1909 St. Petersburg tournament, there were very few who doubted that world champion Emanuel Lasker, who had just defeated Siegbert Tarrasch in a world championship match, would be the winner. But, Lasker was cautious in his predictions and answered such questions with a smile: "Yes, but there will be two stones against me." He meant Akiba Rubinstein and Ossip Bernstein, whose surnames end in "stein," which is German for "stone." And his apprehension was not misplaced because it was precisely Rubinstein who proved to be his main competitor in the tournament and shared first and second places with him. Bernstein drew his game with Lasker in 1909 and won it in 1914. Incidentally, that was his only loss, which nearly cost him a place in the final part of the tournament. Therefore, it was not by accident that the world champion spoke of Bernstein in such a flattering way: "He is an original talent... and has a rare gift for finding original ideas." It is interesting that the two "stones" were to play a match for the title of Russian champion, but it never took place.

Ossip Bernstein was ten years Alekhine's senior. It is known that as early as in 1909 they, playing as a duo, had won a consultation game from dangerous opponents, Akiba Rubinstein and Alexei Goncharov. And, when they became opponents in games of this kind, Alekhine twice suffered defeat, first playing in consultation with Blumenfeld (1909) against Bernstein and Goncharov, and a second time when playing together with Rozanov (1910) against Bernstein and Urayev. It is true, though, that Alekhine took his revenge in their *vis-à-vis* encounters.

Bernstein and Alekhine's paths first crossed, in tournament play, at the All-Russia Masters Tournament in Vilno (1912), where the two defeats inflicted by Alekhine deprived Bernstein of first prize, even though in the end he came only a half-point behind the winner of the tournament, Akiba Rubinstein.

Two years later, at St. Petersburg (1914), Bernstein and Alekhine drew their game. Their rivalry continued in Paris, where they both emigrated, leaving Soviet Russia almost simultaneously. On the banks of the Seine River, the old acquaintances played two small matches: in 1922 their match of two games was won by Alekhine (+1 =1) and, in 1933, their four-game match was drawn (+1 -1 =2). Surprisingly, the latter match was the first competition that world champion Alekhine failed to win (See, Matches with Bernstein).

After emigrating to France, Bernstein lived in Paris, where he mostly practiced as an advocate – he obtained the degree of Doctor of Law from Heidelberg University in 1906 – but devoted relatively little time to chess. It was only in the early 1930s that he was able to return to chess for a while, coming second at Ponte (1930) and participating in two tournaments in Switzerland: Bern (1932, 5th-6th places) and Zürich (1934, 6th-7th places). In both these tournaments Alekhine finished first and, in Zürich, was able to exploit the advantage of being up the exchange in their encounter (two rooks vs. rook and knight). Subsequently, he spent many hours analyzing endings with this balance of material and wrote a special essay on it.

*Ossip Bernstein*

**(48) Alekhine – Bernstein**
Zürich 1934
Queen's Gambit Declined [D53]

**1.d4 d5 2.c4 e6 3.♘c3 ♘f6
4.♗g5 ♗e7 5.e3 h6 6.♗f4 c6
7.♘f3 ♘bd7 8.c×d5 ♘×d5 9.♗g3
♕a5 10.♕b3 0-0 11.♗e2 ♘7f6?**
This slow regrouping is the source of
the following problems. Simplification
with 11...b6 12.0-0 ♗a6 is called for.
**12.♘d2! c5 13.♘c4 ♕d8 14.d×c5
♗×c5 15.♗f3 b6 16.0-0 ♕e7
17.♘b5** 17.♘a4 is also very strong.
**17...a6 18.♘bd6 ♗d7?!** (D) 18...b5
19.♘×c8 ♖a×c8 20.♘e5 ♗d6 was the
lesser evil.

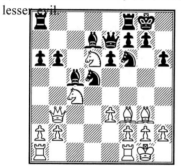

**19.e4?** Black can now drive White's
mighty knights away. The prophylactic
19.a4 ♗c6 20.♖fc1 gives White a
strong initiative. **19...b5! 20.e×d5** (D)

**20...b×c4?** Bernstein misses the surprising *zwischenzug* 20...e×d5 21.♘e3

♗×d6 22.♘×d5 ♘×d5 23.♗×d5 ♖ad8
24.♖fe1 ♕f6, which is more or less
completely equal. **21.♘×c4 ♘×d5?!**
21...e×d5 22.♘b6 ♗×b6 23.♕×b6
♖fe8 is the lesser evil. **22.♖fe1 ♕d8
23.♖ad1 ♕c8 24.♖c1** (D)

**24...♖a7?** 24...♕d8 was the only
move. **25.♘d6 ♕c6 26.♘e4 ♖b7
27.♖×c5** 27.♕d1 ♖b5 28.b4 wins as
well. **27...♖×b3 28.♖×c6 ♖×f3
29.♖d6 ♖×g3 30.h×g3 ♗b5
31.♘c5 ♖c8 32.♖c1 g5 33.♘b3?!**
The resulting endgame is technically
won, but here the domination strategy
with 33.b3 was even stronger, e.g.,
33...g4 34.f3 g×f3 35.g×f3 a5 36.a4
♗e2 37.♔f2+−. **33...♖b8 34.♘d4
♔g7 35.♘×b5 a×b5 36.♖c5 b4
37.♖a6 ♘f6 38.♔f1 ♘e4 39.♖c7
♔g6 40.♔e2 ♖b5 41.♔e3 ♘f6
42.♖c4 h5 43.f3 ♔f5 44.♔d3
♘d5 45.♖a7 f6 46.♖e4 ♖b6
47.g4+** ("A deep conception. Alekhine
intends to start a queenside advance, but
first he secures his position on the
other flank. To this end, he eliminates
the h5-pawn and with it the threat of
h5-h4 followed by the thrust of the
knight to f4." – Kotov) **47...♔g6**
47...h×g4 48.f×g4+ ♔g6 49.g3+−
**48.g×h5+ ♔×h5 49.g3 ♔g6
50.♔c4 f5 51.♖e2 ♔f6 52.♔c5
♖b8 53.♖a6 ♖e8 54.♖d6 f4
55.g×f4 ♘×f4 56.♖ed2 ♖a8**

**57.b3 ♔e5 58.♖d8 ♖a7** 58...♖×d8
59.♖×d8 ♘d5 60.♖f8 +− **59.♔×b4
♘d5+ 60.♔c5 ♖c7+ 61.♔b5 ♖c3
62.♖e2+ ♔f4 63.♖f8+ ♔g3
64.♖e5 ♘f4 65.♖×g5+ ♔×f3
66.♖e5 ♖e3** (D)

**67.♖×f4+** and Black resigned as
White's a-pawn queens first after
67...♔×f4 68.♖×e3 ♔×e3 69.a4 +−. **1-0**

Most surprisingly, almost twenty years
passed before Bernstein could again
return to big-time chess. In 1954, he
led the French team (yet another crossing of his and Alekhine's fates) at the
world chess Olympiad in Amsterdam.
Then, he shared 2nd-3rd places with
Miguel Najdorf in the tournament at
Montevideo (1954), defeating him in
their individual game in crushing style.
Two years later, what Alekhine was
dreaming of in the pre-war years had
come true for Bernstein, who came to
Moscow as leader of the French team
in the 12th Olympiad. However, because of illness, he did not play a single
game there.

Their last encounter occurred in Paris,
in early 1940, and, although each of
them had one consultant to help (I.G.
Zabludovsky with Bernstein and I.L.
Budovsky with Alekhine), it is clear that

Ossip Samoilovich and Alexander
Aleksandrovich had the starring roles.

**(49) Bernstein – Alekhine**
Consultation Game, Paris 1940
Queen's Pawn Game [A49]

**1.d4 ♘f6 2.♘f3 b6 3.g3 ♗b7
4.♗g2 g6 5.0-0 c5 6.♘c3 c×d4
7.♕×d4 ♗g7 8.e4 d6?** 8...♘c6 is
more prudent. **9.e5! ♘fd7 10.♕c4?**
(D) Bernstein misses the beautiful shot
10.♗h6!! ♗×h6 (10...d×e5 11.♕h4
♗f6 12.♕g4) 11.e×d6 ♘f6 12.♕h4
♗g7 13.d×e7 ♕c7 14.♖fe1 with a tremendous attack in both cases.

Here Alekhine thought for 40 minutes
and did not find the solution to his
problems: **10...0-0?** 10...♗×e5??
11.♘g5 +−; 10...♗×f3! 11.♗×f3 ♘e5
12.♕b5+ ♘bd7 13.♗×a8 ♕×a8
14.♕d5 ♕c8 gives Black good compensation for the exchange. **11.e×d6
e×d6 12.♖d1 ♕c8?! 13.♕h4**
13.♕×c8!? ♖×c8 14.♘b5 is also very
strong and was probably the better
choice against Alekhine. **13...♘e5
14.♘d5 ♗×d5** 14...♘bc6? is met by
15.♘×e5 (but not 15.♘f6+? ♗×f6
16.♕×f6 ♘×f3+ 17.♗×f3 ♘e5
18.♗×b7 ♕×b7 19.♗h6 ♘f3+ 20.♔f1
♘×h2+ 21.♔e2? ♖fe8+ (21...♕e4+?
22.♔d2 and White wins) 22.♔d2
♕d5+ 23.♔c1 ♕e5 and Black is pref-

erable) 15...dxe5 16.♘f6+ ♗xf6 17.♕xf6 ♕f5 18.♕xf5 gxf5 19.♖d7 ♖ab8 20.♖xb7 ♖xb7 21.♗xc6 ♖c7 22.♗a4+−. **15.♖xd5 ♘bd7 16.♖xd6 ♕c5 17.♘g5 h5 18.♘e4 ♕xc2 19.f4?** Bernstein fatally weakens his king position as a result of a miscalculation. He should just develop with 19.♗g5±. **19...♘d3 20.♗e3?** (D) 20.♖xd7 ♖ae8 21.f5 gxf5 22.♗e3 ♕e2 23.♕g5 fxe4 24.♗f1 ♕g4 25.♕xg4 hxg4 26.♖d1 is more active.

**20...♕e2?** The surprising 20...♖ae8! 21.♖xd7 ♕e2 makes better use of Black's initiative, e.g., 22.♖xd3 ♕xd3 23.♗f2 ♖xe4 24.♗xe4 ♕xe4 25.♖e1 ♕d5. **21.♘f2 ♘e1!** 21...♕xe3? 22.♖xd3+− **22.♗xa8 ♖xa8 23.♕e7 ♗f8 24.♕e4** (D)

**24...♖d8?** As noted by Bernstein, Black had drawing chances after **24...♗xd6 25.♕xa8+ ♔h7?** (25...♗f8 is stronger and leads more

or less by force to a draw: 26.♖d1 ♘f6 27.♖d8 ♘f3+ 28.♔g2 ♘e1±) **26.♕e8 ♗c5 27.♕xf7+ ♔h8 28.♗xc5** (28.♕e8+ ♘f8 29.♗d4+ is even better) **28...♘xc5 29.♖d1?** (29.♕f6+ ♔h7 30.f5 +−) **29...♘cd3 30.♖xd3 ♘xd3 31.♘xd3 ♕xd3. 25.♖dd1 ♘c2 26.♖d2 ♕xe3 27.♖xc2 ♗c5 28.♕xe3 ♗xe3 29.♖d1 ♔f8 30.♔g2 ♗c5 31.♘e4 ♔e7 32.♖e2 1-0**

## Alekhine-Bernstein Matches, 1922 and 1933

These two Russian players, who almost simultaneously immigrated to France, played two small matches in Paris. From February 2-5, 1922, they played a two-game match. The first game was a Ruy Lopez Exchange Variation and was drawn on move 26. In the second, Alekhine adopted the Vienna Game, seized the initiative and, having won a pawn, exploited his advantage on move 40. Their second match, this time of four games, took place eleven years later, in 1933. This time Alekhine, already the world champion, was unable to overcome the stubborn resistance of his longtime rival, and the match was drawn (+1 -1 = 2). The result was possibly an effect of Alekhine's accumulated fatigue. Alekhine circumnavigated the world and participated, as leader of the French team, in the Olympiad in Folkstone (England).

The game won by Alekhine proved the shortest in the match, lasting merely sixteen moves. In the Steinitz Defense Deferred, Bernstein, who had the white pieces, blundered after a series of exchanges in the center, lost a piece and resigned at once. In the remaining three games, the fight continued until all the resources had been exhausted. In his victorious game, Bernstein, with White, had outplayed his formidable opponent in the Petroff in sixty-six moves! In both drawn games (in 50 and 47 moves respectively) Alekhine had the white pieces. In the first case, he tested his opponent in the Ruy Lopez, in the second, in the Lasker Variation of the Queen's Gambit Declined. In both cases, Bernstein defended faultlessly. The following game typifies the evenness of the match.

**(50) Alekhine – Bernstein**
Paris m(4) 1933
Queen's Gambit Declinied [D56]

**1.d4 d5 2.c4 e6 3.♘c3 ♘f6 4.♗g5 ♗e7 5.e3 h6 6.♗h4 ♘e4 7.♗×e7 ♕×e7 8.♕b3 ♘×c3 9.♕×c3 0-0 10.♘f3 c6 11.♗d3 ♘d7 12.0-0 d×c4 13.♗×c4 b6 14.a4 ♗b7 15.a5 c5 16.♗e2 c×d4 17.♘×d4 ♖ac8 18.♕d2 ♕d6 19.a6 ♗a8 20.♖fd1 ♘c5 21.♕b4 ♕e7 22.♕a3 ♖fd8?!** 22...e5 23.♘b5 ♗c6 is more precise. **23.f3!** Restricting Black's minor pieces. **23...e5 24.♘f5 ♕f6 25.e4 ♔h7 26.♕e3 ♘e6 27.♖×d8 ♖×d8 28.♖c1 h5** (D)

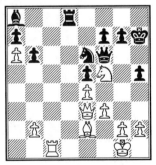

**29.♗c4?!** Alekhine violates the principle "do not rush." A waiting move, like

29.♗f1, is more unplesant for Black as the rook can use the c-file directly. **29...♘d4 30.♘×d4 ♖×d4 31.h3 ♖d6 32.♗d5 ♗c6** 32...♗×d5 33.e×d5 ♕d8 34.♕×e5 ♖×d5 is playable as well. **33.♕b3 ♔g6?!** 33...♔g8 is more natural. **34.♕c4** The alternative 34.♕b4!? looks very attractive, but Black might be able to hang on by the skin of his teeth: 34...♗e8 (34...♗×d5? runs into 35.e×d5 ♕d8? [35...♖×d5? 36.♕e4+ +–] 36.♕×d6+ ♕×d6 37.♖c6 ♕f6 38.h4+– and Black will fall into *zugzwang* sooner or later) 35.♖c8 ♗d7 36.♖c7 ♔h7 37.♕c3 (37.♖×a7? runs into 37...♗×h3!! 38.g×h3 ♕×f3 39.♕×d6 ♕d1+ with a perpetual) 37...b5 38.♔h2 ♕f4+ 39.g3 ♕f6 40.h4 g5 and Black has some counterplay. **34...♗×d5 35.e×d5 ♕d8** (D)

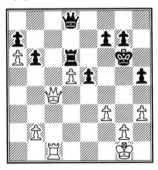

**36.♖d1** Black also defends after 36.♕c2+ ♔f6 and 36.♕e4+ ♔h6 37.♕f5 ♖d7 38.♕×e5 ♖×d5=. **36...f5 37.b4 ♔h7 38.b5 ♕g5 39.♖e1** 39.♕c7 is parried by 39...♖g6 40.♕c2 ♖d6=. **39...♕f4** The rook endgame is drawn but Black can also play 39...♕g3=. **40.♕×f4 e×f4 41.♖e7 ♖×d5 42.♖×a7 ♖×b5 43.♖b7 ♔h6 44.a7 ♖a5 45.♖×b6+ g6 46.♖b7 ♔g5 47.♖g7 ½-½**

**Piestany Tournament, April 7-29, 1922**

Five major international tournaments were held in Europe in 1922, and Alekhine participated in four of them. In Piestany, nineteen participants, both veterans of chess battles such as Siegbert Tarrasch and Georg Marco, and players of the younger generation such as Bogoljubow, Tartakower, Grünfeld, Réti, Euwe, Przepiorka, and Sämisch, gathered. The younger generation, by this time, had announced loud and clear their presence in the chess elite, both because of their sporting achievements and also their searches for new creative approaches to the art of chess. The young players showed exceptionally good results at Piestany. For example, in 1912, Spielmann had scored 11½ points out of 18 and finished second; this time, with a better score (14½ points out of 19), he was only able to share 2nd-3rd places with Alekhine. Bogoljubow garnered first place by scoring 15 points! However, Alekhine also could regard himself as a moral winner of the event because of two brilliancy prizes he won for the excellently played games against Tarrasch and Wolf.

**(51) Tarrasch – Alekhine**
Bad Pistyan 1922
Blumenfeld Countergambit [E10]

**1.d4 ♘f6 2.c4 e6 3.♘f3 c5 4.d5 b5 5.d×e6 f×e6 6.c×b5 d5 7.e3** 7.g3!? is considered to be more critical. **7...♗d6 8.♘c3 0-0 9.♗e2 ♗b7 10.b3?! ♘bd7 11.♗b2 ♕e7 12.0-0 ♖ad8 13.♕c2 e5 14.♖fe1?** 14.♘d2 e4 15.♘a4 to meet 15...♘e5 with 16.♘×c5 offers more counterplay, e.g., 16...♘fg4 17.♘d×e4 d×e4

18.♘×b7 ♕×b7 19.h3. **14...e4 15.♘d2 ♘e5** (D)

**16.♘d1?** This passive retreat gives Black a free hand on the kingside. 16.h3 is called for. **16...♘fg4 17.♗×g4** 17.h3 can even be answered by 17...♘h2!. **17...♘×g4 18.♘f1 ♕g5 19.h3 ♘h6 20.♔h1 ♘f5 21.♘h2 d4 22.♗c1?** Too passive. 22.e×d4? also loses quickly because of 22...c×d4 23.♕c4+ ♔h8 24.♗×d4 ♘×d4 25.♕×d4 ♗×h2–+; 22.♖b1 is more tenacious. **22...d3 23.♕c4+ ♔h8 24.♗b2 ♘g3+ 25.♔g1 ♗d5 26.♕a4 ♘e2+ 27.♔h1 ♖f7 28.♕a6 h5 29.b6 ♘g3+!** The motif repeats itself. **30.♔g1** 30.f×g3? ♕×g3 31.♘f1 ♖×f1+ 32.♖×f1 ♕h2#. **30...a×b6 31.♕×b6 d2 32.♖f1 ♘×f1 33.♘×f1 ♗e6 34.♔h1?!** (D)

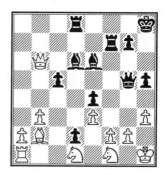

**34...♗×h3!!** The final blow. **35.g×h3 ♖f3 36.♘g3 h4 37.♗f6 ♕×f6 38.♘×e4 ♖×h3+ 0-1**

**London Tournaments, 1922, 1932.**
**July 1922**

The London tournament brought together many well-known figures of the chess world. Capablanca marked his first appearance as world champion by putting forward a document of twenty-two items, intended to regulate future world championship matches. The reaction of the players to these regulations for world championship cycles was, on the whole, positive, but some conditions, and particularly the necessity to secure a prize fund of $10,000, caused discontent. The "London Agreement" was signed by Capablanca, Alekhine, Bogoljubow, Vidmar, Rubinstein, future world champion Euwe, and other grandmasters.

In London, Alekhine and Capablanca met again after an eight-year hiatus and became the main rivals in the struggle for first prize. For a while, they kept abreast, both having five points after five rounds! They met in the ninth round, but there was no fight in that game. Capablanca, who had the black pieces, skillfully neutralized his opponent's initiative, equalized, and a draw was agreed on move 17. The spectators were naturally dissatisfied. "I traveled over 200 miles to watch the game!" exclaimed one disappointed Englishman. However, Alekhine was possibly under the pressure of their previous encounters, and also the time for principled fights between them in tournaments had not yet come.

**London, 1922**

Neither Capablanca nor Alekhine suffered a single loss in the tournament. However, Alekhine made three draws too many and the Cuban, having scored 13/15, took first prize; Alekhine was second with 11½ points.

**(52) Alekhine – Yates, Frederick**
London 1922
Queen's Gambit Declined [D64]

**1.d4 ♘f6 2.c4 e6 3.♘f3 d5 4.♘c3 ♗e7 5.♗g5 0-0 6.e3 ♘bd7 7.♖c1 c6 8.♕c2 ♖e8 9.♗d3 d×c4 10.♗×c4 ♘d5 11.♘e4** The main line runs 11.♗×e7 ♕×e7 12.0-0. **11...f5?** This weakens the dark squares too much. Instead, 11...♕a5+, as played later in Grünfeld-Yates, Merano 1926, is called for. **12.♗×e7 ♕×e7 13.♘ed2 b5 14.♗×d5 c×d5 15.0-0 a5 16.♘b3** (D)

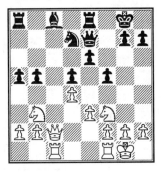

**16...a4?** 16...♗a6, with the idea of 17.♘×a5 b4 18.♖fe1 ♗b5 to get some counterplay is more in the spirit of the position. **17.♘c5 ♘×c5?** In the following endgame, Black has no counterplay and can only sit and wait for the execution, which will come in the form of an invasion on the dark squares. 17...♘b6 offers better practical chances. **18.♕×c5 ♕×c5 19.♖×c5 b4 20.♖fc1 ♗a6 21.♘e5 ♖eb8 22.f3 b3 23.a3 h6 24.♔f2** Alekhine activates the last weapon – his king. **24...♔h7 25.h4 ♖f8 26.♔g3**

117

## London 1922

| | | 1 | 2 | 3 | 4 | 5 | 6 | 7 | 8 | 9 | 10 | 11 | 12 | 13 | 14 | 15 | 16 | Total |
|---|---|---|---|---|---|---|---|---|---|---|---|---|---|---|---|---|---|---|
| 1 | Capablanca | X | ½ | 1 | ½ | 1 | 1 | ½ | ½ | 1 | 1 | 1 | 1 | 1 | 1 | 1 | 1 | 13 |
| 2 | Alekhine | ½ | X | ½ | 1 | ½ | ½ | ½ | ½ | 1 | 1 | 1 | 1 | ½ | 1 | 1 | 1 | 11½ |
| 3 | Vidmar | 0 | ½ | X | 0 | 1 | ½ | 1 | ½ | 1 | ½ | 1 | 1 | 1 | 1 | 1 | 1 | 11 |
| 4 | Rubinstein | ½ | 0 | 1 | X | ½ | ½ | 1 | 1 | ½ | 0 | 1 | ½ | 1 | 1 | 1 | 1 | 10½ |
| 5 | Bogoljubow | 0 | ½ | 0 | ½ | X | ½ | 1 | 1 | 0 | 1 | ½ | 0 | 1 | 1 | 1 | 1 | 9 |
| 6 | Réti | 0 | ½ | ½ | ½ | ½ | X | ½ | ½ | 1 | 1 | ½ | 1 | 0 | 1 | 0 | 1 | 8½ |
| 7 | Tartakower | ½ | ½ | 0 | 0 | 0 | ½ | X | ½ | 1 | 0 | 1 | 1 | 1 | ½ | 1 | 1 | 8½ |
| 8 | Maróczy | ½ | ½ | ½ | 0 | 0 | ½ | ½ | X | 1 | ½ | ½ | 1 | ½ | 0 | 1 | 1 | 8 |
| 9 | Yates | 0 | 0 | 0 | ½ | 1 | 0 | 0 | 0 | X | 1 | 1 | 1 | 1 | 1 | ½ | 1 | 8 |
| 10 | Atkins | 0 | 0 | ½ | 1 | 0 | 0 | 1 | ½ | 0 | X | 0 | 1 | ½ | ½ | 0 | 1 | 6 |
| 11 | Euwe | 0 | 0 | 0 | 0 | ½ | ½ | 0 | ½ | 0 | 1 | X | 0 | 1 | 0 | 1 | 1 | 5½ |
| 12 | Znosko Borovsky | 0 | 0 | 0 | ½ | 1 | 0 | 0 | 0 | 0 | 0 | 1 | X | 1 | ½ | 1 | 0 | 5 |
| 13 | Wahltuch | 0 | ½ | 0 | 0 | 0 | 1 | 0 | ½ | 0 | ½ | 0 | 0 | X | 1 | 1 | ½ | 5 |
| 14 | Morrison | 0 | 0 | 0 | 0 | 0 | 0 | ½ | 1 | 0 | ½ | 1 | ½ | 0 | X | 0 | 1 | 4½ |
| 15 | Watson | 0 | 0 | 0 | 0 | 0 | 1 | 0 | 0 | ½ | 1 | 0 | 0 | 0 | 1 | X | 1 | 4½ |
| 16 | Marotti | 0 | 0 | 0 | 0 | 0 | 0 | 0 | 0 | 0 | 0 | 0 | 1 | ½ | 0 | 0 | X | 1½ |

買fb8 27.買c7 奧b5 28.買1c5 奧a6
29.買5c6 買e8 30.曾f4 曾g8 31.h5
奧f1 32.g3 奧a6 33.買f7 曾h7
34.買cc7 買g8 35.⊘d7 曾h8
36.⊘f6 買gf8 (D)

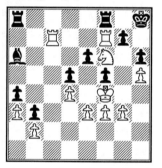

Now, the scene is set for the final small combination: **37.買×g7 買×f6 38.曾e5** Yates resigned because he cannot rescue his rook with 38...買af8 because of 39.買h7+ 曾g8 40.買cg7#.
**1-0**

### February 1-15, 1932

Alekhine won this strong tournament. The distinguishing feature of Alekhine's style was, as before, sparkling combinations that crown his consistently implemented strategic plans. Of special interest was his first encounter with the women's world champion Vera Menchik.

**(53) Menchik,Vera – Alekhine**
London 1932
Queen's Indian Defense [E14]

**1.d4 ⊘f6 2.c4 e6 3.⊘f3 b6 4.e3 奧b7 5.奧d3 奧b4+ 6.奧d2 奧×d2+ 7.⊘b×d2 d6 8.0-0 ⊘bd7 9.曾c2 曾e7 10.買fd1 0-0 11.⊘e4 g6 12.買d2 ⊘×e4 13.奧×e4 c6 14.曾a4 買fc8 15.奧d3 c5 16.曾d1 ⊘f6 17.d×c5 b×c5 18.曾e2 ⊘h5 19.買ad1 買f8 20.e4?** This weakens the dark squares and allows Black's knight to invade for no good reason. 20.奧c2 was called for. **20...⊘f4 21.曾e3 e5 22.奧f1 買ad8 23.b4?! ⊘e6** The alternative, 23...c×b4!? 24.曾×a7 ⊘e6 25.曾e3 ⊘c5 26.奧d3 買a8, gives strong positional pressure. **24.買b2 奧a8 25.b×c5 ⊘×c5 26.⊘d2 f5 27.e×f5 g×f5 (D)**

### London 1932

| | | 1 | 2 | 3 | 4 | 5 | 6 | 7 | 8 | 9 | 10 | 11 | 12 | T |
|---|---|---|---|---|---|---|---|---|---|---|---|---|---|---|
| 1 | Alekhine | x | ½ | ½ | 1 | ½ | 1 | 1 | 1 | ½ | 1 | 1 | 1 | 9 |
| 2 | Flohr | ½ | x | ½ | ½ | 1 | 0 | 1 | 1 | 1 | 1 | ½ | 1 | 8 |
| 3 | Kashdan | ½ | ½ | x | ½ | 0 | ½ | 1 | 1 | 1 | 1 | 1 | ½ | 7½ |
| 4 | Sultan Khan | 0 | ½ | ½ | x | 0 | 1 | ½ | 1 | 1 | 1 | 1 | 1 | 7½ |
| 5 | Maróczy | ½ | 0 | 1 | 1 | x | ½ | ½ | ½ | ½ | ½ | ½ | ½ | 6 |
| 6 | Tartakower | 0 | 1 | ½ | 0 | ½ | x | 1 | 1 | 0 | 0 | 1 | 1 | 6 |
| 7 | Koltanowski | 0 | 0 | 0 | ½ | ½ | 0 | x | ½ | 1 | 1 | ½ | 1 | 5 |
| 8 | Menchik | 0 | 0 | 0 | 0 | ½ | 0 | ½ | x | 1 | ½ | 1 | 1 | 4½ |
| 9 | Thomas | ½ | 0 | 0 | 0 | ½ | 1 | 0 | 0 | x | ½ | ½ | ½ | 3½ |
| 10 | Milner Barry | 0 | 0 | 0 | 0 | ½ | 1 | 0 | ½ | ½ | x | ½ | ½ | 3½ |
| 11 | Berger | 0 | ½ | 0 | 0 | ½ | 0 | ½ | 0 | ½ | ½ | x | ½ | 3 |
| 12 | Winter | 0 | 0 | ½ | 0 | ½ | 0 | 0 | 0 | ½ | ½ | ½ | x | 2½ |

**28.f3?** The plan to protect the kingside and the invade with the rooks on the queenside does not really solve the problems of the position. It is better to fight against Black's attack in the center with 28.♘b3 f4 29.♔h3 ♘e6 30.♔c3, but Black still has the initiative after 30...♘g5. **28...♕g7 29.♖db1?! ♔h8 30.♘b3 ♘e6 31.♖d2 ♘g5 32.♔h1 ♖g8 33.♖f2 ♖de8 34.♖d1 ♖e6 35.f4?** Opening all roads for Black's attack, but there is no defense in the long run anyway. **35...e×f4 36.♕d4 ♖e5** 36...♘h3 37.♕×g7+ ♖×g7 38.♖fd2 f3 wins as well. **37.c5 d×c5 38.♘×c5 ♘h3 39.♖c2 f3 40.g3 f2+** and White resigned in view of 41.♗g2 ♖e1+ 42.♖×e1 f×e1♕+ 43.♕g1 ♕×g1#. "The longest check given with a bishop which I have ever seen in my life," was Alekhine's comment on the last move. **0-1**

One of Alekhine's beautiful sacrifices – the one made against American master George Koltanowski – has entered the golden treasury of chess art.

**(54) Alekhine – Koltanowski**
London 1932
Ruy Lopez [C73]

**1.e4 e5 2.♘f3 ♘c6 3.♗b5 a6 4.♗a4 d6 5.♗×c6+ b×c6 6.d4 e×d4 7.♘×d4 ♗d7 8.0-0 g6 9.♘c3 ♗g7 10.♖e1 ♘e7 11.♗f4 0-0 12.♕d2 c5 13.♘b3 ♘c6 14.♗h6 ♗e6 15.♗×g7 ♔×g7 16.♘d5 f6 17.♖ad1 ♖b8 18.♕c3 ♕c8 19.a3 ♕b7 20.h3 ♖f7 21.♖e3 ♕b5?** (D) If Koltanowski had seen the following shot coming, he would have chosen 21...♖e8 with approximate equality.

**22.♘×c7!!** A powerful blow that demolishes the outer wall of Black's house. **22...♖×c7 23.♖×d6 ♗c4?** 23...♖e8 was forced, but White keeps the initiative after 24.a4 ♕b7 25.♘×c5 ♕c8 26.b4 ♘e5 27.♖×a6. **24.a4!** The first powerful pawn move. **24...♕×a4 25.♘×c5 ♕b5 26.♕×f6+ ♔g8 27.♘d7 ♖d8 28.♖f3 ♕b4?!** (D)

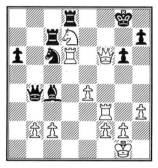

And now Alekhine destroys the defensive setup with another little pawn move with great explosive power: **29.c3!** **♕b5 30.♘e5 ♖dc8 31.♘×c6** and because of 31...♖×c6 32.♖d8+ ♖×d8 33.♕×d8+ ♔g7 34.♕f8#. Koltanowski threw in the towel. **1-0**

**Hastings Tournaments, 1922, 1925-26, 1933-34, 1936-37**
The first of these tournaments was not a traditional Christmas chess congress. It just followed the tournament at London.

**September 10-21, 1922**
The participants of this small double round-robin event were the veteran Tarrasch, two challengers (Alekhine and Rubinstein), Bogoljubow, and the two strongest British masters (Thomas and Yates). A real gem of the tournament was the game Bogoljubow-Alekhine (See, Celebrities).

**December 18, 1925-January 5, 1926**
This tournament, and the tournament at Birmingham, were crucial growth periods for Alekhine. As he admits:

*Since none of these tournaments had any major sporting significance, I was mainly concerned (when playing there) with perfecting my style of play further. It was necessary to disclose, and then eliminate the shortcomings still inherent in my play vis-à-vis Capablanca's play. In my games against Yates, Znosko-Borovsky and Janowsky, I especially paid attention to the moment of transition from the opening to the middlegame. The last of these games, just as my game against Colle (in Scarborough), gave me the chance to study the character of the struggle in ♕+♖ vs. ♕+♖ positions. My knowledge of this field subsequently proved very useful in my match with Capablanca.*

**(55) Janowski,Dawid – Alekhine**
Hastings 1926 (D)

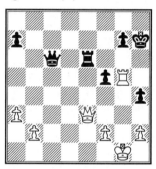

**34.♕c3?** Equivalent to capitulation because White's rook is too misplaced. Janowski could save himself with 34.♖h5+ ♔g8 35.♕b3=. **34...♕×c3 35.b×c3 g6!** White's rook really has a difficult life on g5. **36.♔f1 ♖c6 37.♖g1 ♖×c3 38.♔e2 ♖×a3 39.♖c1 ♔h6 40.♖c7 ♔g5 41.♖c6 a5 42.♖a6 a4 43.h3 ♔f4 44.♖×g6 ♖a2+ 45.♔f1** (D)

Now, a mating attack follows: **45...♔f3! 46.♔g1 ♖×f2 47.♖c6 ♖e2 48.♖c3+** 48.♖a6 ♔g3 49.♔f1

### Hastings 1922

|   |            | 1    | 2    | 3    | 4    | 5    | 6    | Total |
|---|------------|------|------|------|------|------|------|-------|
| 1 | **Alekhine**   | X    | ½1   | 11   | 11   | 1½   | 0½   | 7½    |
| 2 | **Rubinstein** | ½0   | X    | ½1   | 11   | 1½   | ½1   | 7     |
| 3 | **Thomas**     | 00   | ½0   | X    | ½½   | ½½   | 11   | 4½    |
| 4 | **Bogoljubow** | 00   | 00   | ½½   | X    | 1½   | 11   | 4½    |
| 5 | **Tarrasch**   | 0½   | 0½   | ½½   | 0½   | X    | 1½   | 4     |
| 6 | **Yates**      | 1½   | ½0   | 00   | 00   | 0½   | X    | 2½    |

♖e4–+ **48...♖e3 49.♖c5 f4 50.♖a5
a3 51.♔f1 ♖b3 52.♔e1 ♔g2 0-1**

### 1933-1934

The only one of the four tournaments at Hastings in which he played where Alekhine finished behind the winner, Flohr, by half a point, sharing 2nd-3rd places with Lilienthal.

### 1936-1937

The year that Alekhine was to play his return match with Euwe started well for him. He was victorious at the Hastings tournament, scoring eight points out of nine (+7 -0 =2), including the one against his principal competitor in the struggle for the first prize, American grandmaster Reuben Fine.

### Margate Tournaments, 1923, 1937, 1938

Three times Alekhine had the chance to play at this English resort, where, beginning in 1923, small international events were held in spring.

### 1923

Being out of form, Alekhine only scored 4½ points out of 7 and shared 2nd-5th places behind Grünfeld.

### 1937

This time he finished third with 6/9 (+6 -3 =0), behind Keres and Fine, who tied for first and second.

### (56) Alekhine - Foltis
Margate 1937 (D)

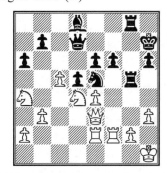

Alekhine opens the way for his inactive a4-knight with **32.c6!? b×c6?** 32...♘xc6 33.♘c5 ♕c8 34.♘dxe6 ♖e5 fights better against White's mighty knights, but Alekhine remains on top after 35.♕f4 of course. **33.♘c5 ♕d6 34.♘c×e6 ♖g3?** (D)

The prophylactic 34...罝5g6! 35.e×d5 罬b6± is called for. **35.營×h6+!** A mighty blow as Alekhine's attack will continue even without queens. **35...營×h6 36.仑f5+ 會h7 37.仑×d6 仑d3?! 38.罝f1 d×e4 39.仑×e4 罝3g6 40.仑×d8** and Black resigned in view of 40...罝×d8 41.仑×f6+ 會h8 (41...會h6 42.罝e6+−) 42.罝e7 罝g7 43.罝e4 罝g5 44.仑e8 會h7 45.罝f8+−. **1-0**

### 1938

Again playing in a tournament of ten, Alekhine this time improved his result, winning first prize with the score +7 -1 =2.

### (57) Alekhine – Golombek,Harry
Margate 1938
Nimzo-Indian Defense [E20]

**1.d4 仑f6 2.c4 e6 3.仑c3 罬b4 4.g3 d5 5.罬g2 0-0 6.仑f3 c5 7.c×d5 仑×d5 8.罬d2 仑c6 9.a3** 9.仑×d5 營×d5 10.罬×b4 仑×b4 11.0-0 is played most often. **9...仑×c3 10.b×c3 罬a5 11.0-0 c×d4 12.c×d4 罬×d2 13.營×d2 營e7 14.營b2 罝d8 15.罝fc1 營d6?** 15...罬d7 was better because 16.營×b7? can be met by 16...仑a5=. **16.e3!** This frees the knight for the attack. **16...罝b8 17.仑g5 罬d7 18.營c2 f5?** (D) 18...g6 was forced.

**19.d5!!** Alekhine now immediately seizes the moment in his typical way: **19...仑e7** 19...e×d5 20.罬×d5+ 營×d5 21.罝d1 營e5 22.營a2+ 罬e6 23.仑×e6 罝×d1+ 24.罝×d1 營f6 25.罝d7 仑e7 26.仑g5+ 會h8 27.仑f7+ 會g8 28.仑h6+ 會h8 29.罝d6 營f8 (29...營×d6?? runs into the famous motif 30.營g8+ 仑×g8 31.仑f7#) 30.仑f7+ 會g8 31.仑e5+ 會h8 32.營e6 罝e8 33.罝d7 仑g6 34.仑×g6+ h×g6 35.營×g6 罝e7 36.營d6+− **20.d×e6 罬×e6 21.罝d1 營e5 22.罬×b7 h6?** 22...罬f7 is more tenacious. **23.仑×e6 營×e6 24.營c7 罝×d1+ 25.罝×d1 罝e8 26.罬f3 a6 27.罝d6 營e5 28.營c4+ 會h7 29.罝×a6 罝c8 30.營f7 罝c1+ 31.會g2 1-0**

**Fine, Reuben** (October 11, 1914, New York-March 26, 1993, New York) An American player and author, international grandmaster (1950), and one of the challengers to the world title. He learned to play at eight years old and joined the Marshall Chess Club in New York at age 15. He devoted all his spare time to studying the works of Nimzowitsch and Tarrasch, and these studies were not in vain.

His first appearances in master tournaments, New York State Championship 1931 (2nd), Pasadena 1932, where he drew his game against Alekhine, playing for the national team at three Olympiads (1933, 1935, 1937), proved that America had a highly promising player. Alexander Alekhine published "Nasha Smena" ("Our Reserve") in the Russian newspaper *Posl_edniye Novosti* on the eve of 1934, in which he singled out promising young talents, among them Reuben Fine. He was "so bold as to predict that the 19-year old New Yorker Fine has a quite extraordinary future in chess." And Alekhine was not wrong. The sensational successes achieved by Fine between 1936 and 1938 could be compared with Morphy and Pillsbury's first successes in Europe.

"The Master of Maneuvering" was the admiring appellation of the chess celebrities at Nottingham 1936 about the performance shown there by the 21-year-old New Yorker. The young master impressed them by his solid, strictly positional play and excellent knowledge of theory, going through this super-tournament without any losses and sharing 3rd-5th places, ahead of Alekhine, Lasker and Flohr. That same year, he won the tournaments at Zandvoort and Amsterdam. And, in 1937, he shared 1st-2nd prizes with Keres at Margate, 1½ points ahead of Alekhine, and demonstrated that he could handle sharp tactical positions with the same confidence.

**(58) Fine – Alekhine**
Margate 1937
Dutch Defense [A90]

**1.d4 e6 2.c4 f5 3.g3 ♞f6 4.♗g2 ♗b4+ 5.♗d2 ♗e7 6.♞c3 ♞c6?!** The main line is 6...0-0. **7.d5 ♞e5**

**8.♕b3 0-0 9.♞h3 ♞g6?! 10.d×e6 d×e6 11.♖d1 c6 12.0-0 e5?** This finally goes too far; the light squares in Black's camp are too weak. In order to reduce the pressure, Black needed to play 12...♕b6. **13.c5+ ♔h8 14.♞g5 ♕e8 15.♞e6 ♗×e6 16.♕×e6 (D)**

**16...♗×c5?** 16...♞d7! 17.b4 a5 18.a3 e4 limits the damage. **17.♕×f5 ♖d8 18.♕c2 ♕e6 19.♞a4 ♗e7 20.a3 ♖d4 21.h3 b5?! 22.♞c3 a5 23.♗e3 ♖×d1 24.♖×d1 b4 25.a×b4 a×b4 26.♞a4 ♞d5 27.♗c5 ♕f7 28.e3 ♖c8 29.♕c4 ♕f8 30.♗×e7 ♞g×e7 31.e4 ♞f6 32.♕×b4 ♖d8 33.♖×d8 ♕×d8 34.♞c5 ♕d6 35.♕c3 h6 36.♞d3 ♞d7 37.h4 ♞g6 38.♗h3 ♞gf8 39.b4 h5?! 40.♞c5 ♞f6** 40...♞×c5 41.b×c5 ♕e7 42.♕a5 ♞e6 43.♕a8+ ♞d8 44.♗f5 +– **41.♕c4 ♕e7 42.♞b3 ♕d6 43.♞a5 ♕d2 44.♞×c6 ♕e1+ 45.♗f1 ♞×e4 46.♕e2 ♕×e2 47.♗×e2 g6 48.♞×e5 ♞c3 49.♗d3 ♔g7 50.f4 ♞d5 51.b5 ♔f6 52.♔f2 ♞b6 53.♔e3 ♞a4 54.♔d4 ♞e6+ 55.♔d5 ♞c7+ 56.♔c6 ♞e6 57.b6 ♞d8+ 58.♔d7 ♞e6 59.b7 ♞ac5+ 60.♔c8 1-0**

A year later, in the famous double round-robin AVRO tournament (1938),

*Reuben Fine*

Reuben won more games (including his two games against Alekhine) than any other participant, once again sharing 1st-2nd places with Keres. The chess world recognized him as one of the challengers to the chess crown. However, upon his return from Europe, he played less frequently in tournaments, devoting more time to psychoanalytic problems and studies in chess theory.

In 1948, Fine was invited to play in the world championship match-tournament, but he declined, having made the final choice in favor of science. Subsequently, he repeatedly returned to chess but only as an author and analyst. He devoted his scientific studies to the analysis of the psychology of chess, world championship candidate matches, and the 11th world champion Robert Fischer.

Selected Works:
*Basic Chess Endings.* Philadelphia, 1941.

*The Ideas Behind Chess Openings.* Philadelphia, 1943.
*Chess – The Easy Way.* New York, 1942.
*Chess Marches On!.* Philadelphia, 1945.
*Schaak verovert de wereld!.* Amsterdam, 1946.
*The World's a Chessboard.* Philadelphia, 1948.
*The Middlegame in Chess.* 1953.
*Lessons From my Games.* New York, 1958.
*The Psychology of a Chessplayer.* New York, 1967.
*The Final Candidates Match, Buenos Aires, 1971, Fischer-Petrosian.* Jackson, 1971.
*Bobby Fischer's Conquest of the World's Chess Championship.* 1975.

## Portsmouth Tournament, August 12-15, 1923

Before undertaking his first voyage across the ocean, Alekhine took part in a tournament at the small English town of Portsmouth, where he won first prize (10½ points out of 11), 2½ ahead of the Hungarian master Arpad Vajda, who finished second. Of Alekhine's creative achievements at Portsmouth, two stand out: his games against Vajda and Drewittt. In the former, Alekhine's knights worked like virtuosos. In the latter, the double-bishop sacrifice brings to mind the well-known game Lasker-Bauer (1889).

### (59) Alekhine – Vajda, Arpad
Portsmouth 1923 (D)

**26.♘gh5!** Alekhine's knight will rule the world soon. **26...♕d7 27.♕b8 b5 28.g4 ♔f7?** 28...a4 was better, but

White can continue pressing with 29.♘d3. **29.♘d3 a4** 29...♕b7? 30.♕d8± **30.♘c5 ♕e7 31.♕b6 ♗e8 32.♘f4 g5 33.♘fd3 h5 34.♘b7 h×g4 35.h×g4 ♔g7?! 36.♘dc5?!** (D)

The direct 36.♘d6 is more precise. **36...e5?** Vajda does Alekhine's job and opens lines. He had to sit tight with a move like 36...♗d7. **37.♘d6 ♗g6 38.♘×b5 ♘d7?** Allowing the decisive invasion, but Black is lost in any case. **39.♕c7 ♗e8 40.♘d6 ♔f8 41.♘f5 ♕h7 42.♘e6+ ♔f7 43.♕d8 1-0**

**(60) Alekhine – Drewitt,John**
Portsmouth 1923
Sokolsky Opening [A00]

**1.♘f3 d5 2.b4 e6 3.♗b2 ♘f6 4.a3 c5 5.b×c5 ♗×c5 6.e3 0-0 7.c4**

♘c6 **8.d4 ♗b6 9.♘bd2 ♕e7 10.♗d3 ♖d8 11.0-0 ♗d7 12.♘e5 ♗e8 13.f4 ♖ac8 14.♖c1 ♘d7?!** 14...♗a5, in order to meet 15.♘df3 with 15...♘e4, gives Black's pieces more active options. **15.♘×c6 ♖×c6?** 15...b×c6 is forced. **16.c5 ♘×c5** 16...♗a5 17.♘b3 ♗c7 18.♗b5± **17.d×c5 ♗×c5 18.♘f3 ♗×a3?** This invites the coming disaster, but Black's compensation is hardly sufficient in any case. **19.♖×c6?** The direct 19.♗×h7+ wins by force: 19...♔×h7 20.♖h3+ ♔g8 21.♕h5 f6 22.♕h7+ ♔f8 23.♖g3 g6 24.♕h8+ ♔f7 25.♖h3+−. **19...♗×c6?** (D) Giving Alekhine another chance, which will not be missed. 19...♗×b2 20.♖c2 ♗a4 21.♗×h7+ ♔f8± had to be played.

**20.♗×h7+! ♔×h7 21.♖h3+ ♔g8 22.♗×g7** Alekhine chooses to complete the double bishop sacrifice, and so Black resigned. The alternative, 22.♕h5, wins as well: 22...f6 23.♗×a3 ♕×a3 24.♕h8+ ♔f7 25.♕×d8 ♕c1+ 26.♘f1 ♗b5 27.♖f3+−. Some sample lines to prove that White wins: 22...f6 (22...♔×g7 23.♕g4+ ♔f8 24.♖h8#) 23.♗h6 ♕h7 24.♕h5 ♗f8 25.♕g4+ ♔f7 26.♗×f8 ♕g6 27.♕×g6+ ♔×g6 28.♖h6++−. **1-0**

## New York Tournaments, 1924, 1927
## March 16-April 18, 1924

Ten years after the great St. Petersburg 1914 tournament, the three celebrated chess musketeers of the first half of the 20th century (Emanuel Lasker, José Raúl Capablanca, and Alexander Alekhine) met again at the chessboard. Along with this splendid trio, the event attracted other outstanding masters of the time: Bogoljubow, Tartakower, Réti, Maróczy, Marshall, Janowsky, Edward Lasker, and Yates. Altogether there were eleven participants, the same number as ten years before in St. Petersburg.

The opening ceremony was held March 16 in the Japanese Hall of the Alamac Hotel, decorated with the national flags of the participants' countries. The games of the first round were played on the same day. The first round was successful for Alekhine. In the initial game, in which he was Black, he defeated the "unyielding" Yates, to whom he had previously lost twice (at Hastings and Carlsbad) in the last eighteen months.

## (61) Yates,Frederick – Alekhine
New York 1924
Ruy Lopez [C76]

**1.e4 e5 2.♘f3 ♘c6 3.♗b5 a6 4.♗a4 d6 5.0-0 g6 6.c3 ♗g7 7.d4 ♗d7 8.♗g5 ♘ge7 9.d×e5 d×e5 10.♕d3** 10.♘bd2 and 10.♕c1 are the main lines. **10...h6 11.♗e3 ♗g4 12.♕e2 0-0 13.♘bd2 f5 14.h3 ♗h5 15.♗b3+ ♔h8 16.e×f5?!** The following plan is very risky because many roads to White's king open. **16...g×f5 17.g4 f×g4 18.♘e1 ♘d5** 18...♕c8!? **19.h×g4 ♘×e3 20.f×e3 ♕g5 21.♗e6 ♗×g4 22.♕×g4?**

**22.♗×g4 h5 23.♘e4 ♕g6 24.♖×f8+ ♖×f8 25.♘f2** stabilizes the position and is almost equal. **22...♕×e3+ 23.♔h1 ♕×d2 24.♖g1 ♕g5 25.♕h3?!** Objectivly, 25.♕×g5 h×g5 26.♖×g5 is better, but keeping the queens on the board also has its practical advantages of course. **25...♕f6 26.♗d5 ♘e7?!** 26...♖ad8 is more direct. **27.♗e4 ♘f5?** 27...♕f4 28.♗×b7 ♖ad8 29.♖g4 ♕f1+ 30.♕×f1 ♖×f1+ 31.♔g2 ♖f6 gives Black a solid extra pawn. **28.♘f3?** This allows Alekhine to dislodge the central bishop. 28.♘d3 ♘d6 can be met by 29.♖g6. **28...♘d6! 29.♗d5** Now 29.♖g6? runs into 29...♘×e4 30.♖×f6 ♘f2+ –+. **29...c6?** (D) 29...♕f5 30.♕g2 ♗f6 31.♕h2 ♕f4 and Black should be able to defend.

**30.♖×g7??** Yates miscalculates. He should bring his remaining forces into the attack with 30.♘h4! c×d5 31.♖af1 ♕×f1 32.♖×f1 ♖×f1+ 33.♕×f1 ±. **30...♔×g7 31.♖g1+ ♔h8 32.♘×e5 c×d5 33.♕h5** 33.♖g6 ♕f1+ –+ **33...♘e4 34.♘g6+ ♔h7 35.♕×d5 ♘g3+** and Yates resigned in view of 36.♖×g3 ♕f1+ 37.♔h2 ♖f2+ 38.♖g2 ♖×g2+ 39.♕×g2 ♕×g2+ 40.♔×g2 ♔×g6–+. **0-1**

In the second round, all games except the one between Alekhine and Maróczy

*New York 1924: Sitting (left to right): Yates, Capablanca, Janowsky, Ed. Lasker, Em. Lasker. Standing: Marshall, Tartakower, Maróczy, Alekhine, Réti, and Bogoljubow.*

### New York 1924

|    |            | 1   | 2   | 3   | 4   | 5   | 6   | 7   | 8   | 9   | 10  | 11  | Total |
|----|------------|-----|-----|-----|-----|-----|-----|-----|-----|-----|-----|-----|-------|
| 1  | **Lasker**     | X   | ½0  | 1½  | ½1  | 11  | 11  | 11  | ½1  | ½1  | ½1  | 11  | **16**    |
| 2  | **Capablanca** | ½1  | X   | ½½  | ½½  | 01  | ½1  | 11  | 11  | 1½  | ½1  | ½1  | **14½**   |
| 3  | **Alekhine**   | 0½  | ½½  | X   | ½½  | 10  | 1½  | ½½  | ½½  | 11  | ½½  | 11  | **12**    |
| 4  | **Marshall,**  | ½0  | ½½  | ½½  | X   | ½1  | 0½  | 01  | ½0  | ½1  | 1½  | 11  | **11**    |
| 5  | **Réti**       | 00  | 10  | 01  | ½0  | X   | ½½  | 01  | 11  | 10  | 10  | 11  | **10½**   |
| 6  | **Maroczy**    | 00  | ½0  | 0½  | 1½  | ½½  | X   | 01  | ½½  | 11  | ½1  | 10  | **10**    |
| 7  | **Bogoljubow** | 00  | 00  | ½½  | 10  | 10  | 10  | X   | 01  | 11  | ½1  | 01  | **9½**    |
| 8  | **Tartakower** | ½0  | 00  | ½½  | ½1  | 00  | ½½  | 10  | X   | 10  | ½0  | ½1  | **8**     |
| 9  | **Yates**      | ½0  | 0½  | 00  | ½0  | 01  | 00  | 00  | 01  | X   | 11  | ½1  | **7**     |
| 10 | **Lasker**     | ½0  | ½0  | ½½  | 0½  | 01  | ½0  | ½0  | ½1  | 00  | X   | 0½  | **6½**    |
| 11 | **Janowski**   | 00  | ½0  | 00  | 00  | 00  | 01  | 10  | ½0  | ½0  | 1½  | X   | **5**     |

were drawn. Alekhine, who adopted his namesake defense, again won and thereby became leader, offering an occasion for the journalists to report about his excellent form.

However, in the third round, playing Lasker, he failed. He seemed to be un-able to take the right attitude to fight the man whom he (one can almost say) worshipped, whose games he had carefully studied, and to whom he twice lost ten years before at St. Petersburg.

"In a big tournament, one should not fear losing a game, but rather fear the psychic depression associated with the loss," Alekhine wrote. The next game, with Capablanca, showed the full measure of his resilience. Just before the tournament, the world champion had a bout with the flu and now was getting back into shape with some difficulty. In the game with Alekhine, he was determined to fight it out. However, in the rook-and-pawn ending, Alekhine demonstrated very refined technique, neatly neutralized all the threats of his opponent, and the game ended in a draw.

In the next three rounds, Alekhine scored 2½ points, defeating Janowsky and Réti and drawing against Marshall. Annotating his game with Réti for the local press, he wrote that "[t]his is my best game after eight rounds of the tournament."

**(62) Alekhine – Réti**
New York 1924
King's Indian Defense [E62]

**1.d4 ♘f6 2.c4 g6 3.g3 ♗g7 4.♗g2 0-0 5.♘c3 d6 6.♘f3 ♘c6 7.d5 ♘b8?!** Very provocative. The main line is 7...♘a5. **8.0-0 ♗g4 9.h3 ♗×f3 10.e×f3 e6 11.f4 e×d5 12.c×d5 c5?** This just opens the game for Alekhine's bishops and rooks. 12...♘bd7 is more in the spirit of the position. **13.d×c6 ♘×c6 14.♗e3 ♕d7 15.♕a4 ♖ac8 16.♖ad1 b6 17.b3 ♖fd8 18.♖d3 ♘e7 19.♘b5 d5 20.♘×a7 ♖a8 21.♗×b6 ♕×a4 22.b×a4 ♖d7 23.♘b5 ♖×a4 24.♘c3 ♖a6 25.♖b1 ♖b7 26.♗c5 ♖×b1+ 27.♘×b1 ♘c6 28.♘c3 ♖a5 29.♗b6?! ♖a6?!** 29...♖a3 is called for. **30.♗c5 ♖a5 31.♗e3 ♘b4 32.♖d2 h6?!** 32...♖a3 is again more tenacious. **33.a4 ♘e4?** Leading

to a lost endgame. But good advice is hard to give in any case. **34.♘×e4 d×e4 35.♖d8+ ♔h7 36.♗×e4 ♖×a4 37.f5 ♖a6** (D)

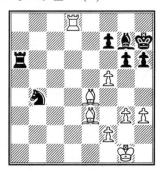

**38.h4!** The next battering ram is brought up. **38...h5 39.g4 ♖a5** 39...♗f6 40.♖c8 h×g4 41.f×g6+ f×g6 42.h5 ♖e6 43.♖c4+− **40.f×g6+ f×g6 41.g×h5 ♖×h5 42.♗g5 ♗c3 43.♖d7+ ♔g8** 43...♗g7 44.♗f6+− **44.♗×g6 1-0**

Black resigned because, after the return of the rook to its original square, White's h-pawn would begin its terrible advance.

Having drawn three more games at the finish of the first leg of the tournament, Alekhine was in second place with 6½ points, a point behind Lasker, but a half-point ahead of Capablanca and Réti. In the second half of the tournament, Alekhine suffered a defeat at the hands of Réti, having made two positional blunders in a row. One of them, on move 19, he called a hallucination, the other, on move 20, suicide. In the next round, having an overwhelming advantage in the game with Maróczy, Alekhine decided to force matters in order to see the sensation of the round, viz., how Capablanca was winning against Lasker. However, haste in chess often backfires. Alekhine's resourceful opponent was able to extricate himself, and the game was drawn. As he had done ten years before, he finished third, after Lasker and Capablanca.

Could he have performed better? Apparently not. And there were several reasons for that. One of them was revealed by Eugene Znosko-Borovsky, who painfully reacted to his friend's results:

> *One should not play on nerves, one should not squander one's fantasy and inventiveness on each game; finally, one should not fritter away one's strength on all possible tours, countless exhibitions, blindfold exhibitions. This is called burning the candle at both ends and with such a behavior, if one even attains colossal strength, it is not for long.*

> *Just before the tournament Alekhine had made a very big tour of America, where he played hundreds of games, many of them blindfold. So, is it really surprising that, after the first half of the tournament, he was physically exhausted, so much so that he drew seven games out of the last ten.*

Another serious reason for his relative failure was his literary chores: he was preparing the tournament book for publishing. Hence his desire to be aware of all the vicissitudes of the struggle in the other participants' games, to witness the crucial moments of the most important games being played. All this could do nothing except take its toll on his own play. Turning to the history of chess, we can notice a curious phenomenon: authors of tournament books, which subsequently became chess best sellers, have never won these tournaments. For example, Siegbert Tarrasch with his book on St. Petersburg 1914 tournament and David Bronstein with his excellent book on Zürich 1953.

**February 9-March 25, 1927**
"Prologue to the Struggle in Buenos Aires." That is how Alekhine labeled this international tournament in New York. The participants of this quadruple round-robin tournament were world champion Capablanca, challenger Alekhine, and such top-class grandmasters as Nimzowitsch, Vidmar, Spielmann, and Marshall. Its format resembled the 1895/96 St. Petersburg tournament. And, although much water had flowed under the bridge in the three decades that passed since then, Lasker still remained one of the strongest players in the world. That is why the chess community was wondering why Lasker had not been invited to participate.

Alekhine's participation was also uncertain mostly because of the organizers' attempt to impose the stipulation that the winner of the tournament, or the second-place finisher should the winner be the world champion, would be recognized as the official world championship challenger. Alekhine, who had gained the support of the Argentinians and Capablanca's consent with such difficulty, could not accept this condition. And he declared outright that he would not participate unless it was removed.

Yet, he eventually agreed to play, thereby showing himself to be a deep strategist of chess diplomacy. First of all, he would be able to see the champion in action one more time and use the information in the preparation for the coming duel. Moreover, he would be able to give the champion a false impression of his form and state of preparation for the match. Should the Cuban succeed in the tournament, he would be overconfident confident as a result of his easy success.

There were also two more immediate reasons for Alekhine to accept the invitation. First, Capablanca had delayed giving the final assent to the repeated queries by Alekhine and the Argentinian chess club, and, in his letters and telegrams, unambiguously hinted that Alekhine should come to New York in order to reach an agreement with him. The other reason was that, as Alekhine himself put it, his "refusal to participate in the tournament could be wrongly understood by the chess world – namely, as a manifestation of fear of Capablanca, which could, as a result, offer him an easy alternative (if he so wished) of replacing me by the first or second place finisher of the tournament, thus ruining the Buenos Aires project."

The start of the tournament was indeed Capablanca's week. In the first cycle of the tournament, he defeated Alekhine, Nimzowitsch, and Marshall and, having scored four points out of five, was confidently leading. Nimzowitsch was a half-point behind, while Alekhine, who had scored only 2½ points, was third. In the second cycle, Alekhine, who lost to Nimzowitsch, fell behind even more, whereas the grandmaster from Copenhagen was demonstrating confident performance and even overtook

the leader. However, he, too, was unable to avoid a dark streak in the competition: in the tenth round he lost to Vidmar, and, in the eleventh, Alekhine had his revenge.

In the second part of the contest, Alekhine played much more confidently, winning three games without losing any. Moreover, he was awarded a second prize for the best game for his game against Marshall.

**(63) Alekhine – Marshall,Frank**
New York 1927
Queen's Gambit Declined [D38]

**1.d4 ♞f6 2.♞f3 e6 3.c4 d5 4.♗g5 h6 5.♗×f6 ♛×f6 6.♞c3 ♗b4 7.♛b3 c5 8.c×d5 c×d4?!** 8...e×d5 is the main line. **9.♛×b4 d×c3 10.d×e6 ♗×e6 11.♛×c3 ♞c6 12.e3?!** 12.♛×f6 g×f6 13.e3 is more principled. **12...♛×c3+ 13.b×c3 ♖c8 14.♗d3 0-0 15.♞d4 ♗d5 16.f3 ♞e5 17.♔d2 ♖c5 18.e4 ♗c4 19.♗×c4 ♞×c4+ 20.♔e2 ♞a3?!** 20...♖fc8 is more precise. **21.♖ac1 ♖fc8 22.♞f5 ♖8c7 23.♖hd1** (D)

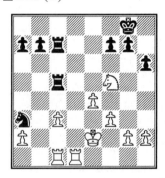

**23...♞b5?** This gives White a dangerous initiative, which is significant, with rooks and knight versus rooks and knight because those pieces do not like passivity at all. Black should keep the

*Participants and Organizers of New York Tournament, 1927.*

*New York 1927*

|  | 1 | 2 | 3 | 4 | 5 | 6 | T |
|---|---|---|---|---|---|---|---|
| **Capablanca** | x x x x | 1 ½ ½ ½ | 1 ½ 1 ½ | ½ ½ 1 ½ | ½ ½ 1 ½ | 1 1 ½ 1 | **14** |
| **Alekhine** | 0 ½ ½ ½ | x x x x | ½ 0 1 ½ | ½ ½ ½ ½ | 1 ½ ½ 1 | ½ 1 ½ 1 | **11½** |
| **Nimzowitsch** | 0 ½ 0 ½ | ½ 1 0 ½ | x x x x | 1 0 0 ½ | 1 1 ½ ½ | 1 ½ ½ 1 | **10½** |
| **Vidmar** | ½ ½ 0 ½ | ½ ½ ½ ½ | 0 1 1 ½ | x x x x | ½ ½ ½ ½ | ½ 0 1 ½ | **10** |
| **Spielmann** | ½ ½ 0 ½ | 0 ½ ½ 0 | 0 0 ½ ½ | ½ ½ ½ ½ | x x x x | ½ ½ 1 ½ | **8** |
| **Marshall** | 0 0 ½ 0 | ½ 0 ½ 0 | 0 ½ ½ 0 | ½ 1 0 ½ | ½ ½ 0 ½ | x x x x | **6** |

*Alekhine, Vidmar, Spielmann, and Nimzowitsch
analyzing a game. New York, 1927.*

131

light-square blockade with 23...♘c4.
**24.c4! ♘a3** 24...♖×c4 25.♖×c4 ♖×c4
26.♖d8+ ♔h7 27.♖d7± **25.♘e3
♔h7 26.♖d5 ♖5c6 27.♔d3 b5
28.c5** (D)

**28...b4?!** 28...♘c4!? offers better
pratical chances after 29.♘×c4 ♖×c5
30.♖×c5 ♖×c5 31.♔d4 ♖c7 32.a4
b×c4 33.♖×c4 ♖d7+ because of the
drawish nature of rook endings in general. But this should be won for White
in view of his activity. **29.♘f5! ♖g6
30.♘d4 ♖×g2 31.c6 ♖×a2
32.♖d7 ♖c8** 32...b3 33.♖×c7 b2
34.♖b1 ♘×b1 35.♖b7 ♘d2 36.c7+–
**33.♖×a7 b3 34.♘×b3 ♘c2
35.♖×a2 ♘b4+ 36.♔d4 ♘×a2
37.♖c4** Alekhine dominates the
knight. **37...♔g6 38.♔c5 ♔f6
39.♖d4 ♘c3 40.♖c4 ♘e2** 40...♘a2
41.♘a5 ♔e7 42.♖c2+– **41.♔b6
♖b8+ 42.♔a7 ♖×b3 43.c7 ♖a3+
44.♔b7 ♖b3+ 45.♔c6** 1-0

Commenting on the 1927 New York
tournament and its relation to his coming world championship match against
Capablanca, Alekhine was optimistic:

*As prologue to the struggle for
world championship, the New
York Tournament 1927 had a two-
fold and very real significance.
Contrary to the opinion of the*
*entire chess world about this
event, its outcome offered an occasion for Lady Luck to give the
Cuban hero an ambiguous smile
in which, with some external encouragement, a cautious warning
could be seen and surely she is
not to blame that this time her
favorite could not guess its meaning. In addition, the tournament
made it possible for his future rival to verify, directly before the
decisive struggle, the observations of the past years with a series of new examples, and thus
derive correct conclusions.*

### Baden-Baden Tournament, April 16-May 13, 1925

The tournament, held at this German
resort gathered twenty-one players,
representing the "flowers of the chess
world," among them Alekhine,
Rubinstein, Bogoljubow, Nimzowitsch,
Spielmann, Grünfeld, Réti, Marshall,
Tartakower, Tarrasch, Sämisch, Torre,
Mieses, and that is apart from
Capablanca and Lasker; these were all
the best.

Alekhine played in this tournament with
ease and with special elegance. Drawing with Carlos Torre in the first round,
he then won nine consecutive games,
winning in that run with Black against
such titans of chess as Tarrasch,
Nimzowitsch, and Réti. A surprising
coincidence was that, like in New York
the previous year, he again met Réti in
round 8, and again it was his best game
in the tournament; this time perhaps his
best ever! (See, Celebrities).

After ten rounds, he had a fantastic 9½
points, 1½ points ahead of Rubinstein,

who was second. The other competitors were Sämisch, Bogoljubow, Tartakower and Marshall. The game with the last was central in the seventeenth round. Among the spectators in the tournament hall watching the encounter between the American and European champions were also their "better halves." "Yesterday's seventeenth round," Saviely Tartakower wrote in his correspondence, "was one of the hardest-contested, for the closeness of the finish made all the participants play for a win. The main attraction was, of course, the game Alekhine-Marshall and, like in Homer, their spouses, who were present, infused in the opponents, who had not yet lost a single game in the tournament, new strength. In this hurricane-like game, after marvelous combinations, Alekhine smashed the transatlantic Frank."

**(64) Alekhine – Marshall,Frank James**
Baden-Baden 1925
Queen's Gambit Declined [D06]

**1.d4 d5 2.c4 ♘f6 3.c×d5 ♘×d5 4.e4 ♘f6 5.♗d3** 5.♘c3 is the main line. **5...e5** This is very risky against Alekhine because it gives him slight initiative. Instead, 5...e6 is played most often. Of course, not 5...♕×d4?? 6.♗b5+. **6.d×e5 ♘g4 7.♘f3 ♘c6 8.♗g5 ♗e7 9.♗×e7 ♕×e7 10.♘c3 ♘c×e5 11.♘×e5 ♕×e5 12.h3 ♘f6 13.♕d2 ♗d7 14.♕e3 ♗c6 15.0-0-0 0-0 16.f4 ♕e6 17.e5 ♖fe8 18.♖he1 ♖ad8 19.f5 ♕e7 20.♕g5** (D)

**20...♘d5?** Running into a devastating attack. The best defense is the surprising retreat 20...♕f8! with the point that

21.e×f6?! (21.♔b1!?) 21...♖×e1 22.♖×e1 ♖×d3 gives counterplay. **21.f6 ♕f8 22.♗c4! ♘×c3 23.♖×d8 ♖×d8 24.f×g7 ♘×a2+** (D) 24...♕e8 25.b×c3 ♗d5 26.♖d1 c6 27.♖d4 ♖d7 28.♗d3+-

**25.♔b1!** 25.♗×a2? allows Black's major pieces to coordinate the defense with 25...♕c5+ 26.♔b1 ♖d7. **25...♕e8 26.e6 ♗e4+ 27.♔a1** Good technique, but 27.♖×e4 ♖d1+ 28.♔c2 ♖c1+ 29.♕×c1 wins as well. Of course, not 27.♔×a2?? ♕a4#. **27...f5** 27...f×e6 28.♗×e6+ ♕×e6 29.♕×d8+ ♔×g7 30.♕d4++- **28.e7+ ♖d5 29.♕f6 ♕f7 30.e8♕+ 1-0**

Alekhine had already secured first prize before the start of the last round. Here are the results at the top of the Baden-Baden 1925 Tournament: 1st – Alekhine with 16/20 (twelve wins and eight draws); 2nd – Rubinstein (14½);

*Baden Baden 1925*

| | | 1 | 2 | 3 | 4 | 5 | 6 | 7 | 8 | 9 | 10 | 11 | 12 | 13 | 14 | 15 | 16 | 17 | 18 | 19 | 20 | 21 | Total |
|---|---|---|---|---|---|---|---|---|---|---|---|---|---|---|---|---|---|---|---|---|---|---|---|
| **1** | **Alekhine** | X | ½ | 1 | ½ | ½ | 1 | 1 | ½ | 1 | ½ | 1 | 1 | ½ | ½ | 1 | 1 | ½ | 1 | 1 | 1 | 1 | **16** |
| **2** | **Rubinstein** | ½ | X | ½ | ½ | 0 | ½ | ½ | ½ | ½ | 1 | ½ | 1 | 1 | 1 | 1 | ½ | 1 | 1 | 1 | 1 | 1 | **14½** |
| **3** | **Sämisch** | 0 | ½ | X | 1 | ½ | 0 | ½ | ½ | 1 | ½ | 1 | 1 | 1 | ½ | 1 | 0 | ½ | 1 | 1 | 1 | 1 | **13½** |
| **4** | **Bogoljubow** | ½ | ½ | 0 | X | 1 | 0 | 0 | 0 | 1 | 1 | 1 | 1 | 1 | ½ | 0 | ½ | 1 | 1 | 1 | 1 | 1 | **13** |
| **5** | **Tartakower** | ½ | 1 | ½ | 0 | X | ½ | ½ | ½ | 1 | ½ | ½ | ½ | ½ | ½ | 1 | ½ | 1 | ½ | 1 | ½ | 1 | **12½** |
| **6** | **Marshall** | 0 | ½ | 1 | 1 | ½ | X | 1 | ½ | ½ | ½ | 0 | ½ | ½ | ½ | ½ | 1 | ½ | 1 | ½ | 1 | 1 | **12½** |
| **7** | **Rabinovich** | 0 | ½ | ½ | 1 | ½ | 0 | X | ½ | 0 | ½ | ½ | ½ | 1 | 1 | ½ | 1 | 1 | 1 | ½ | ½ | 1 | **12** |
| **8** | **Grünfeld** | ½ | ½ | ½ | 1 | ½ | ½ | ½ | X | ½ | 0 | 0 | 1 | ½ | 1 | 0 | 1 | ½ | 0 | 1 | 1 | 1 | **11½** |
| **9** | **Nimzowitsch** | 0 | ½ | 0 | 0 | 0 | ½ | 1 | ½ | X | ½ | 1 | 0 | ½ | 1 | ½ | ½ | 1 | 1 | 1 | ½ | 1 | **11** |
| **10** | **Torre** | ½ | 0 | ½ | 0 | ½ | ½ | ½ | 1 | ½ | X | ½ | 0 | ½ | 0 | 1 | ½ | ½ | ½ | 1 | 1 | 1 | **10½** |
| **11** | **Réti** | 0 | ½ | 0 | 0 | ½ | 1 | ½ | 1 | 0 | ½ | X | ½ | 1 | 1 | ½ | ½ | ½ | 0 | 1 | 0 | 1 | **10** |
| **12** | **Treybal** | 0 | 0 | 0 | 0 | ½ | ½ | ½ | 0 | 1 | 1 | ½ | X | ½ | 1 | 0 | ½ | ½ | 1 | 1 | ½ | 1 | **10** |
| **13** | **Spielmann** | ½ | 0 | 0 | 0 | ½ | ½ | 0 | ½ | ½ | ½ | 0 | ½ | X | 1 | 1 | 0 | 1 | 1 | ½ | 1 | 1 | **10** |
| **14** | **Carls** | ½ | 0 | ½ | ½ | ½ | ½ | 0 | 0 | 0 | 1 | 0 | 0 | 0 | X | 0 | 1 | 1 | ½ | 1 | 1 | 1 | **9** |
| **15** | **Yates** | 0 | 0 | 0 | 1 | 0 | ½ | ½ | 1 | ½ | 0 | ½ | 1 | 0 | 1 | X | 0 | 0 | 0 | 1 | 0 | 1 | **8** |
| **16** | **Tarrasch** | 0 | ½ | 1 | ½ | ½ | 0 | 0 | 0 | ½ | ½ | ½ | ½ | 1 | 0 | 1 | X | 0 | ½ | 0 | 0 | ½ | **7½** |
| **17** | **Rosselli** | ½ | 0 | ½ | 0 | 0 | ½ | 0 | ½ | 0 | ½ | ½ | ½ | 0 | 0 | 1 | 1 | X | 1 | 0 | ½ | ½ | **7½** |
| **18** | **Colle** | 0 | 0 | 0 | 0 | ½ | 0 | 0 | 1 | 0 | ½ | 1 | 0 | 0 | ½ | 1 | ½ | 0 | X | 0 | 1 | 1 | **7** |
| **19** | **Mieses** | 0 | 0 | 0 | 0 | 0 | ½ | ½ | 0 | 0 | 0 | 0 | 0 | ½ | 0 | 0 | 1 | 1 | 1 | X | 1 | 1 | **6½** |
| **20** | **Thomas** | 0 | 0 | 0 | 0 | ½ | 0 | ½ | 0 | ½ | 0 | 1 | ½ | 0 | 0 | 1 | 1 | ½ | 0 | 0 | X | ½ | **6** |
| **21** | **Te Kolste** | 0 | 0 | 0 | 0 | 0 | 0 | 0 | 0 | 0 | 0 | 0 | 0 | 0 | 0 | 0 | ½ | ½ | 0 | 0 | ½ | X | **1½** |

3 – Sämisch (13½); 4th – Bogoljubow (13); 5th-6th – Marshall and Tartakower (12½).

Alekhine won more games than any other participant, and he also was the only one who did not lose a single game. His splendid performance at Baden-Baden inspired Tartakower to another of his famous paradoxes: "Capablanca has the title, Lasker, the results, but only Alekhine has the style of a real world champion."

## Paris Tournaments, 1925, 1933

Between 1925 and 1938, the capital of France hosted five minor international events. Alekhine, then a resident of Paris, participated and won two of them.

## February 11-22, 1925

Although with only five players – Alexander Alekhine, Saviely Tartakower, Eugene Znosko-Borovsky, Karel Opocensky, and Edgard Colle – the double round-robin tournament brought more than a few theoretical novelties. Alekhine tested his novel ideas in two games, one with Colle in the Queen's Gambit Declined: Chigorin Defense and with Opocensky in the Slav Defense. Having scored 6½ points, he finished first, two points ahead of Tartakower in second place. Alekhine "played this time with great facility. Everything seemed simple and natural to [him]; correct plans were born as if by themselves and were executed without any strain. [He] finished first without a single loss."

## (65) Alekhine – Colle
Paris 1925
Chigorin Defense [D07]

**1.d4 d5 2.c4 ♘c6 3.♘f3 ♗g4 4.♕a4 ♗×f3 5.e×f3 e6 6.♘c3 ♗b4?!** The other main option, 6...♘ge7, scores better. **7.a3 ♗×c3+ 8.b×c3 ♘ge7 9.♖b1 ♖b8 10.c×d5 ♕×d5 11.♗d3 0-0 12.0-0 ♕d6 13.♕c2 ♘g6 14.f4 ♘ce7 15.g3 ♖fd8 16.♖d1 b6 17.a4 ♘d5 18.♗d2 c5 19.f5** The alternative,19.d×c5!? ♕×c5 20.c4, might be even stronger. **19...e×f5 20.♗×f5 c×d4 21.c×d4 ♘de7 22.♗b4 ♕f6 23.♗×e7 ♕×e7 24.♖bc1 ♖d5 25.♗e4 ♖d7 26.d5 ♕f6 27.♖e1 ♖bd8 28.♕c6 ♕g5?** (D) Colle should create luft with 28...h6 to solve the problem of his weak back rank.

**29.♗×g6! h×g6?** Allowing Alekhine to show his tactical genius by weaving an unexpected mating net. 29...f×g6! was forced, when White is preferable but to prove a win is another matter of course, e.g., 30.♕e6+ ♖f7! [30...♔f8? 31.♖c4 ♖×d5 32.♖f4+ ♖f5 33.♖e5 +– (Kasparov)] 31.♖c8 ♖×c8 32.♕×c8+ ♖f8 33.♕e6+ ♖f7 (33...♔h8? 34.d6 ♕d2 35.♖e2 ♕d1+ 36.♔g2 h6 37.d7 ♔h7 38.♕e8+–) 34.♕c6 ♖f8 35.♖e8 ♕f6 36.♖×f8+ ♔×f8 37.♕c8+ ♔e7 38.♕c7+ ♔e8 39.♕×a7±; 29...♕×g6? 30.♕×d7 +–. **30.♕×d7!! ♖×d7 31.♖e8+ ♔h7 32.♖cc8 ♖d8 33.♖e×d8 1-0**

**October, 1933**

This time, the number of participants doubled and again, with eight points out of ten, Alekhine, who had been world champion for the past six years and who viewed this small competition as a training session before his world championship match with Bogoljubow, finished first. Tartakower was two points behind in second. The young Hungarian masters Lilienthal and Barcza were both ½ point behind Tartakower, sharing 3rd-4th places.

**Dresden Tournaments, 1926, 1936**
**February 4-14, 1926**

In a nine-round event, Alekhine, although he achieved a fine result of seven points, finished second, one and a half points behind Nimzowitsch. "I put forth in Dresden a lot of valuable (ideas)," Alekhine later wrote, "but Nimzowitsch had even more, maybe because he had shown more will to do so. His magnificent victory deserves universal recognition."

**(66) Alekhine – Tartakower,Saviely**
Dresden 1926
Czech Indian [A44]

**1.d4 c5 2.d5 d6 3.e4 e5 4.♘c3 ♗e7 5.♗d3 ♗g5 6.♘f3 ♗xc1 7.♕xc1 ♘h6 8.h3 f5?** Black should develop his pieces first. **9.♕g5 0-0 10.♕xd8 ♖xd8 11.♘g5 g6?** Again, a developing move like 11...♘a6 is called for. **12.f4 exf4?!** This wastes valuable time and opens roads for Alekhine's attack, but good advice is already hard to give. **13.0-0 ♘a6 14.♖xf4 ♘b4 15.♖h4 ♘xd3** (D)

*Alexander Alekhine, 1933.*

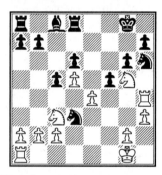

**16.♖xh6!?** Alekhine chooses a direct attack with as many pieces as possible. The more technical solution 16.cxd3 ♘f7 17.♘xf7 ♔xf7 18.♖xh7+ should win as well. **16...♘xb2 17.♖xh7 ♘c4 18.exf5 ♗xf5 19.♖xb7 ♖e8** 19...♖db8 20.♖e7 ♖e8 21.♖ae1 ♖xe7 22.♖xe7 ♗xc2 23.♘e2±; 19...♖d7 20.♖xd7 ♗xd7 21.g4± **20.♘h7 ♖e3 21.♘f6+ ♔f8 22.♘h7+ ♔g8 23.♘b5** (D)

**23...g5?** 23...a6! was relatively best, but White's attack continues after 24.♘a7 ♗xc2 25.♘f6+ ♔f8 26.♘c6;

*Dresden 1926*

| | | 1 | 2 | 3 | 4 | 5 | 6 | 7 | 8 | 9 | 10 | Total |
|---|---|---|---|---|---|---|---|---|---|---|---|---|
| 1 | Nimzowitsch | X | ½ | 1 | 1 | 1 | 1 | 1 | 1 | 1 | 1 | 8½ |
| 2 | Alekhine | ½ | X | 1 | 1 | ½ | ½ | ½ | 1 | 1 | 1 | 7 |
| 3 | Rubinstein | 0 | 0 | X | ½ | 1 | 1 | 1 | 1 | 1 | 1 | 6½ |
| 4 | Tartakower | 0 | 0 | ½ | X | ½ | 1 | ½ | ½ | 1 | 1 | 5 |
| 5 | Von Holzhausen | 0 | ½ | 0 | ½ | X | 0 | 1 | 1 | 0 | 1 | 4 |
| 6 | Johner | 0 | ½ | 0 | 0 | 1 | X | 0 | 1 | 0 | 1 | 3½ |
| 7 | Yates | 0 | ½ | 0 | ½ | 0 | 1 | X | 0 | 1 | 0 | 3 |
| 8 | Sämisch | 0 | 0 | 0 | ½ | 0 | 0 | 1 | X | ½ | 1 | 3 |
| 9 | Blümich | 0 | 0 | 0 | 0 | 1 | 1 | 0 | ½ | X | 0 | 2½ |
| 10 | Steiner | 0 | 0 | 0 | 0 | 0 | 0 | 1 | 0 | 1 | X | 2 |

23...♗xc2? 24.♘f6+ ♚f8 25.♖c1 ♗d3 26.♘d7+ ♚g8 27.♖xc4 ♗xc4 28.♘xd6+– **24.♘f6+ ♚h8 25.♖f1!** The sting of the scorpion. Black can not avoid losing material. **25...♗xc2 26.♖c1 ♘a5** 26...♗d3 27.♖xc4 ♖f8 28.♘xd6 ♖xf6 (28...♗xc4?? 29.♖h7#) 29.♖xc5+– **27.♖c7 ♗g6 28.♘xd6 ♖f8 29.♘g4 ♖e2 30.♖xa7 ♖xa2 31.♖xc5 ♘b3 32.♖xa2 ♘xc5 33.♘e5 ♚g7 34.♖a7+ ♚h6 35.♖c7 ♘d3 36.♘xd3 ♗xd3 37.♘f7+ ♚h5 38.d6 ♗g6 39.d7 ♗xf7 40.♖c8 ♗e6 41.♖xf8 ♗xd7 42.♖f7 ♗a4 43.♚f2 ♚g6 44.♖a7 ♗c2 45.♖a6+ ♚g7 46.♚e3 ♚f7 47.♚d4 ♚g7 48.♚e5 ♗d3 49.♖a3 ♗c2 50.♖g3 ♚g6 51.h4 ♚h5 52.♖xg5+ ♚xh4 53.♚f4 ♗d1 54.g3+ ♚h3 55.g4 1-0**

**June 1936**
Ten years later, Alekhine again played at Dresden in a tournament with ten participants. He placed first with 6½ points, a half-point ahead of Engels, a full point ahead of Maróczy and Stahlberg, and one and a half points ahead of Bogoljubow.

**Euwe, Machgielis (Max)** (May 20, 1901, Vatergrafsmer-November 26, 1981, Amsterdam)
Dutch Grandmaster, fifth world chess champion. Euwe was only 11 years old when he began to play in club tournaments and also compose chess problems and studies. This fascination remained in the years of his studies at the mathematics department of the University of Amsterdam. Upon graduation, Euwe became a teacher of mathematics at a high school for girls, and he received his doctorate in mathematics. His first successes were achieved in 1921 when he became the Dutch champion and also finished second in the international tournament at Vienna. After that, he mostly played during his vacations. He became particularly successful in the late 1920s and early 1930s. Thus, in 1928, he took second prize at The Hague in a tournament of

sixteen players (+10 -1 =4) and then shared 3rd-4th places with Rubinstein in the strong tournament at Kissingen. In the early 1930s, he successfully played at Hastings (1930/31), where he finished ahead of Capablanca, and at Berne (1932), where he shared 2nd-3rd places. At that time, Euwe had already been deemed one of the world's best players. He proved himself as an especially tenacious match player. He drew short matches (usually of ten games) against Maróczy (1921) and Flohr (1932), defeated Colle (1924) and Spielmann (1932), but marginally lost to Alekhine (1926/27, +2 -3 =5). The match's course was rather interesting. After Euwe's win of the eighth game, the score was even.

### (67) Euwe – Alekhine
Amsterdam m(8) 1926
Réti Opening [A09]

**1.♘f3 d5 2.c4 d4 3.b4 g6?!** 3...f6 scores better. **4.e3 a5 5.b5 c5 6.e×d4 ♗g7 7.d3 c×d4** 7...♗×d4? 8.♘×d4 ♕×d4 9.♕c2!± (Euwe). **8.g3 ♘d7 9.♘bd2 ♘c5?!** 9...♘gf6 is more prudent because the knight can help the blockading forces more quickly, but White has a dangerous strategical initiative in any case. **10.♘b3 ♕b6 11.♘×c5 ♕×c5 12.♗g2 ♘h6 13.0-0 0-0 14.a4 ♖e8 15.♖e1 ♗f5?! 16.♗a3 ♕c7 17.c5 ♖ad8** 17...♗e6? runs into 18.♖×e6 f×e6 19.♘g5+–. **18.♘g5** 18.♘d2!? ♗×d3 19.♕f3 ♗c2 20.♕×b7 ♕×b7 21.♗×b7 d3 22.c6± **18...♗f6 19.♘e4 ♗g7 20.♕d2 ♘g4 21.b6 ♕c8** (D)

**22.c6** 22.♕×a5 ♘e5 23.c6 might objectivly be even stronger but is much more complicated. **22...b×c6?** The

queens help White because Black's queen is not a good blockader. Exchanging queens with 22...♕×c6 23.♘d6 (23.♕×a5 ♖a8 24.♕b5 ♕×b5 25.a×b5 ♘e5) 23...♕c3 24.♕×c3 d×c3 25.♘×e8 ♖×e8 26.♗c5 ♘e5 offers more resistance. **23.♕×a5 ♘e5 24.♕d2** 24.♘c5!? **24...♕a6 25.a5 ♘×d3 26.♘c5** 26.♗f1?? is met by 26...♘×e1 27.♗×a6? ♘f3+–+ (Euwe). **26...♘×c5 27.♗×c5** (D)

**27...♕b5?** Alekhine should keep his important central pawn with 27...e5 28.♗×c6 ♖e6 29.♗g2 h5±. **28.♗×e7 ♖c8 29.♗f1 ♕b3** 29...d3 30.♖ab1+– (Euwe) **30.♖a3 ♕d5 31.b7 ♖b8 32.a6 ♗c8 33.b×c8♕ ♖b×c8 34.♗g2 ♕d7 35.♗c5 ♖×e1+ 36.♕×e1 h5 37.a7 ♖a8 38.♕e4 d3 39.♖×d3 ♕b7 40.♕×c6 ♕b1+ 41.♗f1 ♖×a7 42.♗×a7 1-0**

*Max Euwe*

guished by universality. Along with profound strategic plans in the spirit of the classical principles of positional play, he felt at home in sharp tactical positions. But, as he himself admitted, he especially liked to play "with the wind blowing in his sails," that is, in sharp situations when at least a small advantage was on his side.

Euwe also proved himself a remarkable chess researcher and author, turning out a number of books devoted to the basic principles, as well as the strategy and tactics of the game. In his *Course of Chess Lectures* (1929) that had many editions and was translated into many languages, he showed himself a staunch supporter of the positional teachings of Wilhelm Steinitz.

After the ninth game was drawn, the score remained even with just one game remaining. And only by winning that last game was Alekhine able to end the match in his favor. Euwe also marginally lost his matches with the then challenger Bogoljubow (1928, +2 -3 =5 and 1928/29, +1 -2 = 7) and the third world champion Capablanca (1931, +0 -2 =8).

All these successes provided the basis for the leading chess clubs of the Netherlands to combine their efforts in order to organize a world championship match between Alekhine and their compatriot. So, in 1934, an organizing committee was established, a challenge sent to Alekhine, and the start for a marathon contest of thirty games set for the autumn of the following year.

Euwe was almost ten years younger than his famous rival. His style was distin-

During the preparation for the match, Euwe paid great attention to opening theory. "I had the inclination," he later wrote, "to study openings. I understood the logic and interrelation of various lines, and this served as an excellent foundation for building a broad opening repertoire." Physical training (swimming, boxing, tennis, and gymnastics) and competitive play also played an important role in his match preparation. At Zürich, 1934, he shared 2nd-3rd prizes with Flohr, scoring 12 points in 15 games. Only Alekhine, whom he defeated in their individual encounter, finished ahead of him. After his unsuccessful performance at Leningrad, where he finished in the middle of the final standings, Euwe won a splendid victory at Hastings (1934/35), equal with Flohr and Thomas and ahead of Capablanca and Botvinnik.

From October to December 1935, the world championship match between Alekhine and Euwe was held in different Dutch cities (See Alekhine-Euwe Match 1935). It was a hard fought contest. Alekhine won the first game, and, after ten games, the score was 6-4 in his favor. However, Euwe soon managed to even the score at 7-7. Then Alekhine again took the lead, surging two points ahead. The turning point of the match came in the twentieth game.

**(68) Euwe – Alekhine**
World Championship (20) Amsterdam 1935
Slav Defense [D17]

**1.d4 d5 2.c4 c6 3.♘f3 ♘f6 4.♘c3 d×c4 5.a4 ♗f5 6.♘e5 ♘bd7 7.♘×c4 ♕c7 8.g3 e5 9.d×e5 ♘×e5 10.♗f4 ♘fd7 11.♗g2 f6 12.0-0 ♖d8 13.♕c1 ♕b8?** This just wastes valuable time. 13...♗e6 is the main line. **14.♘e4 ♗e7 15.♕c3 0-0 16.♖ad1 ♗e6 17.♘×e5!** Even better than 17.♖×d7 ♖×d7 18.♘×e5 f×e5 19.♗×e5 ♗b4 20.♗×b8 ♗×c3 21.♘c5 ♗×b2 22.♗f4 ♖×f4 23.g×f4 ♖e7 24.♖b1, when White is only slightly better. **17...♘×e5 (D)**

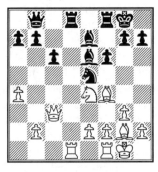

**18.♘g5! f×g5?!** 18...♗f7?! 19.♘×f7 ♖×f7 20.♖×d8+ ♗×d8 21.♖d1 ♗c7

22.♕b3±; 18...♕c8 19.♗×e5 f×e5 20.♕×e5 ♗×g5 21.♕×g5 ♗c4 22.♗f3 ♖de8 is relatively best and also fits Alekhine's active style. **19.♗×e5 ♗f6 20.♗×b8 ♗×c3 21.♗d6 ♖f7 22.b×c3 ♖fd7 23.♖b1!** The point of Euwe's combination. **23...♖×d6 24.♖×b7 ♖8d7 (D)**

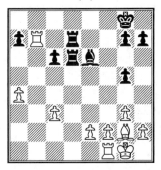

**25.♖×d7?!** Exchanging the active rook reduces the pressure considerably. 25.♖b8+ ♔f7 26.f4 g×f4 27.♖×f4+ ♔e7 28.♔f2±. **25...♗×d7 (D)**

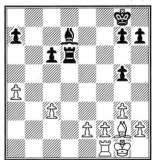

**26.♗e4?** This inaccuracy reduces White's advantage. 26.♖b1 and 26.f4 are much more critical tries to activate the rook first. **26...c5?!** 26...♖d2! with the idea 27.♗d3?! ♗h3 28.♖b1 g4! was more active. **27.c4** 27.♗c2 ♖d2 28.♗b3+ ♔f8 29.♖d1 ♖×d1+ 30.♗×d1 a5! is probably also only drawn as the a4-pawn is now fixed on a light square. **27...♗×a4?** This greedy capture either leads to total passivity or activates White's rook. Instead,

140

Black's rook should be sent into White's camp with 27...♖d2. **28.♗d5+ ♔f8 29.♖a1 ♖a6 (D)**

29...♗c6? 30.♖a6+− **30.♖a2!!** Very subtle prophylaxis. **30...♔e7?!** The unpinning 30...♗b5? now runs into 31.c×b5+−. But, 30...g4 is better because mobilizing White's kingside majority is now more difficult. **31.f4 g×f4 32.g×f4 ♔f6 33.e4 g5 34.f5 h5 35.h4!?** Euwe opens a kingside road for his king. **35...g×h4 36.♔h2 ♔g5 37.♔h3 ♖a5** 37...♖b6 38.♖×a4 ♖b3+ 39.♔g2 ♖b2+ 40.♔f3 ♖b3+ 41.♔e2 ♖b2+ 42.♔d3 h3 43.♖×a7 h2 44.♖a1+− **38.♗b7!** The greedy 38.♗c6? ♗×c6 39.♖×a5 ♗×e4 40.♖×c5 ♗×f5+ only leads to a draw in view of the reduced winning potential. **38...♔f6 39.♗d5 ♔g5 40.♗b7 ♔f6 41.♗c8** The sealed move, but Alekhine had seen enough and resigned. **1-0**

According to Alekhine, this game was the best in the match. Reeling, the champion also lost the next game, in which he played White. After the 26th game, in which, according to Garry Kasparov, who subjected it to a detailed analysis, "Euwe played courageously, creatively and ingeniously," the score became 14-12 in favor of the challenger. Finally, a draw in the 30th game ended the competition with the score

15½-14½, and Euwe became the fifth world champion in the history of chess. In this contest, he showed the best qualities of a strong-willed fighter, strategist, and tactician, as well as a talented theorist (in particular, he showed himself an expert in the Slav Defense and the Open Variation of the Ruy Lopez).

The entire country honored the winner as a national hero. "Holland went mad with joy," Euwe wrote in his reminiscences of the two matches with Alekhine. "Everyone greeted me in the streets, and, for several days, I was in a state of intoxication with my victory. A week later, the usual calm was restored, and I returned to my duties at school."

And how could it be otherwise? The new champion had not received a single penny of the prize fund; it was paid out to Alekhine alone. In his memoirs, Euwe also challenged the wrong belief that Alekhine's defeat was the result of his alcohol abuse. "In fact, he had only turned to alcohol when the match had reached a critical point – apparently before the 18th and certainly before the 21st and 30th games…The true criterion of the significance of a match is the quality of its games. If the games played in the match of 1935 can compare with the best creations in the history of chess, this will suffice." However, if one of the reasons for Euwe's victory was the excellent preparation for the match and, at the same time the underestimation of his potential by Alekhine, who said before the match "I do not believe in Euwe as a future world champion," before the return match the situation was exactly opposite.

As is known, Euwe had confirmed the reputation of a worthy champion in the tournaments at Zandvoort, Nottingham (1936), and Bad Nauheim (1937), and the score of his personal encounters with Alekhine became 3-1 in favor of Euwe. Therefore, Euwe's optimistic mood before the return match was understandable. "Honestly speaking, at the time, I had no doubts about my victory over Alekhine." As a result, his theoretical preparation turned out to be insufficient. For example, Alekhine completely surprised Euwe by switching from 1.e2-e4 to 1.d2-d4 openings. And of course, to play the return match in his native country proved an unbearable psychological burden for Euwe. Salo Flohr, in his article devoted to the results of the match, drew attention to the psychological stress Euwe faced. Since "[c]hess is not soccer, nor is it boxing where the cheers of the spectator invigorate the sportsmen. Chessplayers need silence and the possibility of concentrating. Making his way to the chess table before a game, Euwe had to answer the greetings from the packed seats of his supporters. This, of course, is a trifle but it distracts a chessplayer from his thoughts about the game and abates his fighting spirit."

The return match started in October 1937 in Holland (See, World Championship Matches). Alekhine played in it as in his best years and proved to be well-prepared, both physically and theoretically. Already by the 25th game he had scored the 15½ points required for winning the match and thus regained the world champion title. However, according to the match regulations the match had to continue until all 30 games had been played. In the remaining five games, Euwe scored 3 points and the match summarily ended with the score 17½-12½ in favor of Alekhine. Yet, this contest was hard-fought, too. Vladimir Kramnik justifiably believes that "[i]n the return match, as in the first one, the struggle was equal" and "the myth that the victory in the return match was easily gained by Alekhine should be dispelled."

The same opinion was expressed by Alekhine himself in an article published after the return match in the *Manchester Guardian*. Alekhine cautioned that "[t]he six-point difference gives a somewhat exaggerated notion of the difference in the quality of our play. This difference was mainly due to psychological reasons in the last games of the match." However, in the first twenty games "Euwe did not play weaker, but even somewhat better than in the match of 1935."

After the match, Euwe continued to work persistently on chess theory and appeared in tournaments more often. In 1938, he again won the Dutch Championship and shared 4th-6th places in the AVRO Tournament (+4 -4 =6). Subsequently, he finished first in small international tournaments at Bournemouth and Amsterdam (1939) and at Budapest (1940). In the postwar years, Euwe was again among the world's top players. In 1946, he performed brilliantly in the tournaments at London (first prize, +9 -1 =1), Groningen (second behind Botvinnik, +11 -2 =6), and Zaandam (first place, +9 -1 =1). Somewhat more unexpected was the decline of his playing strength in the 1948 world championship match/tournament at The Hague-Moscow, in which he finished in last (fifth) place.

During the 1950s, Euwe repeatedly played in international tournaments, sometimes even coming first or second. He also led the Dutch team at the world chess Olympiads at Dubrovnik (1950), Amsterdam (1954), and Munich (1958). He was one of the participants of the famous candidates tournament at Zürich in 1953. Euwe himself believed that his game against Miguel Najdorf in the 9th round was the best in his career.

**(69) Euwe – Najdorf,Miguel**
Zürich 1953
King's Indian Defense [E61]

**1.d4 ♘f6 2.c4 g6 3.g3 ♗g7 4.♗g2 0-0 5.♘c3 c5 6.d5 e5** 6...d6 is more normal. **7.♗g5 h6 8.♗×f6 ♕×f6 9.d6!?** Euwe goes all in. The pawn may become weak later. Therefore, he has to start an attack to compensate for it and to use his space advantage. **9...♘c6 10.e3 b6 11.♗d5 ♔h8 12.♘e4 ♕d8 13.h4 f5 14.♘g5 ♗b7 15.g4!** Euwe plays aggressively. The greedy 15.♘f7+? runs into 15...♖×f7 16.♗×f7 ♘b4 with strong counterplay. **15...e4 16.♘e2 ♗×b2 17.♘f4 ♕f6** 17...♗×a1? is countered by 18.♘×g6+ (18.♕×a1+? is parried by 18...♕f6) 18...♔g7 19.g×f5! ♗c3+ 20.♔f1 ♖×f5 21.♘×e4 ♖×d5 22.♕×d5 ♔×g6 23.♖g1+ ♔h7 24.♕d3+- (Kasparov). **18.g×f5! ♗×a1?** Too greedy. Black must bring in more defenders with 18...g×f5! 19.♕h5 ♘e5!= (19...♗×a1? as Kasparov has shown, is refuted by a direct attack: 20.♘g6+ ♔g7 21.♖g1 ♕c3+ 22.♔f1 ♖f6 23.♘f4 ♕c1+ 24.♔g2 ♕b2 25.♘f7

(25.♘×e4 wins as well.) 25...♘e5 26.♘×e5 ♗×d5 (26...♕×e5 27.♕f1+ ♔h7 28.♖g6 ♕×f4 29.♖×f6! ♗×d5 30.♕g6+ ♔h8 31.e×f4+-) 27.♔h1+ ♔h8 (27...♔h7 28.♖g6! ♖×g6 29.♕×g6+ ♔h8 30.♕×h6+ ♔g8 31.♕g6+ ♔h8 32.♕f6+ ♔g8 33.♘×d5 ♕×e5 34.♘e7++-) 28.♘eg6+ ♔h7 29.♘×d5 ♖g8 (29...♕×f2 30.♘×f6+ ♗×f6 31.♘f8+!+-) 30.♘ge7!! ♖×g1+ 31.♔×g1 "and the black pieces have to watch helplessly while their king perishes under the fierce attack of the enemy cavalry, lead by a dauntless amazon" (Kasparov)! **19.♘×g6+ ♔g7 20.♘×e4 ♗c3+** 20...♕b2? 21.♖g1+- **21.♔f1 ♕×f5 22.♘f4** (D)

**22...♔h8!!** Najdorf finds the last chance to resist. The bishop cannot be saved with 22...♗e5? because of 23.♘g3 ♕h7 24.♕g4+ ♔h8 25.♘g6+-. **23.♘×c3 ♖ae8?!** Najdorf should try to exchange attacking potential with 23...♘a5! 24.♗×b7 (24.♖g1? can be met by 24...♖g8! 25.♗×g8 ♖×g8 26.♖×g8+ ♔×g8 27.♕e2 ♗a6 28.♘cd5 ♔h7 with counterplay) 24...♘×b7 25.♘cd5 ♖ae8 26.♖g1 ♔h7, but White can reach a favorable endgame with 27.♕a1 ♕e5 28.♕×e5 ♖×e5 29.♘g6 ♖ef5 30.♘×f8+ ♖×f8 31.h5 ♘×d6 32.♖g6 ♘c4 33.♔e2 because the initiative counts for much more in endings with rook and knight versus rook and knight. **24.♘ce2! ♖g8** 24...♗a6 25.♖g1 ♘e5 26.♕a1 ♕f6 27.♕c3 ♔h7 28.h5± **25.h5!?** Euwe continues to attack. He could also transition into a favorable endgame with 25.♕a1+ ♕e5 (25...♖g7? 26.♖g1 ♕e5 27.♕b1 ♖×g1+ 28.♔×g1 ♖g8+ 29.♘g3 ♕×d6 30.♕e4+–) 26.♕×e5+ ♖×e5 27.♗×g8 ♔×g8 28.♖g1+ ♔f7 29.♘g3±. **25...♖g5 26.♘g3?** This allows Black to simplify the position. After 26.♖h4!, Black has difficulties finding a good move, e.g., 26...♗a8 27.♘g6+ ♔g7 28.e4 ♕f3 29.e5 ♕f5 30.f4±. **26...♖×g3!** 26...♕f6? 27.♘g6+ ♔g7 28.♖h4± **27.f×g3 (D)**

**27...♖×e3?** This greedy capture opens the major invasion route for White's heavy pieces. The last chance to offer resistance was 27...♘a5! in order to reduce the pressure through exchanges, e.g., 28.e4 ♖×e4 29.♗×e4 ♗×e4 30.♖h4 ♘×c4 31.♔g1 ♘e5 32.♘g6+ ♘×g6 33.h×g6 ♕e5. **28.♔f2! ♖e8 29.♖e1 ♖×e1 30.♕×e1 ♔g7** 30...♘e5 31.♕×e5+ ♕×e5 32.♘g6++– **31.♕e8** The decisive penetration. **31...♕c2+ 32.♔g1 ♕d1+ 33.♔h2 ♕c2+ 34.♘g2 ♕f5 35.♕g8+ ♔f6 36.♕h8+ ♔g5 37.♕g7+ 1-0** "and the king hunt is complete – Black resigned. A very im-

pressive victory based on pure intuitive belief in White's unlimited attacking resources. I bet that even Tal wouldn't have refused to be the author of this masterpiece" (Kasparov)!

"Fortunately," Euwe wrote, "time does not weaken either the understanding of the game or interest in chess theory, but rather sharpens them." These words were completely true of Euwe himself. At that time and subsequently, he remained one of the outstanding chess theoreticians. His analyses were published in many volumes by the Hamburg publishers "Chess Archive." Concurrently, Euwe made a very large contribution to the popularization of chess throughout the world while serving as FIDE President from 1970 to 1978.

All along Euwe never abandoned his activity as a mathematician, being a professor of mathematics at the University of The Hague and director of The Hague Computing Center. He was actively involved in the development of computer chess programs, and he believed that even if people would produce "a mechanical miracle that would beat man, all the same such a machine would not be able to harm chess. Chess has lived, and will live for millennia," he wrote in 1969, "giving people joy and benefiting the human society."

His works:
*Chess Master vs. Chess Amateur.*
*The Logical Approach to Chess.* (with M. Blaine, J. F. S. Rumble).
*The Middlegame.* 2 vol. (with H. Kramer).
*Judgement and Planning in Chess.*
*Meet the Masters.*

References:

*The Tournament of Masters with the Participation of M.Euwe and H.Kmoch*, Moscow and Leningrad, 1935 (in Russian).

*World Championship Return Match Alekhine-Euwe*, Moscow and Leningrad, 1939 (in Russian).

*Max Euwe.* (World's Outstanding Players series), Moscow, 1979 (translated from Dutch into Russian).

V.I., Linder and Linder I.M. "Max Euwe." *The Kings of the Chess World.* Moscow, 2001.

—. *Max Euwe: Life and Career.* Moscow, 2006.

Kasparov, G. "Max the Fifth." *My Great Predecessors.* Vol. 2. Everyman Chess: London, 2003.

## Euwe-Alekhine Match, December 22, 1926-January 8, 1927

Well aware that the match struggle differs from the tournament one, Alekhine decided to play – by way of preparation for his world championship match with Capablanca – a ten-game match with Max Euwe. The arrangement had been made the previous year. The match was hard fought, and its winner was only determined in the concluding, tenth game, which Alekhine won in a sharp dramatic battle. The total score was thus 5½-4½ in Alekhine's favor.

Worn out by his four-month tour, Alekhine was unable to show his best qualities; he even had oversights, which was rather unusual for him. The time control adopted for the match was also unusual: two and a half hours for 40 moves (subsequently, this rate of play became standard and was used for all

world championship matches). Also, it was during this match that Alekhine received that notorious telegram from New York informing him of the additional requirement to be met to participate in the next world championship match: the player who comes first (or second if Capablanca was first) in the 1927 New York tournament would be regarded as the challenger. This cast doubt upon the agreement between Alekhine and Capablanca. "To settle this matter I had to interrupt my games with Euwe and go to Paris, which, of course, unfavorably affected my performance." However, everything ended well: the New York organizers abandoned this condition. While in Amsterdam, Alekhine victoriously finished his match.

Here is one of the most consistently and logically played games of the match.

### (70) Euwe – Alekhine
Amsterdam m(2) 1926
Nimzo-Indian Defense [E21]

**1.d4 ♞f6 2.c4 e6 3.♞c3 ♝b4 4.♞f3 b6 5.g3 ♝b7 6.♝g2 0-0 7.0-0 ♝×c3 8.b×c3 d6 9.d5?!** This advance is probably too early because White is not well-mobilized. 9.a4 is played most often. **9...e×d5 10.♞h4 ♞e4?!** 10...♞bd7 11.c×d5 ♜e8 is more natural. **11.c×d5 ♜e8 12.♝b2 b5?!** Too optimistic and weakening. Finishing development with 12...♞d7 is better. **13.a4** 13.♛c2!? ♝×d5 14.♞f5 g6 15.♞h6+ ♚f8 16.c4 is very interesting as well. **13...♛g5?** 13...b×a4 14.♜×a4 ♞c5 15.♜a1 ♞bd7 is the lesser evil. **14.a×b5 ♛×d5** (D)

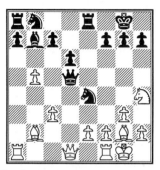

**15.♕a4?** Black's queen is active – and annoying – now. After 15.♕xd5 ♗xd5 16.♘f5, White has a very strong initiative, e.g., 16...♘f6 (16...♗b7 17.♖a3 a6 18.c4 g6 19.♘h6+ ♔f8 20.♖fa1±; 16...♘d7 17.c4 ♗xc4 18.♖fc1 ♘b6 19.♘xg7±) 17.♗xd5 ♘xd5 18.c4 ♘b6 19.♗xg7±. **15...♘d7 16.c4 ♕d2 17.♕a2 a6** (D)

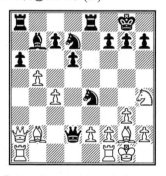

**18.♗c1?** Too passive. Euwe misses 18.b6!! ♘xb6 19.♘f5 with strong counterplay on the dark squares. **18...♕xa2 19.♖xa2 axb5 20.♖b2 ♖ab8** (D)

**21.cxb5?** This gives Alekhine a strong initiative on the light squares. 21.♖xb5 is more active, but Black is still preferable after 21...♘dc5 (21...♗a6?! is answered by 22.♖xb8 ♘xb8 23.♘f5) 22.♖b2 ♘c3 23.e3 ♘3a4 24.♖c2 ♘d3 25.♗d2 ♗xg2 26.♔xg2 ♖b2 27.♖xb2 ♘axb2 28.♗c3 ♘xc4 29.♖a1. **21...♘c3 22.♗c6 ♖xe2 23.♖b3 ♗xc6 24.♖xc3 ♗xb5 25.♖xc7 ♘e5 26.♘f5?** Losing more or less by force. After 26.f4 ♘g4 27.h3 ♘f6 28.♖f2 ♖e1+ 29.♔h2 ♘d5 30.♘g2, White can still fight on. **26...♘f3+ 27.♔g2 ♘e1+ 28.♔h3** (D)

28.♔g1 ♗d3 29.♘e7+ ♔h8 30.h4 ♖e6–+ **28...♖e5** The surprising blow 28...♖c2!? is even stronger. **29.♖h1?!** 29.♖xe1 ♖xe1 30.♘xd6 makes Black's technical task harder but, in the long run, loses as well. **29...♘d3! 30.♘e7+ ♔f8 31.♗a3 ♘xf2+ 32.♔g2 ♘xh1?!** After 32...♖e2, Black's attack comes first. **33.♗xd6?** 33.♘g6+ ♔g8 34.♘xe5 dxe5 35.♔xh1 offers more resistance. **33...♖e6** 33...♖e2+ 34.♔xh1 ♖e8 is also very strong because 35.♘f5? runs into 35...♗c6+ 36.♖xc6 ♖b1+ 37.♖c1 ♖xc1#. **34.♗c5 ♖e8 35.♘f5+ ♔g8 36.♘e7+** 36.♘d6 ♗d3 37.♘xe8 ♗e4+–+ **36...♔h8 37.♔xh1 ♗d3 38.♔g2 h6 39.♔f3 ♔h7 40.h4 h5 0-1**

**Nimzowitsch, Aron** (November 7, 1886, Riga-March 16, 1935, Copenhagen)

A potential world title challenger in the 1920s and 30s, chess theoretician, and author. Aron was 8-years old when his father, a strong player himself, introduced him to the game. His extraordinary combinative talent had become apparent already in his early years. He began to take the game seriously when studying at Berlin University.

After the failure in the 1905 Barmen tournament, where he suffered eight losses in seventeen games and was able to win only three, Nimzowitsch started seriously to think about his style of play. He began to investigate the problems of chess strategy, paying special attention to studying the games of masters of positional play. By the end of 1906, he took first prize in the Munich tournament (8½ points out of 10), two points ahead of Spielmann who finished second. This success brought him the title of master. The next time he took the first prize was 17 years later at Copenhagen (1923). In all these years, he had persistently studied the principles governing the chess struggle. In 1925, the chess world was stirred by his books *Blockade* and *My System*, which were highly praised by Emanuel Lasker: "Nimzowitsch is a bold pioneer who blazes new original paths in the jungles of chess possibilities."

His deep penetration into the secrets of the chess art enabled Nimzowitsch to score convincing successes in practice. Between 1925 and 1933, he won nine first prizes in major events, including such super tournaments as Marienbad (1925), Dresden (1926),

London (1927), Berlin (1928), and Carlsbad (1929). In the major tournament at Semmering (1926), he managed to defeat Alekhine after a sharp fight.

**(71) Nimzowitsch – Alekhine**
Semmering 1926
Alekhine's Defense [B02]

**1.e4 ♞f6 2.♞c3 d5 3.e5 ♞fd7 4.f4 e6 5.♞f3 c5 6.g3 ♞c6 7.♗g2 ♗e7 8.0-0 0-0 9.d3 ♞b6?!** The main lines are 9...f6, 9...♖b8 and 9...a6. **10.♞e2 d4 11.g4** Nimzowitsch starts the typical attack on the kingside, so Alekhine has to react by opening up the center. **11...f6 12.e×f6 g×f6?!** Exposing the king's shelter is extremely risky. The more solid 12...♗×f6 13.♞g3 ♞d5 was required. **13.♞g3 ♞d5 14.♛e2 ♗d6 15.♞h4 ♞ce7 16.♗d2** 16.♞e4!? **16...♛c7 17.♛f2?!** Quite a slow approach. 17.♞h5!? ♗d7 18.♔h1 ♔h8 19.f5 applies more pressure. **17...c4 18.d×c4 ♞e3?!** 18...♛×c4 and only after 19.♞f3, is 19...♞e3 more precise. **19.♗×e3** 19.♞e4!? ♞×f1 20.♖×f1 gives White very dangerous compensation and might even be better than the game continuation. **19...d×e3 20.♛f3** 20.♛×e3?? ♗c5 –+ **20...♛×c4 21.♞e4 ♗c7 22.b3 ♛d4?! 23.c3 ♛b6** (D)

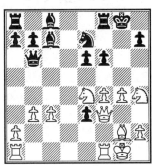

**24.♔h1!** Strong prophylaxis. **24...♘d5?!** This runs into a thunderstorm, but Black's defense looks very shaky in any case. **25.f5?** The wrong advance. Instead, 25.g5! fxg5 (25...f5 26.♕h5; 25...♗d7 26.♕h5) 26.♘xg5 gives White a winning attack. **25...♘f4 26.♖fd1?** Too slow and artificial. The natural 26.♖ae1 e2 27.♖xe2 ♘xe2 28.♕xe2 gives White full compensation for the exchange. 26.♕g3 is also an interesting option. **26...♔h8?** Alekhine misses 26...e2! (H.Wolf) 27.♖d2 exf5 28.gxf5 ♖f7 followed by ♗d7. **27.♗f1 exf5 28.gxf5?!** 28.♘xf5 is more natural. **28...♗e5 29.♖e1?** 29.♗c4 ♕c7 30.♕xe3 ♗d7 31.♗e2 ♗c6 (31...♘xe2? meets with 32.♘g6+) 32.♗f3 is a better way to deal with the pressure on the light squares. **29...♗d7 30.♖xe3 ♗c6 31.♖ae1** Black's bishop also make a powerful impression after 31.♗c4 ♕c7 32.a4 a6 33.a5 ♖fe8. **31...♘d5 32.♖d3 ♘xc3?** Alekhine miscalculates. He should bring his rooks into play with 32...♖g8 33.♗g2 ♖ae8–+. **33.♘g6+** 33.♖xc3? ♗xc3 34.♕xc3 ♕f2–+ **33...hxg6 34.♕g4!!** (D) 34.fxg6? ♔g7–+

**34...♖f7?** Here, the rook cannot help effectively enough. 34...♖g8! ensures that Black always has counterplay, e.g., 35.fxg6 ♔g7 36.♖d7+ ♗xd7

37.♕xd7+ ♔xg6 38.♗d3 ♔h6 39.♕h3+ ♔g7 40.♖g1+ (40.♘xc3 ♕c6+ 41.♘e4 ♗d4) 40...♕xg1+ 41.♔xg1 ♘xe4 42.♗xe4 ♖ac8; 34...♕c7? 35.♖h3+ ♔g8 36.♗c4+ ♘d5 37.♕xg6+ ♔g7 38.♕h5+–. **35.♖h3+ ♔g7** 35...♔g8 36.♗c4 ♗d5 37.♗xd5 ♘xd5 38.♕h4 ♔f8 39.fxg6 ♖g7 40.♕h8+ ♖g8 41.♖h7 ♖xh8 42.g7++–; 35...♖h7 36.fxg6+– **36.♗c4 ♗d5 37.fxg6 ♘xe4?** This loses directly, but 37...♖c7 does not hold the game either: 38.♖h7+ ♔g8 39.♕h5 f5 40.♗xd5+ ♘xd5 41.♖f7 ♖xf7 42.gxf7+ ♔g7 43.♖g1+ ♕xg1+ 44.♔xg1 fxe4 45.♕xe5+ ♘f6 46.♕g3+ ♔xf7 47.♕c7++–. **38.gxf7+ ♔f8 39.♖xe4 ♗xe4+ 40.♕xe4 ♔e7** (D)

**41.f8♕+!** The final blow, crowning the attack. **41...♖xf8 42.♕d5 ♕d6** 42...♕c6 43.♖h7+ ♔e8 44.♗b5+– **43.♕xb7+ ♔d8 44.♖d3 ♗d4 45.♕e4 ♖e8 46.♖xd4 1-0**

Nimzowitsch had the greatest satisfaction from winning first prize at Dresden (1926), where he scored 8½ points out of 9, one and a half points ahead of Alekhine. In 1929, he also won the major international event at Carlsbad ahead of Capablanca, Spielmann, Vidmar, Euwe, Bogoljubow and other top players of the time. Alekhine, who was present at the event as the *New York Times* correspondent, emphasized that "Nimzowitsch first prize is the greatest success in his chess career" and that "the quality of his play was significantly higher than that of the others."

Encouraged by this victory, Nimzowitsch raised the question of organizing a world championship match with Alekhine. In the tournament book he felt that "[t]he chess world should organize a match between the world champion and the winner of the Carlsbad tournament – this is its moral obligation. And should it be deaf to its obligation, it would be an entirely unjustified omission, which would invite a severe reproach."

The world, however, was found to be deaf to this appeal. Then the grandmaster hung on his Copenhagen apartment door a plate with the inscription "World Championship Challenger A. Nimzowitsch." When somebody asked him if he was afraid of forgetting it, he said: "No, but I want the chess world to remember this!"

In their rare tournament encounters in those years, the world champion usually had the upper hand. As regards the match between them, it never materialized. Impractical and lonely, Nimzowitsch was unable to find patrons ready to put up $10,000 for the match. The tormenting sense of hopelessness, mental depression and illness took their toll – he died not yet 49 years old.

Alekhine: "Only those who are acquainted with his books may get the true impression of Nimzowitsch. His last book [*My System*] is especially interesting."

Tigran Petrosian: "Every time I reread *My System*, I seem to discover anew those dicta by Nimzowitsch which, as I now understand, formed the basis for my views on chess."

Key works by Nimzowitsch include: *Blockade, My System, Praxis, The Great International Tournament at Kissingen, How I became Grandmaster, Selected Games of the International Tournament at Carlsbad.*

Bibliography:
Keene, R. *Grandmaster Nimzowitsch*.
Nielsen, B. *A. Nimzowitsch: 100 partier*. Aalborg 1945
Reinfeld, F. *Nimzovich the Hypermodern*. Philadelphia 1948.

**Semmering Tournament, March 8-30, 1926**
Richard Réti, while reflecting on his participation in this major tournament held at the Austrian resort, recalled that "Alekhine, whose victory was conceded almost in advance, fell behind somewhat. And yet, let us get it straight: we should regard him not only as the strongest of all Semmering participants, but (we will be so bold as to pronounce our own opinion, even though it runs counter to the generally recognized chess hierarchy) as the most outstanding contemporary master."

At Semmering, Alekhine preferred open combinational clashes to positional battles. Therefore, it was no accident that he was awarded three prizes there: one for the most wins and two brilliancy prizes, awarded to him for the games that he won against the Dutch master Davidson and grandmaster Rubinstein.

**(72) Davidson,Jacques – Alekhine**
Semmering 1926
Semi-Slav Defense [D46]

**1.d4 d5 2.♘f3 ♘f6 3.c4 c6 4.e3 e6 5.♘c3 ♘bd7 6.♕c2 ♗d6 7.♗d3 0-0 8.0-0 ♕e7 9.e4 d×c4 10.♗×c4 e5 11.♖d1 e×d4 12.♘×d4 ♘b6 13.♗f1 ♖d8 14.h3 ♗c7 15.♗e3 ♖e8 16.♗d3 ♘h5 17.♘ce2 g6 18.♖e1** 18.♖ac1!? is more natural. **18...♘d7 19.♘f3 ♗b6 20.♗g5 ♕c5** (D)

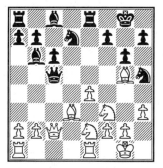

**21.♘c3?** Running into a surpringly strong attack out of the blue. 21.♘ed4, on the other hand, gives White a pleasant initiative. **21...♘e5! 22.♘×e5 ♕×e5 23.♗e3 ♗c7 24.♘e2?** 24.g3 was forced but White's position is in ruins after 24...♗×h3 25.f4 ♕e6. **24...♕h2+ 25.♔f1** (D)

**25...♗×h3!** The decisive blow. **26.g×h3 ♕×h3+ 27.♔g1 ♗h2+ 28.♔h1 ♘f4 29.♘×f4** 29.♗×f4? ♗g3+ 30.♔g1 ♕h2+ 31.♔f1 ♕×f2# **29...♗×f4+ 30.♔g1 ♗h2+ 31.♔h1 ♕f3+ 32.♔×h2 ♖e5 33.♕c5 ♖×c5 34.♗×c5 ♕h5+ 35.♔g2 ♕×c5 36.♖e3 ♖e8**

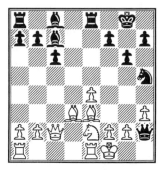

**37.♖ae1 ♕e5 38.♖1e2 ♖e6 39.b3 ♖f6 40.♖g3 ♔g7 41.♗b1 ♖f4 42.♗d3 ♖h4 43.♔f3 ♕f4+ 44.♔g2 ♕c1 45.♔f3 h5 46.♖c2 ♕d1+ 47.♔e3 ♖h1 48.♔d4 h4 49.♖e3 ♖e1 50.♖×e1 ♕×e1 51.♖e2 ♕a1+ 52.♔c4 b5+ 0-1**

**(73) Alekhine – Yates, Frederick**
Semmering, 1926 (D)

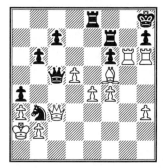

Alekhine forces mate by violent means:
**63.♖×h7+! ♔×h7** 63...♖×h7 64.♕×f6+ ♖g7 65.♕×g7# **64.♖×f6+ ♔g7 65.♖g6+ ♔f8** 65...♔h7 66.♖g4+ ♖×f5 67.♕g7# **66.♕h8+ ♔e7 67.♖e6+ ♔d7 68.♕×e8# 1-0**

**World Championship Matches**
From 1927 to 1937, Alexander Alekhine played five world championship matches: one against José Raúl Capablanca (1927), two against Efim Bogoljubow (1929 and 1934), and two

*Semmering 1916*

| | | 1 | 2 | 3 | 4 | 5 | 6 | 7 | 8 | 9 | 10 | 11 | 12 | 13 | 14 | 15 | 16 | 17 | 18 | Total |
|---|---|---|---|---|---|---|---|---|---|---|---|---|---|---|---|---|---|---|---|---|
| 1 | **Spielmann** | X | ½ | 1 | 1 | 1 | 0 | ½ | ½ | 1 | 1 | 1 | 1 | 1 | ½ | 1 | ½ | ½ | 1 | **13** |
| 2 | **Alekhine** | ½ | X | 0 | 0 | 1 | 1 | 1 | 1 | 1 | ½ | 1 | ½ | 1 | 0 | 1 | 1 | 1 | 1 | **12½** |
| 3 | **Vidmar** | 0 | 1 | X | 1 | 1 | ½ | 0 | 1 | ½ | 1 | 1 | ½ | 1 | 1 | ½ | 1 | ½ | ½ | **12** |
| 4 | **Nimzowitsch** | 0 | 1 | 0 | X | ½ | 1 | ½ | 1 | 0 | 1 | ½ | 1 | 1 | 1 | ½ | ½ | 1 | 1 | **11½** |
| 5 | **Tartakower** | 0 | 0 | 0 | ½ | X | ½ | 1 | 0 | 1 | 1 | 1 | 1 | ½ | 1 | 1 | 1 | 1 | 1 | **11½** |
| 6 | **Rubinstein** | 1 | 0 | ½ | 0 | ½ | X | ½ | 1 | 1 | 0 | ½ | 0 | 1 | ½ | 1 | ½ | 1 | 1 | **10** |
| 7 | **Tarrasch** | ½ | 0 | 1 | ½ | 0 | ½ | X | 1 | 0 | 0 | 0 | 1 | ½ | 1 | 1 | 1 | 1 | 1 | **10** |
| 8 | **Réti** | ½ | 0 | 0 | 0 | 1 | 0 | 0 | X | 1 | 1 | 1 | 0 | ½ | 1 | 1 | ½ | 1 | 1 | **9½** |
| 9 | **Grünfeld** | 0 | 0 | ½ | 1 | 0 | 0 | 1 | 0 | X | 0 | ½ | ½ | 1 | 1 | 1 | 1 | ½ | 1 | **9** |
| 10 | **Janowski** | 0 | ½ | 0 | 0 | 0 | 1 | 1 | 0 | 1 | X | ½ | 0 | ½ | 0 | 1 | 1 | 1 | 1 | **8½** |
| 11 | **Treybal** | 0 | 0 | 0 | ½ | 0 | ½ | 1 | 0 | ½ | ½ | X | 1 | 1 | 1 | 0 | 1 | ½ | ½ | **8** |
| 12 | **Vajda** | 0 | ½ | ½ | 0 | 0 | 1 | 0 | 1 | ½ | 1 | 0 | X | 0 | ½ | ½ | ½ | ½ | 1 | **7½** |
| 13 | **Yates** | 0 | 0 | 0 | 0 | ½ | 0 | ½ | ½ | 0 | ½ | 0 | 1 | X | ½ | ½ | 1 | 1 | 1 | **7** |
| 14 | **Gilg** | ½ | 1 | 0 | 0 | 0 | ½ | 0 | 0 | 0 | 1 | 0 | ½ | ½ | X | ½ | 0 | ½ | 1 | **6** |
| 15 | **Kmoch** | 0 | 0 | ½ | ½ | 0 | 0 | 0 | 0 | 0 | 0 | 1 | ½ | ½ | ½ | X | 1 | ½ | 1 | **6** |
| 16 | **Davidson** | ½ | 0 | 0 | ½ | 0 | ½ | 0 | ½ | 0 | 0 | 0 | ½ | 0 | 1 | 0 | X | 1 | 1 | **5½** |
| 17 | **Michel** | ½ | 0 | ½ | 0 | 0 | 0 | 0 | 0 | ½ | 0 | ½ | ½ | 0 | ½ | ½ | 0 | X | 1 | **4½** |
| 18 | **Rosselli** | 0 | 0 | ½ | 0 | 0 | 0 | 0 | 0 | 0 | 0 | ½ | 0 | 0 | 0 | 0 | 0 | 0 | X | **1** |

*The participants and organizers of the tournament at Semmering, 1926. Sitting (from left to right) are: Nimzowitsch, Alekhine, Grünfeld, Tarrasch, Mittel, Vidmar, Rubinstein. Standing are: Spielmann, Kmoch, Treybal, Davidson, Réti, Vajda, Yates, Tetz, Gilg, Tartakower, Wolf, and NN.*

against Max Euwe (1935 and 1937). He is the only player in chess history to die while holding the world title.

**Capablanca, José Raúl** (November 19, 1888, Havana-March 8, 1942, New York)

A Cuban chessplayer, third world chess champion (1921-1927). "The Wonder of Havana!" asserted respected señors and caballeros when speaking about how the four-year-old Raúl who, without any outside help and only watching the games his father played, learned how to play chess. When he was 13, he defeated the Cuban champion Juan Corzo.

Raúl showed extraordinary aptitude for mathematics, took great interest in philosophy and history, played the violin, and was an excellent baseball player. Having moved to the USA to get higher education there (he studied at the chemical engineering department of Columbia University), he nevertheless enthusiastically continued to be involved in chess. In early 1909, Capablanca made a triumphal tour of America (+540 -13 =18 !), and, in April and June of the same year, he met and virtually crushed the well-known American grandmaster and U.S. champion Frank Marshall (+8 -1 =14).

He soon achieved success in Europe as well. It all started at San Sebastian in 1911, where all the top players of the time, except for world champion Emanuel Lasker, participated. After his spectacular victory there and second place in St. Petersburg in 1914, the chess world regarded him as the principal challenger for the world title. But, the latter tournament became significant both in the history of chess and Capablanca's chess career because it determined his eternal rival in the struggle for world championship in the years to come. And, if fate had decided that Capablanca would be the third chess champion of the world, it also decided that Alekhine would be the fourth. Incidentally, in the lives of both these chess geniuses there is much in common, sometimes surprisingly similar or even mysteriously coinciding...

*José Raúl Capablanca*

Both Alekhine and Capablanca were the younger sons of well-off families. Both were well-educated; Capablanca became a diplomat, Alekhine a lawyer. However, all their dreams and aspirations from their younger years were only associated with chess. And, as both of them admitted, the magic of chess enchanted them at about the same age and thanks to the same magician, the hero of Hastings 1895, Harry Nelson Pillsbury.

It was his magnificent tours with blindfold simultaneous exhibitions in Havana 1899 and Moscow 1902 that made such an overwhelming impression on the young players and predetermined their life's choice. Alekhine and Capablanca first met in St. Petersburg in 1913. Both were young, handsome, sincere, and talented! In November

1913, when the challenger first came to St. Petersburg, Alekhine played two training games with him. The admiration he felt for the Cuban made it impossible for him to show all he was capable of, and he lost both these games. It is true that he was not upset very much by this. On the contrary, the young men (Capablanca only was four years older than Alekhine) soon became friends. Often, they could be seen together visiting people, in museums, theaters, playing blitz games.

Many years later, when Capablanca was no longer alive, Alekhine, flooded with the memories of his youth, told about his past sympathies and his admiration of the Cuban chess phenomenon. Speaking about "his genuine, incredible talent," Alekhine said that "[n]ever before and never afterwards [had he] seen – and [he could not] even imagine – such a flabbergasting quickness of chess comprehension as Capablanca then had… It must be added that Capablanca was always in excellent spirits, had very good health, and was the darling of the ladies – indeed, a dazzling vision!"

Seven long years had passed since the historic St. Petersburg tournament when Capablanca's dream came true; in 1921, he met Emanuel Lasker in Havana in a world championship match and, having defeated him (+4 -0 =10), became the third world chess champion. He held the title for six years, and, all this time, his "pal of St. Petersburg," Alexander Alekhine, was preparing for the battle of his life – with Capablanca. And how he was preparing!

He subjected Capablanca's games to a careful analysis, in the attempt to locate vulnerable spots in the seemingly impeccable play of the world champion. And, since the challenger was, as Capablanca himself recognized, an excellent analyst, what was "secret" to the rest of the world became "obvious" to Alekhine.

Thus, he was able to discover that the champion, despite his relatively limited opening repertoire, had almost never come out of the opening phase in an inferior position and any attempt to obtain an advantage by adopting some unexpected idea in that phase would fail because of Capablanca's infallible intuition. In such cases, concluded Alekhine, Capablanca "exerts himself to the utmost and invariably finds the only correct solution." Therefore, the challenger decided not to prevent Capablanca from using his method of simplifications. Moreover, he decided to use this method himself when playing as Black but, unlike the world champion, not in every position.

Alekhine was ready to study his rival's games for days on end; he worked very hard, systemizing Capablanca's play, placing special emphasis on the endgame. And, he came to the same conclusion as Lasker: in the middlegame, which was the strongest aspect of Capablanca's play, the tactician in him was much inferior to the strategist. In the endgame, he also discovered missed chances or even wrong decisions in Capablanca's play. All this was the result of his "gradual abandonment of searching for the absolute and satisfaction with only good moves," which became typical of "the present stage in Capablanca's chess career."

During these years Capablanca played in four tournaments: London 1922, New York 1924, Moscow 1925, and New York 1927, winning decisively in two of them, in the presence of the principal challenger, Alexander Alekhine, in London and New York 1927.

The start of the world championship match in Buenos Aires was unlucky for Capablanca, who lost the very first game, which was, incidentally, his first loss to Alekhine ever! In the third game, however, he equalized and, in general, was quite satisfied with his performance: "The entire game was played by me vigorously. Alekhine obtained an inferior game early but then he defended very well."

**(74) Capablanca – Alekhine**
World Championship (3) 1927
Queen's Indian Defense [A47]

**1.d4 ♘f6 2.♘f3 b6 3.g3 ♗b7 4.♗g2 c5 5.0-0 c×d4 6.♘×d4 ♗×g2 7.♔×g2 d5?!** The main lines are 7...♕c8 and 7...g6. **8.c4! e6?** 8...d×c4 is more or less forced. **9.♕a4+ ♕d7 10.♘b5! ♘c6 11.c×d5 e×d5 12.♗f4 ♖c8 13.♖c1 ♗c5** 13...♘e4 is also met by 14.b4!±. **14.b4! ♗×b4? (D)**

14...♘×b4 15.♘d6+ ♔d8 16.♕×d7+ ♔×d7 17.♘×c8 ♖×c8± (Lasker) was forced. **15.♖×c6!** A small combination in typical Capablanca style. 15.♘c7+? is wrong because of 15...♖×c7 16.♗×c7 ♗c5!. **15...♖×c6 16.♕×b4 ♘e4 17.♘d2?** This allows Black to reduce the pressure through exchanges. 17.f3 ♘c5 18.♘1c3 ♘e6 19.♖d1 +− is stronger. **17...♘×d2 18.♕×d2 0-0 19.♖d1 ♖c5 20.♘d4 ♖e8 21.♘b3 ♖cc8 22.e3 ♕a4?!** Black should try to exchange major pieces. Therefore, 22...h6 23.♕×d5 ♕d5+ 24.♖×d5 g5 25.♗e5 ♖cd8 is called for. **23.♕×d5 ♖c2 24.♖d2 ♖×a2?** (D) 24...♕×a2 25.♕d7 ♖f8 26.♖×c2 ♕×c2 is similar to the game continuation and denies White the option to keep the rooks on the board.

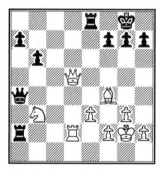

**25.♖×a2?** Capablanca exchanges attacking potential. He should keep and activate his rook with 25.♖d4 ♕a6 26.♖c4 h5 27.♖c7 ♖f8 28.♗d6 ♕e2 29.♕f5+−. **25...♕×a2 26.♕c6 ♖f8 27.♘d4 ♔h8?** Too artificial and passive. 27...♖d8 28.e4 h6 29.♗e3 ♕a1 30.♕c4± offers more resistance. **28.♗e5 f6?!** Opening inroads. But after 28...♕a5 29.♗d6 ♖g8 30.e4 ♕a1 31.♘f5 ♕f6 32.♕b7, White will also win in the long run. **29.♘e6 ♖g8 30.♗d4 h6** 30...a5 31.♘×g7 ♖×g7

32.♕×f6 ♕g8 33.h4 +− **31.h4!**
**♕b1?!** (D) This allows the direct blow.
But Black is lost in any case. One
sample line runs 31...♔h7 32.e4 ♕e2
33.♕d5 ♖e8 34.♕f5+ ♔h8 35.♗×f6
♖×e6 36.♕×e6 g×f6 37.♕×f6+ ♔h7
38.♕f7+ ♔h8 39.♕f8+ ♔h7 40.♕f5+
♔h8 41.e5 +−.

**32.♘×g7!** **♕g6** 32...♖×g7 33.♕×f6
♕e4+ (33...♔h7 34.♕f8+ ♕g8
35.♗×g7++−) 34.♔g1 ♕g4
35.♕×h6+ ♔g8 36.♕×g7+ ♕×g7
37.♗×g7 ♔×g7 38.♔f1 +− **33.h5**
**♕f7 34.♘f5 ♔h7 35.♕e4 ♖e8**
**36.♕f4 ♕f8 37.♘d6 ♖e7** 37...♖d8
38.♕f5+ ♔g8 39.♕e6+ ♔h7 40.♗×f6
♖×d6 41.♕f5+ ♔g8 42.♕g6+ ♕g7
43.♕×g7 # **38.♗×f6 ♕a8+ 39.e4**
**♖g7 40.♗×g7 ♔×g7 41.♘f5+ ♔f7**
**42.♕c7+ 1-0**

Subsequently, Alekhine again seized the
initiative and, after two and a half
months of struggle, convincingly won
the match (+6 -3 =25). The match went
down in chess history as one of the
peaks of chess art.

After his failure in the match,
Capablanca won first place in a num-
ber of major international tournaments:
Berlin 1928, Budapest 1928 and 1929,
Barcelona 1929, Hastings 1929-30,
and Moscow 1936. In 1936, he tied for

1st-2nd places with Botvinnik at
Nottingham, ahead of world champion
Euwe, former champions Alekhine and
Lasker, as well as young grandmasters
Reshevsky, Fine, and Flohr. In the
AVRO tournament held in Holland, he
played his last game with Alekhine. On
that day, the Cuban turned 50 and was
not in a fighting mood. Alekhine, as if
having a premonition that it would be
his last chance to even the score in their
historical confrontation, won that
game. So the ultimate score in all their
encounters became +7 -7 =33.

For over a quarter-century, Capablanca
had remained one of the protagonists
in the history of the struggle for the
world chess championship. Of his last
successes, the first prize at Paris 1938
and the best result on first board in the
chess Olympiad in Argentina 1939 are
noteworthy. Between tournament and
match games, he played 603 games, and
achieved the best result ever in the history of chess (+318 -34 =251).

Capablanca's style harmoniously combined the logic of plans, high technique
of exploiting a positional advantage,
resoluteness in attack and coolness in
defense, and fine handling of the
endgame. "His play produces an irre-
sistible artistic impression. In it, the
tendency to simplicity prevails, and it
is in this simplicity that the unique
beauty of the true depth (of understanding chess) lies" (Botvinnik).

With regard to what is of the greatest
importance in the game of chess,
Capablanca formulated his credo as
follows: "I consider the height of chess
strategy consistently implemented in
a given game and the knowledge of how

to play the endgame to be the criteria in evaluating chess mastery." To both these fields of chess creativity, Capablanca contributed new ideas and methods, and, in many games, he had demonstrated the highest mastery. For example ...

**(75) Capablanca – Tartakower,S.**
New York 1924
Dutch Defense [A85]

**1.d4 e6 2.♘f3 f5 3.c4 ♘f6 4.♗g5 ♗e7 5.♘c3 0-0 6.e3 b6 7.♗d3 ♗b7 8.0-0 ♕e8 9.♕e2 ♘e4 10.♗×e7 ♘×c3 11.b×c3 ♕×e7 12.a4 ♗×f3 13.♕×f3 ♘c6 14.♖fb1 ♖ae8 15.♕h3 ♖f6 16.f4 ♘a5 17.♕f3 d6 18.♖e1 ♕d7 19.e4 f×e4 20.♕×e4 g6 21.g3 ♔f8 22.♔g2 ♖f7 23.h4 d5 24.c×d5 e×d5 25.♕×e8+ ♕×e8 26.♖×e8+ ♔×e8 27.h5 ♖f6 28.h×g6 h×g6 29.♖h1 ♔f8 30.♖h7 ♖c6 31.g4 ♘c4?!** 31...♘b3 is more precise. **32.g5 ♘e3+ 33.♔f3 ♘f5?** The knight must remain on the board with 33...♘d1 34.♔e2 ♘×c3+ 35.♔d2 ♘a2 36.♗b5 ♖c3 with drawing chances because White's king is not so easy to activate. **34.♗×f5 g×f5 (D)**

The following rook endgame is a famous textbook example. **35.♔g3!** Capablanca activates his king with de-

cisive effect and is willing to sacrifice two pawns. **35...♖×c3+ 36.♔h4 ♖f3?!**, 36...a6 provides more counterplay, but White's king still enters with decisive effect: 37.♔h5 b5 38.♔g6 ♔g8 (38...b×a4 39.♔×f5 a3 40.♖h6+– ) 39.♖g7+ ♔f8 40.♖f7+ ♔g8 41.♖f6+– (I.Zaitsev). **37.g6!** Opening the way for the king **37...♖×f4+ 38.♔g5 ♖e4** 38...♖×d4 39.♔f6 ♔g8 40.♖d7+– **39.♔f6 ♔g8 40.♖g7+ ♔h8 41.♖×c7 ♖e8 42.♔×f5!** Now the f-pawn is not needed as a shield anymore and could provide counterplay by advancing, so it is time to eliminate it. **42...♖e4 43.♔f6 ♖f4+ 44.♔e5 ♖g4 45.g7+ ♔g8** 45...♖×g7 46.♖×g7 ♔×g7 47.♔×d5 ♔f7 48.♔c6+– **46.♖×a7 ♖g1 47.♔×d5 ♖c1 48.♔d6 ♖c2 49.d5 ♖c1 50.♖c7 ♖a1 51.♔c6 ♖×a4 52.d6 1-0**

Although in his mature years, the Cuban grandmaster appeared to the chess world as a player of positional style, his combinative gift continually surfaced in a number of spectacular finales and fine combinative concepts. For the following game, Capablanca was awarded a brilliancy prize.

**(76) Capablanca – Zubarev,Nikolay**
Moscow 1925 (D)

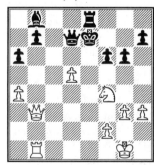

**33.♕×b7    ♗×f4**    33...♕×b7
34.♖×b7+ ♔d6 35.♖×h7 g5 36.♘h5
is also lost in the long run. **34.♖e1+
♗e5 35.d6+!!** The point of
Capablanca's combination. Black's king
can run, but it cannot hide without losing the queen. **35...♔e6** 35...♔d8?
36.♕b6+ ♔c8 37.♖c1++– **36.♕b3+
♔f5 37.♕d3+ ♔g5 38.♕e3+ ♔f5
39.♕e4+ ♔e6 40.♕c4+ ♔×d6**
40...♔f5? 41.♕g4# **41.♖d1+ ♔e7
42.♖×d7+ ♔×d7 43.♕×a6 1-0**

Characterizing Capablanca's natural
gift, his intuition, his contemporaries
noted the astonishing ease with which
he grasped the most complex strategic
and tactical decisions. Richard Réti
believes that "[i]n Capablanca's style of
play, one is, at first sight, taken by his
huge confidence – the almost complete
absence of oversights or misjudgments
in positional valuation. This is without
a doubt owing to the fact that he already
learned to play chess in early childhood: it has become his 'native
tongue.'"

The Moscow chess master Alexander
Ilyin-Genevsky, while recalling the
game he played with the Cuban in the
Moscow tournament 1925, paints a
vivid portrait of the third world champion:

*Sometimes Capablanca starts se-
riously to ponder the position.
Then, I raise my head and start
to examine his features. He is indeed handsome. A persistent
thought is visible on his open and
attractive face. He is struggling
but at the same time calmly and
majestically thinking... Sometimes, I too begin to ponder. Then
Capablanca slowly stands up to*
*take a stroll between the tables
of other players. It looks as if he
were resting. In fact, his eyes are
burning with some inner
fire...He is thinking about the
game.*

Capablanca felt a constant need to share
his knowledge and experience with a
wide audience, publishing articles, lec-
turing, and writing a number of books
in which he revealed himself to be a
wonderful teacher and author. *My
Chess Career* (1920), *Chess Fundamentals* (1921), *A Primer of Chess*
(1935) are still instructing aspiring
chess players. His series of chess lectures (1941), which were published
posthumously, have many merits. And
they reflect his faith that the game of
chess will, for a long time, serve to the
benefit of people on our planet. "I
think," Capablanca used to say, "that
chess should be included in school cur-
ricula in all countries." At the same
time, he stressed the role of chess as a
means for the "further strengthening of
social and spiritual bonds, cordial re-
lationships between peoples."

José Raúl Capablanca died March 8,
1942 in New York. While at the Manhattan Chess Club the day before, he
suddenly felt very unwell, and, several
hours later, he died without regaining
consciousness. He outlived (by only
one year) Emanuel Lasker who had died
after a simultaneous exhibition given
at the same club. And four years later
Alexander Alekhine died in Portugal.

Not long before his death Alekhine decided to write a book about his predecessor, but only had time to write an
introductory essay. In it he professed

that "Capablanca was too soon snatched from the chess world. With his death we lost the greatest chess genius, an equal to whom we will never see."

**His works:**
Capablanca, José Raúl. *Chess Funda mentals*. 1921.
—. *Last Chess Lectures*. 1941.
—. *My Chess Career*. 1920.
—. *A Primer of Chess*. 1935.

**References**
Alekhine, Alexander, ed. *World Cham pionship Match Alekhine – Capablanca, Buenos Aires, Sep tember – November*. 1927. Kharkov, 1928 (In Russian).
Euwe, Max and L. Prins. *Capablanca – Chess Phenomenon*.
Kasparov, Garry. "José Raúl the Third." *On My Great Predecessors*. Vol.1. Moscow, 2003.
Lasker, Emanuel. *My Match with Capablanca*. 2nd ed. L., 1925.
Levenfish, G.Ya. and P.A. Romanovsky. *World Championship match Alekhine- Capablanca*. L., 1928.
Linder, I. and V. Linder. *Capablanca in Russia*. Moscow, 1988.
—. "José Raúl Capablanca." *The Kings of the Chess World*. Moscow, 2001.
Panov, V.N. *Capablanca*. 3rd ed. Mos cow, 1970.

**Capablanca-Alekhine, September 16-November 29, 1927**
Alekhine was preparing for this great trial for thirteen years. Four years had been enough for Lasker to surpass Steinitz, while fate had given Capablanca seven years to learn the secret of the invincible Lasker and, si multaneously, to change his style of play radically.

The long years of Alekhine's creative daring and struggle on the road to the world title passed amidst less favorable circumstances than his two predeces sors had faced. He experienced the hardship and misery of the first World War and revolution in Russia, had to change jobs several times, and had been through many vicissitudes in his private life. Faced with all that, he was entirely obsessed with one goal: to become the first player in the chess kingdom. All of his theoretical and practical activi ties were aimed at achieving this ob jective. He untiringly studied how his future rival handled the various phases of the game, observed his behavior un der different circumstances, including unpredictable ones.

In so doing, Alekhine came to a num ber of important conclusions. For ex ample, he decided that it would be wrong to attempt to surprise Capablanca with an opening novelty, for "his im peccable intuition" would suggest the best way out for him. At the same time, Alekhine worked out the tactics of play ing against Capablanca so as to resolve "the problems of the opening, along the simplifying ways familiar to him." He also gave Capablanca his due regarding the middlegame, noting that his rival's play was distinguished, above all, by his extraordinary swiftness of conception and an almost unfailing intuitive posi tional grasp. At the same time, Alekhine was able to see something else, namely, that the Cuban did not always verify his assessment by calculating concrete variations, which sometimes led to no ticeable mistakes. Somewhat unexpect edly, Alekhine also found out that in the endgame, where Capablanca's mastery

*Alekhine–Capablanca Buenos Aires, 1927*

was deemed legendary, his rival was far from impeccable, especially in dynamic positions. Finally, in analyzing Capablanca's games played in different periods of his chess career, Alekhine discovered that with time, Capablanca lost the necessary ability to concentrate his attention to the utmost and also that when his opponent put up a stout resistance, Capablanca's confidence waned. Alekhine had also made more than a few valuable observations in his creative laboratory while preparing to achieve the main goal of his life.

Forecasts were not lacking before this "match of the giants," as it was referred to regularly in the world press. Thus, Spielmann, Bogoljubow, and Maroczy, based on their catastrophic results in the encounters with the world champion (0-4!), argued that Alekhine would not win a single game in the match. Only Lasker and Réti had complete faith in his genius. Lasker had already repeatedly stated that Alekhine was capable of winning the title of world champion

because he could show more creative fantasy.

And in "Capablanca and Alekhine," Lasker, for the first time, voiced the idea that these two great chess masters had much in common in their approach to chess: "Both of them have retained their freshness and youthful energy. Neither Capablanca nor Alekhine plays routinely. Their individuality is so pronounced that the chessboard with its 64 limited squares unwittingly seems too narrow for them. The unknown does not frighten them and both are ready to test their strength against it if it seems interesting. Both are looking for new ways, seeking to find something abundant and buoyant." At the same time, their attitude to chess praxis itself is what they have in common. "Abstract ideas, philosophic reasoning, and generalities are alien to them. Both wish to deal with theories successfully tested in practice, which, if needed, may be tested a hundred times (*Kalendar shakhmatista* 1926).

And what did the rivals themselves say in anticipation of their duel? "I cannot conceive how I can win six games from Capablanca, but I do not think that Capablanca can win such a large number of games from me." The world champion's statement made before the match was more definite and not without a dose of complacency. Characterizing his rival as an opponent in the match, he came to the conclusion that Alekhine lacks the temperament required for match-play. Capablanca erroneously believed that his challenger had no fighting spirit as an end in itself. "Moreover," stressed Capablanca, "Alekhine is extremely nervous, which may be detrimental in a long and stubborn struggle against a cool and well prepared opponent. However," he added, "Alekhine has an excellent opportunity to refute this in the forthcoming world championship match with me." This statement suggested that Capablanca remained in a state of euphoria after his magnificent success in the 1927 New York tournament and was far from objectively assessing either his own or his rival's potential.

On September 7, Alekhine arrived in Buenos Aires. In a brief interview, he said that he was grateful to the Republic of Argentina for organizing the match, while he did not want to make any assumptions about the outcome of the match. Capablanca arrived after touring Brazil for two weeks. He stated that his health was better than ever before, that he felt a surge of energy, and he expected a difficult struggle. To the questions of his rival, the Cuban said that "the world had not yet seen such a harmonious player, but Alekhine was especially great as an analyst and annotator – in that field he had no equals...."

On the eve of the match, the rules and regulations were published. The most important of them were: (1) the match to be for six won games, draws not counting; (2) if each player wins five games, the match is considered drawn and Capablanca retains the title; (3) the rate of play is two hours for the first forty moves and then one hour for the next fifteen moves; and (4) the games were to be played six times a week, each uninterrupted session lasting five hours.

Finally, September 16 arrived – the day when all preparations, predictions, and interviews were left behind; the day on which the first game of the long-awaited match was played at the club Argentino de Ajedrez; the day on which Alekhine defeated Capablanca for the first time ever!

The world champion and the challenger sat down at the chessboard. Sitting on one side is José Raúl Capablanca, a handsome dark-haired man who can conceal his passions. During the match, he will be 39 years old. On the other side of the board is Alexander Alekhine, with his dark hair swept back. He will also celebrate his 35th birthday in Buenos Aires. They must answer the question which for over forty years has excited millions of devotees of this ancient and wise game: who is the chess king? Behind the doors, passions are raging, bets are being placed, toasts are being made. While they, having renounced the world, are sitting bent over the black-and-white checkered wooden board with thirty-two wooden men standing on it, and appear to be worshipping...

In the first game, Capablanca was White, and the choice of the opening

160

was mostly his choice. He opened with 1.e2-e4, being sure that the Russian grandmaster who had come from Paris would adopt the French Defense. And he was right: as it had more than once happened in their previous encounters, Alekhine replied 1...e7-e6. This time Black equalized easily and even gained a small spatial advantage. Quite unexpectedly, on move 16, Capablanca overlooked the loss of a pawn. True, it was far from simple to exploit this advantage in the ending with major pieces. But Alekhine proceeded vigorously and won the game.

**(77) Capablanca – Alekhine**
World Championship (1) Buenos Aires 1927
French Defense [C01]

**1.e4 e6 2.d4 d5 3.♘c3 ♗b4 4.e×d5 e×d5 5.♗d3 ♘c6 6.♘ge2 ♘ge7 7.0-0 ♗f5 8.♗×f5 ♘×f5 9.♕d3 ♕d7 10.♘d1?!** 10.♗f4 is the main line. **10...0-0 11.♘e3 ♘×e3 12.♗×e3 ♖fe8 13.♘f4 ♗d6 14.♖fe1?!** 14.c3!? **14...♘b4 15.♕b3 ♕f5 16.♖ac1?** (D) A tactical oversight. 16.♘d3! ♘×d3 17.♕×d3 ♕×d3 18.c×d3 (Capablanca) was much more tenacious.

**16...♘×c2!** Surprisingly 16...a5!? is also very strong, e.g., 17.c3 a4 18.♕d1 ♘a2 19.♖a1 ♗×f4. **17.♖×c2** 17.♕×c2 is met by 17...♕×c2 18.♖×c2

♗×f4. **17...♕×f4! 18.g3 ♕f5 19.♖ce2 b6 20.♕b5 h5** The battering ram is moving forward. **21.h4 ♖e4!** (D)

**22.♗d2** Giving up the weak pawn is relatively best because, against passive defense, Alekhine's attack on the kingside prevails, e.g., 22.♕d3? ♕f3 23.♕d1?! ♖×h4 24.g×h4 ♕g4+ 25.♔f1 ♕h3+ 26.♔g1 ♕h2+ 27.♔f1 ♕h1#. **22...♖×d4 23.♗c3 ♖d3 24.♗e5 ♖d8 25.♗×d6 ♖×d6 26.♖e5 ♕f3** 26...♕g6?? 27.♖g5!+− **27.♖×h5** (D)

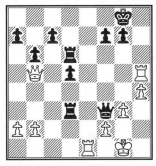

**27...♕×h5?** Alekhine exchanges his active d3-rook for the intruder on h5. 27...♖e6?? is, of course, totally wrong because of 28.♕e8+! ♖×e8 29.♖×e8#. But 27...♖h6!, to exchange the passive rook, is more logical, e.g., 28.♖×h6 g×h6 29.♕c6 ♖d2 30.♖f1 ♖×b2 with good winning chances. **28.♖e8+ ♔h7 29.♕×d3+ ♕g6 30.♕d1?** Too passive. 30.♕f3 makes White's counterplay more dangerous, e.g.,

30...c6 31.h5 ♕b1+ 32.♔g2 ♖f6 33.♕e2 ♕f5 34.♖e5. **30...♖e6 31.♖a8?!** ♖e5? Too slow. Averbakh's 31...d4! is stronger: 32.♖×a7 (32.♕×d4?? ♖e1+ 33.♔h2 ♕c6−+) 32...d3 33.♖a3 ♖d6 and Black should win in the long run as he can combine the advance of his d-pawn with an attack against White's king. **32.♖×a7 c5** 32...♕e6? is met by 33.♕d3+ f5 34.♖×c7±. **33.♖d7?** Capablanca loses very valuable time. He can still defend with 33.♕f3 ♖f5 34.♕d3 d4 35.♖b7. **33...♕e6! 34.♕d3+ g6 35.♖d8?! d4** (D)

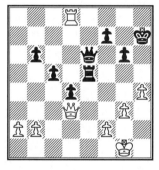

**36.a4?** This loses directly. The prophylactic 36.♔g2! ♕×a2 37.♕b5 ♕e6 38.♕d7 holds out longer. **36...♖e1+ 37.♔g2 ♕c6+ 38.f3** 38.♕f3 ♖g1+−+ **38...♖e3 39.♕d1 ♕e6 40.g4** 40.♔f2 ♕h3 41.♕g1 ♖b3−+ (Becker) **40...♖e2+ 41.♔h3 ♕e3 42.♕h1 ♕f4 43.h5 ♖f2 0-1**

This game served as an emotional stimulant for Alekhine, whereas Capablanca, obviously puzzled by such a beginning, took a timeout. In the second game, after nineteen moves, each player had only two rooks, a knight and six pawns; they agreed to a draw. After the third game, the score became even, Alekhine failing in the Queen's Indian Defense. In the games to follow, they concentrated all their efforts in an ocean of Queen's Gambit Declined variations. Incidentally, there had never before been such constancy in the history of world championship matches, in which thirty-two games out of thirty-four were contested in the same opening, the Queen's Gambit Declined. Explaining the mistakes that he had made in the opening of the third game, Alekhine admitted that "that game is the only one in the match in which I was unable to keep my nerves under complete control." The next three games were only drawn after full-blooded struggles, having exhausted all resources.

In those days, Alekhine showed remarkable resilience, playing on despite suffering from a severe toothache. However, before the fifth game, he had to take a respite. He played the next few games with a swollen cheek, several of his teeth having been removed.

On September 30, in the seventh game, Capablanca adopted a novelty in the opening and won the game in spectacular style, taking the lead in the match. That was his best achievement in the contest. Inspired, Capablanca yearned to build on his success; however, all his efforts in the following three games failed against Alekhine's stout resistance.

In the ninth game, as in the seventh, Alekhine again adopted the Cambridge Springs Variation. The world champion came up with another novelty, thus gaining a positional advantage. The impression was that the black queen, adrift on the queenside, would not be able to escape the pursuit of White's army. However, Alekhine, finding "only" moves every time, was able to keep the game balanced. His fantastic resistance overwhelmed Capablanca. All attempts to break through Black's defense were in vain, and the black queen, having finally escaped capture, had her revenge in perpetually checking the opposing king. As fate would have it, the main events in the first third of the match occurred in odd-numbered games. In the eleventh game played a pivotal role, with Alekhine again adopting the Cambridge Springs Variation.

That game proceeded with a complicated maneuvering struggle. The finale of this hard-fought encounter, which ended with Alekhine declaring mate when there were four (!) queens on the board, was so unexpected, so spectacular, and so impressive, that, naturally, it caused the players, as well as analysts, to scutinize the twists and turns of that practically decisive game of the match in greater depth. In particular, a real debate broke out around this game in master Nikolai Grigoriev's chess column in the Moscow newspaper *Izvestiya*, which Capablanca himself was sending brief annotations to the games. And, almost four decades later, the newspaper again brought up the subject by publishing this game with annotations by grandmaster David Bronstein in his article "The Battle of the Equals" (March 25, 1965). We gladly present this monumental game to you not only with Karsten Müller's comments, but also with comments by Alekhine, Capablanca, Bronstein, and Levenfish and Romanovsky, taken from their book on the match.

**(78) Capablanca – Alekhine**
World Championship (11) Buenos Aires 1927
Queen's Gambit Declined [D52]

**1.d4 d5 2.c4 e6 3.♘c3 ♘f6 4.♗g5 ♘bd7 5.e3 c6 6.♘f3 ♕a5 7.♘d2 ♗b4 8.♕c2 d×c4 9.♗×f6 ♘×f6 10.♘×c4 ♕c7 11.a3 ♗e7 12.♗e2 0-0 13.0-0 ♗d7 14.b4 b6 15.♗f3 ♖ac8 16.♖fd1 ♖fd8 17.♖ac1 ♗e8 (D**

"Alekhine has built a position à la Steinitz. The four bishops are lying low, waiting for the diagonals to open. Accordingly, Capablanca is carrying out his attack in the center and on the flanks slowly" (Bronstein). **18.g3 ♘d5 19.♘b2 ♕b8 20.♘d3 ♗g5 21.♖b1 ♕b7 22.e4 ♘×c3 23.♕×c3 ♕e7 24.h4 ♗h6 25.♘e5 g6 26.♘g4 (D)**

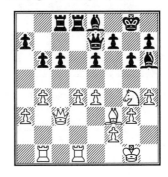

"And now White makes a mistake! Only by playing 26.♘c4!, threatening e4-e5 and ♘d6, could he consolidate his advantage. True, after 26...♗g7 27. e5 h5! 28. ♘d6, Black could obtain excellent counter-chances with the exchange sacrifice 28...♖×d6" (Alekhine). **26...♗g7 27.e5 h5 28.♘e3 c5! 29.b×c5 b×c5 30.d5 e×d5 31.♘×d5 ♕e6 32.♘f6+** "On the 32nd move, I blundered: instead of ♘f6+? I should have played ♖b7! whereupon Black hardly has, in my opinion, a satisfactory defense" (Capablanca). I agree with Capablanca, who believes that precisely this move is – in the exact meaning of the word – the decisive mistake. Better chances were offered by 32.♖b7 ♗×e5 33. ♕a5, though even in that case Black's game should be preferred. From a practical point of view, the move in the game also left White some drawing chances because the position now becomes very complicated" (Alekhine). **32...♗×f6! 33.e×f6 ♖×d1+ 34.♖×d1** (D)

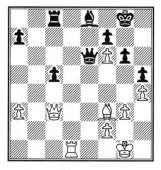

**34...♗c6!** "A quiet and very strong move: after the remaining minor pieces are exchanged, the role of the passed c-pawn will increase. At the same time, it would be very difficult for the white queen to penetrate in the vicinity of the g7-square" (Bronstein). **35.♖e1 ♕f5**

**36.♖e3 c4 37.a4 a5 38.♗g2 ♗×g2 39.♔×g2 ♕d5+ 40.♔h2 ♕f5 41.♖f3 ♕c5** (D)

At this point, the game was adjourned. In the analysis, White finds the best defensive chance. **42.♖f4! ♔h7** Having encountered the unexpected plan of White's defense, Alekhine commits an inaccuracy. Stronger, in his opinion, would be 42...♕b6!. **43.♖d4 ♕c6 44.♕×a5** "During the adjournment analysis, Capablanca found an amazing defense. That is why he is not afraid of the apparently unstoppable march of the black passed pawn to the first rank" (Bronstein). **44...c3 45.♕a7 ♔g8** Alekhine pondered over this move for 65 minutes, rejecting many variations, in particular, 45...♕×f6, 45...♖c7, and 45...♕c7. **46.♕e7 ♕b6 47.♕d7?** (D)

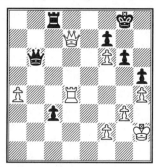

**47...♕c5!** "The move 44. ♕×a5 was very good and should have led to a draw. Unfortunately, later, I again made a mistake, after which I lost. Instead of

47.♕d7, it was necessary to play the rook to that square (47. ♖d7!). I, however, overlooked Black's simple reply, 47...♕c5!" (Capablanca).

Indeed, that was one of the key moments not only of the game but of the whole match. The best analysts tried to find here either a win for Black or a draw for White. As a result, it has been found that 47. ♖d7! indeed led to a draw. On 47...♕×f2+ 48.♔h1! ♕a2 48.♖d8+ ♖×d8 49.♕×d8+ ♔h7 50.♕f8, Black has to give a perpetual, as he is unable to capture the pawn at f6; or 47...♖f8 48.♕e3 (indicated by Tarrasch) 48...♕c6 (♕×f6) 49.♖c7!. As Levenfish and Romanovsky admonish, "[o]ne should hardly rebuke Capablanca for, with the limited time he had for thinking, not daring to embark on an unknown voyage."

**48.♖e4! ♕×f2+ 49.♔h3 ♕f1+ 50.♔h2 ♕f2+ 51.♔h3 ♖f8 52.♕c6 ♕f1+ 53.♔h2 ♕f2+ 54.♔h3 ♕f1+ 55.♔h2 ♔h7** Threatening 56...♖d8 with a mating attack. "Alekhine lays a trap: 56.♕×c3 ♕f2+ 57.♔h1 ♖d8 58.♕e1 ♕f3+ 59.♔h2 ♖d1 60.♕e3 ♕d5 61.♖e5 ♕a2+ 62.♖e2 ♕b1 63.♕f2 ♖h1+ 64.♔g2 ♕b7+ 65.♕f3 ♖h2+; with the king on g8, Capablanca would be able not only to escape but even to win by 60. ♖e8+" (Bronstein). **56.♕c4! ♕f2+ 57.♔h3 ♕g1 58.♖e2 ♕f1+** "Correct," notes Alekhine, "was 58...♕h1+ 59.♖h2 ♕f3! 60.♕f4 ♕d1." **59.♔h2 ♕×f6 60.a5** (D)

**60...♖d8** Alekhine activates his rook; 60...♕f1 wins as well. "60...♕f1! 61.♕e4 ♖d8 would decide matters at once. The text move is inaccurate, and should have at least greatly impeded the

win" (Alekhine). **61.a6?!** 61.♔g2 is met by 61...♕f5, and Black's rook will invade with decisive effect, e.g., 62.♕×c3 ♖d3−+. **61...♕f1! 62.♕e4** 62.a7 ♖d2 63.♖×d2 ♕×c4−+ **62...♖d2 63.♖×d2 c×d2 64.a7 d1♕ 65.a8♕** With such firepower on the board, the safety of the king's become the all important issue, so Black wins quickly: **65...♕g1+ 66.♔h3 ♕df1+** and Capablanca resigned, since 67.♔g2 is met by 67...♕h1#. **0-1**

"Alekhine played the concluding phase of the game excellently. The finale itself is distinguished by subtlety and elegance," Capablanca admitted and nobly added "I cannot win that way."

In the next, Capablanca's fatigue from the strain of the preceding encounter made itself felt. Having equalized the game, he did not find the best course of action, while the pseudo-active maneuver of his rook resulted in its loss. Capablanca resigned without resuming play.

Moscow magazine *Shakhmaty* journalist Vyacheslav Rakhmanov described, in "Dnevnik," the situation in and around the match, compiled on the basis of responses in the world press:

*Two losses in a row. What is going on with the public! During today's game, messengers on bikes and motorbikes drove up every minute to find out how the game was going. This was for those who for some reason or other could not get into the club. And what about the telephone calls! One telephone was continuously connected with the apartment of some ailing old man who was unable to go outside. His doctor has come to request the club board to allow this [the open telephone line]: his patient may die if he remains out of touch. The request of the old man was met.*

The excitement around the match had, by then, reached its climax. Few expected such developments. With only twelve games played, Alekhine has already achieved half the required number of wins. Now, Capablanca felt that he had been wrong for the London Regulations to include the requirement of an unlimited match until one player was six games up.

Meanwhile, Alekhine, seeing that his rival lacked confidence, decided to resort to a new sporting tactics when the score of the match was 3-2 in his favor, viz., to unnerve his opponent with a long series of draws. In this case, Capablanca would sooner or later seek to change the score and would have to take a risk. And so it happened: starting from the 13th game, one draw followed another, agreed on moves 27, 25, 30, and 24.

However, for their sheer beauty and sharpness, the draws in games 17 and 20 were as good as any won game. After the 17th game, Capablanca bitterly remarked that "[i]f I were unable to win this game, then I would not be able to win the match."

Indeed, in that encounter, the world champion could hope for a win. After the 24th move, the situation on the board was such that Black's pawn chain on the kingside was broken into several isolated pawns (or "islands"), while his center pawns were reliably blockaded by the white knights. Black's white-bound bishop, tied to the defense of the center pawn, was immobile, and on the whole, Black's position seemed to be in ruins. For thirty-five moves, Capablanca was doing his utmost to exploit his positional advantage, but all his efforts to break through the black defense were in vain...

**(79) Capablanca – Alekhine**
World Championship (17) Buenos Aires 1927
Queen's Indian Defense [E12]

**1.d4 d5 2.c4 e6 3.♘c3 ♘f6 4.♗g5 ♘bd7 5.e3 ♗e7 6.♘f3 0-0 7.♖c1 a6 8.a3 b6 9.c×d5 e×d5 10.♗d3 ♗b7 11.0-0 c5 12.d×c5 b×c5 13.♕e2 ♖e8 14.♗c2 ♕b6 15.♖fd1 ♖ad8 16.♘a4 ♕b5?!** 16...♕e6 fits Alekhine's active style better. **17.♕×b5 a×b5 18.♘c3 ♗c6 19.♗d3 c4?!** Positionally, a very risky move. 19...♖b8 20.♗f5 b4 is more active, e.g., 21.a×b4 ♖×b4 22.♗×d7 ♘×d7 23.♗×e7 ♖×e7 24.♘×d5 ♗×d5 25.♖×d5 ♖×b2 with good drawing chances because White has only pawns on the kingside.

**20.♗f5?!** The *zwischenzug* 20.♘d4!? is more precise because, after 20...♗b7 21.♗c2 b4 22.axb4 ♗xb4, the pin 23.♗a4 is very annoying. **20...b4 21.axb4 ♗xb4 22.♘d4 ♗b7 23.♗xd7 ♖xd7 24.♗xf6 gxf6** (D)

**25.♘de2?** There is no need to take the passive route. 25.♘f5 creates much more direct pressure. **25...♗d6 26.♖c2 ♗e5 27.♖cd2 ♖c7 28.♖a1 ♔g7 29.g3 ♖c5 30.♖a7 ♖b8 31.♘d4 ♔g6 32.f4?!** Capablanca rushes. 32.♘ce2 ♗c8 33.♔g2 is more unpleasant for Black. **32...♗c7 33.♔f2 ♖a5 34.♖xa5 ♗xa5 35.g4 h5!?** Alekhine eliminates his weakness and opens roads for his rook. **36.gxh5+ ♔xh5 37.♔f3 ♖g8** (D)

**38.♖g2?!** After exchanging rooks, the draw is more or less clear. Capablanca could have fought on with 38.♖d1. The objective result should still be a draw of course, but White has better practical chances with rooks on the board. **38...♖xg2 39.♔xg2 ♔g4 40.h3+ ♔h4 41.♘f5+ ♔h5 42.♔g3** 42.♘d6 ♗xc3 43.bxc3 d4+ 44.♔f2 (44.♘xb7? runs into 44...dxc3-+) 44...dxc3 45.♔e1= **42...♗b4 43.♘d4 ♔g6 44.♔g4 f5+ 45.♔g3** 45.♘xf5?? ♗c8 46.♘xd5 ♗xf5+-+ **45...♔f6 46.♘f3 ♗c5 47.♔f2 ♗b4 48.♘e5 ♗d6 49.♘f3 ♗b4 50.h4 ♔g6 51.♘e2 ♗c8 52.♘g3 ♗e6 53.h5+ ♔h6 54.♔e2 ♗e7 55.♔d2 ♗d8 56.♘d4 ♗c8 57.♔c2 ♗a5 58.♔d1** 58.♘dxf5+ ♗xf5+ 59.♘xf5+ ♔xh5 60.♘e7 ♔g4 61.♘xd5 ♔f3= **58...♗b4 59.♔e2 ♗d7 ½-½**

In the 20th game, Alekhine again was on the brink of defeat. The world champion played the opening excellently and soon won the exchange. However, in severe time trouble, both players made mistakes, and the game was eventually drawn. In the next game, Capablanca declined to exchange queens on move 14 and started playing for a win in a position where such an ambitious decision was hardly justified. Thus, the series of eight draws had psychologically prepared a catastrophe for the world champion in one of the decisive encounters.

### (80) Capablanca – Alekhine
World Championship (21) Buenos Aires 1927
Queen's Gambit Decined [D63]

"However, before this came the 21st game, which came as a shock to both the champion and the entire chess world: no one had yet defeated

Capablanca in such a way." (Kasparov)
**1.d4 d5 2.c4 e6 3.♘c3 ♘f6
4.♗g5 ♘bd7 5.e3 ♗e7 6.♘f3 0-
0 7.♖c1 a6 8.a3 h6 9.♗h4 d×c4
10.♗×c4 b5 11.♗e2** The main line
is 11.♗a2. **11...♗b7** 11...c5!? **12.0-
0** Playing for a bind with 12.b4 is answered by 12...a5 13.♕b3 a×b4
14.a×b4 ♘d5=. **12...c5 13.d×c5
♘×c5 14.♘d4 ♖c8 15.b4?!** This
weakens the important c4-square.
15.♗f3 ♕b6 16.♕e2= (Alekhine) was
called for. **15...♘cd7 16.♗g3 ♘b6
17.♕b3 ♘fd5 18.♗f3 ♖c4!?
19.♘e4 ♕c8 20.♖×c4** 20.♕b1!?
might be more precise, but Black keeps
a slight pull with 20...♖×c1 21.♖×c1
♘c4 (Kasparov). **20...♘×c4 21.♖c1
♕a8** (D)

**22.♘c3?** The following exchanges
leave White with passive pieces.
"Capablanca lost this game, only because he did not realize in time the dangers of his position" (Alekhine).
Capablanca should have tried the active
22.♘c5! with counterplay, e.g.,
22...♗×c5 23.b×c5 ♖c8 24.e4 ♘f6
25.a4 ♖×c5 26.♕b4 ♘d7 27.a×b5
a×b5 28.♘b3=. **22...♖c8 23.♘×d5
♗×d5 24.♗×d5 ♕×d5 25.a4 ♗f6
26.♘f3 ♗b2 27.♖e1** 27.♖b1? runs
into 27...♘a3!!−+. **27...♖d8 28.a×b5
a×b5 29.h3 e5! 30.♖b1** 30.e4 is
answered by 30...♕d3 31.♕×d3 ♖×d3

32.♖b1 f6−+. **30...e4 31.♘d4
♗×d4** (D)

**32.♖d1?** 32.e×d4 ♕×d4 33.♗f4 g5
34.♕g3 ♕d3 35.♖a1 offers more resistance. **32...♘×e3!** and Capablanca
resigend in view of 33.♕×d5 ♖×d5
34.f×e3 ♗×e3+−+. "Along with the
34th game, I consider this game to be
the best in the whole match" (Alekhine).
**0-1**

In his commentaries for *Izvestiya*
Capablanca wrote that "[t]his game was
won by Alekhine in great style. I was
playing for a win all along but confused
moves and got an inferior position.
Alekhine made good use of the advantages of his position, and, when I blundered on move 32, he at once forced
me to resign."

So, Capablanca lost as White for the
third time and the score in the match
became 4-2 in favor of Alekhine. The
next game lasted eighty-six moves, thus
becoming the longest in the match. This
time, it was Alekhine who had the initiative, but Capablanca neatly defended
and did not allow the challenger to
build on his success. After this draw,
there followed six more.

It was only in the 29th game that
Capablanca was able to win for the third

time, but his failure to win the 31st game, in which he had a big advantage completely demoralized him. He was virtually overwhelmed by Alekhine's fantastic resistance.

The impression was that the challenger was not all that tired, but sought to fight every game, striving for a win! After an interesting struggle and an impeccably played ending, Alekhine won the 32nd game on move 63 and, in fact, sealed the fate of the match because the score became critical: 5-3 in his favor. The short draw (28 moves) in the 33rd game showed that Capablanca had no energy left to attempt to change the course of the battle. At this point, many believed that the next game would be the last in this match between the giants. And so it happened. Alekhine opened vigorously, gained a positional advantage, then won a pawn and, in spite of Capablanca's heroic resistance – the game was adjourned twice – brought the game, and the match, to a successful conclusion.

**(81) Alekhine – Capablanca**
World Championship (34) Buenos Aires 1927
Queen's Gambit Declined [D51]

**1.d4 d5 2.c4 e6 3.♘c3 ♘f6 4.♗g5 ♘bd7 5.e3 c6 6.a3 ♗e7 7.♘f3 0-0 8.♗d3 d×c4 9.♗×c4 ♘d5 10.♗×e7 ♕×e7 11.♘e4 ♘5f6** 11...♘5b6 12.♗a2 e5 was the alternative. **12.♘g3 c5** 12...b6!? **13.0-0 ♘b6 14.♗a2 c×d4 15.♘×d4 g6 16.♖c1 ♗d7 17.♕e2** 17.♖c7? is met by 17...♕d6! 18.♖×b7? ♗c8 trapping the rook. **17...♖ac8 18.e4 e5 19.♘f3 ♔g7 20.h3 h6 21.♕d2** threatening the nasty double

attack ♕a5. **21...♗e6!?** Capablanca chooses a bold active defense, which seems to work. It is only later that he misses the correct continuation of this strategy. **22.♗×e6 ♕×e6 23.♕a5 ♘c4 24.♕×a7 ♘×b2 25.♖×c8 ♖×c8 26.♕×b7** (D)

**26...♘c4?** This misplaces the knight. After 26...♘d3 27.a4 ♖c3 28.a5 ♖a3 29.♖d1 ♘d7, Black's raging activity fully compensates for the missing pawn. **27.♕b4 ♖a8 28.♖a1 ♕c6 29.a4** 29.♖c1?! is met by 29...♖a4 30.♕e7 ♕d6 31.♕×d6 ♘×d6 32.♘e5 ♘f×e4 33.♘×e4 ♖×e4, and Black has good chances to defend. **29...♘×e4?** (D) Bringing the knight into play is correct, but Black is not ready to open the position. 29...♘e8 30.♕c3 ♕c5 31.a5 ♘ed6 makes it more difficult for White's knights to enter the game.

**30.♘×e5?** Surprisingly, it was better to choose the alternative 30.♘×e4 ♕×e4 31.a5 because Black cannot deal with the a-pawn and the defense of his king, e.g., 31...♕d5 (31...♕d3 32.♖c1 ♘xa5 33.♘xe5 ♕d5 [33...♕d8 34.♘xf7 ♔xf7 35.♕f4+ ♔g8 36.♖c7 ♕xc7 37.♕xc7+−] 34.♕b2 ♕b7 35.♕c3 ♔h7 36.♘g4+−) 32.a6 e4 33.♕c3+ f6 (33...♔h7 34.♘d4 ♖a7 35.♖a4 ♘e5 36.♖a5 ♕d6 37.♘b5 ♕f6 38.♕c5 ♖a8 39.♘c3 ♘d3 40.♘xe4+−) 34.♘d4 ♖a7 35.♖a4 ♘b6 36.♖a5+−. **30...♕d6** It is very hard to say if the resulting major piece endgame or the following one with rooks and knights offers more practical drawing chances: 30...♘xe5 31.♘xe4 ♕c4 32.♕xc4 ♘xc4 33.g3±. **31.♕xc4 ♕xe5 32.♖e1 ♘d6 33.♕c1!** The point of Alekhine's combination. 33.♕b4? ♖xa4= **33...♕f6** 33...♕d4? 34.♖d1 ♕b6 35.a5+− **34.♘e4 ♘xe4 35.♖xe4 ♖b8?** The blockade must be maintained with 35...♖a5. **36.♖e2?** Passed pawns must be pushed, and this is no exception. So, 36.a5! is correct because 36...♕f5 can be met by 37.♕a1+ ♔g8 38.♖e1 ♖a8 39.♖e5±. **36...♖a8 37.♖a2 ♖a5 38.♕c7 ♕a6?** Capablanca decentralizes his queen, which allows Alekhine to activate his forces vigorously. Kasparov's suggestion, 38...♖g5 39.♖a3 ♖f5 40.♕c2 ♖a5, makes it much more difficult to break the blockade. **39.♕c3+ ♔h7** (D)

**40.♖d2!** "Skilfully relieving the blockade of the passed pawn"(Alekhine). **40...♕b6** 40...♖xa4? 41.♖d8 g5 42.♖h8+ ♔g6 43.♖g8+ ♔f5 44.♕f3+ ♖f4 45.♕d5+ ♔f6 46.♕d8+ ♔e5 47.♖e8++− **41.♖d7** The sealed move. **41...♕b1+?** Since Black has to enter a rook ending later anyway, 41...♖f5 42.♕d4 ♕xd4 43.♖xd4 ♖a5 was better. **42.♔h2 ♕b8+ 43.g3 ♖f5 44.♕d4 ♕e8 45.♖d5!** 45.♖d8? runs into 45...♖xf2+. **45...♖f3 46.h4 ♕h8 47.♕b6 ♕a1** 47...♕a8 48.♖d8 ♖xf2+ (48...♕xa4 49.♕b2+−) 49.♕xf2 ♕xd8 50.♕xf7+ ♔h8 51.♕xg6 ♕d2+ 52.♔h3 ♕d7+ 53.♕g4+− (Tartakower). **48.♔g2 ♖f6** 48...♖a3? 49.♖d7 ♔g7 50.♕b7 ♕f6 51.♖xf7+ ♕xf7 52.♕b2+− **49.♕d4 ♕xd4 50.♖xd4 ♔g7** 50...♖a6 51.♔f3 ♔g7 52.♔e4 ♖a5 53.♔d3 ♔f6 54.♔c3+− **51.a5 ♖a6 52.♖d5 ♖f6 53.♖d4 ♖a6 54.♖a4 ♔f6 55.♔f3 ♔e5 56.♔e3 h5 57.♔d3 ♔d5 58.♔c3 ♔c5 59.♖a2 ♔b5 60.♔b3 ♔c5 61.♔c3 ♔b5 62.♔d4!** White will now win on the kingside. **62...♖d6+ 63.♔e5 ♖e6+ 64.♔f4 ♔a6** 64...f6 65.a6 ♖xa6 66.♖xa6 ♔xa6 67.♔e4+− (Tartakower). **65.♔g5 ♖e5+ 66.♔h6 ♖f5 67.f4** The game was adjourned for the second time here. **67...♖c5 68.♖a3 ♖c7 69.♔g7 ♖d7** (D)

**70.f5** 70.♔f6!? is easier: 70...♖c7 71.f5 gxf5 72.♔xf5 ♖c5+ 73.♔f6 ♖c7 74.♖f3 ♔xa5 75.♖f5++− (Alekhine). **70...gxf5 71.♔h6 f4 72.gxf4 ♖d5 73.♔g7 ♖f5 74.♖a4 ♔b5 75.♖e4 ♔a6 76.♔h6 ♖xa5 77.♖e5 ♖a1 78.♔xh5 ♖g1 79.♖g5 ♖h1 80.♖f5 ♔b6 81.♖xf7 ♔c6**

**82.罝e7 1-0** Here the game was again adjourned. The following day, in the morning of November 29, 1927, Alekhine was handed Capablanca's letter written in French.

"Dear Alekhine, I resign the game. Thus you are world champion. Please accept my congratulations upon this success and my best wishes. Please also congratulate Mrs. Alekhine for me. Sincerely yours, J.R.Capablanca."

The same evening Capablanca went to congratulate the new champion. The American Telegraph Agency mentioned, in particular, that

*...when both the opponents entered the hall where the match was played, the large audience that gathered there gave them an ovation. Capablanca, as everyone expected, made a short speech in which he remarked about his resigning the 34th game and proclaimed Alekhine world champion. Next, Capablanca expressed his certitude that Alekhine would remember their struggle with good feeling. He himself especially appreciates*

*that it was Alekhine who defeated him.*

*The words of gratitude Alekhine said in reply to Capablanca were met with a stormy applause by the audience. In conclusion, both the opponents shook hands and embraced each other, thus inviting a fresh explosion of greetings from those present.*

A week later, on December 8, a special celebration was held to honor Alekhine at the Buenos Aires chess club, where he was awarded the world champion's gold medal. Capablanca was not present at this ceremony. In a brief speech, the new champion thanked the organizers, who, incidentally, had spent $15,000 (USD) on the match. Thus, having won the match with the score +6 -3 =25, Alekhine became the fourth world champion in the history of chess.

"For the first time in my entire chess career, I was faced, in Buenos Aires, with the unique opportunity of the highest sporting achievement and... I played as never before," Alekhine said. And, many years later, after Capablanca had died, Alekhine, in an outline for a book about him, sincerely admitted, "How did it happen that he lost the match? I must confess that even now I cannot answer exactly this question, for, in 1927, I did not believe that I was superior to Capablanca. Perhaps the chief reason for his defeat was the overestimation of his own powers arising out of his overwhelming victory in the 1927 New York Tournament, and his underestimation of mine."

### 1927 World Chamionship Match

| | 1 | 2 | 3 | 4 | 5 | 6 | 7 | 8 | 9 | 10 | 11 | 12 | 13 | 14 | 15 | 16 | 17 | 18 |
|---|---|---|---|---|---|---|---|---|---|---|---|---|---|---|---|---|---|---|
| Alekhine | 1 | ½ | 0 | ½ | ½ | ½ | 0 | ½ | ½ | ½ | 1 | 1 | ½ | ½ | ½ | ½ | ½ | ½ |
| Capablanca | 0 | ½ | 1 | ½ | ½ | ½ | 1 | ½ | ½ | ½ | 0 | 0 | ½ | ½ | ½ | ½ | ½ | ½ |

| 19 | 20 | 21 | 22 | 23 | 24 | 25 | 26 | 27 | 28 | 29 | 30 | 31 | 32 | 33 | 34 | T |
|---|---|---|---|---|---|---|---|---|---|---|---|---|---|---|---|---|
| ½ | ½ | 1 | ½ | ½ | ½ | ½ | ½ | ½ | ½ | 0 | ½ | ½ | 1 | ½ | 1 | 18½ |
| ½ | ½ | 0 | ½ | ½ | ½ | ½ | ½ | ½ | ½ | 1 | ½ | ½ | 0 | ½ | 0 | 15½ |

A month later, in the Uruguayan journal *Mundial* published an "Article about Master José Raúl Capablanca" and the recent match (December 1927). The journal was then received by many outstanding players who were the members of the Editorial Board. Along with Capablanca, there were Alekhine, Emanuel Lasker, Réti, Tarrasch, Grünfeld, Tartakower, Vidmar and others.

"It was a long and hard struggle," stated Capablanca. Characterizing the play of the winner, he was brief: in the openings Alekhine had not surpassed him; in the middlegame, he played well; but where he excelled was the endgame, which he obviously plays better than everyone else and better than the other phases of the game. "Overall Alekhine played in this match better than I, and, therefore, he deserves the success he has achieved."

So, how did the chess world take the outcome of this unprecedented competition – without parallel in the degree of passions, fierceness, and stubbornness of struggle? Naturally, the reaction was different in different countries and among different fans. Some were glad and others, disappointed; some were elated because of the victory of the man whose creativity they admired, others could not understand why their idol had suffered a fiasco...

Responses from Soviet Russia, where the course of the battle was followed so closely and with such sympathy, were optimistic. All the twists and turns of the contest in the far-off Argentina were covered on the pages of the major newspapers, *Pravda* and *Izvestiya*, as well as the chess magazines *Shakhmaty, Shakhmatny listok, 64* (See, Russia).

In the articles and books by Romanovsky, Levenfish, Ilyin-Genevsky and other Soviet masters, it was emphasized that Alekhine's victory was, on one hand, the fulfillment of the old dream that had existed in Russia ever since the battle of Chigorin with Steinitz for the world championship, and, on the other hand, the triumph of the more progressive creative approach toward the art of chess, in which the might of a genius of combination combined with the theoretical achievements of modern chess thought and the perfection of technique.

Among the responses, there were also emotional outbursts of emigrant friends, who rejoiced at the victory of the Russian grandmaster. Alekhine was acclaimed by the well-known chessplayers who then lived in France

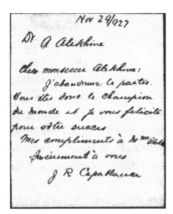

*Capablanca's letter of November 29, 1927*

grandmaster Ossip Bernstein and master Eugene Znosko-Borovsky (See, France).

Alekhine's victory was also hailed by the second world champion Emanuel Lasker who emphasized that "both rivals were in their prime (one can even say at the apogee of their powers!) and the games were almost without exception very valuable, representing a series of stubborn and sharp fights...The conclusions to be drawn by the entire chess world are tremendously important: the rejuvenation of not only strategic principles or theoretical variations but also the culture of the game itself, the rejuvenation that was already becoming necessary in order to avoid the stagnation that threatened our art!"

In special articles devoted to the results of the match, published in the magazines *Shakhmaty* and *Shakhmatny listok*, Richard Réti noted that Alekhine's victory was quite a natural and logical outcome because

*"The dream of my life has come true. Now – new tasks, new responsibility" Alexander Alekhine, 1927.*

*[i]n all games won by Alekhine, under the icy cover of modern chess technique, there burns a passionate search for new ways...With the present match, Alekhine has proven, though we have known before, that he is the better psychologist than Capablanca...The victory has only turned out possible as a result of a long struggle with incessant pressure of various alternat-*

*ing threats, complications and combinations – such that only an artist with an inexhaustible imagination is capable, i.e., Alekhine, who did not for a minute allow Capablanca to resort to his favorite method of simplifications, bringing the game to the level of pure technique, where without a doubt he is the greatest master.*

The historical match Capablanca-Alekhine continues to attract the attention and research from the creative heritage of the two great champions even today. Goldin, Fridstein, I. Zaitsev, Lilienthal, and Kasparov have contributed to the analysis of a number of games from the match. Grandmasters Hübner and Timman showed much interest in the match at the turn of the century. While Kasparov, in the first volume of his work *My Great Predecessors*, has considered it from both the point of view of Capablanca and that of the winner, Alekhine. Among the chief reasons for the fall of the champion, he mentions "the excessive complacency and, as a consequence, weak preparation, the habitual desire to win without straining himself to calculate 'dangerous variations'..." On the other hand, the triumph of Alekhine's creative creed, that "was once and for all formulated" in Buenos Aires, is evident.

The factors that decided the outcome of the match were "Alekhine's superiority in assessing complicated, dynamic positions, in fusing positional and tactical ideas and, last but not least, in using psychology."

**Bogoljubow, Efim Dmitriyevich** (April 14, 1889, Stanislavchik Village, Kiev Governorship-June 18, 1952, Triberg, Germany)

An international grandmaster who played two world championship matches (1929 and 1934) with Alekhine. He, to the chagrin of his parents, stopped studying theology and refused to follow in his father's footsteps of joining the clergy. At 18-years old, he entered the Kiev Polytechnic Institute but dropped out two years later because of his passionate involvement with chess. He soon became one of the leading Ukrainian players. In the summer of 1914, he participated in the the German Chess Congress, an international tournament held in Mannheim, where he was interned when the First World War erupted. In Germany, he found his love and happiness, having met Frieda Kaltenbach in Triberg. He remained a Russian citizen until 1926, twice becoming Russian champion (1924, 1925). In 1925, he achieved the finest success of his life by placing first (ahead of Capablanca and Lasker) in the great Moscow tournament. Then, the chess world recognized him as the new challenger to the world title. And, soon after Alekhine won the world champion title, Bogoljubow challenged him to a world championship match. By mutual agreement, the match would being in September 1929. By that time, Bogoljubow had already become a naturalized German citizen. His daughters, Sonya and Tamara, had grown up. It was three years since he had been stripped of his Russian champion's title, and he refused Soviet citizenship. The reason for that was his intention to participate in a tournament in Italy (Meran

1926), where Mussolini was in power. On April 14, 1929, the grandmaster celebrated his 40th birthday; he was in his prime and dreamed of winning the world title.

The distinguishing feature of Bogoljubow's talent was his rich imagination, revealed in combinational complications and great optimism. According to Rudolf Spielmann, "the main feature of his (Bogoljubow's) character is boundless optimism." Analyzing Bogoljubow's games and credo, Alekhine wrote, in an article about the coming match, that "Bogoljubow is aggressive and inventive. I agree that we have something in common in understanding the essence of the game of chess, but we have entirely different views of both the life and the principles of struggle. He views his opponent as an excellent experimental field for the application of his art and never attempts to study his opponent. He often relies on wonder where knowledge is necessary."

And twice the wonder failed to materialize. Bogoljubow was defeated in his world championship matches with Alekhine in 1929 and 1934; both times the winner had to score the majority of points in thirty games. The first of the matches was held in a number of German and Dutch cities, ending with the score 9½-15½, the second in eight German cities. It started in Baden-Baden on April 1, 1934 and ended on June 14, 1934 in Berlin with a score of 10½-15½ (See, World Championship Matches).

Bogoljubow was champion of Germany (1925, 1931 and 1933) and of West Germany (1949). He won a number of

*Efim Bogoljubow*

international tournaments: Stockholm (1919), Berlin (1919, 1926, 1928), Bad Kissingen (1928), Bad Nauheim (1935), and Stuttgart (1939) among others.

Bogoljubow made his contribution to opening theory, having worked out new lines in the King's Gambit and the French Defense, some systems in the Queen's Gambit and the Queen's Indian Defense. "I feel a special attachment to Bogoljubow's best games," Emanuel Lasker used to say. "He is an unusually gifted chessplayer."

### (82) Alekhine – Bogoljubow
World Championship (22) Mannheim 1934
Nimzo-Indian Defense [E35]

**1.d4 ♘f6 2.c4 e6 3.♘c3 ♗b4 4.♕c2 d5 5.c×d5 e×d5 6.♗g5 h6 7.♗h4 ♘bd7 8.e3 0-0 9.♗d3 c5 10.d×c5 ♘×c5 11.♘ge2 ♘×d3+ 12.♕×d3 ♗e6 13.0-0 ♗e7**

**14.♖fd1?!** 14.♘f4! is more critical.
**14...♕a5 15.♘d4** 15.♗xf6?! ♗xf6
16.♘xd5 ♗xb2 17.♖ab1 ♖ad8
18.♘ef4 ♗e5= **15...♖fc8 16.♖ac1**
16.♘xe6!? fxe6 17.e4 uses White's
intiative directly, e.g., 17...dxe4
18.♘xe4 ♘xe4 19.♗xe7 ♕f5 20.f3
♘f6 21.♕xf5 exf5 22.♗xf6 gxf6
23.♖d7. **16...♖c4 17.b3** 17.♘xe6
fxe6 18.e4 ♔h8= **17...♖c5**
17...♖xc3? 18.♖xc3 ♘e4 19.b4+-
(Bogoljubow) **18.♘a4 ♖xc1**
**19.♖xc1 ♖c8 20.♖xc8+ ♗xc8**
**21.♕c3 ♕d8!** Bogoljubow keeps his
queen, which can help apply pressure
on the dark squares. **22.f3 ♗d7**
**23.♘b2 ♕b6 24.♘d3** (D)

**24...♘e4!?** A good way to reduce the
pressure and obtain counterplay.
**25.fxe4** 25.♕e1 is met by 25...♘g5
because 26.f4 can be answered by
26...♘h3+ 27.gxh3 ♕g6+ 28.♕g3
♗xh4 29.♕xg6 fxg6. **25...♗xh4**
**26.exd5 ♕g6 27.♕d2?!** 27.♘f3
♗f6 28.♕d2 ♗g4 29.♘fe1 is more
critical, but Black's compensation
should be sufficient. **27...♕e4**
**28.♘f3?!** ♕xd5!? A small combination. **29.♘xh4 ♗b5!** Black's point.
**30.♘f3 ♗xd3 31.♔f2 ♕f5?!** (D)
31...f6!?

**32.g4!** In his typical style, Alekhine
grabs the initiative immediately.

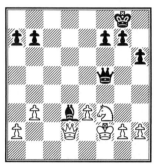

**32...♕e4 33.♕a5 ♗a6** 33...♕xg4??
34.♕d8++- **34.♕d8+ ♔h7**
**35.♕d4 ♕c2+ 36.♔g3 ♗f1**
36...♕xa2 37.♕e4+ g6 38.♕d5=
**37.♕d5 ♕c7+ 38.♔f2 ♗a6**
**39.♕e4+ ♔g8 40.♕e8+ ♔h7**
**41.♕e4+ g6 42.h4 ½-½**

Literary works: *Selected Games*
(Leningrad, 1925), *The 1925 Moscow
International Chess Tournament*,
parts 1 and 2 (Leningrad, 1925), *M. I.
Chigorin's Selected Games*
(Leningrad, 1926).

Bibliography
Brinckmann, A. *Grossmeister
Bogoljubow*. Berlin, 1953.

### Alekhine-Bogoljubow, September 6-November 12, 1929

The 5th FIDE Congress (1927) proclaimed Bogoljubow the "FIDE Champion." At that time, a major international tournament was held at the resort of Kissingen, in which Capablanca,
Bogoljubow, Euwe, Nimzowitsch, Réti,
Marshall, Tartakower, Spielmann, and
Tarrasch participated. Bogoljubow won
first prize, coming a full point ahead
of Capablanca. Encouraged by his victory, Bogoljubow sent a letter to the

world champion on August 28, challenging him to a match.

Having sent his query (written in Russian), he soon received a reply (written in French): "With these lines I make it known to you that, in principle, I accept your challenge, the first since I have won the title, and that, on my part, there are no objections to the match being held in 1929. It goes without saying that the match can only take place on the conditions worked out in London in 1922, incidentally signed by both of us."

The final agreement to hold the match between Alekhine and Bogoljubow was signed in Wiesbaden on July 9. Interestingly enough, it diverged from the London Agreement on many points. The match was determined by the best score out of thirty games. The winner had to score 15½ with at least six wins. Regardless of the outcome, Alekhine was to receive $6,000. Bogoljubow was playing for the title of world champion. It was decided to hold the match in those German and Dutch cities whose chess devotees contributed donations for the match.

Preparing for the match with Alekhine, Bogoljubow decided to take Max Euwe, one of the strongest European players, as his sparring partner. That training match ended with a marginal success for Bogoljubow (+2 -1 =7). Also, Bogoljubow decided, on the eve of the match, to participate in the Carlsbad Tournament where, except for Alekhine and Lasker, all the leading grandmasters of the time participated. When Bogoljubow failed in that tournament, having finished only eighth, Alekhine remarked that it would be frivolous on his part to draw conclusions from this that were "too optimistic."

The interest in the match was increased by a number of circumstances. An individual world championship competition had not taken place in Europe for nineteen years, since the Lasker-Schlechter and Lasker-Janowsky matches. Also, the match was to be played by two Russians who, not long before, had been champions of Soviet Russia and had since immigrated; Alekhine was now a French citizen, and Bogoljubow was now a German citizen. Their roads to "big chess" differed. Muscovite Alekhine became a chess master when only 16 years old, whereas Kiev's Bogoljubow used to receive the odds of a pawn and a move from first-category players even at 19. With their natural talent, both gravitated toward combinative play. However, their approach to the game was diametrically opposed. Characterizing his rival, Alekhine said that Bogoljubow

*...often relies on a miracle when the exact knowledge is necessary... He regards his personal satisfaction as the chief objective of the struggle. My understanding of struggle, however, has always been opposite. I believe that for success the following three factors are necessary: first, understanding of one's strength and one's weakness; second, an exact understanding of the opponent's strengths and weaknesses; and third, a higher objective than a moment's satisfaction. This aim I see in the scientific and artistic achievements that place the*

177

*game of chess among the other arts.*

The match started in Wiesbaden. German master Adolf Kramer described the atmosphere of the match for *Shakhmaty*:

*Alekhine and Bogoljubow are close friends and know the strong and weak spots of each other very well. Bogoljubow is an optimistic, sanguine man. Like a massive ship, he sits immovably at the board, while the nervous Alekhine knocks his finger on the table all the time and moves his feet.*

*At first the match was played in the beautiful kurhaus of Wiesbaden. But, the sounds of music could be heard there. This irritated the champion, and, at his request* (Alekhine's desire is the law, Kramer writes), *the match venue was moved to the quiet Paulinen Schlosschen located in an elevated part of the city, in a small room where only the seconds and the Chairman of the German Chess Union Hild could enter. For the spectators, there was a special demonstration hall, but one could not analyze games in it.*

*Without a word, with a spring to his step, the world champion moves through the crowd of spectators. Sometimes, he drops in the room for journalists and then he occasionally lets out one or two short phrases. "If I had more time, I could have played ♕c2," he*

*says about the 40th move of the second game. Or: "He offered a draw, but we will yet play for two hours more." Sometimes he comes to his wife, who is usually in the room for the journalists, and says a few words in Russian to her.*

*The corpulent Bogoljubow gets up from his chair much less frequently. His good nature does not allow him to answer spectator's queries with silence, so he hurries along to hide from them in the journalists' room. There is always an affable smile on his face, and the journalists will always hear a few phrases from him: "What does he want: even if I sacrifice the pawn at a7, it will be a draw all the same," or "He has declined to draw, well, let him remain annoyed for a few more moves.*

*O tempora, o mores*! So much spontaneity, so much sincerity! For the authors, who have witnessed the world chess championship battles in the Hall of Columns of the House of Unions, filled with thousands of Moscow spectators, in the Chaikovsky Concert Hall, in the Pushkin theatre, in the majestic Congress Halls of Baguio and Lyon, on the stages of Meran and Seville, the above described scenes appear as almost family-like health resort battles.

Having won the first game, Alekhine seized the initiative at the very start of the match. The challenger, who mishandled the Slav Defense, fell under the pressure of the white pieces. Alas! Even the wasp that stung the champion on move 18 did not help. The doctor was called for, gave him the emergency aid and the irritated champion played on furiously, forcing the resignation of the challenger on move 26. The second and third games were more stubborn, being drawn in fifty-one and seventy moves, respectively.

The next five games were all decided. At first, the rivals took turns winning – Bogoljubow, Alekhine, and again Bogoljubow, Alekhine… However, in the eighth game, the champion again won, and the overall score of the Wiesbaden part of the match became +4 -2 =2 in his favor. The most typical game of this period was the eighth, where the inexact opening play of the challenger enabled Black to seize the initiative and win by direct attack on the white king.

**(83) Bogoljubow – Alekhine**
World Championship (8) Wiesbaden 1929
Queen's Indian Defense [A50]

**1.d4 ♘f6 2.c4 b6?! 3.♘c3 ♗b7 4.f3 d5 5.c×d5 ♘×d5 6.e4 ♘×c3 7.b×c3 e6 8.♗b5+ ♘d7 9.♘e2 ♗e7 10.0-0 a6 11.♗d3 c5 12.♗b2?! ♕c7 13.f4 ♘f6 14.♘g3 h5!? 15.♕e2 h4 16.♘h1 ♘h5 17.♕g4?** Probably based on a miscalculation. The position of the dark-square bishop should be improved by 17.♗c1. **17...0-0-0 18.♖ae1** 18.f5 is met by 18...♗d6 19.e5 ♗×e5 20.d×e5 ♖×d3. **18...♔b8 19.f5?! e5 20.d5?** Bringing the knight back with 20.♘f2 has a much higher priority. **20...c4 21.♗c2 ♗c5+ 22.♘f2 g6!** Alekhine wants to open lines for his attack. **23.f×g6 ♖dg8 24.♗c1 ♗c8**

**25.♕f3 ♖×g6 26.♔h1?** (D) The queen sacrifice 26.♗d1 ♗g4 27.♕×g4 ♖×g4 28.♗×g4 was the best practical chance, but Black will win after 28...♘g3 29.h×g3 h×g3−+.

**26...♘g3+!  27.h×g3**  27.♔g1 ♗g4−+  **27...h×g3+ 28.♘h3 ♗×h3 29.g×h3 ♖×h3+ 30.♔g2 ♖h2# 0-1**

According to the previous arrangement, after eight games a two-week break in the match was announced, thereby allowing Alekhine to attend the regular FIDE Congress in Venice as the representative of the French Chess Federation. The match was resumed on October 3rd. It was moved from Wiesbaden to Heidelberg, where three more games were played. Two of them were drawn, and Alekhine won one, increasing his lead. Then, six games were played in Berlin at the "Café Koenig unter den Linden." Here the match jury was headed by Emanuel Lasker. The players were not isolated from the public, and the chess lovers who paid five marks for their seats were in the immediate proximity of the contestants. According to witnesses, the Berliners rather sympathized with Bogoljubow and met his victories in games 13 and 14 with applause. Nevertheless, in Berlin, too, Alekhine won one game more than his opponent, winning games 12,

16, and 17. Perhaps the culmination of the match was reached in the 15th game, in which Bogoljubow, who gained a positional advantage, overestimated his chances and refused to simplify the game. Alekhine, who was in severe time-trouble, sacrificed a pawn and, after the necessary exchanges, managed to force a draw.

Characterizing the situation at the match, master Adolf Seitz reported to *Shakhmaty* that

*Alekhine is extremely nervous – more than usual. He spends a lot of time in the opening and subsequently he is almost always in extreme time pressure. Then, he keeps looking at the clock all the time, as if piercing the dial with sparkling eyes. When it is the turn of his opponent to think, he strides around the hall with big steps, sometimes stopping before the demonstration board and scrutinizing it most closely, as if hoping to notice something new...Alekhine gave up smoking a long time ago (and therefore feels much better now), while Bogoljubow incessantly smokes thick "Havanas" or cheap Swiss cigarettes. One can always observe his characteristic gestures: now he is sitting, pondering over the position, now a few short fast draws on the cigar or cigarette and immediately after that a swiftly made move. On the other hand, Alekhine makes his move slowly and cautiously...*

**(84) Alekhine – Bogoljubow**
World Championship (17) Berlin 1929
Grünfeld Defense [D70]

**1.d4 ♘f6 2.c4 g6 3.f3 d5 4.c×d5 ♘×d5 5.e4 ♘b6 6.♗e3 ♗g7 7.♘c3 ♘c6 8.d5 ♘e5 9.♗d4 f6?** This weakens the light squares too much. 9...0-0 is the main line. **10.f4 ♘f7 11.a4 e5 12.d×e6 ♗×e6 13.a5 ♘d7 14.a6 b6 15.♗b5 ♕e7 16.♘ge2 c5 17.♗f2 0-0-0?!** Extremely risky, especially against the attacking genius Alekhine. But, White is also preferable after 17...0-0 18.♘d5 ♗×d5 19.♕×d5 ♖ad8 20.0-0±. **18.♕a4** 18.♘d5!? ♕d6 19.♕a4 ♗×d5 20.♖d1± **18...f5 19.e5 g5 20.♗c4! ♘d×e5 21.♗×e6+ ♕×e6 22.f×e5 ♘×e5 23.0-0 ♕c4?!** (D) 23...♘d3 is preferable but cannot stop Alekhine's attack either, e.g., 24.♘b5 ♖d7 25.♖ad1 ♕×e2 26.♘×a7+ ♖×a7 27.♕c6+ ♖c7 28.♕a8+ ♔d7 29.♕d5+ ♔c8 30.♖×d3 ♕e4 31.♕d6 ♕c6 32.♕g3±.

**24.b4!?** A very inspired move – a typical Alekine trademark. 24.♘b5 is also very strong because 24...♕×e2? runs into 25.♘×a7+ ♔b8 26.♘c6+ ♔a8 27.♘×d8 ♖×d8 28.♕b3+–. **24...♕×b4** 24...c×b4? 25.♘b5! ♔b8 26.♗×b6+– **25.♕c2?!** As usual, Alekhine goes for the direct attack. But here, the endgame after 25.♕×b4!? c×b4 26.♘b5 ♔b8 27.♖ab1± is even preferable. **25...♘d3 26.♖fb1** 26.♖fd1 ♗c3 27.♘×c3 ♕b2

28.♕×b2 ♘×b2 29.♖e1 also promises White an enduring initiative, but, if Alekhine had wanted an endgame, he would have chosen 25.♕×b4. **26...♕c4 27.♖a4 ♕e6 28.♘b5** (D)

**28...♔b8?** Running into a mighty blow. Bogoljubow had to reduce the number of attackers first by 28...♘×f2, but White is still better after 29.♔×f2 (29.♘×a7+? ♔b8 30.♕×c5 ♘h3+ 31.g×h3 ♖d1+–+) 29...♔b8 30.♖a3 becasue of his solid blockade on the light squares. **29.♘ed4! ♕e4** 29...♗×d4 30.♗×d4 ♖×d4 31.♖×d4 ♕e3+ 32.♔f1 +– **30.♘c3 ♕e8 31.♕×d3 c×d4 32.♗×d4 ♕e6 33.♕f3 ♕f7 34.♗×b6! 1-0**

After the seventeen games played in Germany, the score was +8 -4 =5 in Alekhine's favor. Had the match been played according to the London Agreement, it would have finished after a mere twelve games, when Alekhine scored his sixth win. It was becoming evident that with the uncompromising attitude of the players, the planned thirty games would hardly be played.

From Berlin, the match moved to The Netherlands. "The match on wheels" continued in The Hague, Rotterdam, Amsterdam, and again The Hague. The Dutch found Bogoljubow looking "fresh," while Alekhine, who arrived

with his wife, "tired." The longest games of the match were played in The Netherlands: the 24th, drawn in eighty-three moves, and the 19th won by Alekhine on move 77. Here, Bogoljubow also decided to subject his opponent to new trials, starting to open with 1.e2-e4. He was successful in the French Defense, but lost in the Ruy Lopez

### (85) Bogoljubow – Alekhine
World Championship (22) Amsterdam 1929
Ruy Lopez [C76]

**1.e4 e5 2.♘f3 ♘c6 3.♗b5 a6 4.♗a4 d6 5.c3 ♗d7 6.d4 g6 7.♗g5 f6 8.♗e3 ♘h6 9.0-0 ♗g7 10.h3 ♘f7 11.♘bd2 0-0 12.d×e5** 12.♖e1 is the main line. **12...d×e5 13.♗c5 ♖e8 14.♗b3 b6 15.♗e3 ♕e7 16.♕e2 ♘cd8 17.♗d5 ♗c6** 17...c6? 18.♗×f7+ ♘×f7 19.♗×b6± **18.c4 ♗×d5 19.c×d5 f5! 20.♘c4 ♘b7 21.♖ac1 ♖ad8 22.d6 ♘b×d6 23.♘×d6 ♖×d6 24.♕×a6 ♕d7 25.♖c2 c5 26.a4 f4 27.♗d2 g5 28.♕b5!?** Bogoljubow stops Alekhine's kingside attack. **28...♕×b5 29.a×b5 ♖d3!? 30.♖a1 ♘d6 31.♖a6 ♖b8** (D)

**32.♗c3?** The first step in the wrong direction. White should fight against Black's central invasion with 32.♖c3

c4 33.♖a4 ♖d8 34.♔f1=. **32...♘×e4 33.♗×e5?** 33.♖a4 ♖d1+ 34.♔h2 ♘d6 35.♘×g5 ♘b5 36.♘e4 offers more resistance. **33...♗×e5 34.♘×e5 ♖d1+ 35.♔h2 ♘d2! 36.h4** 36.b4?? ♘f1+ 37.♔g1 ♘g3+ 38.♔h2 ♖h1# **36...♖e8** (D)

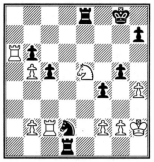

**37.♘f3?** The last chance to resist was 37.♘g4, but Black's attack continues: 37...♖ee1 38.♘h6+ ♔g7 39.♔h3 ♔×h6 40.♔g4 ♖e6 41.h×g5+ ♔g6 42.♖×c5 f3 43.g×f3 ♖g1+ 44.♔f4 h6 45.g×h6 ♖f6+ 46.♔e3 b×c5−+. **37...♘×f3+ 38.g×f3 ♖ee1 39.♔h3 h5** The pawn closes the mating net, so Bogoljubow resigned. **0-1**

This game turned out to be the last decided game in the match. The score now became 14-8 (+11 −5 =6) in favor of Alekhine, and, in order to be declared winner, he had to gain merely 1½ points in eight games. But, only three games were necessary, all of which were drawn. Thus, winning before the planned limit, Alekhine retained the title of world champion.

After the match ended, Bogoljubow told the Düsseldorf newspaper *Der Mittag* that Alekhine had no rivals, and, in some years to follow, he would defeat any challenger. Despite that, he would again challenge Alekhine in four

or five years. "I do not agree to admit that I am vanquished after just one defeat," he declared. This match had also shown soothing else, viz., that it is much easier for Alekhine to struggle against players with well-defined combinative style. And, although his struggle with Bogoljubow fascinated the spectators, it was still inferior to that in Buenos Aires, as far as the depth of concepts was concerned.

### Alekhine-Bogoljubow, April 1-June 14, 1934

In the four and a half years that had elapsed since the first match, Bogoljubow had not achieved any new convincing successes. On the contrary, his results had become less and less impressive. He finished in second place in Stockholm (1930) and Bled (1930) and shared 5th-6th places in Bern (1932). In 1932, he also lost a match to Spielmann in Semmering (+3 -4 =3).

So, why was Bogoljubow again selected by Alekhine as the challenger? One of the reasons was that he met the financial requirements. Moreover, considering himself obliged to play a world championship match once in a few years, he had no doubts about winning that match. The curious thing about the second match is that, at Bogoljubow's insistence, it was pompously called a return match.

The conditions under which the second match was played were the same as the first, i.e., it was played for the majority of points to be scored out of thirty games. The match lasted for two and a half months, and it was held in twelve German cities, starting in Baden-Baden and finishing in Berlin.

There have been several books on the match, published in different languages, including the one by Bogoljubow (German) and the other by Lasker (English and Russian). In the foreword to the Russian edition, the former world champion felt that "[t]he games played between Alekhine and Bogoljubow in their return match are of great interest for students of the game. Although these games are far from being faultless, the struggle in them was very tense."

**(86) Alekhine – Bogoljubow**
World Championship (2) Baden-Baden 1934
Semi-Slav Defense [D48]

**1.d4 ♘f6 2.c4 c6 3.♘f3 d5 4.e3 e6 5.♗d3 ♘bd7 6.♘c3 d×c4 7.♗×c4 b5 8.♗d3 a6 9.0-0 c5 10.a4 b4 11.♘e4 ♗b7 12.♘ed2 ♗e7 13.a5?!** 13.♕e2 is played more often and is more critical. **13...0-0 14.♘c4 ♕c7 15.♕e2 ♘g4!** A strong counterattack. **16.e4** 16.h3?? ♗×f3–+ **16...c×d4 17.h3 ♘ge5?!** 17...♘gf6! 18.♗g5 h6 19.♗h4 ♘c5 20.♗g3 ♕d8 21.♘fd2 ♘fd7 creates more pressure. **18.♘f×e5 ♘×e5 19.♗f4 ♗d6 20.♗×e5** 20.♘b6? runs into 20...♘×d3! 21.♘×a8? ♘×f4–+; the alternative, 20.♘×e5!? ♗×e5 21.♖fc1 ♕b8 22.♗×e5 ♕×e5 23.♖c4, gives White a pleasant initiative and is easier to play. **20...♗×e5 21.♘b6 ♖a7 22.♖ac1 ♕d6 23.♖c4 f5?** Ultimately, this just opens the e-file for White. Black should just hold the position with 23...♗h2+ 24.♔h1 ♗f4=. **24.e×f5 e×f5 25.♖e1 ♕g6 26.f3** (D)

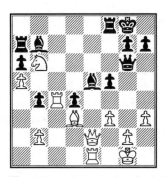

**26...♖e8?** Based on a miscalculation. 26...♗f4? is refuted by 27.♖×d4 ♕g3 28.♗c4+ ♔h8 29.♕e7+–. However, two other lines deserve attention: (a) 26...♗g3 27.♘d7 ♗×f3 28.♘×f8 ♗×e2 29.♘×g6 ♗×d3 30.♖c8+ ♔f7 31.♘e5+ ♗×e5 32.♖×e5; (b) 26...♗d6!? 27.♕e6+ ♕×e6 28.♖×e6 ♖d8 29.♗×f5 ♔f7 30.♖e1. In both cases, White keeps winning chances. **27.f4! ♕g3 28.f×e5 ♖×e5** 28...♗×g2 29.♕f2 ♕×d3 (29...♕×h3 30.♕×g2 ♕×d3 31.♖c8 ♕b5 32.♖ec1+–) 30.♔×g2+–. **29.♖c8+!!** Alekhine's point. **29...♔f7** 29...♗×c8 30.♕×e5 ♕×d3? 31.♕e8#. **30.♕h5+ g6 31.♕×h7+ ♔f6** 31...♔e6 32.♕d7+ ♔f6 33.♕d8+ ♔g7 34.♕f8+ ♔h7 35.♕h8#. **32.♖f8+ ♔g5** 32...♔e6 33.♕d7#. **33.h4+ ♔f4** 33...♕×h4 34.♕×h4+ ♔×h4 35.♖×e5+–. **34.♕h6+ g5 35.♖×f5+! ♖×f5 36.♕d6+ ♔g4 37.♗×f5+ 1-0** and Black resigned in view of 37...♔×f5 38.♕e6+ ♔f4 39.♕f6+ ♔g4 40.♕×g5#.

After the 4th game, the score was 3-1 in favor of Alekhine.

**(87) Alekhine – Bogoljubow,Efim**
World Championship (4) Willingen 1934
Semi-Slav Defense [D31]

**1.d4 d5 2.c4 c6 3.♘c3 ♘f6 4.e3 e6 5.♗d3 ♘bd7 6.f4?!** Positionally very risky beause Black can sooner or later attack the center with c5. **6...d×c4 7.♗×c4 b5 8.♗d3 ♗b7 9.♘f3 a6 10.a4 b4 11.♘e2 c5 12.0-0 ♗e7 13.a5?!** White does not have time for this ambitious advance. 13.b3 0-0 14.♗b2 is more natural. **13...0-0 14.♘g3 g6 15.♕e2 c×d4 16.e×d4** (D)

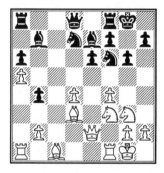

**16...♘b8!** A very strong and typical redeployment of the knight. **17.♘e5** 17.f5? is calmly met by 17...e×f5 18.♗×f5 ♘c6. **17...♘c6!** The greedy 17...♕×d4+? 18.♗e3 ♕d8 19.♗b6 ♕e8 20.♗c2 plays into White's hands. **18.♘×c6 ♗×c6 19.♗c4?** Alekhine simply has to take the pawn with 19.♗×a6, but Black has pleasant play in this case as well. **19...♗b7** "Black has a strategically won position" (Lasker). **20.♗e3 ♕d6 21.♖ad1 ♖fe8 22.b3 ♗f8 23.♖d3 ♕c7 24.♕a2 ♗d6 25.♗d2 ♕c6 26.♗e1 ♖ad8 27.♖d2 ♗e7 28.♕b2 ♖d7 29.♖c2 ♕d6?** 29...♘g4! is more powerful because 30.f5 runs into 30...♘e3 31.f×e6 f×e6 32.♖e2 ♘×c4 33.b×c4 ♕×c4−+; but not 29...♖×d4? because of 30.♗×a6!. **30.♘e2 ♘d5** 30...♘g4!? **31.♕c1 ♗d8 32.♗g3 ♕e7?** The following regrouping is very slow. 32...♕c6!

33.♖f3 (33.♗d3? ♘c3−+) 33...♗f6 is a more hamonious set-up. **33.♖a2 ♕f6 34.♕d2 ♕f5 35.♗d3 ♕f6 36.♗c4 ♗e7 37.♕d3 ♖ed8?!** The pawn sacrifice is not correct, so 37...♖a8 is called for. **38.♗e1?!** Alekhine should grab the pawn with 38.♗×a6 ♗×a6 39.♕×a6 ♕f5 40.♗f2. **38...♕f5 39.♕d2** Now, 39.♗×a6? can be met by 39...♗×a6 40.♕×a6 ♕b1 41.♖d2 ♘e3−+. **39...♕e4 40.♗d3 ♕e3+ 41.♗f2** The sealed move. **41...♕×d2 42.♖×d2 ♖c8 43.♗c4 ♔g7 44.g3 ♖cd8 45.♖c1 h6 46.♗d3 f5 47.♖dc2 g5** (D)

**48.g4!?** Alekhine tries to confuse matters in his typical style and is immediately successful. Lasker finds that this "combination ... is very beautiful." **48...♗×f4?** Bogoljubow had at least two better alternatives in 48...f×g4 49.f5 ♗d6 50.f×e6 ♖e7 51.♘g3 ♘f4, and 48...♗f8 49.g×f5 e×f5 50.f×g5 h×g5, when Black is preferable in both cases. **49.♘×f4 g×f4 50.g×f5 e5 51.♖e1 e×d4?** (D)

51...♖×d4 52.♗×d4 ♖×d4 53.♖c7 ♔f6 54.♖×e5 ♗d5 55.♖×e7 ♖×d3 with good drawing chances because of Black's activity. **52.♖×e7+!! ♖×e7 53.♗h4 ♔f7 54.♗×e7 ♔×e7 55.♖c7+ ♖d7 56.f6+ ♔e8 57.♗g6+ ♔d8 58.f7! ♔×c7**

*1934 World Championship Match*

| | 1 | 2 | 3 | 4 | 5 | 6 | 7 | 8 | 9 | 10 | 11 | 12 | 13 | 14 |
|---|---|---|---|---|---|---|---|---|---|---|---|---|---|---|
| **Alekhine** | ½ | 1 | ½ | 1 | ½ | ½ | ½ | ½ | 1 | 0 | 1 | ½ | ½ | ½ |
| **Bogoljubow** | ½ | 0 | ½ | 0 | ½ | ½ | ½ | ½ | 0 | 1 | 0 | ½ | ½ | ½ |

| 15 | 16 | 17 | 18 | 19 | 20 | 21 | 22 | 23 | 24 | 25 | 26 | T |
|---|---|---|---|---|---|---|---|---|---|---|---|---|
| ½ | 1 | 1 | ½ | ½ | ½ | 1 | ½ | 0 | 0 | 1 | ½ | 15½ |
| ½ | 0 | 0 | ½ | ½ | ½ | 0 | ½ | 1 | 1 | 0 | ½ | 10½ |

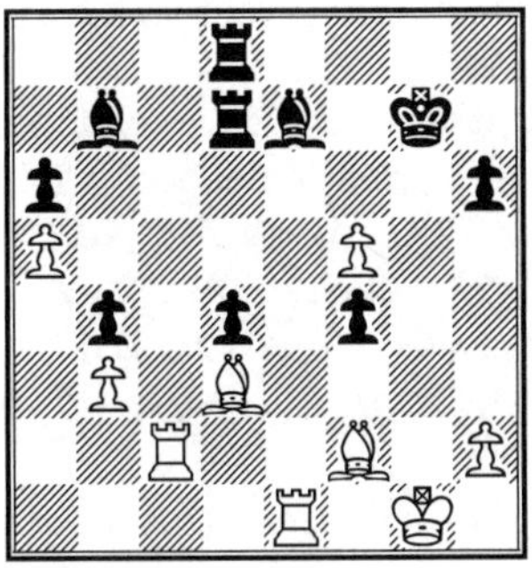

**59.f8♕ f3 60.♕×b4 ♖d6 61.♗d3 1-0**

After the 17th game, played in Kissingen, the champion's lead reached five points (+6 -1 =10). It was clear that the "return" would never take place. Alekhine was stronger in all phases of the game. He played more spontaneously and was not subjected this time to the "old malady" of having time trouble. Having scored the required 15½ points in twenty-six games, Alekhine again won the match before the game limit, retaining the world title.

**Alekhine-Euwe, October 3-December 5, 1935**

Just as Capablanca in his time, Alekhine was full of optimism and believed in his star. As far back as 1933, he had proposed a ten-game match to Max Euwe on board a steamship sailing from The Netherlands to Indonesia, and he

even agreed to consider it a world championship match. The prudent Dutchman was thinking... Teaching math at one of Amsterdam's gymnasia for girls, Euwe did not play often, and, when he did, it was only short matches. And, although he had no ambition to become a professional player, Caissa, the muse of chess, did not let him go.

Euwe wrote to Alekhine that a match aboard a ship would hardly be feasible, but, should he agree, it would be possible to hold a world championship match of thirty games in The Netherlands in the autumn of 1935.

In May 1935, the official agreement to hold the match was signed. Although Alekhine was sure of the outcome, he showed enough prudence that he insisted on a return-match clause guaranteeing, which, in the event Euwe won, had to be held within two years after the finish of the first match. In August, Alekhine again played for France in the world chess Olympiad in Warsaw, and, for the first time, did not take first prize on board one, ceding it to Flohr. At last, all the preparations for the match had been completed, Hans Kmoch having been appointed the Chief Arbiter. The opponents' seconds were Geza Maróczy for Euwe and Salo Landau for Alekhine.

185

The first game of the match was held October 3 in Amsterdam at the Carlton Hotel, where the world champion was staying. In this game, Alekhine convincingly appeared to demonstrate his superiority.

**(88) Alekhine – Euwe**
World Championship (1) Amsterdam 1935
Slav Defense [D17]

**1.d4 d5 2.c4 c6 3.♘f3 ♘f6 4.♘c3 d×c4 5.a4 ♗f5 6.♘e5 ♘bd7 7.♘×c4 ♕c7 8.g3 e5 9.d×e5 ♘×e5 10.♗f4 ♘fd7 11.♗g2 ♗e6?!** 11...g5 and 11...f6 are the main lines. **12.♘×e5 ♘×e5 13.0-0 ♗e7 14.♕c2! ♖d8** 14...♕a5? runs into **15.♘b5±. 15.♖fd1 0-0 16.♘b5 ♖×d1+ 17.♖×d1 ♕a5?** This meets with a beautiful refutation. 17...♕b6 18.♘d4 ♘g4 19.e3 ♗c8 20.♘f5 ♗×f5 21.♕×f5 ♘f6 is the lesser evil. **18.♘d4 ♗c8** (D)

**19.b4!! ♕c7** 19...♗×b4 is met by 20.♘b3 ♕c7 21.♕e4 ♗c3 (21...♗d6 22.♕d4 [Alekhine] 22...g5 23.♗×g5 ♗e7 24.♗×e7 ♕×e7 25.♕×a7±) 22.♖c1 ♗b2 (22...f5 23.♕e3±) 23.♖b1 g5 24.♗×g5 ♗a3 25.♗f6±. **20.b5 c5 21.♘f5 f6?! 22.♘e3 ♗e6?!** (D) 22...g5 23.♘d5 ♕d6 24.♗c1±

**23.♗d5!** Alekhine exchanges the most important defender of the light squares. **23...♗×d5 24.♖×d5 ♕a5?! 25.♘f5 ♕e1+ 26.♔g2 ♗d8 27.♗×e5 f×e5 28.♖d7 ♗f6 29.♘h6+ ♔h8 30.♕×c5 1-0**

Already in the second game, in which Alekhine adopted the Grünfeld Defense, Euwe fought back. So, the beginning of the match promised a very sharp struggle indeed, not a single draw in the first four games! The third game was a French Defense, and Alekhine again won the opening battle. After four games, the score was 3-1 in favor of the champion. And after ten games it was +5 -3 =2 in Alekhine's favor.

After four more games, the score had already been evened at 7-7! Alekhine looked tired. He was also somewhat annoyed by the necessity to move all the time from one city to another. At this point, the physical condition of the players became an important factor. While Euwe, who continued doing physical exercises and taking cold showers was in excellent form, Alekhine clearly looked unhealthy; he appeared nervous, smoked a lot, and also drank, not just mineral water...

*1935 World Championship Match*

| | 1 | 2 | 3 | 4 | 5 | 6 | 7 | 8 | 9 | 10 | 11 | 12 | 13 | 14 | 15 |
|---|---|---|---|---|---|---|---|---|---|---|---|---|---|---|---|
| **Euwe** | 0 | 1 | 0 | 0 | = | = | 0 | 1 | 0 | 1 | = | 1 | = | 1 | = |
| **Alekhine** | 1 | 0 | 1 | 1 | = | = | 1 | 0 | 1 | 0 | = | 0 | = | 0 | = |

| 16 | 17 | 18 | 19 | 20 | 21 | 22 | 23 | 24 | 25 | 26 | 27 | 28 | 29 | 30 | T |
|---|---|---|---|---|---|---|---|---|---|---|---|---|---|---|---|
| 0 | = | = | 0 | 1 | 1 | = | = | = | 1 | 1 | 0 | = | = | = | 15½ |
| 1 | = | = | 1 | 0 | 0 | = | = | = | 0 | 0 | 1 | = | = | = | 14½ |

In spite of this the struggle, there were no reprieves from the match. Only once, feeling unwell, did Alekhine ask for a postponement, a half-hour before the 21st game. Kmoch refused his request. "There are two thousand spectators gathered in the hall," he said, "they would not understand." Alekhine complied with this decision. He lost the game.

After twenty-four games the score was, as before, even, 12-12. Only six games remained. It was precisely the 24th game that Euwe considered the culmination of the match. In that game, Alekhine botched a relatively simple win in a pawn ending. In game 25, Alekhine sacrificed two pawns in order to obtain, as subsequent analyses have shown, a winning position. Suddenly, he initiated an incorrect combination on move 20 and, as a result, lost any chance even for a peaceful outcome.

After the 26th game, Euwe was already leading by two points. By unbelievable force of will, Alekhine managed to win the 27th game, reducing the gap. However, he had no strength left. Two draws followed and the last game was played in the largest concert hall of Amsterdam on December 15. It was Sunday, and the game started in the daytime. Alekhine came dressed in a frockcoat. Euwe said that he would agree to a draw at any time. It was already clear, after the opening, that Alekhine would be unable to win that game. After 40 moves of struggle, he extended his hand to Euwe and proclaimed in French, "Long live World Champion Euwe! Long live Chess Holland!"

What happened next? The champion's country rejoiced, and a song was composed about the new champion, "But Our Euwe Won." Leaving The Netherlands, Alekhine said that "[n]othing awful has happened. Let us assume that I loaned the title to Euwe for two years!" Thus, the Dutch player Max Euwe became the fifth world champion in chess history.

Emanuel Lasker, speaking before an audience at the Leningrad Philharmonic Hall on January 6, 1936, also touched on the Alekhine's loss in Holland, reminding everyone that

> *[e]ach defeat is a valuable lesson for the loser: he who never loses, never progresses. Alekhine*

187

*is, therefore, faced with the problem of learning the lesson of his defeat, and he who wishes to assure him that the present defeat is less deserved by him than his earlier victories is not his friend... Alekhine is a virtuoso in such positions where weak points are present both in attack and counterattack or defense. But positions with insufficient tension, without fine points, which are normally considered boring, conceal problems he was not prepared to face. Therefore, in the future, he should pay attention to exactly such positions. This is a matter of training, a task worthy of his chess past. He is also morally obliged to combine this task with taking care of his health, of his way of life...Now Alekhine is offered an opportunity to show the clarity of his thought by not becoming depressed, getting down to work in order to establish objectively the deficiencies of his style and systematically liquidate them.*

### Alekhine-Euwe, October 5-December 7, 1937

It was the second return match in history. Forty years before, Lasker had defeated Steinitz in their return match, after which there had been no comeback for the former champion. Lasker himself never claimed a return match. His successor, Capablanca, having initiated the historical London Agreement, never envisaged the possibility of a return match. Alekhine corrected his mistake.

Were the hopes of the former champion to be fulfilled this time? Many

columnists doubted that, basing their opinion on the physical condition of the rivals, the difference in age, and, lastly, their recent results. Everything appeared to be going Euwe's way. But, strangely enough, it all turned against him. The Dutch grandmaster was a good mathematician but a poor psychologist. He understood very clearly Alekhine's style as it was in 1935 but never expected to encounter Alekhine as he was in 1937.

On Alekhine's side was his great experience in match-play, including that on the highest level. And, for the second match with Euwe, he was preparing not only by thoroughly analyzing his games, preparing surprises in the openings, and carefully working out the match strategy but also was able, by a tremendous effort of will, to get rid of his own weaknesses and harmful habits. Also, he had another incentive to win: he wanted to come back to Russia as the world champion (See, Russia).

The opening ceremony was held in The Hague. At the ceremony, the Dutch Minister of Sciences and Arts, Slotemaker de Bruin, was present. The following day the Chief Arbiter Geza Maróczy started Euwe's clock; he had drawn the white pieces in the first game. Alekhine adopted the Slav Defense. On the 14th move, White came up with a novelty. While participating in the 1937 world chess Olympiad in Stockholm, shortly before the match, Euwe had noticed the game Turn-Oyanen. Alekhine was not there and adopted an ineffective plan and, in spite of desperate resistance, had to resign on the 50th move. Already in the second game, in which the Slav Defense was again adopted, Alekhine evened the score. The Slav Defense occurred rather often in the match – in eleven games, Alekhine playing as Black in eight of them. After two decisive games, there followed two draws, and, in the fifth game, Euwe again took the lead. Two days passed, and Alekhine restored the status quo. The score became 3-3. In that game, Euwe resigned on the 23rd move.

**(89) Alekhine – Euwe**
World Championship (6) Haarlem 1937
Slav Defense [D10]

**1.d4 d5 2.c4 c6 3.♞c3 d×c4 4.e4 e5 5.♗×c4?** As the following sacrifice is not correct, this goes too far from an objective point of view. The main options are 5.♞f3, 5.d×e5, and 5.d5. **5...e×d4 6.♞f3!?** This bold sacrifice is logical and "a fantastic move, which, perhaps, won...the match." (Kasparov). **6...b5?** Euwe miscalculates. The sacrifice can only be refuted by accepting it: 6...d×c3 7.♗×f7+ ♚e7 8.♕b3, and now 8...c×b2! (8...♞f6? runs into 9.e5 ♞e4 10.0-0 ♕b6 11.♕c4! with a strong attack.) 9.♗×b2 ♕b6! 10.♗a3+ (10.♗×g8 is met by 10...♖×g8 11.♕×g8 ♕b4+) 10...c5 11.♗×g8 ♖×g8 12.♗×c5+ ♕×c5 13.0-0. (D)

*Analysis Diagram*

Now comes the point of the refutation, found by Gontscharov and published in *64* in 1938. 13...♕h5!! 14.♕×g8 (14.♕b4+!? is more critical, but Black is still on top after 14...♚e8 15.♕c4 ♞c6 16.♕×g8 h6) 14...♗e6 15.♕h8 ♞c6 and Black is clearly better. **7.♞×b5 ♗a6** 7...c×b5 8.♗d5 +− **8.♕b3 ♕e7** 8...♗×b5? 9.♗×f7+ ♚d7 10.♞×d4 ♕b6 11.♗f4 ♕a5+ 12.♗d2 ♕b6 13.♕e6+ ♚c7 14.♞×b5+ ♕×b5 15.a4 ♕b6 16.♗×g8+− **9.0-0 ♗×b5 10.♗×b5 ♞f6** 10...c×b5 11.♕d5+− **11.♗c4 ♞bd7 12.♞×d4 ♖b8 13.♕c2 ♕c5 14.♞f5 ♞e5** (D)

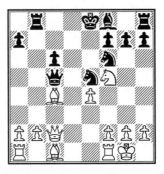

**15.♗f4!?** 15.♞×g7+ ♚d8 (15...♗×g7?? 16.♗×f7+ ♚×f7 17.♕×c5+−) 16.♞f5 ♕×c4 17.♕×c4 ♞×c4 18.♗g5 ♗e7 19.♖ac1 ♞e5 20.f4 ♞ed7 21.♞×e7 ♚×e7 22.e5 wins as well. **15...♞h5 16.♗×f7+** 16.♗×e5 ♕×e5 17.♕a4 ♕c7 18.♗d5+− is even stronger. **16...♚×f7 17.♕×c5 ♗×c5 18.♗×e5 ♖b5** 18...♖be8 19.♗d6 ♗b6 20.♖fe1+− **19.♗d6 ♗b6 20.b4 ♖d8 21.♖ad1 c5 22.b×c5 ♗×c5 23.♖d5 1-0**

After such a cruel defeat, Euwe discarded the Slav Defense and chose the Nimzo-Indian Defense, Catalan Opening, Réti Opening, and Queen's Gambit. It also seemed that Alekhine's rejection of 1.e2-e4 was a surprise for him.

Euwe's catastrophe in the sixth game shattered him so much that, in the next four games, he was able to score only a half-point. Having moved from Groningen to Amsterdam after the 11th game, Alekhine, in the best of spirits, celebrated his 45th birthday with a glass of apple juice!

But Euwe was not yet defeated, and his will to fight not yet broken. In the next nine games, he won two, lost one, and drew six. The score of the match became 11-9 in favor of Alekhine. But, after the defeat in the 21st game, Euwe was no longer able to resist.

### (90) Euwe – Alekhine
World Championship (21) Amsterdam 1937
Queen's Indian Defense [E16]

**1.d4 ♞f6 2.c4 e6 3.♞f3 b6 4.g3 ♝b7 5.♝g2 ♝b4+ 6.♝d2 ♝e7 7.♞c3 ♞e4?!** The main line is 7...0-0. **8.0-0 0-0 9.d5! ♞×d2 10.♛×d2 ♝f6 11.♖ad1?!** 11.♞d4 creates more pressure. **11...d6 12.d×e6** 12.♞e1!? **12...f×e6 13.♞d4 ♝×g2 14.♔×g2** 14.♞×e6? runs into 14...♛e7 15.♞×f8 ♝×c3 16.b×c3 ♝c6. **14...♛c8 15.♛e3** 15.♛c2!? **15...♝×d4 16.♖×d4 ♞c6 17.♖e4 ♖f6 18.f4?!** Too ambitious. Advancing the pawns in front of the king can easily backfire. The normal 18.♖f4 ♖×f4 19.♛×f4 ♛d7 20.♛e4 is slightly better for White. **18...♛d7 19.g4?! ♖af8** (D)

**20.g5?** This weaknens the king's haven and the light squares irreparably.

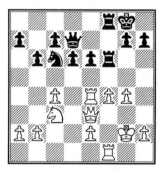

Instead, the light squares should be strengthened by 20.h3. **20...♖f5 21.h4?!** 21.♖×e6? ♞e5–+ **21...♛f7 22.♖f3?! ♔h8?** Unneccessary prophylaxis. The direct 22...d5! is stronger: 23.♖×e6 d4 24.♛e4 d×c3 25.b×c3 [25.♖×c6? c×b2–+ (Alekhine)] 25...♞d8 26.♖e7 ♛g6 with the point that 27.♖×c7?? ♖×g5+–+ (Botvinnik) is clearly better for Black. **23.♛d3?** (D) 23.♖×e6? runs into 23...♞e5 24.f×e5 ♛×e6–+; 23.♞b5! was necessary, when the position is more or less equal.

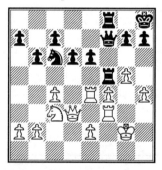

**23...d5!** Finally, Alekhine seizes the moment to open the position. **24.♖×e6?!** 24.c×d5 is more tenacious, but Black should win in the long run after 24...e×d5 25.♖a4 d4 (Alekhine) 26.♞b5 ♛e8 27.♞×d4 ♖×f4. **24...♞b4! 25.♛e3 ♞c2 26.♛d2 ♛×e6 27.c×d5 ♛f7?!** 27...♛d6 is more precise. **28.♛×c2** 28.♔g3 ♞e1

190

*1937 World Championsip Match*

| | 1 | 2 | 3 | 4 | 5 | 6 | 7 | 8 | 9 | 10 | 11 | 12 | 13 |
|---|---|---|---|---|---|---|---|---|---|---|---|---|---|
| Euwe | 1 | 0 | = | = | 1 | 0 | 0 | 0 | = | 0 | = | = | 1 |
| Alekhine | 0 | I | = | = | 0 | 1 | 1 | 1 | = | 1 | = | = | 0 |

| 14 | 15 | 16 | 17 | 18 | 19 | 20 | 21 | 22 | 23 | 24 | 25 | T |
|---|---|---|---|---|---|---|---|---|---|---|---|---|
| 0 | = | = | 1 | = | = | = | 0 | 0 | = | 0 | 0 | 9½ |
| 1 | = | = | 0 | = | = | = | 1 | 1 | = | 1 | 1 | 15½ |

29.♖f2 ♘g2 30.e3 ♘xh4 31.♔xh4 h6–+ (Alekhine) **28...♖xf4 29.♕d3 ♕h5 30.♖xf4 ♖xf4 31.♕h3 ♖g4+ 32.♔f2 h6! 0-1**

In the next four games, Alekhine scored 3½ points and thus reached the required 15½ points after twenty-five games, regaining the world title. In accordance with the match regulations, the opponents were to play all thirty games, but the remaining five games, in which Euwe scored three points, were not to be taken into account in the final result. Therefore, Alekhine won the match with the score 15½ (+10 -4 =11). "I have done in this match all I could," said Euwe "but Alekhine played better."

Soon after the match, articles by the participants devoted to the outcome, were published in the *Manchester Guardian*. Alekhine noted Euwe's erudition in the opening phase and his combinative talent. "But," Alekhine remarked, "here is a tactician who resolved to become, at any cost, a good strategist." The title of Euwe's article was symbolic – "Obituary." As always, Euwe was humble, acknowledging that "Alekhine played amazingly, and I am definitely not ashamed to be defeated by such an opponent."

**Kecskemet Tournament, June 25-July 14 1927**

After his match with Euwe and the tournament in New York, the outcome of which was quite favorable for Alekhine's psychological preparation for the coming world championship match with Capablanca, Alekhine felt dissatisfaction with his play, and lack of fighting spirit. To ameliorate such unpleasant feelings, he made a somewhat risky decision by agreeing to participate in a major international tournament in Hungary, to be held in less than three months before the match with Capablanca.

Subsequently, Alekhine explained that he had entered the competition at Kecskemet because it was to be a last trial of his form, and it would answer several tormenting questions but mainly whether his work of many years on improving his style of play had been fruitful. As became apparent, he was reassured that he could play quite confidently, and was in excellent sporting form. Therefore, the match would be hard-fought and exciting. The following games against Tartakower and Asztalos, which was awarded a brilliancy prize, are noteworthy. Not even the grueling 50-degree-Celsius heat impeded the creation of these master-pieces.

### (91) Alekhine – Tartakower
Kecskemet 1927
Caro-Kann Defense [B15]

**1.e4 c6 2.d4 d5 3.♘c3 d×e4 4.♘×e4 ♘f6 5.♘g3 e5?!** Tartakower's speciality, but Alekhine will obtain an annoying initiative. A slight advantage in developement is often very dangerous in near symmetrical positions with an open center because it is very difficult to generate counterplay. 5...h5 is played most often. **6.♘f3 e×d4 7.♘×d4 ♗c5 8.♕e2+!? ♗e7 9.♗e3 c5 10.♘df5 0-0 11.♕c4 ♖e8 12.♗d3 b6?** Black just does not have time for this. 12...♕a5+ is called for, which keeps White's advantage minimal. **13.0-0-0 ♗a6?!** (D) This runs into a thunderstorm, but good advice is already hard to give, e.g., 13...♗xf5 14.♘xf5 ♘bd7 15.♘xg7 ♚xg7 16.♗f5 ♕c7 17.♗xd7 ♖ed8 18.♗h3+–; 13...♗e6 14.♕h4+–.

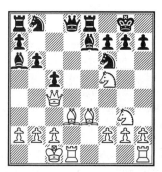

**14.♘h6+!! g×h6** 14...♚h8? allows a smother mate by 15.♘xf7+ ♚g8 16.♘h6+ ♚h8 17.♕g8+ ♘xg8 18.♘f7#. **15.♗×h7+ ♘×h7** 15...♚h8 16.♕xf7 ♘bd7 17.♘f5 ♗f8 18.♘h4 ♗g7 19.♗f5+–; 15...♚xh7?

16.♕×f7+ ♚h8 17.♖×d8+– **16.♕g4+ ♚h8 17.♖×d8 ♖×d8 18.♕e4** The final point as Black loses more matrial. **18...♘c6 19.♕×c6 ♗f8 20.♘f5 ♗c4 21.♗×h6 ♗d5 22.♕c7 ♖ac8 23.♕f4 ♖c6 24.♗×f8 ♖×f8 25.♕e5+ ♘f6 26.♘d6 1-0**

### (92) Alekhine – Asztalos,Lajos
Kecskemet 1927
Semi-Slav Defense [D43]

**1.♘f3 d5 2.c4 e6 3.d4 ♘f6 4.♗g5 h6 5.♗×f6 ♕×f6 6.♘c3 c6 7.♕b3 ♘d7 8.e4 d×e4 9.♘×e4 ♕f4 10.♗d3 ♗e7 11.0-0 0-0 12.♖fe1 ♖d8 13.♖ad1 ♕c7 14.♘g3 ♘f8 15.♕c3 a5 16.a3 a4 17.♘e5 ♕a5 18.♕c1 ♗d7** 18...♖xd4? 19.♗h7+ ♚xh7 20.♖xd4± **19.c5 b5 20.♗e4 ♕c7 21.♕c3** 21.♘h5 ♗e8 22.♕f4 was the alternative. **21...♗e8 22.♘e2 ♖a6 23.♘c1 ♘d7 24.♘×d7** 24.♘cd3!? **24...♖×d7?** Allowing White's knight to enter the center with tempo. After 24...♕xd7, White has more difficulties organizing his kingside play. **25.♘d3 ♖d8 26.♘e5 ♗f8 27.h4 ♖aa8 28.♗b1 h5 29.♕f3 g6** (D)

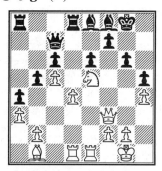

**30.g4!** The can opener. White's attack cannot really be stopped. **30...h×g4 31.♕×g4 ♗g7 32.♗a2** 32.h5!?

g×h5 33.♕×h5 f6 34.♕h7+ ♔f8 35.♘g6+ ♗×g6 36.♗×g6 and the bishops of opposite color favor White because of his raging attack. **32...b4 33.♗c4 b×a3 34.b×a3 ♕a5 35.♕e4 ♕c7** 35...♖ab8 36.♖e3± **36.♕f4?** (D)

This loses valuable time. Alekhine should implement his plan directly with 36.h5 g×h5 37.♔h1. **36...♖ab8?** Now White's attack will crash through; 36...♕e7, to answer 37.♘×g6 with 37...♕f6, was forced. **37.h5** The battering ram moves forward. **37...g×h5 38.♔h1! ♖b7?! 39.♖g1 ♕e7 40.♖×g7+! ♔×g7 41.♖g1+ ♔h7** (D)

**42.♘×f7** and, after this shot, Asztalos resigned in view of 42...♕×f7 43.♗d3+ ♕g6 44.♗×g6+ ♗×g6 45.♕f6 ♖g8 46.♕×e6+−. But, objectivly, the retreat 42.♘f3! was even stronger than the violent blow. **1−0**

Finishing the tournament without a loss, Alekhine scored 12 points out of 16 and finished first, a half-point ahead of Nimzowitsch and L. Steiner.

### San Remo Tournament, January 16-February 5, 1930

Giving his assent to participate in the major chess competition of the year, Alekhine specified that his appearance fee should be 20,000 liras, and, if Capablanca were to participate, he would want 40,000 liras. For that reason, the organizers failed to invite the Cuban. San Remo had already been known to chessplayers as the venue of a minor tournament held in 1911. At that time, the field included, along with the young players Réti and Kostic, the seasoned veteran Gunsberg. However, it was the relatively unknown Swiss player Hans Fahrni who won. This time the Italian seaside resort attracted many top players.

Of the luminaries, Lasker, Capablanca, and Euwe were absent. Among the future winners of the tournament, the press mentioned the names of Nimzowitsch, who won at Carlsbad, 1929; Bogoljubow, winner at Kissingen, 1928; Spielmann, the hero of Semmering, 1926 and, of course, the world champion and the winner at Baden-Baden 1925, Alekhine. Of the tournaments listed above (all of which, incidentally, were held at health resorts), Alekhine only played at Semmering, where he finished second, a half-point behind the winner. Alekhine arrived in San Remo with a single purpose, to win. Moreover, he wanted an even more convincing success than Capablanca had achieved in London 1922 and New York 1927. Playing with great inspiration, he achieved his aim. He won thirteen games and drew only two, against Bogoljubow and Spielmann. Nimzowitsch finished second, 3½ points behind!

**(93) Alekhine – Nimzowitsch,Aron**
San Remo 1930
French Defense [C17]

**1.e4 e6 2.d4 d5 3.♘c3 ♗b4 4.e5 c5 5.♗d2 ♘e7 6.♘b5 ♗×d2+ 7.♕×d2 0-0 8.c3 b6?!** The main line is 8...♘bc6. **9.f4 ♗a6 10.♘f3 ♕d7 11.a4 ♘bc6 12.b4 c×b4 13.c×b4 ♗b7 14.♘d6 (D)**

**14...f5?** Too slow. Black must fight for space on the queenside with 14...a5! 15.♗b5 a×b4 16.0-0 ♘c8 17.♘×b7 ♕×b7 18.♗×c6 ♕×c6 19.♖fc1 ♕b7 20.♕×b4 ♘e7= (Kasparov). **15.a5! (D)**

**15...♘c8?** After this mistake, the game is effectivly over because the

light squares in Black's camp are too weak, and he cannot stop the penetration of White's major pieces in the long run. Better practical chances were offered by 15...b×a5 16.b5 ♘d8± and 15...a6 16.a×b6 ♘c8 17.♘×b7 ♕×b7 18.♕c3 ♘×b6 19.♗×a6 ♖×a6 20.♖×a6 ♘×d4±. **16.♘×b7 ♕×b7 17.a6! ♕f7 18.♗b5 ♘8e7 19.0-0 h6 20.♖fc1 ♖fc8 21.♖c2 ♕e8** 21...♘d8 22.♖ac1 ♖×c2 23.♖×c2 ♖c8?! 24.♖×c8 ♘×c8 25.♕c3+– (Alekhine). **22.♖ac1 ♖ab8 23.♕e3 ♖c7 24.♖c3** Alekhine starts to load his gun by tripling on the c-file with the queen behind the rooks. **24...♕d7 25.♖1c2 ♔f8 26.♕c1 ♖bc8 (D)**

**27.♗a4!** "The last link of the positional attack" (Alekhine). **27...b5 28.♗×b5 ♔e8 29.♗a4 ♔d8 30.h4** and since Black will fall into *zugzwang* sooner or later. Nimzowitsch resigned. **1-0**

**Tournaments of Nations**
Before World War II, there were eight world chess Olympiads held that were named "Tournaments of Nations." World champion Alexander Alekhine participated in five of them on the first board for the French team, and finished first in the tournament of first boards in four events, the 1939 Olympiad being the only exception.

*Participants and organizers of the tournament at San Remo, 1930.*

*San Remo 1930*

| | | 1 | 2 | 3 | 4 | 5 | 6 | 7 | 8 | 9 | 10 | 11 | 12 | 13 | 14 | 15 | 16 | Total |
|---|---|---|---|---|---|---|---|---|---|---|---|---|---|---|---|---|---|---|
| **1** | **Alekhine** | X | 1 | 1 | ½ | 1 | 1 | ½ | 1 | 1 | 1 | 1 | 1 | 1 | 1 | 1 | 1 | **14** |
| **2** | **Nimzowitsch** | 0 | X | 0 | 1 | ½ | 1 | ½ | ½ | ½ | ½ | 1 | 1 | 1 | 1 | 1 | 1 | **10½** |
| **3** | **Rubinstein** | 0 | 1 | X | 0 | 1 | ½ | 0 | 1 | 1 | ½ | 1 | 0 | 1 | 1 | 1 | 1 | **10** |
| **4** | **Bogoljubow** | ½ | 0 | 1 | X | ½ | 0 | 1 | ½ | 1 | 1 | 0 | 1 | 1 | 0 | 1 | 1 | **9½** |
| **5** | **Yates** | 0 | ½ | 0 | ½ | X | ½ | 1 | 1 | 0 | ½ | 0 | 1 | 1 | 1 | 1 | 1 | **9** |
| **6** | **Ahues** | 0 | 0 | ½ | 1 | ½ | X | 1 | ½ | 0 | 1 | 0 | ½ | 1 | 1 | ½ | 1 | **8½** |
| **7** | **Spielmann** | ½ | ½ | 1 | 0 | 0 | 0 | X | ½ | ½ | ½ | 1 | 1 | ½ | 1 | 1 | 0 | **8** |
| **8** | **Vidmar** | 0 | ½ | 0 | ½ | 0 | ½ | ½ | X | ½ | ½ | 1 | 1 | ½ | 1 | ½ | 1 | **8** |
| **9** | **Tartakower** | 0 | ½ | 0 | 0 | 1 | 1 | ½ | ½ | X | ½ | 0 | 0 | 1 | ½ | 1 | 1 | **7½** |
| **10** | **Maroczy** | 0 | ½ | ½ | 0 | ½ | 0 | ½ | ½ | ½ | X | ½ | ½ | ½ | 1 | 1 | 1 | **7½** |
| **11** | **Colle** | 0 | 0 | 0 | 1 | 1 | 1 | 0 | 0 | 1 | ½ | X | 0 | ½ | 1 | 0 | ½ | **6½** |
| **12** | **Kmoch** | 0 | 0 | 1 | 0 | 0 | ½ | 0 | 0 | 1 | ½ | 1 | X | ½ | 0 | 1 | 1 | **6½** |
| **13** | **Araiza** | 0 | 0 | 0 | 0 | 0 | 0 | ½ | ½ | 0 | ½ | ½ | ½ | X | ½ | ½ | 1 | **4½** |
| **14** | **Monticelli** | 0 | 0 | 0 | 1 | 0 | 0 | 0 | 0 | ½ | 0 | 0 | 1 | ½ | X | ½ | ½ | **4** |
| **15** | **Grau** | 0 | 0 | 0 | 0 | 0 | ½ | 0 | ½ | 0 | 0 | 1 | 0 | ½ | ½ | X | ½ | **3½** |
| **16** | **Romi** | 0 | 0 | 0 | 0 | 0 | 0 | 1 | 0 | 0 | 0 | ½ | 0 | 0 | ½ | ½ | X | **2½** |

**Hamburg, July 13-17,1930**

The 3rd Chess Olympiad was held in Hamburg to honor the centennial of the local chess club. Alekhine won all nine games, playing in the matches against the strongest teams only.

**(94) Stahlberg,Gideon – Alekhine**
Hamburg 1930
Nimzo-Indian Defense [E23]

**1.d4 ♘f6 2.c4 e6 3.♘c3 ♗b4 4.♕b3 c5 5.d×c5 ♘c6 6.♘f3 ♘e4 7.♗d2 ♘×c5 8.♕c2 f5 9.a3 ♗×c3 10.♗×c3 0–0 11.b4 ♘e4 12.e3 b6 13.♗d3 ♘×c3 14.♕×c3 ♗b7 15.0–0 ♘e7 16.♗e2 ♕e8 17.♖fd1 ♖d8 18.a4 f4 19.a5 f×e3 20.♕×e3 ♘f5 21.♕c3 d6 22.a×b6 a×b6 23.♘e1?** The knight should go to the center: 23.♘d4 ♕g6 24.♕h3 ♘×d4 25.♖×d4 ♕f6 26.♕e3, and

White is certainly not worse. **23...e5 24.♖a7 ♘d4 25.♕e3 ♖d7 26.♖a2?!** Retreating the active rook is hardly the solution to White's problems, but good advice is already hard to give. One interesting try is 26.♗d3!? because the shot 26...♗xg2 27.♖xd7 ♕xd7 28.♘xg2 ♕g4 can be met by 29.♖e1! (but not 29.♖c1? ♘f3+ 30.♔f1 ♘xh2+ 31.♔g1 ♘f3+ 32.♔f1 h5 with a strong attack) 29...♘f3+ 30.♔f1 ♘xh2+ 31.♔g1 ♘f3+ 32.♔f1 ♘xe1 33.♘xe1, and White defends. **26...♖df7 27.f3 ♖f4 28.♗d3 ♕h5 29.♗f1 ♕g5** Against the surprising try 29...♕g4, White defends with 30.♗e2 ♘xe2+ 31.♕xe2 ♖xf3 32.♘xf3 ♗xf3 33.♕d3 ♗xd1 34.♕d5+ ♔h8 35.♖a8 ♕f5 36.♖xf8+ ♕xf8 37.♕xd1 with drawing chances. **30.♖f2 h6 31.♔h1?** (D) Running into a mighty blow. 31.♗d3 was necessary.

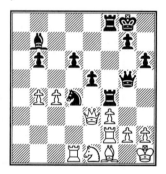

**31...♖xf3!!**, and Stahlberg resigned in view of 32.♕xg5 (32.♖xf3 ♕xe3 33.♖xe3 ♖xf1#) 32...♖xf2−+. **0-1**

**Prague, July 11-26, 1931**
The 4th Olympiad. Alekhine again had the best result on the first board. This time he played all eighteen games, scoring 13½ points (+10 -1 =7).

**Folkstone, June 12-23, 1933**
The 5th Olympiad. He scored 9½ points in twelve games. One of the best games played in that event was his win against the Latvian master Fricis Apsenieks (1894-1941).

**(95) Alekhine – Apsenieks**
Folkestone 1933
Queen's Gambit Declined [D30]

**1.d4 ♘f6 2.c4 c6 3.♘f3 d5 4.e3 e6 5.♗d3 a6 6.♘bd2 dxc4?** This activates White's knight. The main lines are 6...c5 and 6...♘bd7. **7.♘xc4 b5 8.♘ce5 h6 9.a4 ♗b7 10.♗d2 ♘bd7 11.♕c2 ♖c8?** (D) 11...♘xe5 12.♘xe5 ♗d6 13.♘xc6 ♕b6 is the lesser evil.

**12.♗g6!!** Alekhine strikes at Black's Achilles' Heel with decisive effect **12...♘xe5** 12...fxg6 13.♕xg6+ ♔e7 14.♗b4+ c5 15.dxc5 ♖xc5 16.♖d1 +- **13.♘xe5 ♖c7 14.♗a5 fxg6 15.♕xg6+ ♔e7 16.♘f7** After 16.♗b4+ c5 17.♗xc5+ ♖xc5 18.♕f7+, White can castle either way in the ensuing king hunt: 18...♔d6 19.dxc5+ ♔xe5 20.f4+ ♔e4 (20...♔d5 21.0-0-0+ +-; 20...♔f5 21.g4+ ♔xg4 22.♕g6+ ♔f3 23.0-0-0+ ♔xe3 24.♖a3+ ♔d4 25.♕d3+ ♔xc5 26.♖c1+ ♔b6 27.♕e3+ ♔a5 28.axb5+ ♗xa3 29.♕xa3+ ♔xb5 30.♕b3+ ♔a5

31.♖c5#) 21.♕×e6+ ♔d3 22.♖a3+ ♔c2 23.♕b3+ ♔b1 24.0-0+ ♕d1 25.♖×d1#. **16...♕e8 17.♘×h8 ♖c8 18.♗b4+ c5 19.♗×c5+ ♖×c5 20.d×c5 ♗e4 21.♕×e8+ ♘×e8 22.f3 ♗d3 23.a×b5 1-0**

**Warsaw, August 16-31, 1935**
The 6th Olympiad. Alekhine won seven games, drawing ten.

**Buenos Aires, August 24-September 19, 1939**
The 8th Olympiad. For the first time, Alekhine played in an Olympiad in which Capablanca also played. There was no personal encounter. "On the day the France-Cuba match was to take place," remembers the Lithuanian player Vladas Mikenas, "Alekhine had come to the tournament hall a half-hour before the start and walked up and down the podium with a determined air, getting into the proper mood for the game with Capablanca. He was furious when the Cubans entered a reserve player instead of Capablanca. Alekhine crushed him in twenty moves, but could not conceal his anger." The France-Cuba match was drawn (2-2), France eventually finishing tenth in the tournament, Cuba eleventh. Alekhine played sixteen games (+9 -0 =7). However, in the competition between the team leaders, Capablanca was ahead of him, sharing first prize with Keres (8½ points in 11 games). In all, Alekhine played seventy-two games in the Olympiads, scoring 78.5% (+43 -2 =27).

During the Buenos Aires Olympiad the participants learned that World War II had broken out. Many of the European players decided to stay on the other side of the ocean. But Alekhine, after win-

ning minor tournaments at Montevideo and Caracas, decided to return to France.

**Bled International Tournament, August 3-September 28, 1932**
In this double round-robin event, arranged by the famous Yugoslav resort, fourteen leading world players participated, including such seasoned veterans as Alekhine, Bogoljubow (the recent challenger), Nimzowitsch, Vidmar, Spielmann, Tartakower, Maróczy, Kostic, as well as the young, but already recognized talents of Kashdan, Flohr, Stoltz, and Pirc.

Both the beautiful, peaceful Lake Bled and the sunny glades and shadowy quiet alleys to take walks in all enabled the participants to forget about the affairs and problems of everyday life and wholeheartedly give themselves to chess. Alekhine played magnificently. In some games, his opponents could not even last thirty moves, while Nimzowitsch (3rd prize) admitted his defeat (in the French Defense) as early as move 19. Considerably shattered, he said to those players who were not at the board just then: "He treats us as fledglings still in the nest!" Many other participants experienced similar fiascos when playing Alekhine. Lake Bled was the scene of a unique victory over Nimzowitsch in 1931.

**(96) Alekhine – Nimzowitsch**
Bled 1931
French Defense [C15]

**1.e4 e6 2.d4 d5 3.♘c3 ♗b4 4.♘ge2 d×e4 5.a3 ♗×c3+ 6.♘×c3 f5?!** Very risky against Alekhine, who opens the position immediately by sacrificing a second pawn. **7.f3 e×f3 8.♕×f3 ♕×d4 9.♕g3** (D)

**9...♘f6!?** "This bold move is Black's comparatively best chance" (Alekhine). 9...♕d7?! 10.♗f4 ♘f6 11.♖d1 ♕f7 12.♗×c7 ♘c6 13.♗c4 gives White very good compensation for the pawn. 9...c6? runs into 10.♗f4 ♘d7 11.♖d1 ♕f6 12.♖×d7 ♗×d7 13.♗e5 ♕e7 14.♕×g7+−. **10.♕×g7 ♕e5+?!** It was probably better to give back the second pawn immediately as well by again choosing the active solution 10...♖g8!? 11.♕×c7 ♘c6. **11.♗e2 ♖g8 12.♕h6 ♖g6** 12...♖×g2? 13.♗g5+− **13.♕h4 ♗d7?** 13...♖×g2? is also wrong because of 14.♗g5 ♘bd7 15.0-0-0 ♔f7 16.♗h5+ ♔g8 17.♗f3+−; but, after Kasparov's suggestion of 13...♖g4!? 14.♕f2 ♘e4 15.♘×e4 ♖×e4 16.♕f3, White is only slightly better. **14.♗g5?** (D)

Alekhine should bring out even more pieces with 14.♗f4! ♕d4 (14...♕c5

15.0-0-0 ♘c6 16.♗×c7 ♘d4 17.♕×d4 ♕×c7 18.♗h5±) 15.♖d1 when he can no longer castle queenside, but this is not important: 15...♕c5 16.♗g5 ♕f8 (16...♕e5 17.0-0 ♘c6 18.♗h5 ♘×h5 19.♖d8+ ♔f7 20.♕×h5 ♔g7 21.♔h1 ♗×g2+ 22.♔×g2 ♕f6 23.♔h1 ♖×g5 24.♕e8 ♕f7 25.♕×f7+ ♔×f7 26.♘b5+−) 17.♕f4 ♘a6 18.♗×f6 ♕×f6 19.♗h5±. **14...♗c6?** Far too greedy and slow. Black must finish his development with 14...♘c6! 15.0-0-0 0-0-0 16.♖he1 h6 17.♗×h6 ♘g4 18.♗×g4 ♖×g4 (Kmoch) 19.♕×g4 f×g4 20.♖×e5 ♘×e5 21.♗f4 when White is only slightly better. But not 14...h6? 15.♗f4 ♕c5 16.♗h5 ♘×h5 17.♕×h5 ♔f7 18.0-0-0+−. **15.0-0-0 ♗×g2** 15...♘bd7 16.♖he1 ♕c5 17.♖×d7 ♘×d7 18.♗h+− **16.♖he1 ♗e4 17.♗h5 ♘×h5 18.♖d8+ ♔f7 19.♕×h5 1-0**

## (97) Pirc,Vasja – Alekhine
Bled 1931
Queen's Gambit Declined [D32]

**1.d4 d5 2.c4 e6 3.♘c3 c5 4.c×d5 c×d4 5.♕a4+ ♗d7 6.♕×d4 e×d5 7.♕×d5 ♘c6 8.♗g5 ♘f6 9.♕d2 h6 10.♗×f6 ♕×f6 11.e3?** The main line is 11.♘d5. **11...0-0-0 12.0-0-0?** Pirc castles directly into the disaster. But 12.♘f3 ♗g4 13.♕c2 ♗×f3 14.g×f3 ♕×f3 15.♖g1 ♕f6 also gives Black a strong initiative. **12...♗g4 13.♘d5 ♖×d5! 14.♕×d5** (D)

**14...♗a3!!** A killing blow. **15.♕b3** 15.b×a3? ♕a1+ 16.♔c2 ♗×d1+ 17.♕×d1 ♕×a2+ 18.♔c1 ♖d8 19.♗d3 ♕×a3+ −+; 15.♖d2 ♖d8 −+ **15...♗×d1 16.♕×a3 ♕×f2 17.♕d3 ♗g4 18.♘f3 ♗×f3 19.♕f5+** 19.g×f3 ♕e1+ 20.♔d1 ♕×e3+ 21.♔d2 ♕e6 −+ **19...♔b8 20.♕×f3 ♕e1+ 21.♔c2?** 21.♕d1 was absolutely forced. **21...♖c8 22.♕g3+ ♘e5+ 23.♔b3 ♕d1+ 24.♔a3 ♖c5** and, since the rook has closed the mating net, Pirc threw in the towel. **0-1**

**(98) Alekhine – Maróczy,Geza**
Bled 1931
Queen's Gambit Declined [D63]

**1.d4 d5 2.♘f3 ♘f6 3.c4 e6 4.♗g5 ♘bd7 5.e3 h6 6.♗h4 ♗e7 7.♘c3 0-0 8.♖c1 c6 9.♗d3 a6 10.0-0 d×c4 11.♗×c4 c5 12.a4 ♕a5 13.♕e2 c×d4 14.e×d4 ♘b6 15.♗d3 ♗d7 16.♘e5** Alekhine wants to start an attack in his typical stlye. The alternative 16.♗×f6!? ♗×f6 17.♕e4 ♕f5 18.♕×f5 e×f5 19.a5 ♘a4 20.♘×a4 ♗×a4 21.♗×f5 is objectivly better, but Black has good drawing chances after 21...♖ab8. **16...♖fd8 17.f4?!** 17.♕f3 is less committal. **17...♗e8! 18.♘g4 (D)**

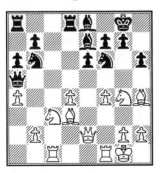

**18...♖×d4?** This greedy capture gives Alekhine a very dangerous attack. Maróczy should bring his b6-knight into play with 18...♘bd5!, when Black is by no means worse. **19.♗×f6 ♗×f6 20.♘×f6+ g×f6 21.♘e4** 21.f5 is met by 21...♕e5. **21...♖ad8?** This counterattack is too slow. Maróczy had to bring another defender to the kingside with 21...♘d5 or 21...♘d7, when he should be able to defend. **22.♘×f6+ ♔f8 (D)**

22...♔h8 23.♕g4 ♗c6 24.♕h3 ♔g7 25.♘g4 ♖h8 26.♕g3 ♔f8 27.f5 +− **23.♘h7+?** Driving Black's king out of the danger zone. Conversely, 23.f5 e5 24.♕e3 wins, e.g., 24...♗c6 (24...♖×d3? 25.♘h7+ ♔e7 26.f6+ ♔e6 27.♘f8+ ♔d6 28.♕×d3+ +− ) 25.♕×h6+ ♔e7 26.♕g5 ♔d6 27.♗e4 ♔c7 28.♕g7 +− **23...♔e7 24.f5 ♖8d6 (D)**

**25.b4!?** An inspired sacrifice to disturb the harmony of the defenders. Black can also fight on after the alternatives 25.fxe6 ♖xe6 26.♕f2 ♕b4 27.♘f6 ♗c6 28.♘h5 ♔d8 and 25.♘f6 ♗c6 26.♘g8+ ♔e8 27.fxe6 fxe6 28.♗e4 ♗xe4 29.♘f6+ ♔d8 30.♘xe4 ♖c6. **25...♕xb4 26.♕e5 ♘d7** Black is also not out of the woods after 26...♘d5 27.♖b1 ♕c5 28.♖xb7+ ♔d8 29.♔h1 ♖xd3 (Kasparov) 30.fxe6 ♖e3 31.♖b8+ ♔c7 32.♕b2 ♖dxe6 33.♕b7+ ♔d6 34.♖d8+ ♔e5 35.♘f8 ♗c6 36.♘xe6 fxe6 37.♕g7+ ♔e4 38.♕xh6, but matters are not completely clear of course. **27.♕h8** (D)

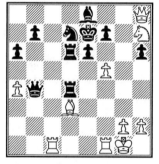

**27...♖xd3?** A blunder. 27...♖c6! 28.♖xc6 bxc6 29.fxe6 fxe6 30.♘f6 ♘xf6 31.♕xf6+ ♔d7 32.♕xh6 ♖d5 (Kasparov) is the only way to continue the fight. After 27...♕b6? on the other hand, one point of the pawn sacrifice is revealed: 28.a5 ♕xa5 29.♖c8+– (Alekhine). **28.f6+** and Maróczy resigned in view of 28...♔d8 (28...♘xf6 29.♕xf6+ ♔d7 30.♘f8#) 29.♕xe8+ ♔xe8 30.♖c8# **1-0**

After losing his second game to Alekhine, Nimzowitsch exclaimed in annoyance that "Alekhine hypnotizes us all!" The old familiar tune! Thirty years before the Bled tournament, a similar reproach was thrown at Emanuel Lasker. Now, it was Alekhine's turn. Thirty more years would pass and the same indictment would be made for another triumphant winner at Bled, Mikhail Tal.

As a matter of fact, Alekhine simply was the strongest. "He could afford experiments, taking risks, playing recklessly," Flohr wrote, because "in those (his best) years, Alekhine not only was the official world champion... he was in a class of his own." In Bled, he set a record, finishing 5½ points ahead of second-place Bogoljubow. Of his thirteen opponents, only Kashdan, Spielmann, and Asztalos managed to draw their micro-matches with him.

According to Kramnik, the great gap between Alekhine and the other players was because, at the time, it was a period of transition. Neither Capablanca nor Lasker played in those tournaments, neither Botvinnik nor Keres had yet reached peak strength, and the "old rivals" were no longer as strong as they used to be. "Of course, Alekhine was an outstanding world champion, but the gap was, I think, really a result of this" (Kramnik).

However, facts are stubborn and Alekhine's record results suggested that he was in splendid form and in the prime of his creativity. This period in the life and chess career of the fourth world champion was named "the golden years of the champion" by Garry Kasparov, who figuratively compared his achievements to those of Napoleon: "Alekhine had clearly reached the peak of his career: those were the times of Austerlitz and Jena! The very style of

*Bled 1931*

| | | 1 | 2 | 3 | 4 | 5 | 6 | 7 | 8 | 9 | 10 | 11 | 12 | 13 | 14 | Total |
|---|---|---|---|---|---|---|---|---|---|---|---|---|---|---|---|---|
| **1** | **Alekhine** | X | 1½ | 11 | ½½ | 1½ | 1½ | 11 | 1½ | ½½ | 1½ | 11 | 11 | ½½ | 11 | **20½** |
| **2** | **Bogoljubow** | 0½ | X | ½0 | 11 | 0½ | 11 | 1½ | 10 | 0½ | 01 | 00 | 11 | ½1 | 11 | **15** |
| **3** | **Nimzowitsch** | 00 | ½1 | X | 00 | ½½ | 11 | 0½ | ½½ | ½1 | ½½ | 1½ | 1½ | 11 | 0½ | **14** |
| **4** | **Kashdan** | ½½ | 00 | 11 | X | ½½ | 0½ | 1½ | 00 | ½½ | 1½ | 10 | 11 | ½½ | ½½ | **13½** |
| **5** | **Vidmar** | 0½ | 1½ | ½½ | ½½ | X | ½0 | ½0 | ½½ | ½0 | 11 | ½½ | ½1 | ½1 | ½½ | **13½** |
| **6** | **Flohr** | 0½ | 00 | 00 | 1½ | ½1 | X | ½½ | 10 | ½1 | 1½ | 11 | ½0 | ½1 | ½½ | **13½** |
| **7** | **Stoltz** | 00 | 0½ | 1½ | 0½ | ½1 | ½½ | X | 11 | ½1 | ½½ | ½1 | 00 | 01 | 1½ | **13½** |
| **8** | **Tartakower** | 0½ | 01 | ½½ | 11 | ½½ | 01 | 00 | X | ½½ | ½0 | ½½ | 11 | ½½ | ½½ | **13** |
| **9** | **Spielmann** | ½½ | 1½ | ½0 | ½½ | ½1 | ½0 | ½0 | ½½ | X | ½½ | 0½ | 00 | 1½ | 11 | **12½** |
| **10** | **Kostic** | 0½ | 10 | ½½ | 0½ | 00 | 0½ | ½½ | ½1 | ½½ | X | ½½ | 01 | 1½ | 11 | **12½** |
| **11** | **Maróczy** | 00 | 11 | 0½ | 01 | ½½ | 00 | ½0 | ½½ | 1½ | ½½ | X | ½1 | ½½ | ½½ | **12** |
| **12** | **Colle** | 00 | 00 | 0½ | 00 | ½0 | ½1 | 11 | 00 | 11 | 10 | ½0 | X | 0½ | 11 | **10½** |
| **13** | **Asztalos** | ½½ | ½0 | 00 | ½½ | ½0 | ½0 | 10 | ½½ | 0½ | 0½ | ½½ | 1½ | X | 0½ | **9½** |
| **14** | **Pirc** | 00 | 00 | 1½ | ½½ | ½½ | ½½ | 0½ | ½½ | 00 | 00 | ½½ | 00 | 1½ | X | **8½** |

his victories is tremendously impressive. Who else in the history of chess won so many serious games by means of brilliant tactical blows?" And to illustrate this opinion, the finales of the games with Flohr and Maróczy and the 19-move miniature with Nimzowitsch have been presented.

### Correspondence Chess

Alekhine had been participated in correspondence chess since he was 11 years old. Playing by correspondence helped to develop his talent. In his later years, when he had no time for correspondence competitions, he still valued its role highly, especially for those who, for various reasons, were unable to play chess over the board. However, even being world champion, he found time to play two correspondence games against the players of the Reykjavik chess club in 1931. These games were started by radio onboard a ship on which Alekhine was sailing from Iceland and so continued up to the 12th move. Then they were resumed by correspondence. One of the games was drawn and the other, in which Alekhine had the black pieces, he won on the 52nd move.

### (99) Reykjavik Chess Club – Alekhine

Corr 1931
Queen's Indian Defense [A47]

**1.d4 ♘f6 2.♘f3 b6 3.g3 ♗b7 4.♗g2 c5 5.e3 e6 6.0–0 ♗e7 7.♘c3?!** Blocking the c-pawn is not good because White has no direct options in the center anymore. **7...0–0 8.♖e1 d5 9.♘e5 ♘c6 10.♘×c6 ♗×c6 11.a4 ♕c8 12.a5?! ♖d8 13.a×b6 a×b6 14.♖×a8 ♕×a8 15.♕e2 ♕b7 16.♗d2 b5 17.♖a1 b4 18.♘d1 ♖a8 19.♖×a8+ ♕×a8** (D)

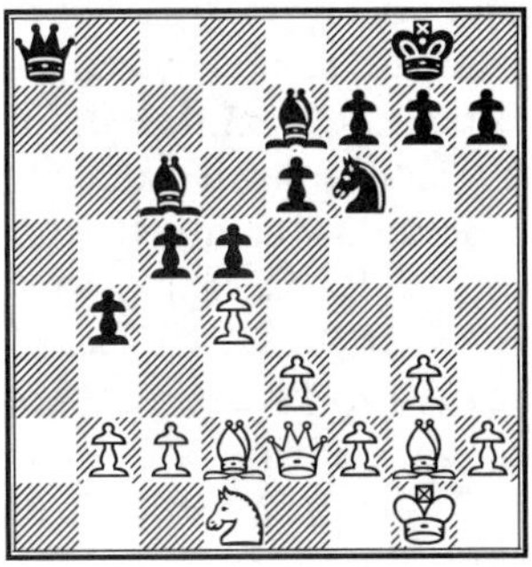

**20.b3?** 20.d×c5 ♗×c5 21.c3 b3 22.c4 was better. **20...c4! 21.e4?** Desperation, as after 21.b×c4 d×c4 22.♗×c6 ♕×c6, Black's queenside pawns look menacing. But this had to be played. **21...c3** Alekhine chooses a dynamic solution. The greedy 21...c×b3 22.c×b3

d×e4 is objectivly even better. **22.e×d5 ♘×d5 23.♗e3** (D)

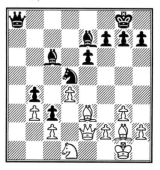

**23...♘f4!** Alekhine's idea is to dominate the light squares. **24.♗×f4** 24.♗×c6?? ♘e2+−+ **24...♗×g2 25.♕b5?!** 25.♘e3 must be played anyway so the right time is now. **25...♗b7?!** 25...♗e4 26.♘e3 ♕a1+ 27.♕f1 ♕a7 28.f3 ♗c6 29.♕c4 ♕b7−+ **26.♘e3 h6 27.♗c7 ♔h7?** This makes Black's job considerably more difficult. The queen should first invade with 27...♕a1+ 28.♕f1 ♕a2 29.♕e2 (29.♕d3 ♗f3) 29...♗g5 30.f4 ♗e7 31.♗b6 ♗e4, and Black should win in both cases. **28.♕a5 ♕e8 29.♕b6 ♗f3 30.h3 ♕d7 31.g4 f6 32.♔h2?** Allowing Alekhine to open the position. The prophylactic 32.♗g3 is better. **32...e5! 33.d×e5?** This runs directly into a deadly attack. 33.d5 ♗×d5 34.♗d6 was a better practical chance, but Black should win in the long run after 34...♗e4 35.♗×e7 ♕×e7 36.♔g1 ♕f8. **33...♕d2 34.♘f5?!** ♕d1 34...♗a8 35.e×f6 ♕d1 36.f3 ♕×f3 37.♘h4 ♕e2+ 38.♔g3 ♗×f6−+ is easier. **35.♘g3** 35.♘×e7? meets with 35...♕h1+ 36.♔g3 g5 37.♕×f6 ♕g2#. **35...♕×c2 36.e×f6 ♗×f6 37.♘h5 ♗h4 38.♗g3** (D)

**38...♕d1!?** A typical amazing Alekhine attacking solution. The normal 38...♗e7 39.♕d4 ♕g6 wins as

well. **39.♗×h4 ♕h1+ 40.♔g3 ♗c6 41.♗d8** 41.♕e3 c2 42.♘f6+ ♔h8!−+ **41...♕f3+ 42.♔h4 c2** (D)

White has no way to stop the pawn because of the mating attack: **43.♕a7** 43.♕c5 is met by 43...g5+ 44.♗×g5 h×g5+ 45.♕×g5 (45.♔×g5? ♕d5+−+) 45...♕×f2+ 46.♘g3 ♗e8!−+ (Alekhine). **43...♕f8 44.♗e7** 44.♘f6+ ♔h8! 45.♗e7 g5+ 46.♔g3 c1♕−+ **44...♕f7 45.♘f6+** 45.♕e3 ♕f3 46.♘f6+ ♔g6 47.♗c5 ♕×f6+ 48.♔g3 ♔f7 49.♗d4 c1♕−+ **45...g×f6 46.♕c5** 46.♕e3 f5 47.g×f5 ♕×f5 48.f4 ♗d7 49.♗d6 c1♕−+ **46...♕g6 47.♔g3** 47.f4 ♕e4−+ **47...♕d3+ 48.♔h4 ♗g2 49.f3 ♕×f3 50.♕×c2+ ♔g7 51.♗f8+ ♔×f8** (D)

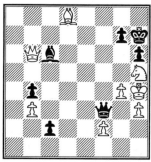

**52.♕c5+?** 52.♕c8+ is much more tenacious, but Black's king can escape with 52...♔e7 53.♕c7+ ♔e6 54.♕c8+

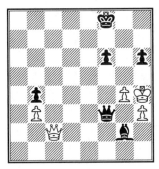

♔d5 55.♕b7+ ♔d6 56.♕×b4+ ♔e6 57.♕b6+ ♔f7 58.♕c7+ ♔g6 59.♕c2+ ♕e4–+. **52...♔f7** and White resigned in view of 53.♕c4+ ♔g7 54.♕c7+ ♔g6 55.♕c2+ ♕e4 56.♕d2 ♗f1 57.♔g3 ♕d3+–+. **0-1**

As far back as in 1936, Alekhine had put forth the idea of holding a correspondence world championship, which was only realized after World War II. In a conversation with the president of the International Correspondence Chess Union (now the ICCF), K. Abonyi, he emphasized that "[c]orrespondence chess and chess over the board complement each other."

**Flohr, Salomon** (November 21, 1908, Gorodenka, Ukraine-July 18, 1983, Moscow)
An international grandmaster (1950), chess journalist. During World War I, Flohr's family moved to Prague. He learned to play chess rather late, at 14. Wishing to surpass his elder brother, to whom he often lost, Salo began to study chess literature.

In the late 1920s, there began to appear witty reports in the press, signed Salo Flohr. Soon, his name could often be seen among participants and then prize winners of international events. Making his debut in the tournament at Rogaska-Slatina (1929), 21-year-old Flohr finished second, behind Rubinstein. Then, there followed victories at Brno (1931), Hastings (1931/ 32, 1932/33, 1933/34), Sliac (1932), Moscow (1935), and Podebrady (1936). In 1931-1933, he played four matches, winning two, one against Stoltz (1931) and one against Sultan Khan (1932), and drawing the two against Euwe (1932) and Botvinnik (1933). His wins over Capablanca, Euwe, and Lasker are a testimony to his chess strength during that period.

### (100) Flohr – Capablanca
Nottingham 1936
Queen's Gambit Declined [D59]

**1.d4 ♘f6 2.c4 e6 3.♘c3 d5 4.♗g5 ♗e7 5.e3 0-0 6.♘f3 h6 7.♗h4 b6 8.c×d5 ♘×d5 9.♗×e7 ♘×e7?!** 9...♕×e7 is the main line. **10.♗e2 ♗b7 11.0-0 ♘d7 12.♕a4** 12.b4!? scores better. **12...a6 13.♖fd1 ♘d5 14.♖ac1 ♖c8 15.♘×d5** 15.♗×a6?? runs into 15...♘×c3 16.♖×c3 ♖a8–+. **15...e×d5 16.♗d3 c5 17.d×c5 ♘×c5** The hanging pawns are too weak after 17...b×c5? 18.♗f5 ♘b6 19.♕a5±. **18.♕d4 ♖e8 19.♗f5 ♖c7 20.♕f4 ♖ce7** (D)

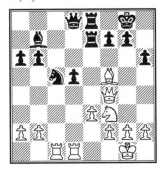

**21.♘d4** Flohr decides to play the middlegame because the alternative, 21.b4!? ♘e4 22.♗×e4 ♖×e4 23.♕c7 ♕×c7 24.♖×c7 ♖8e7 25.♖×e7 ♖×e7 26.♖c1, gives White a very plesant endgame. **21...a5 22.♗d3?!** This allows a regrouping of Black's rooks. 22.a3!? is more precise. **22...♖e5 23.♗b5 ♖8e7 24.♕f3** Against direct tries, Black can defend: 24.♘c6?! is met by 24...♗×c6 25.♗×c6 ♖7e6 and 24.♗c6 by 24...♗a6 25.♘f3 ♖5e6 26.♗×d5 ♖d7 27.♗b3 ♘×b3 28.♖×d7 ♕×d7 29.a×b3 ♖c6. **24...♖g5 25.♕e2 ♖g6 26.♗d3 ♖f6 27.♗b1 ♗a6 28.♕h5 ♗b7 29.a3 a4 30.♕g4 ♖e5 31.♘f3 ♖e7 32.♘d4 ♖e5 33.♘f3 ♖e7 34.♕g3 ♗a6?** (D) 34...♕e8 to sidestep the pin was necessary.

**35.♘d4?** Flohr misses the shot 35.♖×d5!± , which exploits Black's weak back rank. **35...♖d7 36.♗f5 ♖c7?** A very unfortunate square for the rook, which does better to go to e7. **37.♗b1?** The direct 37.e4 is stronger, e.g., 37...h5 38.e5 ♖h6 39.e6± . **37...♕c8?** Walking into a small combination. But Black's task is hard in any case; one better option is 37...♕d6, although he will have to suffer in a long ending. **38.♘f5! ♖g6** 38...♖×f5 39.♗×f5 ♕×f5 40.♕×c7+– **39.♘d6 ♖×g3 40.♘×c8 ♖×g2+ 41.♔×g2**

♖×c8 42.♗a2 ♖c6 43.♗×d5 ♖g6+ 44.♔h1 ♘d3 45.♖c2! ♖d6 46.♗f3 ♖f6 47.♗e4! (D)

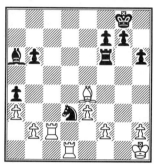

Black is lost, whatever he tries: **47...♖d6** 47...♘×f2+?? 48.♖×f2 ♖×f2 49.♖d8#; 47...♗b7 48.♗×b7 ♘×f2+ 49.♖×f2 ♖×f2 50.♖d4+– **48.♗×d3** 48.♔g1 is even easier. **48...♗×d3 49.f3 ♗×c2 50.♖×d6 b5 51.♔g2 ♗b3 52.♖b6 ♗c4 53.♔g3 ♔f8 54.♔f4 ♔e7 55.♔e5 ♗e2 56.f4 ♗c4 57.♖b7+ ♔f8 58.f5 f6+ 59.♔f4 h5 60.e4 ♗e2 61.e5 f×e5+ 62.♔×e5 ♗c4 63.♔f4 h4 64.♔g5 1-0**

In 1935, Flohr was one of the trainers who helped Euwe in the world championship match against Alekhine. And, two years later, he himself challenged Alekhine, who had regained the world title in the return match with Euwe. In reply to Flohr's challenge of December 8, Alekhine at first declined on the grounds that he had already proposed to play a match with Capablanca in 1939. In his speech at the closing ceremony of his match with Euwe, he mentioned that the negotiations on behalf of some Argentinian organizations were under way and that, although he had not yet received an official challenge from Capablanca himself, he was ready to play the match. And only six months later, after a brief exchange of letters, Alekhine came to Prague.

Flohr described the general guidelines for the match in *64*: "On May 30, we signed a formal agreement about the match. The contest will be held in the autumn of 1939 in the Republic of Czechoslovakia on the same terms as the Alekhine-Euwe match. Only the point about seconds has been changed. In contrast to the aforementioned match, our seconds shall be people who are not chess masters" (June 10, 1938). Flohr evaluated his chances as rather modest:

*Alekhine and Flohr signing the world championship match agreement.*

*Alekhine looks splendid – he weighs 96 kilograms and feels fine. Not only during the preparation for the match with Euwe but also after the match and up to now, he has not drunk a single drop of wine, only milk and apple juice. This extraordinary will power of the world champion is very impressive. To play against such an Alekhine with success is a more than difficult task. Hardly is there anyone else the struggle with whom would leave less hope. I believe that chances, of course, are on Alekhine's side. But to hope is human. During the time that is left before the match I shall have to prepare thoroughly in both the chess and psychological aspects (64 June 10, 1938).*

But the war upset the plans. Flohr moved to Moscow where he became actively involved in the chess life of Russia. In the post-war years, Flohr was no longer able to demonstrate the power that would realistically allow him to fight for the world chess crown.

Then, the former challenger became "a world champion" in chess journalism. Here he achieved indisputable success. His articles, reports, and sketches were laced with humor and irony, historical excursions and brilliant laconic portrayals of chess luminaries. As the Russian writer Yuri Nagibin remarked, "Flohr is just incapable of writing a dry, businesslike newspaper article. His cordiality, his interest in people, his untiring compassion to them will surely break through somewhere and the urgently produced material will shine with the light of humanity, soaring high above the smallness of the task at hand." From time to time, he would revisit his years as a splendid chessplayer, participating in the 16th USSR Championship and the 1948 interzonal tournament, the 1950 candidates tournament, the international tournaments at Göteborg (1958, 1st place), Beverwijk (1960, 4th-5th places), Stockholm (1962, 3rd place), and Amsterdam (1966, 3rd place).

Selected works
*The Clock Has Not Been Stopped.* Moscow, 1984.

*Salo Flohr*

*Through the Prism of a Half-Century.* Moscow, 1986.

*Euwe-Aljechin. Analyse der derting gespeelde partijen om het Wereldkampioeschop.* Amsterdam, 1935.

*Euwe-Aljechin. De derting gespeelde partijen om het Wereldkampioen schop.* Amsterdam, 1937.

*Die 12 Schacholympiade, Moskau, 1957.* (and the same title in En glish and French).

*Weltgeschichte des Schach.* Lfg 33. *Sowjetisches Schach, 1917-1935.* Hamburg, 1960 (co-authored).

*Heiteres Schwarz-Weiss.* Hamburg, 1961.

*Weltgeschichte des Schachs,* Band 6 *Der Intersonenturnier, Amsterdam, 1964.* Hamburg, 1965 (co-authored).

*Petrosjan bleibt Weltmeister.* Amsterdam, 1967.

*Spassky-Weltmeister.* Amsterdam, 1971.

Baturinsky, V.D. ed. *Grandmaster Flohr.* Moscow,1985.

**Berne International Tournament, July 16-30, 1932**

In this open championship of Switzerland, where seven other grandmasters and eight Swiss national masters participated, Alekhine took first place, scoring 12½ points (+11 -1 =3), a full point ahead of Flohr and Euwe.

**(101) Alekhine – Flohr**
Berne 1932
Queen's Pawn Game [D05]

**1.d4 d5 2.♘f3 ♘f6 3.e3 e6 4.♗d3 c5 5.c3 ♘c6 6.♘bd2 ♗e7 7.0-0 ♕c7 8.♕e2 0-0 9.e4 d×e4 10.♘×e4 c×d4 11.♘×d4 ♘×d4 12.c×d4 ♘×e4 13.♗×e4 f5 14.♗f3 ♗f6 15.♖d1 ♖d8?!** 15...♗d7 is more natural. **16.♗e3 f4?** Based on a miscalculation. Black should develop counterplay with 16...♗d7 17.♖ac1 ♕a5 18.♗×b7 ♖ab8 19.♗a6 ♕×a2 in order to keep White's advantage manageable. **17.♖ac1 ♕d6 18.♗d2 ♗×d4?** (D) This greedy capture is refuted on the spot. But good advice is already hard to give.

**19.♗a5! ♖d7** 19...b6 20.♗c3 +- **20.♖×d4 ♕×d4 21.♕×e6+ ♖f7** 21...♔f8 22.♖e1 g6 23.♗c3 +- **22.♖×c8+ ♖×c8 23.♕×c8+ ♖f8 24.♕×b7 ♖e8 25.h3 ♕c5 26.♗c3 ♕e7 27.♗d5+ ♔h8 28.♕×e7 1-0**

## Berne 1932

| | | 1 | 2 | 3 | 4 | 5 | 6 | 7 | 8 | 9 | 10 | 11 | 12 | 13 | 14 | 15 | 16 | T |
|---|---|---|---|---|---|---|---|---|---|---|---|---|---|---|---|---|---|---|
| 1 | Alekhine | x | ½ | 1 | 1 | 0 | 1 | 1 | 1 | 1 | ½ | 1 | 1 | 1 | 1 | ½ | 1 | 12½ |
| 2 | Euwe | ½ | x | ½ | ½ | 1 | ½ | ½ | ½ | 1 | 1 | ½ | 1 | 1 | 1 | 1 | 1 | 11½ |
| 3 | Flohr | 0 | ½ | x | ½ | ½ | ½ | ½ | 1 | 1 | 1 | 1 | 1 | 1 | 1 | 1 | 1 | 11½ |
| 4 | Sultan Khan | 0 | ½ | ½ | x | 0 | 1 | 1 | 1 | 1 | 1 | 1 | 1 | 0 | 1 | 1 | 1 | 11 |
| 5 | Bogoljubow | 1 | 0 | ½ | 1 | x | ½ | 1 | 0 | ½ | 0 | 1 | 1 | 1 | ½ | 1 | 1 | 10 |
| 6 | Bernstein | 0 | ½ | ½ | 0 | ½ | x | 1 | 1 | 0 | 1 | 1 | 1 | 1 | 1 | ½ | 1 | 10 |
| 7 | Johner, H. | 0 | ½ | ½ | 0 | 0 | 0 | x | ½ | 1 | 1 | 1 | 0 | 1 | 1 | 0 | ½ | 7 |
| 8 | Johner, P. | 0 | ½ | 0 | 0 | 1 | 0 | ½ | x | ½ | 1 | ½ | 0 | 0 | 1 | 1 | 1 | 7 |
| 9 | Henneberger | 0 | 0 | 0 | 0 | ½ | 1 | 0 | ½ | x | 0 | ½ | 1 | ½ | 0 | 1 | 1 | 6 |
| 10 | Naegeli | ½ | 0 | 0 | 0 | 1 | 0 | 0 | 0 | 1 | x | 0 | 0 | ½ | 1 | 1 | 1 | 6 |
| 11 | Rivier | 0 | ½ | 0 | 0 | 0 | 0 | 0 | ½ | ½ | 1 | x | 1 | 1 | 0 | ½ | 1 | 6 |
| 12 | Grob | 0 | 0 | 0 | 0 | 0 | 0 | 1 | 1 | 0 | 1 | 0 | x | ½ | ½ | 1 | 1 | 6 |
| 13 | Colin | 0 | 0 | 0 | 1 | 0 | 0 | 0 | 1 | ½ | ½ | 0 | ½ | x | 0 | 1 | 1 | 5½ |
| 14 | Voellmy | 0 | 0 | 0 | 0 | ½ | 0 | 0 | 0 | 1 | 0 | 1 | ½ | 1 | x | ½ | 0 | 4½ |
| 15 | Gygli | ½ | 0 | 0 | 0 | 0 | ½ | 1 | 0 | 0 | 0 | ½ | 0 | 0 | ½ | x | ½ | 3½ |
| 16 | Staehelin | 0 | 0 | 0 | 0 | 0 | 0 | ½ | 0 | 0 | 0 | 0 | 0 | 0 | 1 | ½ | x | 2 |

## Podebrady Tournament, July 4-26, 1936

The former world champion had a good start in this tournament at the Czechoslovakian health resort. "I had no doubt," Flohr recalled, "that Alekhine would win the event, the more so that up to the nineth round he was winning game after game, and in the best style."

**(102) Alekhine – Eliskases,Erich**
Podebrady 1936
Ruy Lopez [C90]

**1.e4 e5 2.♘f3 ♘c6 3.♗b5 a6 4.♗a4 ♘f6 5.0-0 ♗e7 6.♖e1 b5 7.♗b3 d6 8.c3 ♘a5 9.♗c2 c5 10.d3 ♘c6 11.♘bd2 0-0 12.♘f1 ♖e8 13.♘e3 d5?!** The main line is 13...♗f8. **14.e×d5 ♘×d5 15.♘×d5 ♕×d5** (D)

**16.d4!** Alekhine exploits 13...d5?! and opens even more gates, starting a very dangerous attack. **16...e×d4 17.♗e4 ♕d7** 17...♕d6? 18.♗f4± **18.c×d4 ♗f6?!** 18...♗b7 19.d5 ♘d4 20.♘e5 ♕d8 looks suspicious for Black because White has options like ♗×h7+ and ♕h5, but it might be worth investigating in more detail. **19.♗g5! ♖×e4** 19...♗×d4? runs into 20.♗f5! ♖e6 21.♗×e6 f×e6 22.♘×d4 c×d4 23.♕b3±. **20.♖×e4 ♗×d4 21.♘×d4 ♘×d4 22.♕h5?!** The direct 22.♖e7 is better because the counterattack 22...♕c6 23.♖c1 ♗h3 can simply be met by 24.f3±. **22...♗b7?** A miscalculation. 22...g6 23.♕h6 ♗b7 24.♖h4 f6 25.♗×f6 ♘f5 26.♕g5 ♘×h4 27.♕×h4 ♖e8 is almost equal. **23.♖h4 ♕f5!?** 23...h6 24.♗×h6 ♕c6 25.♖g4 g6 26.♗e3± **24.♗e3** (D)

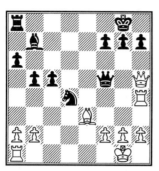

**24...♖d8??** A blunder. Eliskases had two options to continue the fight: 24...♗f3 25.♕×f5 ♘×f5 26.♖f4 ♘×e3 27.♖×f3 ♘c2 28.♖d1 ♘d4±; and 24...♕×h5 25.♖×h5 ♘e6 26.♖e5 c4±. **25.♖×d4** Eliskases resigned in view of 25...♕×h5 26.♖×d8#. **1-0**

**(103) Alekhine – Frydman**
Podebrady 1936 (D)

Alekhine shows good technique and plays against Black's king to win the e5-pawn, when his connected passed pawns will give him victory: **36.b4+!! ♚c4** 36...♚×b4 37.♖e6 ♖h3+ 38.♚f2 ♖h2+ 39.♚f3 ♖×c2 40.♖×e5 ♖c6 41.♖e7+– **37.♖d6 ♖h3+** 37...♖×c2 38.♖d5 ♖c3+ 39.♚e2 ♚×b4 40.♖×e5+– **38.♚e2 ♖h4 39.♚f3 h5** 39...♖f4+ 40.♚e3 ♖f1 41.♖e6 ♖e1+ 42.♚f3 ♚d4 43.c3+ ♚×c3 44.♖×e5+– **40.♖e6 ♖f4+** 40...♚d4 41.c3+ ♚×c3 42.♖×e5 ♖h1 43.♚g2

♖a1 44.f6+– **41.♚e3 h4 42.♖×e5 h3** (D)

**43.♖d5!** Again Alekhine cuts the king off. The greedy 43.♚×f4?? h2 44.f6 h1♕ 45.♖e7 only leads to a draw. **43...♖h4** 43...♖f1 44.♖d2+– **44.♖d4+ ♚c3** 44...♚b5 45.♖d1 h2 46.♖h1 ♚c6 47.c4 ♚d6 48.♚d4+– **45.♖d1 h2 46.♖h1 ♖h3+** 46...♚×b4 47.f6 ♚c5 48.f7 ♖h8 49.♖×h2+– **47.♚f4 ♖h4+ 48.♚e5 ♚d2 49.f6 ♚e3 50.♚d6 ♖×e4 51.♖×h2 ♖d4+ 52.♚e6 1-0**

However, in the second half of the tournament, a crisis arose, and Alekhine, having made one draw too many, suddenly fell a half-point behind Flohr, who finished first.

**Zürich Tournament, July 1934**
This contest in Switzerland became the major international tournament of the year. The field included world champion Alexander Alekhine and candidates for the grandmaster title Flohr, Euwe, Bogoljubow, and Nimzowitsch. The tournament sensation was the performance of the 65-year-old ex-world champion Lasker who had not played in tournaments for nine years.

Fate brought Alekhine and Lasker together in the tournament for the third time in twenty years. In St. Petersburg

*Podebrady 1936*

| | | 1 | 2 | 3 | 4 | 5 | 6 | 7 | 8 | 9 | 10 | 11 | 12 | 13 | 14 | 15 | 16 | 17 | 18 | Total |
|---|---|---|---|---|---|---|---|---|---|---|---|---|---|---|---|---|---|---|---|---|
| 1 | **Flohr** | X | ½ | ½ | ½ | 1 | 0 | ½ | 1 | 1 | 1 | 1 | ½ | 1 | ½ | 1 | 1 | 1 | 1 | **13** |
| 2 | **Alekhine** | ½ | X | 1 | ½ | ½ | 1 | ½ | ½ | 1 | ½ | 1 | ½ | 1 | 1 | 1 | ½ | 1 | ½ | **12½** |
| 3 | **Foltys** | ½ | 0 | X | ½ | ½ | 1 | 0 | 1 | 0 | ½ | 1 | ½ | 1 | 1 | ½ | 1 | 1 | 1 | **11** |
| 4 | **Stahlberg** | ½ | ½ | ½ | X | ½ | 0 | 0 | 1 | ½ | 1 | 1 | ½ | 0 | 1 | 1 | 1 | 1 | ½ | **10½** |
| 5 | **Pirc** | 0 | ½ | ½ | ½ | X | ½ | ½ | ½ | ½ | ½ | ½ | 1 | 1 | 1 | 1 | 1 | 0 | 1 | **10½** |
| 6 | **Eliskases** | 1 | 0 | 0 | 1 | ½ | X | ½ | 1 | ½ | 1 | ½ | ½ | 1 | ½ | 0 | 0 | 1 | ½ | **9½** |
| 7 | **Richter** | ½ | ½ | 1 | 1 | ½ | ½ | X | 0 | ½ | ½ | 0 | ½ | 0 | 1 | 0 | ½ | 1 | 1 | **9** |
| 8 | **Pelikan** | 0 | ½ | 0 | 0 | ½ | 0 | 1 | X | 0 | 1 | 0 | 1 | ½ | 1 | ½ | 1 | 1 | 1 | **9** |
| 9 | **Frydman** | 0 | 0 | 1 | ½ | ½ | ½ | ½ | 1 | X | 0 | ½ | 1 | 0 | 0 | 0 | 1 | 1 | 1 | **8½** |
| 10 | **Petrovs** | 0 | ½ | ½ | 0 | ½ | 0 | ½ | 0 | 1 | X | 1 | ½ | ½ | 1 | 1 | 0 | 1 | ½ | **8½** |
| 11 | **Steiner** | 0 | 0 | 0 | 0 | ½ | ½ | 1 | 1 | ½ | 0 | X | 1 | ½ | 0 | 1 | 1 | ½ | 1 | **8½** |
| 12 | **Opocensky** | ½ | ½ | ½ | ½ | 0 | ½ | ½ | 0 | 0 | ½ | 0 | X | 1 | 0 | ½ | 1 | 1 | 1 | **8** |
| 13 | **Treybal** | 0 | 0 | 0 | 1 | 0 | 0 | 1 | ½ | 1 | ½ | ½ | 0 | X | 0 | 1 | ½ | ½ | ½ | **7** |
| 14 | **Menchik** | ½ | 0 | 0 | 0 | 0 | ½ | 0 | 0 | 1 | 0 | 1 | 1 | 1 | X | 0 | 1 | 0 | 1 | **7** |
| 15 | **Zinner** | 0 | 0 | ½ | 0 | 0 | 1 | 1 | ½ | 1 | 0 | 0 | ½ | 0 | 1 | X | 0 | 0 | 1 | **6½** |
| 16 | **Skalicka** | 0 | ½ | 0 | 0 | 0 | 1 | ½ | 0 | 0 | 1 | 0 | 0 | ½ | 0 | 1 | X | 1 | ½ | **6** |
| 17 | **Fazekas** | 0 | 0 | 0 | 0 | 1 | 0 | 0 | 0 | 0 | 0 | ½ | 0 | ½ | 1 | 1 | 0 | X | 0 | **4** |
| 18 | **Thomas** | 0 | ½ | 0 | ½ | 0 | ½ | 0 | 0 | 0 | ½ | 0 | 0 | ½ | 0 | 0 | ½ | 1 | X | **4** |

1914, the young Russian master drew their game in the preliminary tournament but suffered two cruel defeats in the final. Ten years later, at New York, Alekhine again failed (½-1½). In both events Alekhine only finished third, whereas Lasker was first. So, in Zürich, Alekhine desired a double success: to take first prize and also defeat Lasker. The drawing of colors was favorable for him: he played White. In the Queen's Gambit Declined, Black adopted a new plan for developing his queenside, and almost managed to equalize. However, Lasker's inaccuracy on move 17 resulted in a sudden increase of activity of the white pieces. Alekhine's knight, queen, and rook began demolishing his opponent's kingside, and everything was finished by a spectacular queen sacrifice on move 26!

**(104) Alekhine – Lasker**
Zürich 1934
Queen's Gambit Declined [D67]

**1.d4 d5 2.c4 e6 3.♘c3 ♘f6 4.♘f3 ♗e7 5.♗g5 ♘bd7 6.e3 0-0 7.♖c1 c6 8.♗d3 d×c4 9.♗×c4 ♘d5 10.♗×e7 ♕×e7 11.♘e4 ♘5f6 12.♘g3 e5 13.0-0 e×d4 14.♘f5 ♕d8 15.♘3×d4 ♘e5 16.♗b3 ♗×f5 17.♘×f5 ♕b6?** "Here is where it tells that Lasker was never an openings expert and relied almost exclusively on common sense. It required only one accurate move by Black...and the position would have become a dead draw" (Kasparov). 17...g6 18.♕d4 ♕×d4 19.♘×d4 and a draw was agreed in Euwe-Flohr, Nottingham 1936. **18.♕d6!** Now the queen occupies such a comanding position that Black is in big trouble. **18...♘ed7 19.♖fd1 ♖ad8 20.♕g3 g6 21.♕g5 ♔h8?** The more active 21...♘e4! gives better practical chances, e.g., 22.♕e7 g×f5 23.♖×d7 ♖×d7 24.♕×d7 ♕b5±. **22.♘d6 ♔g7** (D)

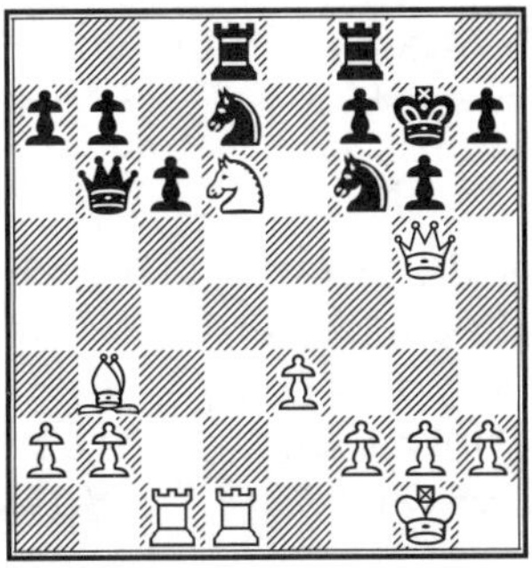

**23.e4! ♘g8 24.♖d3 f6?** Allowing a forced mate. 24...h6? is also wrong because of 25.♘f5+ ♔h7 26.♘xh6+–; but 24...♘df6 still offered some resistance, although White is clearly on top after 25.♖cd1+–. **25.♘f5+ ♔h8 26.♕xg6!** because 26...hxg6 is met by 27.♖h3+ ♘h6 28.♖xh6# Lasker resigned. **1-0**

At Zürich, Alekhine defeated, for the first and only time, his boyhood idol, Emanuel Lasker.

It was in Zürich that Alekhine said, at the closing ceremony banquet, that "Lasker was [his] teacher and without him [he] could not have become what [he is] now. The idea of chess art is unthinkable without Emanuel Lasker." The world champion's significant words of gratitude were heard all over the world.

"Alekhine," remembered Salo Flohr, "believed that the double Devil's dozen – the number 26 – was lucky for him. Once he bet on this number in roulette, and won. The date of his marriage to Grace Wishart was March 26, the second match with Bogoljubow was decided in twenty-six games, the memorable win over Lasker was in twenty-six moves!"

**(105) Alekhine – Rosselli,Stefano**
Zürich 1934
Queen's Pawn Game [D05]

**1.d4 d5 2.♘f3 ♘f6 3.e3 e6 4.♗d3 c5 5.b3 cxd4 6.exd4 ♗d6 7.0-0 0-0 8.♗b2 ♘c6 9.a3 b6 10.♘bd2 ♗b7 11.♕e2 ♕c7 12.♘e5 ♘e7 13.f4 ♖ac8 14.♖ac1**

**g6 15.g4 h5 16.h3 ♔g7 17.c4 ♕d8 18.c5 ♗xe5 19.fxe5** (D)

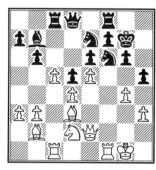

**19...♘d7?** Too passive. 19...♘e4! 20.♘xe4 dxe4 21.♗xe4 ♗xe4 22.♕xe4 hxg4 23.hxg4 ♘d5 gives Black good compensation because of his pressure on the light squares and potential counterplay in the center and against White's king. **20.b4 hxg4 21.hxg4 ♖h8 22.♘f3 bxc5 23.bxc5 ♘c6 24.♕e3 ♕e7 25.♔g2 f5?** Opening many lines for White's attack. 25...♘a5 26.♕g5 ♖ce8 27.♖c2 ♘c4 28.♔g3± keeps the position more closed. **26.exf6+ ♘xf6 27.♕g5 ♖h6 28.♖h1 ♖ch8** 28...♘g8 29.♖xh6 ♕xg5 30.♖h7+ ♔xh7 31.♘xg5+ ♔g7 32.♘xe6++– **29.♖xh6 ♖xh6 30.♖e1 ♘d8 31.♘e5 ♘g8 32.♗c1 ♕e8 33.♖f1 ♗c6** (D)

**34.♖f6!!** White can win in many ways and Alekhine chooses a stylish one.

*Zürich 1934*

| | | 1 | 2 | 3 | 4 | 5 | 6 | 7 | 8 | 9 | 10 | 11 | 12 | 13 | 14 | 15 | 16 | Total |
|---|---|---|---|---|---|---|---|---|---|---|---|---|---|---|---|---|---|---|
| **1** | **Alekhine** | X | 0 | ½ | ½ | 1 | 1 | 1 | 1 | 1 | 1 | 1 | 1 | 1 | 1 | 1 | 1 | **13** |
| **2** | **Euwe** | 1 | X | ½ | 1 | 0 | ½ | 1 | ½ | 1 | 1 | 1 | 1 | ½ | 1 | 1 | 1 | **12** |
| **3** | **Flohr** | ½ | ½ | X | ½ | ½ | ½ | ½ | 1 | 1 | 1 | 1 | 1 | 1 | 1 | 1 | 1 | **12** |
| **4** | **Bogoljubow** | ½ | 0 | ½ | X | 1 | ½ | ½ | ½ | 1 | 1 | 1 | 1 | 1 | 1 | 1 | 1 | **11½** |
| **5** | **Lasker** | 0 | 1 | ½ | 0 | X | 0 | 1 | 0 | ½ | 1 | 1 | 1 | 1 | 1 | 1 | 1 | **10** |
| **6** | **Nimzowitsch** | 0 | ½ | ½ | ½ | 1 | X | ½ | ½ | 0 | 0 | 1 | 1 | ½ | 1 | 1 | 1 | **9** |
| **7** | **Bernstein** | 0 | 0 | ½ | ½ | 0 | ½ | X | 1 | ½ | ½ | ½ | 1 | 1 | 1 | 1 | 1 | **9** |
| **8** | **Stahlberg** | 0 | ½ | 0 | ½ | 1 | ½ | 0 | X | ½ | 1 | 0 | 1 | 1 | ½ | 1 | ½ | **8** |
| **9** | **Johner,H** | 0 | 0 | 0 | 0 | ½ | 1 | ½ | ½ | X | 0 | 1 | 1 | 1 | 1 | ½ | ½ | **7½** |
| **10** | **Henneberger** | 0 | 0 | 0 | 0 | 0 | 1 | ½ | 0 | 1 | X | 0 | 0 | 1 | 0 | 1 | 1 | **5½** |
| **11** | **Gygli** | 0 | 0 | 0 | 0 | 0 | 0 | ½ | 1 | 0 | 1 | X | ½ | 0 | ½ | ½ | 1 | **5** |
| **12** | **Rosselli** | 0 | 0 | 0 | 0 | 0 | 0 | 0 | 0 | 0 | 1 | ½ | X | ½ | 1 | 1 | ½ | **4½** |
| **13** | **Grob** | 0 | ½ | 0 | 0 | 0 | ½ | 0 | 0 | 0 | 0 | 1 | ½ | X | 0 | ½ | 1 | **4** |
| **14** | **Müller** | 0 | 0 | 0 | 0 | 0 | 0 | 0 | ½ | 0 | 1 | ½ | 0 | 1 | X | 0 | 1 | **4** |
| **15** | **Naegeli** | 0 | 0 | 0 | 0 | 0 | 0 | 0 | 0 | ½ | 0 | ½ | 0 | ½ | 1 | X | ½ | **3** |
| **16** | **Joss** | 0 | 0 | 0 | 0 | 0 | 0 | 0 | ½ | ½ | 0 | 0 | ½ | 0 | 0 | ½ | X | **2** |

**34...♘×f6 35.♕×h6+ ♔g8 36.♗g5 1-0**

At Zürich, Alekhine was leading from pole to pole, winning twelve of fifteen, and losing only one to Euwe.

**Nottingham Tournament August 10-28, 1936**

For the first time in history, all four living world champions (Euwe, Lasker, Capablanca, and Alekhine) and four potential challengers, Flohr, Fine, Reshevsky and Botvinnik met in a single competition.

Each of them was capable of winning the tournament. The journalists who covered the event more than once made use of the analogy with another tournament held in England over forty years previously, Hastings 1895, where the flowers of the chess world also were brought together. That tournament was won by one of the youngest participants, Harry Nelson Pillsbury, while Lasker, who had just won the world title, only finished third. So many wondered if Euwe would have more luck now than Lasker did then. Euwe played excellently (as did Lasker in Hastings), was leading for a long time, but after unexpected defeats finished only third.

Chess devotees were also interested in Alekhine's sporting form. Would the winner of San Remo, Bled and Zürich be able to finish ahead of Capablanca at least in a single event? Alekhine behaved in a somewhat restrained manner and was not sociable, preferring the company of his spouse to that of noisy colleagues. While playing, he was chain smoking. Some correspondents even took the trouble to count the number of cigarettes he usually smoked during a game; it was about one hundred. True, some of them were lit for only a few seconds and then extinguished.

When drawing lots, Alekhine drew number one. In the first round, he adjourned the game with Flohr in a winning position. In the second round, he faced Capablanca. In the nine years that had elapsed since their match in Buenos Aires, it was the first time they sat across the board from each other. Alekhine, playing Black, quickly equalized, but, on move 24, he blundered, giving White a material advantage. The last part of the game led to a disagreement. When the game was to be adjourned, there was a dispute about who should seal the move. Alekhine, instead of sealing his move after the gong sounded, made it on the board. Capablanca declined to seal his moved, too. Accordingly, the play was not resumed in this game for a long time, and the conflict was only settled when Black resigned without resuming the play.

In the fifth round, Alekhine faced Botvinnik for the first time. Botvinnik vividly recalls this meeting:

*Alekhine seemed nervous when we were introduced. He was thin, jerky in his movements, and made upon me an impression of a sick man –his eyes flickered from side to side. He seemed to continue drinking... Our actual introduction took place at the chessboard. In a variation of the Sicilian Defense, Alekhine had prepared a highly dangerous line. He was a shrewd psychologist and knew how important it was to suppress the morale of the opponent. So, right up to the critical moment, he played at lightning speed, circling all the time round the board (and his victim) and sitting down at the board only to make his move quickly.*

*It was necessary to suggest to his opponent that everything had been worked out to the end in the quiet of his study and that resistance was therefore useless. Now, I thought for about 20 minutes and found a saving line. True, I would have to sacrifice both knights, but a draw by repetition of moves is guaranteed. So, I sacrificed the knights, but, before repeating moves, I decide to ponder over the position a little – there is no risk for me any longer! Goodness, what has come over Alexander Alexandrovich! He has overlooked Black's counterplay in his analysis ... His tie became undone, his detachable collar shifted to one side, his thinning hair became disheveled. When we agreed to a draw, he was just able to calm down but then, straight away, took on a pose and claimed that he had found the whole line at the board.*

**(106) Alekhine – Botvinnik**
Nottingham 1936
Sicilian Defense [B72]

**1.e4 c5 2.♘f3 d6 3.d4 c×d4 4.♘×d4 ♘f6 5.♘c3 g6 6.♗e2 ♗g7 7.♗e3 ♘c6 8.♘b3 ♗e6 9.f4 0-0 10.g4 d5** 10...♘a5 and 10...♖c8 are the alternatives. **11.f5 ♗c8 12.e×d5 ♘b4** (D)

**13.d6** This leads more or less to a forced draw. 13.♗f3! is the critical continuation. **13...♕×d6 14.♗c5 ♕f4 15.♖f1 ♕×h2 16.♗×b4 ♘×g4 17.♗×g4 ♕g3+** 17...g×f5? 18.♕e2 ♕g3+ 19.♕f2± **18.♖f2 ♕g1+ 19.♖f1 ♕g3+ 20.♖f2 ♕g1+ ½-½**

Meanwhile, after seven rounds, Euwe was leading with six points. Botvinnik was one point behind, and a half-point behind Botvinnik were Reshevsky and Fine. Alekhine, who had lost to Reshevsky and drew several games, had only three points, his win against Flohr in the first round remaining so far the only one. But, the game he won in the ninth round against the world champion became a real stimulus for him. In that hard-fought game, he subtly outplayed his opponent. The game was adjourned three times deep into the queen-and-pawn ending.

**(107) Alekhine – Euwe**
Nottingham 1936
French Defense [C02]

**1.e4 e6 2.d4 d5 3.e5 c5 4.♘f3 ♘c6 5.♗d3 c×d4 6.0-0 f6 7.♗b5 ♗d7 8.♗×c6 b×c6 9.♕×d4 f×e5?!** This makes it easy for White to establish a blockade on the dark squares. The main line is 9...c5. **10.♕×e5 ♘f6 11.♗f4 ♗c5 12.♘c3 0-0 13.♗g3 ♕e7 14.a3?!** Quite slow. 14.♖ae1 ♗c8 15.♘a4 ♗b6 16.c4 is more in the spirit of the position because it solidifies the blockade. **14...a5?!** 14...♘g4 15.♕e2 ♗d6 16.♘e5 ♘×e5 17.♗×e5 ♖f5 is a better way to fight against White's control of the dark central squares. **15.♖fe1 ♖a7 16.♘a4 ♖b7 17.♕c3?!** Too ambitious. 17.♘×c5 ♕×c5 18.♘d4 is not worse for White because 18...♘g4? runs into 19.♘×e6 ♕e7 20.♗h4 ♕f7 21.♕d6. **17...♗a7 18.♕×a5?** Too greedy. 18.♗h4 makes it more difficult for Black to develop an attack. **18...♘e4 19.♕a6?** The prophylactic 19.♖e2, to meet 19...♘×g3 (19...♗e8!?) 20.h×g3 e5 with 21.♕a6, is more prudent. **19...♗e8** 19...♗c8!? was even stronger because 20.♕×c6? runs into 20...♘×g3 21.h×g3 ♖c7 22.♕b5 ♖×c2 23.♖e2 ♗d7−+. **20.b4** (D)

*Nottingham 1936*

| | | 1 | 2 | 3 | 4 | 5 | 6 | 7 | 8 | 9 | 10 | 11 | 12 | 13 | 14 | 15 | Total |
|---|---|---|---|---|---|---|---|---|---|---|---|---|---|---|---|---|---|
| 1 | **Capablanca** | X | ½ | ½ | 1 | ½ | 1 | 0 | ½ | 1 | ½ | ½ | 1 | 1 | 1 | 1 | **10** |
| 2 | **Botvinnik** | ½ | X | ½ | ½ | ½ | ½ | ½ | ½ | 1 | 1 | 1 | 1 | 1 | 1 | ½ | **10** |
| 3 | **Fine** | ½ | ½ | X | ½ | ½ | ½ | ½ | 1 | ½ | ½ | 1 | 1 | 1 | ½ | 1 | **9½** |
| 4 | **Reshevsky** | 0 | ½ | ½ | X | 0 | 1 | ½ | 1 | 1 | ½ | 1 | 1 | 1 | 1 | ½ | **9½** |
| 5 | **Euwe** | ½ | ½ | ½ | 1 | X | 0 | ½ | 0 | 1 | 1 | ½ | 1 | 1 | 1 | 1 | **9½** |
| 6 | **Alekhine** | 0 | ½ | ½ | 0 | 1 | X | 1 | ½ | ½ | 1 | 1 | ½ | 1 | ½ | 1 | **9** |
| 7 | **Flohr** | 1 | ½ | ½ | ½ | ½ | 0 | X | 1 | 1 | ½ | 1 | 0 | 0 | 1 | 1 | **8½** |
| 8 | **Lasker** | ½ | ½ | 0 | 0 | 1 | ½ | 0 | X | ½ | ½ | 1 | 1 | 1 | 1 | 1 | **8½** |
| 9 | **Vidmar** | 0 | 0 | ½ | 0 | 0 | ½ | 0 | ½ | X | ½ | 1 | ½ | 1 | ½ | 1 | **6** |
| 10 | **Tartakower** | ½ | 0 | ½ | ½ | 0 | 0 | ½ | ½ | ½ | X | ½ | 0 | 0 | 1 | 1 | **5½** |
| 11 | **Bogoljubow** | ½ | 0 | 0 | 0 | ½ | 0 | 0 | 0 | 0 | ½ | X | 1 | 1 | 1 | 1 | **5½** |
| 12 | **Tylor** | 0 | 0 | 0 | 0 | 0 | ½ | 1 | 0 | ½ | 1 | 0 | X | ½ | ½ | ½ | **4½** |
| 13 | **Alexander** | 0 | 0 | 0 | 0 | 0 | 0 | 1 | 0 | 0 | 1 | 0 | ½ | X | ½ | ½ | **3½** |
| 14 | **Thomas** | 0 | 0 | ½ | 0 | 0 | ½ | 0 | 0 | ½ | 0 | 0 | ½ | ½ | X | ½ | **3** |
| 15 | **Winter** | 0 | ½ | 0 | ½ | 0 | 0 | 0 | 0 | 0 | 0 | 0 | ½ | ½ | ½ | X | **2½** |

*Alekhine at Nottingham 1936.*

**20...g5?** Attacking is the right concept, but this is too radical. 20...♗h5! 21.♘c5 (21.♖×e4 d×e4 22.♘e5 ♕f6) 21...♗×c5 22.b×c5 ♗×f3 23.g×f3 ♘g5 24.♗d6?! ♕f7 gives Black good play in both cases. **21.♘c5!** Alekhine stops Black short and underscores that he will use the weak squares around Black's king. **21...♗×c5 22.b×c5 ♘×c5 23.♕e2 ♘e4** White also obtains attacking chances after 23...♗h5 24.♕e3 ♗×f3 25.g×f3 ♖a7 26.h4. **24.♕e3 ♗g6 25.♘e5 c5 26.♘×g6 h×g6 27.f3 ♘×g3 28.h×g3 ♔f7! 29.a4 ♖a8 30.♔f2 ♖b2?** 30...♖b4, in order to meet 31.♖h1 with the surprising 31...♔f6, was the last chance to offer real resistance. **31.♖e2 c4 32.♖h1!** (D)

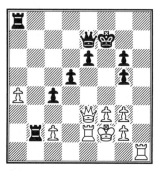

**32...♔g8?** A miscalculation because White's king will always find a safe haven in the following complications. But 32...♕f6 33.♖h7+ ♔g8 34.♖d7 ♖a6 (34...♖×a4? 35.♖d6+−) 35.g4± is also very depressing for Black of course. **33.♕e5! ♕a7+ 34.♔f1 ♖b1+ 35.♖e1 ♖×e1+ 36.♔×e1 ♕g7 37.♕×e6+ ♔f8** 37...♕f7? 38.♖h8+− **38.♕×d5** (D)

**38...♕c3+** After 38...♖e8+? White's king hides in the center with 39.♔d2 ♕f6 40.♖h7 ♖e6 41.♖d7 ♔e8 42.♕d4+−. **39.♔f2 ♖e8** 39...♕×c2+ allows the monarch to find a safe shelter on the kingside: 40.♔g1 ♕b1+ 41.♔h2+−. **40.g4 ♕e3+** 40...♕×c2+ 41.♔g3 ♕c3 42.♕×g5 ♕d4 43.♕f4+−. **41.♔g3 ♕f4+ 42.♔h3 ♖e7 43.♕c5 ♕f6 44.g3! ♕h8+ 45.♔g2 ♕c3 46.♖h7 ♕×c2+ 47.♔h3 ♕e2 48.♖×e7 ♕×e7 49.♕×c4 ♕e1 50.♕c5+ ♔f7**

**51.♔g2 ♕a1?! 52.♔c2?!** 52.♕×g5!?
♕b2+ 53.♔h3 ♕h8+ 54.♕h4 ♕a1
55.♕h7+ ♔f8 56.♕h6+ ♔f7
57.♕f4++− **52...♔f6 53.♕b3
♔e5?! 54.♔f2?!** 54.♕b8+!?, in order
to exploit the insecure position of
Black's king, is more precise: 54...♔d5
55.♕b5+ ♔e6 56.♕e8+ ♔d5
57.♕d7+ ♔c5 58.♕b5+ ♔d6
59.♕×g5+−. **54...♔f6 55.♕b6+
♔g7 56.♕b4 ♕h1?** Putting the
queen offside. It is usually better to
keep it more centralized. Therefore,
56...♕a2+ 57.♔e3 ♕e6+ 58.♔d3
♕a6+ 59.♕c4 ♕b7 is better, but White
should still win in the long run.
**57.♕e1 ♕h2+ 58.♔e3 ♔h7
59.a5 ♕a2 60.♕d2 ♕a1 61.♔e2
♔h6 62.f4 g×f4 63.g×f4 ♕a4
64.♔f2!?** A good prophylactic move
to sidestep checks. **64...♔h7 65.g5
♕a3 66.♕d7+ ♔h8 67.♕c8+
♔h7 68.♕c7+ ♔h8 69.♔e2
♕a2+ 70.♔e3 ♕b3+ 71.♔d4
♕b4+ 72.♔d5 ♕b5+ 73.♔d4
♕a6 74.♕b6 ♕c8 75.♕d6 ♕c2
76.a6 ♕d2+?! 77.♔e5 ♕c3+
78.♔e6 ♕c8+ 79.♔e7 ♔h7
80.♕d7 ♕c3 81.♔e6+** Black resigned because, after any retreat by the
king, the queens are exchanged (e.g.,
81...♔h8 82.♕e8+♔h7 83.♕f7+♔h8
84.♕f6+, etc.). **1-0**

"Euwe loses to Alekhine. It is one of
the most beautiful games of the tournament," as journalist P. Mussuri shares
his impressions with the readers
(*Shakhmaty v SSSR*). Alekhine is satisfied. When asked, "How do you expect to do in the return match with
Euwe?" Alekhine simply replied that he
has "no doubts of winning it."

Of the remaining five games, his game
against Alexander is memorable because it received a special prize "for
the best executed kingside attack" (See,
Attack). His powerful finish almost allowed him to overtake the leading
group.

At the end of the Nottingham event, the
*Manchester Guardian* published
Alekhine's article that assessed the
battles at Nottingham and characterized
the play of some of the participants. In
particular, he expressed his admiration
for Lasker as a personality, chess artist, and thinker. Alekhine felt that
"Lasker should serve as an example for
all chessplayers of this generation and
the next." He also stressed that the success achieved by Botvinnik was not
unexpected. "His achievement at
Nottingham confirms that he is the
most likely candidate for the world
title." Soon after Alekhine published
his annotated book *Nottingham 1936*.

### AVRO 1938

This double round-robin event was held
in the Netherlands. The participants
were the strongest grandmasters of the
day: world champion Alekhine, former
champions Euwe and Capablanca and
the potential challengers Botvinnik,
Fine, Flohr, Keres, and Reshevsky. As
in 1927 in New York, Alekhine objected to the intention of the organizers to declare the winner of the tournament the title challenger. At the opening ceremony, he said that he was prepared to play any well-known grandmaster who would ensure the required prize
fund.

The conditions of play in the tournament were very unfavorable, with almost every round being played in a different town. Alekhine lost three games (two of them to Fine and one to Botvinnik) and also won three games, defeating Reshevsky, Flohr and Capablanca. That was his first tournament win over the Cuban since their title match. Ironically, the game was played on Capablanca's 50th birthday, 19 November 1938. Alekhine was resolute and, according to one the participants, Salo Flohr, he even dropped in at the barber's before the game. To the playful remark of the jokester grandmaster that "today one should look pretty," he reacted nervously: "I will try to do so that there would not be a celebration" (S.Flohr, "Through the Prism of Half a Century," Moscow, 1986). Yes, Alekhine clearly intended to win the game.

### (108) Alekhine – Capablanca
AVRO 1938
French Defense [C06]

**1.e4 e6 2.d4 d5 3.♘d2 ♘f6 4.e5 ♘fd7 5.♗d3 c5 6.c3 ♘c6 7.♘e2 ♛b6 8.♘f3 c×d4 9.c×d4 ♗b4+ 10.♔f1!?** The main line is 10.♗d2. **10...♗e7 11.a3 (D)**

**11...♘f8?** Too slow and too passive. 11...f6 is called for to open the posi-

tion to exploit White's loss of time by moving the king. **12.b4 ♗d7 13.♗e3 ♘d8?! 14.♘c3 a5?! 15.♘a4 ♛a7 16.b5 b6 17.g3 f5 18.♔g2 ♘f7 19.♛d2 h6 20.h4 ♘h7 21.h5 ♘fg5 22.♘h4 ♘e4 23.♛b2 ♔f7?!** The king is not safe here, as Alekhine shows immediately. Perhaps 23...0-0 is better, but White's advantage is of course not in doubt. **24.f3 ♘eg5 25.g4 f×g4 26.♗g6+ ♔g8 27.f4!** The battering ram is coming. **27...♘f3 28.♗×h7+ ♖×h7** 28...♔×h7 29.♛b1+ ♔g8 30.♘g6 ♗e8 31.♔g3+– **29.♘g6 ♗d8 30.♖ac1 ♗e8 (D)**

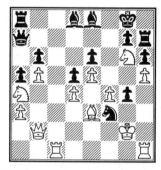

**31.♔g3!** The king itself deals with the problem. **31...♛f7 32.♔×g4 ♘h4** 32...♘g5 33.f×g5 ♛f5+ 34.♔g3 ♗×g5 35.♖hf1+– **33.♘×h4 ♛×h5+ 34.♔g3 ♛f7 35.♘f3 1-0**

Black had overstepped the time limit. With this win in their last encounter in official competitions, Alekhine evened his score against Capablanca (+7 -7 =33). Also, Alekhine, for the first time, stood higher in the tournament, though it was little consolation to him because he only shared fourth-sixth places with Euwe and Reshevsky.

During the AVRO tournament, Botvinnik's negotiations with Alekhine

### AVRO 1938

|   |           | 1   | 2   | 3    | 4   | 5    | 6    | 7    | 8    | Total |
|---|-----------|-----|-----|------|-----|------|------|------|------|-------|
| 1 | **Keres**     | X   | 1½  | ½½   | ½½  | 1½   | ½½   | 1½   | ½½   | 8½    |
| 2 | **Fine**      | 0½  | X   | 1½   | 10  | 10   | 11   | ½½   | 1½   | 8½    |
| 3 | **Botvinnik** | ½½  | 0½  | X    | ½0  | 1½   | 1½   | ½1   | ½½   | 7½    |
| 4 | **Euwe**      | ½½  | 01  | ½1   | X   | 0½   | 0½   | 01   | 1½   | 7     |
| 5 | **Reshevsky** | 0½  | 01  | 0½   | 1½  | X    | ½½   | ½½   | 1½   | 7     |
| 6 | **Alekhine**  | ½½  | 00  | 0½   | 1½  | ½½   | X    | ½1   | ½1   | 7     |
| 7 | **Capablanca**| 0½  | ½½  | ½0   | 10  | ½½   | ½0   | X    | ½1   | 6     |
| 8 | **Flohr**     | ½½  | 0½  | ½½   | 0½  | 0½   | ½0   | ½0   | X    | 4½    |

about their world championship match had begun. "Alekhine, in principle, agreed to play in Moscow," Botvinnik recalls, "provided that 3 months before the start of the match he could play there in a training tournament. In January, 1939, the Soviet government permitted the organization and budgeting of the match, and our correspondence with Alekhine started, but it was interrupted by the Second World War."

**Munich Tournaments, 1941, 1942**
The Nazis called them European Championships.

**September 8-21, 1941**
The Swedish player Gosta Stoltz (1904-1963) won this tournament of sixteen players, who scored twelve points. Alekhine and Lundin (Sweden) shared 2nd-3rd places, 1½ points behind the winner

**(109) Kieninger,Georg – Alekhine**
Munich 1941
Ruy Lopez [C64]

**1.e4 e5 2.♘f3 ♘c6 3.♗b5 ♗c5 4.c3 ♕f6 5.0-0 ♘ge7 6.d3 h6 7.♘bd2** 7.♗e3 is the main line. **7...0-0 8.♘c4?!** 8.b4 ♗b6 9.♘c4 is more precise. **8...♘g6 9.d4?!** Opening the position like this plays into Black's hands because he is better developed and will obtain the bishop pair. **9...e×d4 10.♗×c6 d×c6 11.♘×d4 ♖e8 12.♘b3 ♗f8** 12...♗e6!? **13.♕c2 ♕e6 14.♘cd2 ♘h4 15.f3?! c5 16.♖d1?** (D) Kieninger removes the last defender from the kingside. 16.♖f2 b6 17.♘f1 is more tenacious.

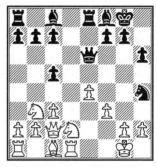

**16...♘×g2?** It is amazing that Black can play like this and obtain a dangerous attack anyway. But, 16...♕g6 17.g3 ♗h3 18.♔f2 f5 simply wins. **17.♔×g2 ♕h3+ 18.♔g1 ♗d6 19.♘f1 ♕×f3 20.♖d3?** This forces, more or less, a technically lost endgame. 20.♖e1 defends, e.g., 20...♗f5 (20...♗h3 21.♕e2) 21.♖e3, and Black has compensation in both cases, but not more. **20...♕×e4 21.♖d2 ♕h4 22.♖g2 ♗h3 23.♕f2 ♕e4 24.♗d2 ♕×g2+ 25.♕×g2 ♗×g2 26.♔×g2 ♖e2+ 27.♔f3 ♖ae8**

## Munich 1942

|    |            | 1 | 2 | 3 | 4 | 5 | 6 | 7 | 8 | 9 | 10 | 11 | 12 | Total |
|----|------------|---|---|---|---|---|---|---|---|---|----|----|----|-------|
| 1  | Alekhine   | X | 1 | ½ | ½ | 1 | 1 | 1 | 0 | 1 | ½  | 1  | 1  | 8½    |
| 2  | Keres      | 0 | X | 1 | ½ | 0 | 1 | ½ | 1 | ½ | 1  | 1  | 1  | 7½    |
| 3  | Foltys     | ½ | 0 | X | 1 | ½ | 1 | 0 | ½ | 1 | 1  | ½  | 1  | 7     |
| 4  | Bogoljubow | ½ | ½ | 0 | X | 1 | 0 | 1 | 1 | ½ | 1  | ½  | 1  | 7     |
| 5  | Richter    | 0 | 1 | ½ | 0 | X | ½ | ½ | 1 | ½ | 1  | 1  | 1  | 7     |
| 6  | Barcza     | 0 | 0 | 0 | 1 | ½ | X | ½ | 0 | 1 | ½  | 1  | 1  | 5½    |
| 7  | Junge      | 0 | ½ | 1 | 0 | ½ | ½ | X | 1 | ½ | 0  | 0  | 1  | 5     |
| 8  | Rellstab   | 1 | 0 | ½ | 0 | 0 | 1 | 0 | X | 0 | ½  | 1  | ½  | 4½    |
| 9  | Stoltz     | 0 | ½ | 0 | ½ | ½ | 0 | ½ | 1 | X | 0  | 0  | 1  | 4     |
| 10 | Rohacek    | ½ | 0 | 0 | 0 | 0 | ½ | 1 | ½ | 1 | X  | ½  | 0  | 4     |
| 11 | Napolitano | 0 | 0 | ½ | ½ | 0 | 0 | 1 | 0 | 1 | ½  | X  | 0  | 3½    |
| 12 | Rabar      | 0 | 0 | 0 | 0 | 0 | 0 | 0 | ½ | 0 | 1  | 1  | X  | 2½    |

**28.罝d1 b6 29.②c1 罝2e6 30.b3 c4!? 31.b×c4 罝f6+ 32.♔g2 罝e4 33.②e3 ♗c5 34.罝e1 ♗×e3 35.罝×e3 罝g4+ 36.罝g3 罝×c4 37.罝f3 罝d6 38.♗f4 罝d1 39.②e2 罝a1 40.♔g3 c5 41.罝e3 罝×a2 42.h4 b5 43.h5 0-1**

**September, 1942**
In this tournament of twelve players, Alekhine finished first, a point ahead of Keres. According to Alekhine, "from the creative point of view, at any rate, this Munich tournament turned out to be more fruitful than the preceding one."

**Madrid Tournaments, 1941, 1945**
**December 1941**
This was a small tournament where, apart from Alekhine, five Spanish masters participated. It was referred to as the "Alekhine tournament," and the champion won it easily, winning all five games.

**March 1945**
Alekhine came to Madrid at the invitation of the Spanish Chess Federation to participate in the jubilee tournament at the close of 1943 but, unfortunately, was late and did not participate in the tournament (won by Keres). However, "El Colosso," as he was nicknamed in Spain, remained there and toured the country throughout the following year (1944), playing in small tournaments, matches and giving simultaneous exhibitions. In 1945, he started coaching the very promising youth from the Canaries, Arturo Pomar, and also took part in a number of tournaments. In the ten-player tournament at Madrid, Alekhine won the first prize, scoring 8½ out of 9 points.

**Salzburg Tournaments, 1942, 1943**
In Mozart's native town, the Austrian town of Salzburg, Alekhine happened to play twice during the war years, Paul Keres being his main competitor in both cases.

**June 9-18, 1942**
This was a double round-robin event, in which six of the strongest players of western Europe participated: world champion Alekhine, the former challenger Bogoljubow, and the new challenger Keres, the German champion

Schmidt, the young German talent Junge, and Stoltz of Sweden. Euwe refused to participate. Alekhine had an unlucky start, losing to Bogoljubow and Junge and drawing with Stoltz. However, beginning in the fourth round, he won all his remaining games, including both games with Keres.

**June 9-18, 1943**

Exactly a year later, the double round-robin tournament with six players ended with Alekhine tying for 1st-2nd places with Keres. Before the tournament, Alekhine proposed a world championship match to Keres, but Keres declined the proposal, explaining his refusal by being unprepared for such a responsible competition. "It seems they are waiting until I am sixty," Alekhine commented not without sarcasm. Among the most interesting games played by Alekhine in this tournament is the game he won against Bogoljubow.

**(110) Bogoljubow – Alekhine**
Salzburg 1943
Queen's Pawn Game [D00]

1.d4 ♘f6 2.♗g5 d5 3.c3 ♘e4 4.♗h4 ♕d6?! 5.♘d2 ♗f5 6.♘gf3 ♘d7 7.♕b3 0-0-0?! 8.♘×e4 ♗×e4 9.♗g3 ♕c6 10.♘d2 ♗g6 11.e3 e6 12.c4 ♕b6 13.c5 ♕a5 14.a3 e5 (D)

15.♕d1! A very strong retreat, getting out of the way of White's rolling queenside pawns. 15...c6 16.d×e5? The highly original 16.f4 makes Black's life very difficult in view of 16...e×d4? 17.b4 ♕c7 18.f5 +– . 16...♕×c5

17.♖c1 ♕b6 18.♗e2? Too bold. The simple 18.b4 gives White good play against Black's king on the queenside. 18...♘c5? The aggressive 18...♕×b2!? is better because 19.e6 can be answered by 19...♘c5 (of course, not 19...f×e6?? 20.♖×c6+ b×c6 21.♗a6+ ♕b7 22.♕a4 +– ). 19.b4 ♘d3+ 20.♗×d3 ♗×d3 21.♘f3?! 21.♕g4+ ♖d7 22.♖c3 ♗a6 23.♘b3 ♗c4 24.♕f4 applies more pressure. 21...♗c4 22.♘d4 a5?! The other rook's pawn should advance, viz., 22...h5 to stop ♕g4. 23.♕g4+ ♖d7 24.♖×c4?! The sacrifice should be prepared by 24.♕f4 and only after 24...♕a7 25.b5 ♗×a3 comes 26.♖×c4 d×c4 27.0-0 with a strong attack. 24...d×c4 25.0-0 c5 26.b×a5? Not the right way to open attacking roads. It should be accomplished by 26.e6 f×e6 27.♘×e6. 26...♕g6 (D)

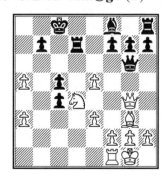

*Salzburg 1943*

| | | 1 | 2 | 3 | 4 | 5 | 6 | Total |
|---|---|---|---|---|---|---|---|---|
| 1 | **Alekhine** | X | 11 | 01 | 11 | 01 | ½1 | 7½ |
| 2 | **Keres** | 00 | X | 1½ | ½½ | ½1 | 11 | 6 |
| 3 | **Junge** | 10 | 0½ | X | ½½ | 01 | ½1 | 5 |
| 4 | **Schmidt** | 00 | ½½ | ½½ | X | 01 | 11 | 5 |
| 5 | **Bogoljubow** | 10 | ½0 | 10 | 10 | X | 00 | 3½ |
| 6 | **Stoltz** | ½0 | 00 | ½0 | 00 | 11 | X | 3 |

**27.a6!?** ♕×a6 Taking the queen, 27...♕×g4?, allows the a-pawn to queen 28.a7=, which gives White a draw. **28.♘e2 ♕e6 29.♕e4 f5 30.♕c2 g5 31.f431 g4?** A strategic mistake because White gains time for his play in the center and on the queenside. After 31...♗e7, followed by a quick activation of the second rook, the extra exchange will count sooner or later. **32.e4! ♖f7?!** The active 32...♖d3 33.e×f5 ♕×f5 34.♕×c4 ♖d2 is the lesser evil. **33.e×f5 ♖×f5 34.♗h4?** The start of a misguided plan. The natural 34.♘c3 gives White a dangerous initiative. **34...♗h6 35.♕e4 ♖hf8 36.g3?** This wastes time and destroys options on the kingside. 36.♖b1 ♖8f7 37.♗g3 ♖d7 38.♘c3 is much more harmonious. **36...♕d7?!** 36...♗g7, in order to open up lines by sacrificing the bishop on e5, was stronger: 37.♖b1 ♖8f7 38.♘c3 ♗×e5−+. **37.♖c1?** The wrong square because the f-pawn is now pinned. The rook should go to b1. **37...♖e8! 38.♔g2?** (D)

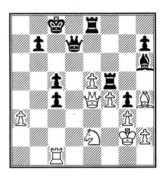

**41.h3 g×h3+ 42.♔h2 ♖f2+ 43.♔g1 ♖g2+ 44.♔h1** (D)

38.♖b1 was forced when, after 38...♖f7 39.♖c1 ♕d3 40.♖×c4 ♕×e4 41.♖×e4 ♔d7 42.♘c3, White keeps practical drawing chances. **38...♖e×e5!** Alekhine rarely missed such shots. **39.f×e5** 39.♕×c4 ♖e8 40.♘d4 ♖d5−+ **39...♗×c1 40.♘×c1 ♕e6**

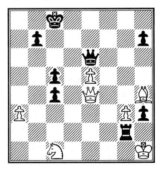

**44...♕d7!** The queen enters the attack and decides the issue because White must exchange into a lost ending. **45.♕f3 ♕d4 46.♕f8+ ♔c7 47.♕e7+ ♔b6 48.♕d6+ ♕×d6 49.e×d6 ♔c6 50.♗e7 ♖c2 51.♗g5 ♔×d6 52.a4 h5 0-1**

**Junge, Klaus** (January 1, 1924, Concepcion, Chili-April 17, 1945, near

Welle, Germany)
One of the most talented German masters of the mid-20th century.

Already in his childhood Klaus had shown extraordinary abilities, learning how to read and write very early. His father, Otto Junge, a passionate lover of chess, was able to instill this love in his son. As early as 12 years old, Klaus frequented the Hamburg chess club, and, at 15, he won the right to participate in a masters tournament. Two years later, Klaus was one of the strongest players in Germany. During World War II, he was able to play in twelve tournaments in which his talent was revealed. Only in two of them was he not among the prize winners. But in major tournaments such as Hamburg (1941), Dresden (1942), and Prague (1942), he finished first. In Prague, he tied for first with Alekhine, who only overtook the Hamburg student by winning their personal encounter in the last round. Junge was named the most talented German player after Emanuel Lasker, and a bright future was predicted for him. But, in 1942, Junge was conscripted and was killed ten days before the end of the war.

**(111) Alekhine – Junge**
Salzburg 1942 (D)

**69...♖b6 0-1**

References:
V.A., Charushin. *A Dance at the Edge of a Volcano (Creations of Klaus Junge)*. Nizhni Novgorod, 1993 (Russian).
E., Budrich and D. Schulte. *Das war Klaus Junge. Partien und Aufzeichnungen*. Berlin, 1956.

**Prague Tournaments, 1942, 1943**
As far back as 1921, Alekhine had made his first tour of the capital of Czechoslovakia. A chess club there was named after him. And there he brilliantly performed at the world chess Olympiad ten years later.

Alekhine enjoyed his first tournament in Prague. He called it the golden city, particularly for chess. For

*[h]ere, it is good to play chess. It stands among the few places in Europe (Berlin, Vienna, Paris, Rome, and Madrid) with a chess tradition of many ages. In Prague, a unique chess school developed. And it is Prague that hosted, in 1931, one of the most representative world chess Olympiads. And this Czech capital gave the world a chessplayer of outstanding class, Oldrich Duras, who sacrificed his profession to take up our cause. At 60, he is a welcome participant or guest of any tournament.*

**December, 1942**
Twelve players competed in this event dedicated to Duras' (1882-1957) 60th birthday. Along with the world cham-

*Participants and organizers of the
international tournament at Podebrady, 1936.*

pion and two German players (Junge
and Sämisch), there were also the well-
known Czech masters Foltys,
Opocensky, Kottnauer, Hromadka,
Podgorny and others. Alekhine met the
talented 18-years-old student from
Hamburg, Klaus Junge, midway through
the tournament. Having defeated him
in the decisive encounter, Alekhine was
able to overtake Junge and, with 8½
points out of 11, share first prize with
him.

**(112) Alekhine – Junge,Klaus**
Prague 1942
Catalan Opening [E03]

**1.d4 d5 2.c4 e6 3.♘f3 ♘f6 4.g3
d×c4 5.♕a4+ ♘bd7 6.♗g2 a6
7.♕×c4 b5 8.♕c6 ♖b8 9.0-0 ♗b7
10.♕c2 c5 11.a4 ♗×f3?!** 11...♕b6
is the main line. **12.♗×f3 c×d4
13.a×b5 a×b5 14.♖d1 ♕b6
15.♘d2 e5?!** 15...♗c5!? 16.♘b3 0-0
17.♘×c5 ♘×c5 (Dvoretsky) is much
safer. **16.♘b3 ♘c5 17.♘×c5**
17.♗g5!? **17...♗×c5** (D) 17...♕×c5?

18.♗c6+ ♔d8 19.♕f5 ♕×c6 20.♕×e5
♘d7 21.♖×d4±

**18.♖a6!?** A very courageous sacrifice.
The alternative, 18.♗g5!? 0-0
(18...♖c8?? 19.b4+–) 19.♗×f6 d3
20.♕×d3 ♕×f6 21.♕e4, gives White a
slight pull. Alekhine probably wants
more. **18...♕×a6 19.♕×c5 ♕e6!**
The queen must help the defense directly. 19...♖c8? 20.♕×e5+ ♕e6
(20...♔f8 21.♕×d4) 21.♕×b5+ ♘d7
22.♗f4 0-0 23.♖×d4 gives White the
initiative in both cases. 19...♘d7?
20.♗c6 ♔d8 (20...♖c8? 21.♕×e5+
♔d8 22.♗×d7+–) 21.♗×d7 ♔×d7
22.♕×e5 ♕e6 23.♕×d4+ ♔e7

24.♕a7+ ♔f6 25.♕c5 +− **20.♗c6+
♘d7!** 20...♔d8? 21.♗d2! b4 22.♕a5+
♔e7 23.♕c7+ ♘d7 24.♗×d7 ♕d6
(24...♕×d7? 25.♕×e5+ ♕e6 26.♕×g7
h6 27.♕×d4 +−) 25.♖c1 ♕×c7
26.♖×c7 ± **21.♗×d7+ ♔×d7
22.♕a7+** (D)

**22...♔c6?** 22...♔d6! 23.♗f4 was already given by Junge as leading to a
draw. (a) 23.♖×d4+? is parried by
23...e×d4 24.♗f4+ ♔d5 25.♗×b8
♖c8; (b) 23.♗d2?! allows Black defends with 23...♕d7! 24.♕a6+
(24.♗b4+? ♔e6 25.♕a6+ ♔f5 −+,
Dvoretsky) 24...♔c6 25.♗b4+ ♔c7
26.♕a2 ♖b7 27.♕×f7+ ♔b8; (c)
23.f4!? is given by Fine in his his book
*Chess Marches On!* (1945). Dvoretsky
gives the defense 23...♕d7 (23...f6?
24.f×e5+ f×e5 25.♗f4! with an attack
is Fine's point.) 24.f×e5+ ♔e6
25.♕a6+ ♔e7 26.♗g5+ ♔e8;
23...e×f4 (23...♖hd8!? is an interesting
try to avoid the direct draw, but White
seems to be able to hold, e.g.,
24.♕×d4+ ♔c6 [24...♔e7 25.♕b4+
♔e8 26.♖×d8+ ♖×d8 27.♕×b5+]
25.♖c1+ ♔b7 26.♕c5 ♖bc8
27.♕×b5+) 24.♖×d4+ ♔c6 (24...♔e5
25.♖×f4 ♔d6 26.♖d4+ ±) 25.♖d1
♖hc8 26.♖c1+ ♔d6 27.♖d1 ±
(Junge); 22...♔c8? 23.♗g5 +−.
**23.♗d2 ♖hc8!** 23...♕d7? 24.♖c1+
♔d6 25.♗b4+ ♔e6 26.♖c7 ♕d5

27.♖×f7 ♖he8 28.♖×g7 ♔f6
29.♖×h7 +−; 23...♔d5? 24.f3 b4
(24...♖a8 25.♕b7+ ♔c4 26.b3+ ♔×b3
27.♕b5+ ♔a2 28.♕b1+ ♔a3
29.♕d3+ ♔b2 30.♖b1+ ♔a2
31.♕c2+ ♔a3 32.♗b4 #) 25.♕a5+
♔d6 26.♗×b4+ ♖×b4 27.♕×b4+ ♔d7
28.♕b7+ ♔d6 29.♖a1 +− **24.e4!** (D)
Alekhine blocks the king's escape
route, which could be used after
24.♖c1+? ♔d5.

**24...♕b3?** The queen will be sorely
missed in the defense. 24...b4! was the
last chance to continue the fight:
25.♖a1 ♕b5 (25...♕e8? 26.♖a6+ +−)
26.b3 ♕b6 27.♕a4+ ♔c5 28.♕d7
♕d8! (28...♕b5? 29.♕×f7 ♔b6
[29...♔c6 30.♗g5 +−] 30.♖a4 ♖c3
[30...♖b7 31.♕e6+ ♖c6 32.♕g8 ♖c3
33.♗×c3 d×c3 34.♕d8+ ♖c7
35.♕d6+ ♔c6 36.♕×b4+ ♕b5
37.♕d6+ ♕c6 38.♕a3 +−]
31.♕×g7 +−) 29.♕a7+ ♔d6
(29...♔c6? 30.♖a5 ♕f8 31.♖×e5 +−)
30.♕×f7 ♖a8 31.♕d5+ ♔c7
32.♕×e5+ ♔b7 33.♖d1 ±. **25.♖a1!
b4 26.♖a6+ ♔b5 27.♖a5+ ♔c6
28.♕c5+ ♔d7 29.♖a7+ 1-0**

Early the following year, Alekhine, then
50 years old, fell ill with scarlet fever
and was placed in the same hospital
where Richard Réti had died in 1929
from the same disease! After being

*Prague 1942*

| | | 1 | 2 | 3 | 4 | 5 | 6 | 7 | 8 | 9 | 10 | 11 | 12 | Total |
|---|---|---|---|---|---|---|---|---|---|---|---|---|---|---|
| 1 | Alekhine | X | 1 | ½ | 1 | ½ | 1 | ½ | ½ | 1 | 1 | ½ | 1 | 8½ |
| 2 | Junge | 0 | X | ½ | ½ | 1 | 1 | 1 | 1 | ½ | 1 | 1 | 1 | 8½ |
| 3 | Foltys | ½ | ½ | X | 0 | ½ | 1 | ½ | 1 | ½ | 1 | ½ | 1 | 7 |
| 4 | Opocensky | 0 | ½ | 1 | X | 0 | 0 | 1 | ½ | 1 | 1 | ½ | 1 | 6½ |
| 5 | Zita | ½ | 0 | ½ | 1 | X | ½ | 0 | 1 | ½ | ½ | 1 | 1 | 6½ |
| 6 | Kottnauer | 0 | 0 | 0 | 1 | ½ | X | 0 | 1 | 1 | 1 | ½ | 1 | 6 |
| 7 | Rejfir | ½ | 0 | ½ | 0 | 1 | 1 | X | ½ | 1 | 0 | 1 | 0 | 5½ |
| 8 | Thelen | ½ | 0 | 0 | ½ | 0 | 0 | ½ | X | 1 | ½ | ½ | ½ | 4 |
| 9 | Podgorny | 0 | ½ | ½ | 0 | ½ | 0 | 0 | 0 | X | ½ | 1 | 1 | 4 |
| 10 | Hromadka | 0 | 0 | 0 | 0 | ½ | 0 | 1 | ½ | ½ | X | ½ | 1 | 4 |
| 11 | Sämisch | ½ | 0 | ½ | ½ | 0 | ½ | 0 | ½ | 0 | ½ | X | 0 | 3 |
| 12 | Prokop | 0 | 0 | 0 | 0 | 0 | 0 | 1 | ½ | 0 | 0 | 1 | X | 2½ |

treated for two months, the world champion recovered and soon took part in a major international tournament with twenty participants, including fifteen Czech masters. This time Junge did not participate (having been conscripted). Instead, Keres played.

**April 10-30, 1943**
Alekhine won the tournament with 17 points out of 19, 2½ points ahead of the Estonian grandmaster. Their game ended in a draw.

In "Fighting Chess of 1943" (published in the *Frankfurter Zeitung*), Alekhine remarked on the development and style of the runner up. He felt that "Keres played confidently and well. His quite faultless technique, remarkable ability to sustain the initiative in the opening, healthy concept of the chess game – all this has secured success for him. And yet it seems that something is lacking, something that in 1937-1938 he had in full measure – that decisive factor of victory which lies in the unshakable confidence in the correctness of the chosen approach to creativity."

Alekhine further characterized the play of the masters who came next. "It is gratifying," he wrote, "to mention the artistic creativity of the 19-year-old Ludek Pachman, who, by his manner of playing and his selfless devotion to chess, somewhat reminds me of Carlos Torre. Moreover, he is able to control his nerves better than the Mexican in his young years."

**(113) Alekhine – Pachman,Ludek**
Prague 1943
Nimzo-Indian Defense [E33]

**1.d4 ♘f6 2.c4 e6 3.♘c3 ♗b4 4.♕c2 ♘c6 5.♘f3 d6 6.♗d2 0-0 7.a3 ♗×c3 8.♗×c3 ♖e8 9.♖d1 ♕e7 10.g3 e5 11.d5 ♘b8 12.♗g2 ♘bd7 13.0-0 ♘f8 14.♘h4 ♘h5 15.♘f5 ♗×f5 16.♕×f5 g6 17.♕c2 f5 18.e3 e4 19.f3 e×f3 20.♗×f3 ♘f6 21.♗d4 ♘8d7 22.b4 ♘e4?** (D) 22...a5, to bring the second rook into play, limits White's advantage.

**23.g4!** A very strong undermining move. **23...f×g4?** Pachman invites White's long-range pieces into the heart of his position. While 23...♕g5

*Prague 1943*

| | | 1 | 2 | 3 | 4 | 5 | 6 | 7 | 8 | 9 | 10 | 11 | 12 | 13 | 14 | 15 | 16 | 17 | 18 | 19 | 20 | Total |
|---|---|---|---|---|---|---|---|---|---|---|---|---|---|---|---|---|---|---|---|---|---|---|
| **1** | **Alekhine** | X | ½ | ½ | 1 | ½ | 1 | 1 | 1 | 1 | 1 | 1 | 1 | ½ | 1 | 1 | 1 | 1 | 1 | 1 | 1 | **17** |
| **2** | **Keres** | ½ | X | ½ | ½ | 1 | 1 | ½ | ½ | ½ | 1 | 1 | ½ | 1 | 1 | 1 | 1 | 1 | 1 | 0 | 1 | **14½** |
| **3** | **Katetov** | ½ | ½ | X | ½ | ½ | ½ | ½ | 1 | ½ | 1 | 1 | ½ | 1 | 1 | 1 | 0 | ½ | ½ | 1 | 1 | **13** |
| **4** | **Sajtar** | 0 | ½ | ½ | X | ½ | ½ | 1 | ½ | 1 | 1 | 1 | 1 | 1 | 0 | ½ | 0 | ½ | 1 | 1 | 1 | **12½** |
| **5** | **Foltys** | ½ | 0 | ½ | ½ | X | ½ | 1 | ½ | 1 | 0 | ½ | 1 | ½ | 1 | ½ | ½ | 1 | 1 | 1 | 1 | **12½** |
| **6** | **Lokvenc** | 0 | 0 | ½ | ½ | ½ | X | ½ | ½ | ½ | 1 | ½ | 1 | ½ | ½ | ½ | ½ | 1 | ½ | 1 | 1 | **11** |
| **7** | **Thelen** | 0 | ½ | ½ | 0 | 0 | ½ | X | ½ | ½ | 1 | 0 | ½ | 1 | 1 | 1 | 1 | ½ | ½ | 1 | 1 | **11** |
| **8** | **Sämisch** | 0 | ½ | 0 | ½ | ½ | ½ | ½ | X | ½ | ½ | ½ | 1 | 1 | 0 | ½ | 1 | ½ | 1 | 1 | 1 | **11** |
| **9** | **Urbanec** | 0 | ½ | ½ | 0 | 0 | ½ | ½ | ½ | X | 1 | 1 | ½ | ½ | ½ | ½ | ½ | 1 | 1 | 1 | 1 | **11** |
| **10** | **Pachman** | 0 | 0 | 0 | 0 | 1 | 0 | 0 | ½ | 0 | X | 1 | 0 | 1 | ½ | 1 | 1 | 1 | ½ | 1 | 1 | **9½** |
| **11** | **Opocensky** | 0 | 0 | 0 | 0 | ½ | ½ | 1 | ½ | 0 | 0 | X | 0 | 1 | ½ | ½ | 1 | 1 | ½ | 1 | 1 | **9** |
| **12** | **Prucha** | 0 | ½ | ½ | 0 | 0 | 0 | ½ | 0 | ½ | 1 | 1 | X | 1 | ½ | ½ | 0 | 1 | 0 | ½ | 1 | **8½** |
| **13** | **Fichtl** | ½ | 0 | 0 | 0 | ½ | ½ | 0 | 0 | ½ | 0 | 0 | 0 | X | 1 | 1 | 1 | 1 | 1 | 1 | ½ | **8½** |
| **14** | **Novotny** | 0 | 0 | 0 | 1 | 0 | ½ | 0 | 1 | ½ | ½ | ½ | ½ | 0 | X | ½ | 0 | ½ | 1 | 1 | 1 | **8½** |
| **15** | **Bartosek** | 0 | 0 | 0 | ½ | ½ | ½ | 0 | ½ | ½ | 0 | ½ | ½ | 0 | ½ | X | 1 | ½ | 1 | 1 | 1 | **8½** |
| **16** | **Florian** | 0 | 0 | 1 | 1 | ½ | ½ | 0 | 0 | ½ | 0 | 0 | 1 | 0 | 1 | 0 | X | 0 | 1 | 0 | 1 | **7½** |
| **17** | **Podgorny** | 0 | 0 | ½ | ½ | 0 | 0 | ½ | ½ | 0 | 0 | 0 | 0 | 0 | ½ | ½ | 1 | X | 0 | 1 | 1 | **6** |
| **18** | **Dietze** | 0 | 0 | ½ | 0 | 0 | ½ | ½ | 0 | 0 | ½ | ½ | 1 | 0 | 0 | 0 | 0 | 1 | X | ½ | ½ | **5½** |
| **19** | **Kubanek** | 0 | 1 | 0 | 0 | 0 | 0 | 0 | 0 | 0 | 0 | 0 | ½ | 0 | 0 | 0 | 1 | 0 | ½ | X | ½ | **3½** |
| **20** | **Sucha** | 0 | 0 | 0 | 0 | 0 | 0 | 0 | 0 | 0 | 0 | 0 | 0 | ½ | 0 | 0 | 0 | 0 | ½ | ½ | X | **1½** |

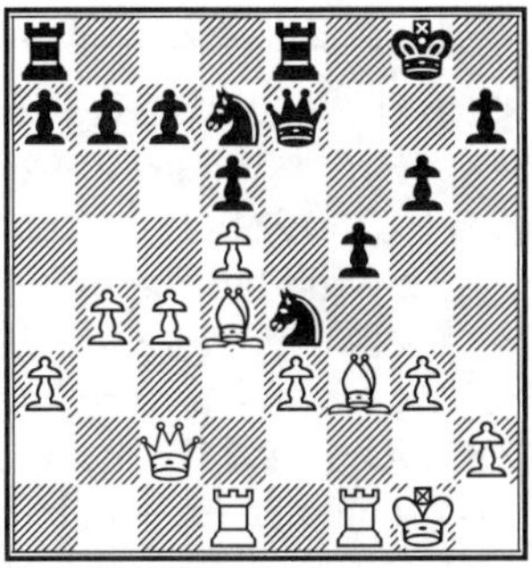

keeps more roads closed, White remains on top after 24.♕g2 (24.♔h1 ♖e7±) 24...a5±. **24.♗×g4 ♕g5** 24...♘g5 25.h4 ♘e5 26.♗×e5 ♕×e5 27.h×g5 ♕×g5 28.♕g2 ♕×e3+ 29.♔h1+–; 24...♘f8 25.♖×f8+ ♕×f8 26.♖f1 ♕h6 27.♖f4 ♘g5 28.h4 ♖f8 29.h×g5 ♕×g5 30.♕g2+– **25.♕g2! ♘f8** 25...♘e5 26.♖f4 ♘×g4 27.♖×g4 ♕h5 (27...♕f5 28.♖f1+–) 28.♖f1 ♘d2 29.♖g5 ♕h6 30.♖f6+– **26.♖f4** The triumph of Alekhine's strategy – the e4-knight is completely encircled. **26...h5 27.h4 ♕h6** 27...♕×h4 28.♗e6++– **28.♗h3 1-0**

Alekhine concluded his article by also touched upon his own form: "According to all chess fans, my creative and sporting achievements turned out to be the same as in my 'best years.'"

**Simultaneous Exhibitions**

Until the last years of his life, Alekhine never ceased to surprise his contemporaries by his beautiful combinative ideas. His first-ever simultaneous exhibition, given at the Moscow Chess Circle on March 4, 1910, soon after winning the All-Russia Amateurs Tournament 1909, lasted 3½ hours and ended in his favor (+15 -1 =6). The money collected from the exhibition went to the fund for building a monument to Mikhail Chigorin. Alekhine gave his last exhibition, on seven boards and with clocks, in Caceres, Spain on December 17, 1945. One of the games from this exhibition (against Moreno Ramos) was preserved; it was drawn on move 38. In his exhibitions given during the tours of European, American and Asian countries, Alekhine had played tens of thousands of games. Thus, for example, While touring the United States and Canada from November 1923 to early April 1924, he gave thirty-three exhibitions, playing 993 games with an 89% winning percentage (+846 -55 =92).

He regularly made such tours in a number of Latin American countries: Argentina (1926), Chili (1927), Mexico (1929, 1932), Puerto Rico (1933), Panama, Brazil and Colombia (1939). No less intense and frequent were his exhibitions in the 1920s and 1930s, given during the tours of many European countries – France, Germany, Switzerland, The Netherlands, Czechoslovakia, Belgium, Denmark, Sweden, Iceland, Italy, Spain, Portugal, Yugoslavia, Bulgaria, etc.

His performance is amazing: in Yugoslavia, from December 1930 to January 1931, Alekhine gave seventeen exhibitions, in which 555 chess devotees participated (+440 -36 =79); in Spain (January-March 1935) 720 amateurs played him (+627 -33 =60). During his global circumnavigation in 1932-33, the world champion visited quite a number of African and Asian countries. Along the way, he played, in all, 1,320 games, earning a 92% win percentage (+1161 -65 =94). Here are two games played in this famous world tour. In one of them, played on March 1, 1933 in Jakarta, Alekhine suffered one of his rare losses. The resolution of his opponent is surprising. He undertook an unexpected advance of his h-pawn and did not stop at sacrificing the exchange against the world champion. Well, as the Russian saying goes, it is the brave who take towns.

**(114) Alekhine – Engelen,JC**
Jakarta 1933 (simul)
Sicilian Defense [B47]

**1.e4 c5 2.♘f3 ♘c6 3.d4 c×d4 4.♘×d4 ♘f6 5.♘c3 a6?! 6.♗e2** 6.♘×c6 is more critical. **6...♕c7 7.0-0 e6 8.♗f3?!** This plan is very slow. **8...b5 9.a3 ♘×d4 10.♕×d4 ♗d6 11.g3 ♗b7 12.♗g2 h5!? 13.♗g5 ♗e5 14.♕d3 h4 15.♗×h4** (D)

**15...♖×h4!** Engelen playes strongly in the style of ... the great Alekhine! **16.g×h4 ♗×h2+ 17.♔h1 ♔e7 18.♕h3?** Misplacing the queen. 18.♖ae1 ♖h8 19.♖e3 ♗e5 20.♖h3 ♘h5 21.♘e2 is much more harmonious. **18...♗e5 19.f4?** Again, one of the rooks should be brougth into play: 19.♖fd1 ♖h8 20.♔g1 g5 21.♕e3 ♖×h4 22.♖d3, but as a result of his pressure on the dark squares, Black is clearly preferable of course. **19...♗×f4 20.e5 ♗×e5 21.♗×b7 ♕×b7+ 22.♕f3 ♕×f3+ 23.♖×f3 ♖h8 24.♖h3 g5 25.♖e1 g4 26.♖d3 ♖×h4+ 27.♔g1 d6 28.b4 g3 29.♘e2 ♘e4 30.♘d4 ♗×d4+ 31.♖×d4 d5 32.a4 f5 33.a×b5 a×b5 34.c4 d×c4 35.♖a1 ♖h2 36.♖a5 ♘c3 0-1**

Alekhine remembered well his offender and, a week later (also in Jakarta), avenged his loss, playing Black this time. It is interesting that Engelen, so resolute when playing Black, became timid and unconvincing when playing White, as though afraid of his former bravery.

**(115) Engelen,JC – Alekhine**
Jakarta 1933 (simul)
Queen's Indian Defense [E14]

**1.d4 ♘f6 2.c4 e6 3.e3 b6 4.♘f3 ♗b7 5.♗d3 ♗b4+ 6.♗d2 ♗×d2+ 7.♘b×d2 d6 8.0-0 ♘bd7 9.♖e1 0-0 10.♖c1 ♕e7 11.♘f1 ♘e4 12.♘3d2 f5 13.f3 ♘×d2 14.♕×d2 e5 15.♘g3 g6 16.♕c2 ♘f6 17.d×e5?!** 17.c5 makes much better use of White's advantage in development. **17...♕×e5 18.♕c3 ♖ae8 19.♖e2 a5 20.♔f2 ♕c5 21.h4?** (D) 21.♕d4 is forced.

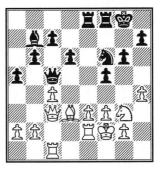

f×e4 23.f4 ♖×f4+ –+ **22...f×e4+ 23.♔e1 e×d3 24.♕×d3 ♗×g2!?** Another hard hit **25.h5 ♕g5 0-1**

**21...♘e4+!** The knight opens lines for Black's long-range pieces, and they cannot be closed. **22.f×e4** 22.♗×e4

Practically the entire chess world had the opportunity to meet Alekhine over the chessboard in different years (for the record of blindfold exhibitions of Alekhine, see Blindfold Play).

## Chapter 3: Chess Creations, Games and Discoveries

**Attack**

Alexander Alekhine was a recognized master of attack. Especially inspiring are his direct attacks against the king, which enabled him to show his combinative talent in all its glory and find the shortest way to win a game. Illustrative of this is a game from the 1926 Dresden Tournament.

**(116) Alekhine – Blümich,Max**
Dresden 1926
Queen's Pawn Game [A48]

**1.d4 ♘f6 2.♘f3 g6 3.♗g5 ♗g7 4.♘bd2 0-0 5.e3 d6 6.♗c4 ♘c6 7.c3 a6 8.♕e2 ♗g4 9.h3 ♗d7 10.♘h2 ♕c8 11.f4 e5?** Far too optimistic; 11...♘a5 12.♗d3 c5 was one way to play. **12.f×e5 d×e5 13.0-0 ♘h5** (D)

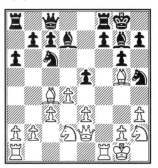

**14.♖×f7!!** A thunderous blow. **14...♖×f7 15.♗×f7+ ♔×f7 16.♕c4+ ♗e6** 16...♔f8 17.♖f1+ ♗f5 18.g4 ♘g3 19.♖f2± **17.d5 ♗×d5?!** Losing directly, but good advice is hard to give. **18.♖f1+?** The wrong order of moves: 18.♕×d5+ ♕e6 19.♖f1+ ♗f6 20.♕f3 ♔g7 21.♘e4 ♗×g5 22.♘×g5 ♕f5 23.♕g4 ♕×g4 24.♘×g4 ♘d8 25.♖d1 ♘f6 26.♖×d8+−. **18...♘f6?** 18...♔e6! was forced, but White's at-

tack goes on after 19.♕g4+ ♔d6 20.♕d1! ♔c5 21.e4 ♗×a2 22.♘b3+ ♗×b3 23.♗e3+ ♘d4 24.♕×b3. **19.♕×d5+ ♕e6** (D)

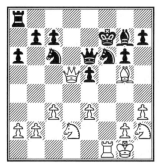

**20.♕f3!** A killing retreat. **20...♕f5** 20...♔g8 21.♗×f6 ♖f8 22.♘e4+− **21.♗×f6** and Blümich resigned in view of 21...♗×f6 22.♘g4 ♕×f3 23.♖×f3 ♖d8 24.♘×f6 ♖×d2 25.♘e4+−. **1-0**

The following game was awarded a special prize "For a kingside attack carried out in the best way."

**(117) Alekhine – Alexander,Conel Hugh**
Nottingham 1936
Queen's Indian Defense [E16]

**1.d4 ♘f6 2.c4 e6 3.♘f3 ♗b4+ 4.♘bd2 b6 5.g3 ♗b7 6.♗g2 0-0 7.0-0 ♗×d2** 7...d5 is played more often. **8.♕×d2 d6 9.b3 ♘bd7 10.♗b2 ♖b8?** Black does not have time for this. The main lines are 10...♕e7 and 10...♘e4. **11.♖ad1 ♘e4 12.♕e3 f5?! 13.d5 e×d5 14.c×d5 ♘df6 15.♘h4! ♕d7** 15...♘×d5? 16.♖×d5 ♗×d5 17.♕d4+−; 15...♗×d5? 16.♗×f6 ♘×f6 17.♗×d5++− **16.♗h3 g6 17.f3 ♘c5 18.♕g5 ♕g7 19.b4 ♘cd7?!** (D)

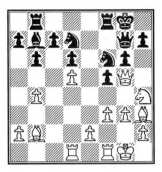

**20.e4!!** Alekhine brings the other bishop into play with great effect and prepares a sacrifice on f5, since after the direct 20.♗×f5? g×f5, White's queen is attacked. **20...♘×e4 21.♕c1** Now the white queen is safe; the same cannot be said about Black's queen. **21...♘ef6** (D)

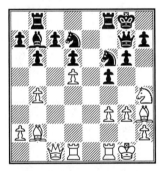

**22.♗×f5! ♔h8** 22...g×f5 23.♘×f5 loses the queen because 23...♕h8 meets with 24.♘h6+ ♔g7 25.♕g5#. **23.♗e6 ♗a6 24.♖fe1 ♘e5 25.f4 ♘d3 26.♖×d3 ♗×d3 27.g4 1-0**

More typical of Alekhine are attacks against the king that are prepared by profound strategic play in the center or on both flanks. For example, his games with Bogoljubow (Hastings, 1922) and Réti (Baden-Baden, 1925), which gave him the most satisfaction (See, Celebrities).

**Aphorisms and Thoughts on Chess**

* Combination is the soul of the game of chess (1935).

* I do not "play" chess; in chess I fight. So, I willingly combine the tactical with the strategic, the fantastic with the scientific, the combinative with the positional, endeavoring to satisfy the demands of each given position (1923).

* Nothing is so harmful as routine. It is always associated with the danger of finding oneself in an inferior position and, undoubtedly, impoverishes the game of chess.

* To me, chess is not a game, but an art... I see its aim in the scientific and artistic achievements, which places chess among the other arts (1929).

* A deep inner drama continually unfolds in the consciousness of every master in the process of chess struggle – a drama, unparalleled in any other form of artistic creation and characterized by the continuous collision between the creative idea which tends towards infinity and the opponent's desire to refute it. For the chess struggle, one needs above all to know human nature, to understand the opponent's psychology. Previously, they only fought against the pieces. We, however, also fight the opponent – his will, nerves, individual features, and last but not least, his vanity (1929).

* By means of chess, I educated my character. Chess, above all, teaches one to be objective. One may become a great chess master only by realizing

one's mistakes and shortcomings. Just as it is in life (1926).

### Opening Discoveries

In the 1920s and early 1930s, Alekhine was rightly regarded as one of the greatest experts in chess theory. For Alekhine, a creative search in theory meant finding new ways and solutions to suit his strategic and combinative aspirations. Grandmaster Alexander Kotov, who studied Alekhine's classical heritage, suggested describing his handling of openings as "concrete and tactical." Especially valuable were Alekhine's ideas in the Ruy Lopez.

To begin, there is his namesake variation of the Ruy Lopez, in which White sacrifices a pawn to better post his pieces and launch a kingside attack.

**1.e4 e5 2.♘f3 ♘c6 3.♗b5 a6 4.♗a4 ♘f6 5.0-0 ♗e7 6.♖e1 b5 7.♗b3 d6 8.c3 ♘a5 9.♗c2 c5 10.d4 ♕c7 11.♘bd2 0-0 12.♘f1 ♗g4 13.♘e3!** (D)

There are also two systems in this opening in which Alekhine contributed ideas for White. One of them is **1.e4 e5 2.♘f3 ♘c6 3.♗b5 a6 4.♗a4 ♘f6 5.♘c3** or **5.♕e2.** He also worked out a number of active lines for Black; for

example, the knight thrust in the Jaenisch Gambit. **1.e4 e5 2.♘f3 ♘c6 3.♗b5 f5 4.♘c3 ♘d4.**

Alekhine also developed the so-called Kecskemet Variation, the idea of which is to regroup the black pieces and to transfer the black queen's bishop to the e8-h5 diagonal in order to fortify the black center. It was first played in the game L.Steiner-Alekhine (Kecskemet, 1927).

**1.e4 e5 2.♘f3 ♘c6 3.♗b5 a6 4.♗a4 ♘f6 5.0-0 d6 6.c3 ♗d7 7.♖e1 ♗e7 8.d4 0-0 9.♘bd2 ♗e8** As Black, Alekhine often fianchettoed his king's bishop in the Ruy Lopez by playing g7-g6 after **1.e4 e5 2.♘f3 ♘c6 3.♗b5** either on the third move (Tarrasch-Alekhine, Carlsbad, 1923) or the sixth **1.e4 e5 2.♘f3 ♘c6 3.♗b5 a6 4.♗a4 d6 5.c3 ♗d7 6.d4 g6** (Fine-Alekhine, AVRO Tournament, 1938). (D)

Another Alekhine variation is still in use:

**1.e4 e5 2.♘f3 ♘c6 3.♗b5 a6 4.♗×c6 d×c6 5.d4 e×d4 6.♕×d4 ♕×d4 7.♘×d4 ♗d7 8.♗e3 0-0-0 9.♘d2 ♘e7 10.0-0-0 ♖e8!** (D)

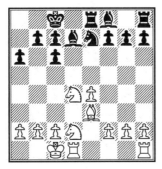

In his younger years, Alekhine also looked for new ideas and lines in other open games: the Petroff Defense, Vienna Game, Danish Gambit, and Scotch Game. His inquisitive mind found possibilities for developing attacks in the center or flanks in many semi-open games as well.

In the French Defense, he introduced, as early as on the fourth move, several novel ideas, based on sacrificing one or several pawns, directed against the so-called Nimzowitsch system, **1.e4 e6 2.d4 d5 3.♘c3 ♗b4 4.a3**, **4.♘ge2, 4.♕g4**, and **4.♗d2**.

Also of interest here is the following line advocated by Alekhine, **1.e4 e6 2.d4 d5 3.♘c3 ♗b4 4.e5 c5 5.a3 ♗a5 6.b4!?**. Grandmaster Paul Keres believed that "[t]he move 6.b2-b4, recommended by Alekhine, is undoubtedly the most vigorous continuation, leading to intricate positions where White's chances are still somewhat better" (*French Defense* [Russian] Moscow, 1958). Subsequently, Alekhine played 3.♘d2 to prevent the Nimzowitsch System (3.♘c3 ♗b4).

Keres named one of the sections in his monograph "The Chatard-Alekhine Attack" to describe the variation first adopted by the French player Chatard but introduced into master praxis by Alekhine at Mannheim in 1914.

**1.e4 e6 2.d4 d5 3.♘c3 ♘f6 4.♗g5 ♗e7 5.e5 ♘fd7 6.h4!** (D)

The idea behind the move is to speed up the mobilization of the white pieces and open the h-file for a kingside attack.

Early in his career Alekhine analyzed and often adopted the sharp MacCutcheon Variation, which requires very accurate and lengthy calculation. **1.e4 e6 2.d4 d5 3.♘c3 ♘f6 4.♗g5 ♗b4** In the line beginning with 5.e5, he found a brilliant continuation:

**5.e5 h6 6.e×f6 h×g5 7.f×g7 ♖g8 8.h4 ♖×g7 9.♕h5 ♘c6 10.♕h8+ ♗f8 11.h5 ♗d7 12.h6 ♖g6 13.h7 ♔e7 14.♕g8 ♗g7 15.♗d3 f5** (D)

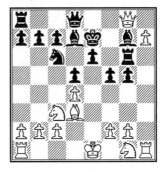

In this seemingly reliable position for Black there follows, as Keres put it, Alekhine's brilliant combination: **16.♗×f5! e×f5 17.♖h6!! ♗×h6 18.♕×g6 ♕f8 19.♘×d5+ ♔d8 20.♕g8**

In the Sicilian Defense, the line introduced by Alekhine in the Dragon Variation is well-known:

**1.e4 c5 2.♘f3 ♘c6 3.d4 c×d4 4.♘×d4 ♘f6 5.♘c3 d6 6.♗e2 g6 7.♗e3 ♗g7 8.0-0 0-0 9.♘b3 a5** (D)

The purpose of this move is to advance the a-pawn further (a5-a4-a3) in order to weaken the dark squares along the a1-h8 diagonal or, should White prevent this by playing 10.a2-a4, post the black knight on b4 (Spielmann-Alekhine, Margate 1938).

In the Caro-Kann Defense, Alekhine developed some lines for White in the Panov-Botvinnik Attack, whose originator proposed to put pressure on the d5-square by playing c2-c4. **1.e4 c6 2.d4 d5 3.e×d5 c×d5 4.c4 ♘f6 5.♘c3 ♘c6 6.♗g5 d×c4 7.♗×c4.** (D)

This system of play, involving the sacrifice of a pawn to seize the initiative, is named the Alekhine Gambit by the authors of the monograph *The Caro-*

*Kann Defense* (Moscow, 1988), Alexander Konstantinopolsky and Aron Veits.

Another method of playing, named the Alekhine Attack, arises after **6.♘f3 ♗g4 7.c×d5 ♘×d5 8.♗d5**.
Alekhine introduced many novelties in the theory of closed games, especially in the Queen's Gambit, Nimzo-Indian Defense, Slav Defense, and King's Indian Defense. There are several lines developed by Alekhine.

**1.d4 d5 2.c4 e6 3.♘c3 ♘f6 4.♗g5 ♗e7 5.e3 0-0 6.♘f3 ♘bd7 7.♖c1 c6 8.♗d3 d×c4 9.♗×c4 ♘d5 10.♗×e7 ♕×e7 11.♘e4** (Alekhine-Treybal, Baden-Baden, 1925). (D)

**1.d4 d5 2.c4 e6 3.♘c3 ♘f6 4.♗g5 ♘bd7 5.c×d5 e×d5 6.e3 c6 7.♗d3 ♗e7 8.♘ge2** (Alekhine –

Capablanca, 1927, 32nd match game). (D)

Alekhine also worked out some new lines in this opening for Black. For example, **1.d4 d5 2.c4 e6 3.♘c3 ♘f6 4.♗g5 ♗e7 5.e3 0-0 6.♘f3 ♘bd7 7.♖c1 c6 8.♖c2 a6** (Grünfeld-Alekhine, Carlsbad 1923). (D)

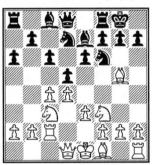

The Alekhine system in the Queen's Gambit Accepted is popular. **1.d4 d5 2.c4 d×c4 3.♘f3 a6 4.e3 ♗g4** (D)

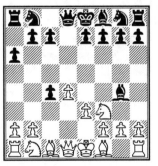

The world champion first adopted this system in his match with Bogoljubow

in 1934. The purpose of this plan is to deploy the queenside forces as fast as possible.

A number of new ideas were also introduced in other closed games.

The Grünfeld Defense: Alekhine Variation: **1.d4 ♘f6 2.c4 g6 3.♘c3 d5 4.c×d5 ♘×d5 5.e4 ♘×c3 6.b×c3 ♗g7 7.♗c4 c5 8.♘e2!** (D)

The move 8.♘e2! was suggested by Alekhine in 1924. Its aim is to prevent the pin 8...♗g4 and finish the development of the pieces while retaining a powerful pawn center. The system was further analyzed by Botvinnik when the pawn center is attacked without the exchange in the center (i.e. after 8...0-0 9.0-0).

Slav Defense: Chigorin-Alekhine System
This was the name that was given to it by Pavel Kondratiev, a chess master and theoretician from Leningrad (now St. Petersburg) in his monograph *The Slav Defense* (Moscow 1985). This system of development had already been introduced into master play by Mikhail Chigorin and then further analyzed and adopted by Alekhine (e.g., in his return match with Euwe, 1937).

**1.d4 d5 2.c4 c6 3.♘f3 ♘f6**

**4.♘c3 e6 5.e3 ♘bd7 6.♗d3 ♗d6** (Chigorin) or **6...♗b4** (D) (Alekhine).

Black continues to dispute the control of the e4-square.

Réti Opening

**1.♘f3 d5 2.c4 d4 3.b4 c5 4.e3 f6 5.e×d4 c×d4 6.c5!** (Played with idea of weakening the a2-g8 diagonal a2-g8) (D)

Queen's Gambit Declined: Chigorin Defense

**1.d4 d5 2.c4 ♘c6 3.♘f3 ♗g4 ♕a5** (Alekhine-Colle, Paris 1925). With this move, suggested by Alekhine, a pawn is sacrificed (4...♗×f3 5.e×f3 d×c4 6.♗×c4 ♕×d4) to develop pieces as fast as possible.

Nimzo-Indian Defense

**1.d4 ♘f6 2.c4 e6 3.♘c3 ♗b4 4.♕c2 d5 5.a3 ♗×c3+ 6.♕×c3 ♘e4 7.♕c2 ♘c6** (Vidmar-Alekhine,

San Remo 1930) (D)

**1.d4 ♘f6 2.c4 e6 3.♘c3 ♗b4 4.g3** (Alekhine-Golombek, Margate 1938).

By fianchettoing his king's bishop, White keeps the center squares e4 and d5 under control. He also refrains from playing e2-e3, which would prevent the development of the c1-bishop.

Among the original opening ideas contributed by Alekhine, the move **2.b4** (after **1.♘f3 d5**), which he made in his game with Drewitt (Portsmouth 1923), deserves mentioning. It allowed White, after **2...c5 3.b×c5**, to gain a pawn preponderance in the center and develop an attack first on one flank and then on the other.

King's Indian Defense

**1.d4 ♘f6 2.c4 g6 3.♘c3 ♗g7 4.e4 0-0 5.♗e3 d6 6.f3 e5 7.d5** (D)

This continuation, adopted by Alekhine in the third game of his training match with Euwe (Amsterdam, 1926), is still considered the best by opening theory.

In the Four Pawns Variation of the King's Indian Defense, Alekhine realized the idea of forming a pawn triangle in the center for the accelerated development of his pieces and gaining a queenside advantage.

**1.d4 ♘f6 2.c4 g6 3.♘c3 ♗g7 4.e4 d6 5.f4 0-0 6.♘f3 e5 7.f×e5 d×e5 8.d5** (D)

Alekhine also searched for new ideas in the Queen's Indian Defense, which involves the flank development of the black queen's bishop.

**1.d4 ♘f6 2.♘f3 b6 3.c4 e6 4.g3 ♗b7 5.♗g2 ♗b4+ 6.♗d2 ♗×d2+ 7.♕×d2 d6 8.0-0 ♘bd7 9.d5** (Alekhine-Johner, Berne 1932) (D)

Alekhine gave his philosophical and practical justification for adopting this opening in his foreword to the monograph by the then French champion Viktor Kahn (1889-1973) *The Queen's Indian Defense* (Paris 1935)

*In former times, Philidor repeated as a leitmotif that pawns constitute the soul of chess. The French master was right and wrong at the same time... He deserves credit for his instinctive realization of the significance of the center, whereas his fallacy lies in his contention that supremacy in the center must necessarily be assured by pawns. A fallacy quite forgivable for that epoch... And only shortly before 1914 did several young players (Nimzowitsch being the first among them) begin to argue that the occupation of the center by pawns alone was not at all necessary for successfully conducting a game. They had demonstrated that it was sufficient to control the center with pieces (even from a distance), as for example, could be done using fianchettoed bishops. What seemed paradoxical a mere twenty years ago has become the truth for all knowledgeable players ... The theme investigated by [Kahn], at the root of which lies the struggle for the center without occupying it with pawns, enables the readers to gain an insight into the modern strategic spirit, being in a sense the only chess truth. His investigation does not refute the principle advanced by Philidor, but it comple-*

235

*ments this principle in the most successful manner. Namely – it is the center that is the soul of chess.*

The relation of this philosophical generalization concerning chess with the specific struggle for the center has found a remarkable embodiment in Alekhine's namesake defense (1.e4 ♘f6). Paradoxically, the great master of attack has immortalized his name in opening theory by developing one of the most popular defenses! In any event, this is hardly accidental. We are reminded that the outstanding players, whose games are permeated with the desire to play actively and attack decisively, have been especially diligent in looking for ways of repulsing such onslaughts. To support this statement, we will mention such openings as the Philidor Defense, Marshall Counterattack in Ruy Lopez, Chigorin Defense, Lasker Defense in the Queen's Gambit, Grünfeld Defense, and Petroff Defense (or Russian Game)...

By the way, the last-mentioned opening, defined by the moves 1.e4 e5 2. ♘f3 ♘f6, is interesting because of its parallels and analogies with the Alekhine Defense. In both these openings, this pawn is attacked by the king's knight – in one case this is done on the first move, in the other, on the second. However, this is enough for entirely different ideas, development of pieces, strategic plans of attack and defense to arise.

Alekhine Defense
**1.e4 ♘f6** (D)

The move 1...♘f6 had already been mentioned in Allgaier's book (1811). At the turn of 1920s, the Moscow player and chess composer Mikhail Klyatskin (1897-1926) started adopting it, but it gained recognition only after its introduction into master play by Alekhine in his game against Endre Steiner at Budapest (1921). "This opening," wrote Lasker, "is a sheet anchor for those players who wish to avoid the well-trodden paths. The positive side of this opening lies in its multifaceted nature. We should be grateful to Alekhine for disclosing the possibilities hidden in the move 1...♘f6."

The idea behind this opening is to weaken the white pawn center by putting pressure on it with the pieces in conjunction with undermining pawn moves (d7-d6, f7-f6, and c7-c5). From the very outset, the battle assumes a sharp and tense character.

The study of Alekhine's discoveries in opening theory enables one to draw a number of conclusions. First of all, it shows the wide spectrum of openings found in the sphere of his analysis and practice. Between 1909 and 1914, open games mostly appear among his theoretical preferences, which is explained by the Chigorin traditions out of which Alekhine had grown. In later years, he repeatedly resorted to 1.d2-d4. The dramatic expansion of his opening repertoire in the 1920s was one of the means by which Alekhine developed an universal style of play, which played a huge role in his successful ascension of chess Olympus. Another important feature of Alekhine's opening ideas was their organic relationship with the subsequent phases of the game. This leads naturally to a third feature of Alekhine's discoveries in the opening: for White they mainly aim at obtaining sharp positions with prospects of creating attacks and combinational solutions; for Black it was the constant creative search for counterplay.

## Defense

Alekhine understood the necessity of mastering the multi-faceted defensive technique as the most important element of his universal style. He felt it acutely in the early 1920s when defense still remained one of his deficiencies. For example, in his game with Rubinstein (Vienna, 1922), Alekhine failed to conceive of a clear-cut plan of defense and, without exhausting all the defensive possibilities, had to resign by move 26.

While perfecting his style during his preparation for the world championship match, Alekhine paid exceptional attention to mastering the high art of defense. He adopted all the best achieved in this field by Steinitz, Lasker, Tarrasch, Schlechter, and Capablanca, fully assimilating the historical experience. Over a relatively short period of time, Alekhine developed into a

*A sketch from* Sahovski Glasnik *magazine (1931).*

great master of defense, which turned out to be one of the main surprises for Capablanca. Defending skillfully, he was able, for example, to salvage the ninth, fifteenth, and twentieth games of his match with Capablanca.

Alekhine also demonstrated high defensive skill in a number of his subsequent world championship match games against Bogoljubow and Euwe. He also repeatedly demonstrated in tournament battles his skill in adopting all methods of defense, from active defense followed by going over to counterattack to stubborn repulsion of attack by preventing dangerous threats and creating the greatest possible obstacles in the way of the opponent's attacking pieces. In the former case, the games abounded in sharp situations where Alekhine's sacrifices and combinations aimed at restoring the balance in the game or wrestling the initiative from his opponent were not infrequent. Finding himself in a pickle, Alekhine sometimes steered the game into the endgame where it would be more difficult for his opponent to exploit his advantage. His AVRO game against the American Samuel Reshevsky is a prime example in which Alekhine made full use of all his resources: his opponent's inaccuracies, his own fine traps, and also the psychological motives associated with the overestimation of his chances by the active side.

**(118) Reshevsky – Alekhine**
AVRO 1938
Nimzo-Indian Defense [E43]

**1.d4 ♘f6 2.c4 e6 3.♘c3 ♗b4 4.e3 0-0 5.♘f3 b6 6.♗d3 ♗b7 7.0-0 ♗×c3 8.b×c3 ♗e4 9.♗×e4?** This gives Black a good game in view of his control of the light squares. 9.♗e2 is the critical main line. **9...♘×e4 10.♕c2 f5 11.♘e5 ♕e8 12.f3 ♘f6 13.♗a3 d6 14.♘d3 c5 15.♘f4 ♘c6 16.e4?** White is not yet ready to open the position, but Black is comfortable in any case. **16...f×e4 17.f×e4** (D)

**17...♘a5?** Alekhine misses the tactical 17...e5! 18.♘d5 e×d4 which gives him strong play against White's weak pawns, e.g., 19.♘c7 (19.♘×f6+ ♖×f6 20.♖×f6 g×f6 21.♗b2 ♕e5) 19...♕×e4

20.♕×e4 ♘×e4 21.♘×a8 ♖×a8 22.c×d4 ♘d2. **18.♕d3! ♘h5** 18...♖f7!? was an alternative, but not the greedy 18...♘a4? because White has 19.♘×e6 ♕×a3? 20.e5 ♘d7 21.♗g5 g6 22.♕h3+−. **19.♘×h5 ♕×h5 20.e5 d×e5 21.d×c5 ♖fd8 22.♕e4 ♕g6 23.♕e2** (D)

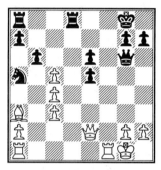

**23...e4?** Alekhine should try to exchange queens with 23...♕d3 in order to take the sting out of White's initiative, e.g., 24.♕×e5 ♖e8 25.♕d4 ♕×d4+ 26.c×d4 ♘×c4, and Black is certainly not worse. **24.♖f4 b×c5?!** 24...e5 is better because 25.♖×e4? can strongly be met by 25...♖d2 26.♕×d2 ♕×e4 27.♖e1 ♘×c4=. **25.♗×c5 ♘c6 26.♖×e4?!** (D) The *zwischenzug* 26.♖af1 is more precise.

**26...♖d2?!** The following dynamics only activate White. The static 26...e5 is more in the spirit of the position because Black's solid set up is too difficult to crack. **27.♕×d2 ♕×e4 28.♖e1 ♕×c4 29.♕d6! ♖c8 30.♕×e6+ ♕×e6 31.♖×e6 ♔f7 32.♖d6 a5 33.♔f2?** Allowing a strong repositioning of the knight, which the prophylactic 33.♖d7+± prevents. **33...♘e7! 34.♗d4 ♘f5 35.♖d7+ ♔e6?** Leaving the kingside pawns very vulnerable. 35...♔g6 keeps them protected. **36.♖a7 ♘×d4 37.c×d4 ♖c2+ 38.♔f3 ♖×a2 39.♖×g7 ♖a3+ 40.♔e4 h5 41.♖g6+ ♔f7?!** 41...♔d7 is more tenacious. **42.♖h6 ♖a2 43.♔f3 ♖a3+ 44.♔f2 ♖d3** 44...♖a2+ 45.♔g3 ♖a3+ 46.♔h4 ♖a2 47.♔h3 ♖d2 48.♖×h5 ♖d3+ (48...a4 49.d5 ♖d3+ 50.♔g4+−) 49.g3 a4 50.♖a5 ♖×d4 51.♖a6+− **45.♖×h5 a4 46.d5 a3** 46...♔e7 47.♖h4 a3 48.♖a4 ♔d6 49.♖a5+− transposes. **47.♖h7+ ♔f6 48.♖a7 ♔e5 49.♖a5 ♖d2+ 50.♔f3 ♖d3+ 51.♔e2 ♖b3 52.♔f2 ♖b2+ 53.♔g3 ♖b3+** (D) 53...a2 54.h4+−

**54.♔h4?** The g-pawn is more valuable, so 54.♔g4 ♖b2 55.g3! is stronger: 55...a2 56.h4 ♔f6 57.h5 ♖b4+ 58.♔h3 ♖b2 59.d6+−. **54...♖b2! 55.♔h3** 55.♖×a3 ♖×g2 56.♔h3 ♖d2 57.♖a5 ♖×d5 58.♖×d5+ ♔×d5 59.♔g4 ♔e6 60.♔g5 ♔f7= **55...a2 56.d6+ ♔×d6 57.g4 ♔c6 58.♔g3 ♔b6 59.♖a8 ♔b5 60.h3** 60.g5

♖b3+ 61.♔g4?? even loses to the standard 61...♖b4+ 62.♔f5 ♖a4 63.♖b8+ ♔a5 64.♖a8+ ♔b4 65.♖b8+ ♔a3−+. **60...♔b4 61.♔f4 ♖c2 62.♖b8+ ♔c3 63.♖a8 ♔b4 ½-½**

## Celebrities

In Alekhine's creative legacy, many games have become widely known because of their deep strategy, of the fantasy and brilliancy of combinative ideas, of the delicate handling of the endgame, or, finally, of the depth of his approach toward the most complex problems of chess struggle. The following games Alekhine "consider[ed] them the most brilliant games in [his] chess career." It is remarkable that in both these games he played Black and that they were played in the early 1920s.

### (119) Bogoljubow – Alekhine
Hastings 1922
Dutch Defense [A90]

**1.d4 f5 2.c4 ♘f6 3.g3 e6 4.♗g2 ♗b4+ 5.♗d2 ♗×d2+ 6.♘×d2 ♘c6 7.♘gf3 0-0 8.0-0 d6 9.♕b3 ♔h8 10.♕c3 e5 11.e3 a5 12.b3 ♕e8 13.a3 ♕h5** "White can reply neither 14.d×e5 d×e5 15.♘×e5 ♘×e5 16.♕×e5 because of 16...♘g4, nor 14.b4? because of 14...e4 15.♘e1 a×b4" (Alekhine). **14.h4 ♘g4 15.♘g5 ♗d7 16.f3?** White plays on the wrong wing. He should opt for 16.b4, to pressurize the queenside. **16...♘f6 17.f4?! e4 18.♖fd1 h6 19.♘h3 d5 20.♘f1 ♘e7 21.a4 ♘c6 22.♖d2 ♘b4 23.♗h1 ♕e8** "A very strong move, which gives Black new advantages: either the possession of the d5-square (in case of 24.cxd5), the opening files on the queenside after 24.c5 b5! or, as happened in the actual game, the winning of a pawn" (Alekhine). **24.♖g2?** 24.♘f2 ♖a6 25.♗g2 is more harmonious. **24...d×c4 25.b×c4 ♗×a4 26.♘f2 ♗d7 27.♘d2 b5 28.♘d1 ♘d3! 29.♖×a5 b4 30.♖×a8** (D)

**30...b×c3!?** 30...♕×a8 31.♕b3 ♕a1 wins easily, but Alekhine chooses a much more beautiful finish. **31.♖×e8 c2 32.♖×f8+ ♔h7 33.♘f2 c1♕+ 34.♘f1 ♘e1!** Threatening mate in one. **35.♖h2 ♕×c4 36.♖b8 ♗b5 37.♖×b5 ♕×b5 38.g4 ♘f3+ 39.♗×f3 e×f3 40.g×f5 ♕e2!** "This move creates a problem-like position, wherein White cannot move any piece without exposing himself to immediate loss. For example, 41.♘h3 ♘g4! [42.♖×e2 f×e2 and the e-pawn will queen.] or 41.♖h1 ♘g4. Hence, after two unimportant moves, he must play e3-e4, which leads to an immediate liquidation, with a won endgame for Black" (Alekhine). **41.d5 ♔g8 42.h5 ♔h7** "A show of strength." (Kasparov). **43.e4 ♘×e4 44.♘×e4 ♕×e4 45.d6 c×d6 46.f6 g×f6 47.♖d2** (D)

**47...♕e2!?** Disrupting the coordination of White's pieces. **48.♖×e2 f×e2 49.♔f2 e×f1♕+ 50.♔×f1 ♔g7 51.♔f2 ♔f7 52.♔e3 ♔e6 53.♔e4 d5+ 0-1**

**(120) Réti,Richard – Alekhine**
Baden-Baden 1925
Réti Opening [A00]

**1.g3 e5 2.♘f3 e4 3.♘d4 d5 4.d3 e×d3 5.♕×d3 ♘f6 6.♗g2 ♗b4+ 7.♗d2 ♗×d2+ 8.♘×d2 00 9.c4! ♘a6! 10.c×d5 ♘b4 11.♕c4 ♘b×d5 12.♘2b3 c6 13.00 ♖e8 14.♖fd1 ♗g4 15.♖d2 ♕c8 16.♘c5 ♗h3 17.♗f3 ♗g4 18.♗g2 ♗h3 19.♗f3 ♗g4 20.♗h1** The psychological duel has ended in Black's favor. Réti, with White, refuses to repeat moves, thereby demonstrating his resolve to play for a win. Having retreated his bishop to h1, he relies on the strong position of his knight on c5 and a queenside pawn assault. Black, however, does not prevent this plan "because he anticipates the possibility of a combination on the kingside" (Lasker). **20...h5!** "Now Black develops his attack with surprising energy, which makes the second part of the game one of the most ingenious, lively and intricate in all chess literature" (Tartakower). **21.b4 a6 22.♖c1 h4 23.a4 h×g3 24.h×g3 ♕c7 25.b5 a×b5 26.a×b5** (D)

**26...♖e3!!** A very bold move, typical of Alekhine's attacking style. **27.♘f3?** This loses control completely. White

also cannot play 27.f×e3?? because of 27...♕×g3+ and 28...♘×e3. Alekhine thought 27.♗f3! ♗×f3 28.e×f3! would have given White better chances to resist because all of White's pieces are well placed for the defense. "The beginning of one of the most beautiful combinations ever created on the chessboard" (Lasker). **27...c×b5 28.♕×b5 ♘c3 29.♕×b7 ♕×b7 30.♘×b7 ♘×e2+ 31.♔h2 ♘e4!!** The second knight enters the attack with decisive effect. "It seems that a herd of horses, not a single horse, has invaded White's camp" (Tartakower). **32.♖c4** 32.♖d8+ ♖×d8 33.f×e3 ♖d5!−+ (Kasparov). "White is up to the mark: the attack and counterattack are equal" (Lasker). **32...♘×f2!** 32...♗×f3? runs into 33.♖×e4!! with drawing chances (Kasparov). **33.♗g2 ♗e6 34.♖cc2 ♘g4+ 35.♔h3 ♘e5+ 36.♔h2 ♖×f3! 37.♖×e2 ♘g4+ 38.♔h3 ♘e3+ 39.♔h2 ♘×c2 40.♗×f3 ♘d4** and Réti resigned because 41.♖f2 ♘×f3+ 42.♖×f3 ♗d5 wins the stranded knight. **0−1**

## Combinations

In carrying out unexpected maneuvers and delivering tactical blows with far-reaching and overwhelming sacrifices, Alekhine's imagination was amazing. Many of his games were awarded bril-

liancy prizes. In his two-volume monograph, *The Chess Heritage of Alekhine*, grandmaster Alexander Kotov divided all Alekhine's combinations into three groups: (1) pawn combinations aimed pawn promotion; (2) combinations based on the awkward position of the opponents pieces; and (3) mating combinations.

The Bogoljubow-Alekhine game from the Hastings 1922 tournament (See Celebrities) belongs to the first group. The ending of another famous game, in which the same motif occurs, he presented in his collections *My Best Games (1908-1923)*:

**(121) Alekhine − Hofmeister**
Petrograd 1917 (D)

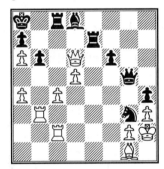

**1.c5! b5 2.a×b5! ♘e4 3.b6! ♘×d6 4.c×d6** A very rare position!: despite his great superiority in material, Black must lose. To prove the point, Alekhine gives the following variations: (1) 4...♖×c2 5.b7+ ♖×b7 6.a×b7+ ♔b8 7.♗×a7+ with mate in two; (2) 4...♖b8 5.b7+ with mate in three; (3) 4...a×b6 5.♖×c8+ ♔a7 and White wins; (4) 4...♗c7! 5.b7+! ♔b8 6.d×c7+ ♖e×c7 (or 6...♖c×c7 7.♗×a7+ and 8.b8♕+). **4...♖ec7 5.b7+ ♔b8 6.d7!! ♕g3+ 7.♔h1 0−1**

241

Mating combinations also occurred in his games rather frequently. As Lasker justly remarked, in attacking the king, Alekhine's imagination is fired, and he played with special inspiration.

It is interesting to hypothesize how Alekhine's "mechanism" of originating such combinations might work. With all their diversity, it is sometimes possible to discover some inherent patterns. A relevant example is his game with the English master Harry Golombek, in which the position of the white knight at g5, the absence of a black pawn at f7, and the possibility of giving a check on the weakened a2-g8 diagonal suggested to Alekhine the idea of a smothered mate with the knight on f7.

**(122) Alekhine – Golombek**
Margate 1938
Nimzo-Indian Defense [E20]

**1.d4 ♘f6 2.c4 e6 3.♘c3 ♗b4 4.g3 d5 5.♗g2 0-0 6.♘f3 c5 7.c×d5 ♘×d5 8.♗d2 ♘c6 9.a3** 9.♘×d5 ♕×d5 10.♗×b4 ♘×b4 11.0-0 is played most often. **9...♘×c3 10.b×c3 ♗a5 11.0-0 c×d4 12.c×d4 ♗×d2 13.♕×d2 ♕e7 14.♕b2 ♖d8 15.♖fc1 ♕d6?** 15...♗d7 was better because 16.♕×b7? can be met with 16...♘a5=. **16.e3!** Freeing the knight for attacking purposes. **16...♖b8 17.♘g5 ♗d7 18.♕c2 f5?** (D) 18...g6 was forced.

**19.d5!!** Alekhine now seizes the moment immediately in his typical way. **19...♘e7** 19...e×d5 20.♗×d5+ ♕×d5 21.♖d1 ♕e5 22.♕a2+ ♗e6 23.♘×e6 ♖×d1+ 24.♖×d1 ♕f6 25.♖d7 ♘e7 26.♘g5+ ♔h8 27.♘f7+ ♔g8 28.♘h6+

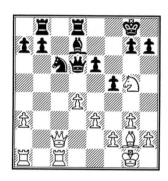

♔h8 29.♖d6 ♕f8 (29...♕×d6?? meets with the well-known motif 30.♕g8+ ♘×g8 31.♘f7#) **30.♘f7+ ♔g8 31.♘e5+ ♔h8 32.♕e6 ♖e8 33.♖d7 ♘g6 34.♘×g6+ h×g6 35.♕×g6 ♖e7 36.♕d6+–**. **20.d×e6 ♗×e6 21.♖d1 ♕e5 22.♗×b7 h6?** 22...♗f7 is more tenacious. **23.♘×e6 ♕×e6 24.♕c7 ♖×d1+ 25.♖×d1 ♖e8 26.♗f3 a6 27.♖d6 ♕e5 28.♕c4+ ♔h7 29.♖×a6 ♖c8 30.♕f7 ♖c1+ 31.♔g2 1-0**

The "typology" of Alekhine's combinations is, of course, conditional. One might just as well divide them into groups by the character of sacrificial combinations, i.e., sacrifice of a queen, rook, bishop, knight, or pawn. Alekhine sacrificed his queen in very different situations. Not infrequently this occurred in his simultaneous exhibition games. Here is an example of such a beautiful ten-move combination:

**(123) Alekhine – Prat,M**
Paris 1913 (simul)
Queen's Gambit Accepted [D24]

**1.d4 d5 2.♘f3 ♘f6 3.c4 e6 4.♘c3 d×c4 5.e3 ♘c6?!** The main lines are 5...a6 and 5...c5. **6.♗×c4 ♗b4 7.0-0 ♗×c3?!** Ceding the bishop pair for no good reason. 7...0-0 is played most often. **8.b×c3 0-0 9.♕c2 ♘e7 10.♗a3 c6 11.e4 h6 12.♖ad1 ♗d7 13.♘e5 ♖e8 14.f4 ♕c7?** 14...b5 15.♗b3 a5± gives more counterplay. **15.f5! ♖ad8?!** (D) 15...b5 16.♗b3 ♗c8 is the lesser evil.

**16.♘×f7!** The knight clears the way for White's powerful central pawn mass. **16...♔×f7 17.e5 ♘eg8?! 18.♗d6 ♕c8 19.♕e2 b5 20.♗b3 a5 21.♖de1 a4** (D)

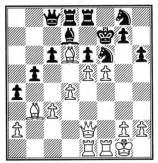

**22.♕h5+!!** A solution in typical Alekhine style. 22.e×f6 ♘×f6 23.f×e6+ ♗×e6 24.♕h5+ ♔g8 25.♖×f6 ♗×b3 26.♗e5 wins as well. **22...♘×h5 23.f×e6+ ♔g6 24.♗c2+ ♔g5 25.♖f5+ ♔g6 26.♖f6+ ♔g5 27.♖g6+ ♔h4** 27...♔f4 28.♖e4+ ♔f5 29.♖eg4# **28.♖e4+ ♘f4 29.♖×f4+ ♔h5 30.g3** and Prat resigned as ♖h4# can not be parried. **1-0**

**(124) Alekhine – Feldt**
Odessa 1916 (Simul)
French Defense [C11]

**1.e4 e6 2.d4 d5 3.♘c3 ♘f6 4.e×d5 ♘×d5 5.♘e4 f5?! 6.♘g5 ♗e7 7.♘5f3 c6?! 8.♘e5 0-0 9.♘gf3 b6 10.♗d3 ♗b7 11.0-0 ♖e8 12.c4 ♘f6 13.♗f4 ♘bd7 14.♕e2 c5?** (D) 14...♘×e5, in order to meet 15.♕×e5 with 15...♕c8 16.♘g5 ♘h5 was necessary.

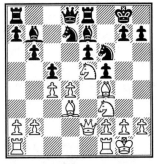

Now one of Alekhine's most famous combinations follows: **15.♘f7!!** ♔×f7 15...♗×f3 16.♕×e6 ♘f8 17.♘h6+ ♔h8 18.♕g8+ ♘×g8 19.♘f7# **16.♕×e6+ ♔g6** 16...♔f8 17.♘g5+-; 16...♔×e6 17.♘g5# **17.g4 ♗e4 18.♘h4# 1-0**

Even a world-class player like Samuel Reshevsky was not immune to the Alekhine queen sacrifice.

**(125) Alekhine – Reshevsky**
Kemeri 1937
Alekhine's Defense [B05]

**1.e4 ♘f6 2.e5 ♘d5 3.d4 d6 4.♘f3 ♗g4 5.c4 ♘b6 6.♗e2 d×e5 7.♘×e5 ♗×e2 8.♕×e2 ♕×d4 9.0-0 ♘8d7 10.♘×d7 ♘×d7?!** 10...♕×d7 is the critical main line. **11.♘c3 c6 12.♗e3 ♕e5 13.♖ad1**

e6 **14.♕f3 0-0-0 15.♗×a7 ♕a5 16.♗d4 ♕f5 17.♕g3** 17.♕×f5 e×f5 18.♘a4 gives White a lasting long-term advantage. But Alekhine, true to his style, plays for an attack. **17...e5 18.♗e3 ♗b4 19.♘a4 ♗a5 20.f4 ♗c7 21.b3 f6?** The knight should be activated with 21...♘f6 because 22.♕×g7? may be countered with 22...♖hg8 23.♖×d8+ ♗×d8 24.♕×f7 ♕h3–+. **22.f×e5 ♕e6 23.h3?** The bold pawn grab 23.♕×g7 cannot be punished: 23...♖hg8 24.♕h6 ♕g4 25.g3 ♗×e5 26.♗f2±. **23...♖hg8 24.♗d4 ♘×e5 25.♕c3 ♘d7 26.c5 ♖ge8 27.b4?** (D) Alekhine overplays his hand. One option is the prophylactic 27.♔h1 to make the defensivee ♗g1 available.

**27...♘b8?** Now the pawn must be taken: 27...♕×a2 28.♖a1 (after 28.♘b6+?, Black has 28...♘×b6 29.c×b6 ♖e2!–+) 28...♕d5 29.♕b2 ♕e4, and Black's well-centralized army gives him strong counterplay. **28.♘b6+ ♗×b6 29.c×b6 ♕×a2?** Now it is too late to grab the pawn. But good advice is hard to find. **30.♕g3 ♖d7?! 31.♗c5?!** 31.♗×f6! wins directly: 31...g×f6 32.♖×d7 ♔×d7 33.♕c7+ ♔e6 34.♖e1++–. **31...♕f7 32.♖a1?!** 32.♗d6! ♖ed8 33.b5 f5 34.b×c6 b×c6 35.♕a3 ♕c4 36.b7+

♖×b7 37.♗×b8 ♖×d1 38.♖×d1 ♕b4 39.♕×b4 ♖×b4 40.♗e5+– **32...♕g6 33.♕h2 ♖e5?** The last chance to fight is 33...♘a6 34.b5 c×b5 35.♖fc1 ♖e2 36.♗f2+ ♖c2 37.♕g3 ♔d8 38.♕b3 ♖×c1+ 39.♖×c1 ♕f7, but Black's position is still very difficult to defend. **34.♖a8 ♖d2?** (D) Allowing a direct mate, but Black is lost in any case, e.g., 34...♕d3 35.♕f4 h5 36.♔h2+–.

**35.♖×b8+!! ♔×b8 36.♕×e5+** "The final attack of this game gave me much more pleasure than a scientifically correct, but purely technical exploitation of a pawn majority on the queenside would do" (Alekhine). **1-0**

## Composition

Alekhine highly valued the idea of problem composition. He mentioned it in his foreword to the collection of chess problems and studies by Lazard. But, as he himself admitted, he "has not produced anything deserving attention." He composed his first problem in 1914, and did it blindfold.

Alekhine 1914 (D)

**1.♕f5! ♗×f5 2.♖a7+ ♔×e6** (2...♔×g6 3.♖g7#) **3.♘f4#** or **1...♗×d4 2.♔d7 ♗×f5 3.♘h8#**.

*White to move and mate in three.*

For a long time, it was believed to be the only problem composed by Alekhine. But recently there has been discovered another three-mover that he published in 1932 in the Italian magazine *Italia Scacchistica*, No. 11.

Alekhine 1932 (D)

*White to move and mate in three.*

**1.♕c4!! ♔d6** (1...d×c3 2.♕f4+! ♔×f4 3.d4#) **2.♕c7+ ♔×c7** (2...♘×c7 3.♘b7#) **3.♘×b5#**

And only once did Alekhine compose a study – a refinement of a game he played in a simultaneous exhibition in Groningen 1932 – which he published in the Dutch magazine *Tijdkrift*. (D)

*White to move and win.*

**1.a6 ♖h4** (1...♖g1 2.a7 ♖a1 3.♖a3) **2.♖d8! ♔×d8 3.a7** and White wins.

## Middlegame

After the opening phase, there comes the decisive stage of struggle in a game, when the individuality of a player, all facets of his/her talent is especially prominent. In all periods of his chess career, Alekhine was regarded by his contemporaries as the rarest master of tactical blows, a wizard of combinations. But many of them would be impossible unless they were preceded by just as brilliant strategy.

One of Alekhine's strategic ideas was to mask the decisive blow on the kingside by preceding operations in the center or on the queenside. The striking examples of such a strategy are, in particular, his games with Bogoljubow (Triberg 1921), Sterk (Budapest 1921), and Rubinstein (Carlsbad 1923). "The main distinguishing feature of all these games," wrote Alekhine, "is the unexpectedness of the rapid decisive attacks invariably prepared far from the point at which they are directed. They are every time preceded by a more or less complicated maneuvering in the center or on the queenside, the purpose of which is to lure the opponent's pieces away from the main sector of struggle. And only then is the lightning blow delivered (in all these games, this is a bishop move) usually involving a sacrifice and leaving no chance of salvation for the opponent. These attacks – of the same character, though occurring in games of an entirely distinct nature – are, in my opinion, highly indicative of and may provide material for judging the style of a player or, at least, the evolution of his style."

### (126) Alekhine – Sterk,Karoly
Budapest 1921
Queen's Gambit Declined [D37]

**1.d4 d5 2.♘f3 e6 3.c4 ♘f6 4.♘c3 ♘bd7 5.e3 ♗d6?! 6.♘b5** 6.c5 is more critical. **6...♗e7 7.♕c2 c6 8.♘c3 0-0 9.♗d3 d×c4 10.♗×c4 c5 11.d×c5 ♗×c5 12.0-0 b6 13.e4 ♗b7 14.♗g5 ♕c8 15.♕e2 ♗b4 16.♗d3 ♗×c3 17.♖fc1 ♘×e4?** A miscalculation. Black should choose the move order 17...♘c5 18.♖×c3 ♗×e4, when he is certainly not worse. **18.♗×e4 ♗×e4 19.♕×e4 ♘c5 (D)**

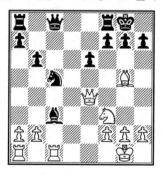

**20.♕e2?** The reatreat 20.♕b1 wins the bishop directly: 20...♗a5 21.b4+–. **20...♗a5 21.♖ab1 ♕a6 22.♖c4 ♘a4?** (D) 22...h6? 23.♗×h6 g×h6 24.♘e5 f5 (24...♔h7 25.♕h5 ♗d2

26.♖d4±) 25.♘d7 ♘×d7 26.♖g4+ f×g4 27.♕×a6 ♗b4 28.♕a4 ♗c5 29.♕×d7 ♖×f2 30.♕×e6+ ♔h7 31.♔h1±; 22...f6! is forced in order to stop White's kingside attack. Black can continue to fight after 23.♗c1 ♖fd8 24.b4 ♗×b4 25.♖b×b4 ♕×a2 26.♖c2 ♕a6.

**23.♗f6!!** The beautiful refutation of Black's concept. **23...♖fc8** 23...g×f6 24.♖g4+ ♔h8 25.♕×a6+– **24.♕e5!** ♖c5 24...♖×c4 25.♕g5 ♖g4 26.♕×g4 g6 27.♕×a4+– **25.♕g3** 25.♖×c5 b×c5 26.♕g5 is even easier. **25...g6 26.♖×a4 ♕d3** 26...♖ac8 27.♖d4 ♖c1+ 28.♖d1+– **27.♖f1 ♖ac8 28.♖d4 ♕f5 29.♕f4 ♕c2?! 30.♕h6 1-0**

Among other strategic methods Alekhine used to employ was to play on all parts of the board at the same time, as happened, for example, in the 34th game of his match against Capablanca, the third game of his match against Euwe (1935), and a number of other games. "Playing on both flanks is my favorite strategy" (Alekhine).

### (127) Alekhine – Euwe
World Championship (3) Netherlands 1935
French Defense [C15]

**1.e4 e6 2.d4 d5 3.♘c3 ♗b4 4.a3 ♗×c3+ 5.b×c3 d×e4 6.♕g4 ♘f6**

**7.♕×g7 ♖g8 8.♕h6 c5 9.♘e2 ♘bd7** "If 9...♘c6, then White would simply reply 10.d×c5!, but 10.♗g5, as Romanovsky played against Botvinnik in the USSR Championship Semi-finals 1938, is also sufficient for equality" (Alekhine). **10.♘g3 ♖g6?!** 10...♕a5 is the critical main line. **11.♕e3 ♘d5?! 12.♕×e4 ♘×c3 13.♕d3 ♘d5 14.♗e2 ♕f6 15.c3 c×d4 16.c×d4 ♘7b6 (D)**

**17.♗h5!** "This bishop maneuver, consisting of four consecutive moves, forces a practically decisive weakening of Black's pawn position. The following play on both wings is very instructive and, I believe, typical of my style" (Alekhine). **17...♗g7 18.♗f3?** Alekhine follows his maneuver. But objectivly, his knight should enter the attack with 18.♘e4 and White wins, e.g., 18...♕e7 19.♗h6 ♖×g2 20.♗×f7+ ♔×f7 21.♕f3++−. **18...♕g6 19.♗e4** 19.♘e4!? **19...f5 20.♗f3 ♔f8 21.a4 ♖c7 22.0-0 ♗d7?** 22...♖c3 23.♕d1 a5± stabilizes the position for the moment. **23.♗a3+?** Alekhine misses the combination 23.a5 ♘c4 24.♘×f5, which either wins material or opens more attacking lines. **23...♔g8 24.a5 ♖c3** 24...♘c4?! 25.♗c5 ♘e5 26.d×e5 ♖×c5 27.♖fc1 ♖ac8 28.♖×c5 ♖×c5 29.♕d4+− (Alekhine). **25.♕b1 ♘a4?** 25...♖×f3 26.g×f3 ♘c4 27.♕×b7

♕e8 offers much more counterplay on the light squares. **26.♗×d5 e×d5 27.♕×b7 ♕c6 28.a6?** Activating the sleeping f1-rook with 28.♖fb1 +− is called for. **28...♘b6?** Alekhine's attack had to be stopped by 28...♕×b7 29.a×b7 ♖b8 30.♖fb1 ♖c6, when Black can still defend tenaciously. **29.♗c5 f4 30.♘f5!** The knight enters the attack with decisive effect. **30...♔h8 31.♘e7 ♕e6 32.♗×b6 ♗c6 33.♘×c6 ♖g8 (D)**

**34.♘e5!** The knight attacks and defends. It is a mighty octopus! **34...♖g7** 34...♕h3 35.♘f7+ ♔g7 36.g×h3 +− **35.♕b8+?!** "Played too hastily, which keeps the fight up for a little while, whereas 35.♗×a7 would force Black to resign at once." (Alekhine). **35...♖c8 36.♘g6+ ♖×g6 37.♕×f4 ♕×b6 38.♕e5+ ♖g7 39.♕×d5 ♖d8 40.♕e5 ♕×d4 41.♕×d4 1-0**

The sacrifice of a pawn to obtain, retain, or develop the initiative occupies an important place in Alekhine's strategic plans. And, in the last decade of his career, Alekhine regularly disturbed the game's balance by sacrificing a pawn for tempestuous complications that would allow his combinative genius to search for winning ways. In this way, he kept masters and grandmasters who had to heighten the level of their positional play dramatically on unsure footing. His game against Reuben Fine at Kemeri is a fine example.

**(128) Alekhine – Fine,Reuben**
Kemeri 1937
Queen's Gambit Accepted [D23]

**1.d4 d5 2.c4 d×c4 3.♘f3 ♘f6 4.♕a4+ ♕d7 5.♕×c4 ♕c6 6.♘a3 ♕×c4 7.♘×c4 e6 8.a3 c5 9.♗f4 ♘c6 10.d×c5 ♗×c5 11.b4 ♗e7 12.b5 ♘b8 13.♘d6+ ♗×d6 14.♗×d6 ♘e4 15.♗c7 ♘d7 16.♘d4 ♘b6 17.f3 ♘d5 18.♗a5 ♘ef6 19.♘c2** 19.e4!? ♘e3 20.♔f2 ♘×f1 21.♖h×f1, with the initiative, is the alternative. **19...♗d7 20.e4 ♖c8 21.♔d2 ♘b6?** Playing against White's bishop pair will be very hard. Therefore, Black should exchange off the a5-bishop for the d5-knight with 21...b6 22.e×d5 b×a5 23.d×e6 f×e6 24.♗d3 ♔e7, when Black has good drawing chances because of his activity. **22.♘e3 0-0 23.a4 ♖fd8 24.♗d3 e5 25.♖hc1 ♗e6 26.♖×c8 ♖×c8 27.♗b4 ♘e8 28.a5 ♘d7 29.♘d5 ♗×d5 30.e×d5** (D)

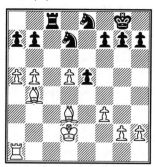

**30...♘c5?** This meets with a tactical refutation, where the bishops show their full power. After 30...♘ef6, it is not so easy to break Black's solid set-

up. **31.♗f5! ♖d8** 31...♘b3+ 32.♔d3 ♖d8 33.♗e7 +- **32.♔c3! b6 33.a×b6 a×b6 34.♗×c5 b×c5 35.b6 ♘d6 36.♗d7! ♖×d7?! 37.♖a8+ ♘e8 38.♖×e8# 1-0**

"This game is perhaps my best purely positional achievement in recent years" (Alekhine).

### Neo-romanticsim and Alekhine

In order to attain superiority over strong rivals, one should search for new ways. This was the conclusion Alekhine arrived at already in the early 1920s. That was a remarkable epoch in the art of chess. It is then that a new creative direction declared itself in a loud voice. Its representatives were such masters as Nimzowitsch, Réti, Breyer, and Tartakower, to name the most prominent ones. "The achievements of these masters," Alekhine wrote in 1929 (in his correspondence sent from the Carlsbad tournament), reflecting on the main trends in the development of chess, "have led to the unexpected flourishing of chess in the postwar years. They have succeeded in demonstrating that even with the extensive development of theory, there is still enough space to show imagination, temperament, and will power. This group of masters one can quite justifiably call 'Neoromanticists.'"

Having declared themselves opponents of the so called classical school of Steinitz and Tarrasch with its "universal" laws, the representatives of the new (or, as they named themselves hypermodern) movement demanded in the first place a concrete assessment of the position and the constant search for exception to the rules. They declared war on the stereotypes, exchanges, and draws! They treated the opening phase as the beginning of the middlegame, where the plan was important from the very first moves. The romantic searches of the adherents of the new doctrine furthered the progress of opening theory and enhanced the role of the aesthetic factor in the chess game. There appear such openings as the Réti Opening, Nimzo-Indian Defense, Grünfeld Defense, and Queen's Indian Defense.

At the same time, the unusually original (by its aims and strategic pattern) Alekhine Defense comes into practice. Understandably, the hypermodernists claimed Alekhine as one of their own. And, although he did not quite agree with this, understanding that "the specificity of the art of chess" in which one's creativity depends "in some measure on the play of the opponent," the followers of the new movement were close to Alekhine of those years, with many of their views and discoveries. Characterizing their leader, Alekhine calls Nimzowitsch "a true representative of the artistic school in chess."

And in Alekhine's style of play one could observe the internal strife between the romanticist he was in his youth and the profound thinker, the scientist who mastered the secrets of positional play in his mature years. According to Pyotr Romanovsky, Alekhine, to a certain extent, remained, as did Chigorin, a romanticist till the end of his life (*Romanticism in Chess Art* Moscow, 1950).

"I want it this way," or "I like it that way" – these motives were not infre- quently present in Alekhine's sacrificial treatment of the game in the last years of his life. Hence, Romanovsky, a chess master and theorist himself, comes to the conclusion that Alekhine's games, in spite of their positional and realistic basis, had not a few features of romanticism. "Alekhine generally had a contradictory nature," Romanovsky stressed. "Two natures always struggled in him: the cool, clever, egoistical calculation and the exciting gamma of moods, enticing him – often contrary to reason – to the sea of stormy emotions and experiences."

However, Alekhine himself, despite his sympathies for the creative neoromantic movement, invariably declined the honor to be counted as its representative. He understood, as Lasker did, the fragility of some of their stands and attitudes, sometimes failing to take into account the specificity of chess art and one of its most important constituent parts, competitiveness. Moreover, his strategic genius suggested to him that there were many undiscovered regularities hidden in chess and that the future of the art of chess lay in the conjunction of artistry and scientific method.

**Style of Play**

Originally, Alekhine appeared before the chess world as an unusually gifted player of combinative style. But, having set himself the goal of ascending chess Olympus, he realized that assimilating all the subtleties of positional play would be the only way to achieve it. And, as a result of constant work to improve his style, Alekhine became one of the greatest masters of strategy. Already in the early 1920s,

Alekhine had come to the conclusion that, first of all, he had to work to understand the secret of the strength of Lasker and Capablanca. And he was not afraid to admit it.

Thus, while working on the 1924 New York Tournament book, he "learned a lot in the process." Alekhine "[w]ith especial interest" set about to "study Lasker and Capablanca's style, which greatly expanded [his] experience and allowed [him] to make important observations." Owing to his colossal ability to work, phenomenal memory, and amazing ability to not only critically assess all movements of chess thought but also to assimilate all that is sound and promising, Alekhine was able to integrate organically positional play with attacking and combinative flavor into his style. During the international tournament at Carlsbad (1923), answering the question of a *Wienerschachzeitung* journalist about his attitude to the "old" and "new" schools, Alekhine said that he did "not 'play' chess; [he] 'struggles.' Therefore, [he] willingly combine[s] the tactical with the strategic, the combinational with the positional, and [he tries] to meet the requirements of position."

While preparing for the match against Capablanca, Alekhine spontaneously assimilated some principles into his style. Master Eugene Znosko-Borovsky, who participated together with Alekhine in the international tournament at Birmingham in the winter of 1926, paid attention to this fact. Their game against each other is an example of Alekhine's Capablanca style of play for advantageous simplifications.

**(129)  Alekhine  –  Znosko-Borovsky,Eugene**
Birmingham 1926
Queen's Indian Defense [E12]

**1.d4 ♘f6 2.c4 e6 3.♘c3 ♗b4 4.♗g5 h6 5.♗×f6 ♕×f6 6.♖c1 b6 7.♘f3 ♗b7 8.e3 0-0 9.♗e2 d6 10.0-0 ♗×c3 11.♖×c3 ♘d7 12.♘d2** Taking into account that his opponent's queenside light squares are weakened, Alekhine intends to swap bishops. This, as he himself emphasizes, will make it possible to worsen Black's pawn structure and "obtain an active game with winning chances." Alekhine's further reasoning is of interest because it reflects Capablanca's influence that one should not artificially cause combinative complications if one can see that the game may be won by simplifications into an advantageous endgame. "Every player," wrote Alekhine, "must, in my opinion, make use of such a possibility and try to solve the problem of winning the game without 'fear' of simplifications. To play for complications is an extreme measure, which a player should resort to only when he cannot find a clear-cut and logical plan. In the given case, however, when White has such a plan, he should endeavor to exploit his advantage even though it would be a task far from easy." **12...e5 13.♗f3 ♗×f3 14.♘×f3 e4 15.♘d2 ♕e7 16.♕a4 f5 17.♕c6 ♘f6 18.b4 a5 19.♖a3 ♕d7 20.♕×d7 ♘×d7 21.b×a5 ♖×a5 22.♖×a5 b×a5 23.♖b1 ♖b8 24.♖×b8+ ♘×b8 25.♔f1 ♘d7 26.♔e2 ♘b6 27.♔d1 a4 28.d5 ♘d7 29.♔c2 ♘e5 30.♔c3 ♘g4 31.♔b4 ♘×f2 32.♔×a4** (D)

**32...f4?** Black plays this trump too early. He should activate his king first with 32...♚f7, but White remains preferable of course because of his outside passed a-pawn. **33.e×f4 e3 34.♘f3 ♘d3 35.♔b5 g5** 35...♔f7 36.♘g1 ♘×f4 (36...♔e7 37.♘e2+−) 37.♔c6 e2 38.♘×e2 ♘×e2 39.a4+− **36.f×g5 h×g5 37.a4 e2** (D)

**38.h3!** Strong prophylaxis. The hasty 38.a5? g4 even loses. **38...♘c5** Black cannot stop the running pawn after 38...e1♛ 39.♘×e1 ♘×e1 40.a5+−. **39.a5 ♘b3 40.♘e1 ♘d4+ 41.♔a4 1-0**

Five years later, in 1931, Alekhine recollected:

*Over the preceding period, I worked on my style a lot, striving for the extreme easiness and outward simplicity that have al-ways been the distinguishing features of style of my future opponent. It seemed to me that in that so striving, I have attained quite satisfactory results. And now, in Birmingham, when talking with Eugene Aleksandrovich on the subject of preparation for the match, I noted his concern as framed in the question: 'Are not you afraid that by artificially drying your style you will lose what has up to now been its essence – the temperament, the fighting roots? And would not this loss be much greater than the acquisition for which you are striving?' This conversation has long dwelled in my mind, begetting a kind of fear for my imagination and apprehension of its, even partial, weakening. The consequence of this apprehension was probably a new subconscious reassessment of values, as a result of which my games, played in the period immediately preceding the match in Buenos Aires, again became brighter and more consistent.*

The amazing ability of Alekhine to creatively synthesize the entire wealth of ideas and styles of the past and contemporary chess thought was also indicated by Emanuel Lasker. Shortly before the match in 1926, he primarily stressed Alekhine's inborn combinative gift. Ten years later, Lasker came to the conclusion that Alekhine's stylistic influences were diverse:

*The origin of Alekhine's style originates with Steinitz and Chigorin; however, he painstak-*

ingly assimilated all the new ideas that were contributed by the diligent, completely trusting in principles put forth by Rubinstein, and the logical, single-minded Capablanca, and the adventure seeker and lover Nimzowitsch and the wholly immersed in the depths of the enigmas posed by Breyer... His attempt to unite this diversity of styles was titanic, but he could count on success, because he is industrious, intelligent, and endowed with extraordinary imagination.

## Alekhine's Pupil

There was only one time in his entire life (1944-1945) in which the first Russian world champion took the patronage of a young player and gave him a number of lessons, and, as a result, the talented pupil achieved considerable sporting successes. That was the Spanish prodigy Arturo Pomar (born Sept 1, 1931 in Palma de Mallorca). Already, at the age of ten, he began playing in adult competitions, and, at twelve, he played in an international tournament (1943). Alekhine praised his playing. At the request of the Spanish chess federation, he started instructing Pomar and wrote down a series of lessons for him, which were subsequently published in Madrid in book form under the title *Legado* (Legacy).

In his book on Alekhine's Spanish period, Pablo Moran published four games that Alekhine had played with Pomar between 1943 and 1945. The first of them is from a simultaneous exhibition with clocks, played October

23, 1943 against eight Spanish players. Arturo resigned on move 31. The second game was played in the tournament at Gijon and was drawn on move 71. Pomar's play beginning with move 19, notes Alekhine, deserves to be highly praised.

**(130) Alekhine – Pomar, Arturo**
Gijon 1944
Ruy Lopez [C84]

**1.e4 e5 2.♘f3 ♘c6 3.♗b5 a6 4.♗a4 ♘f6 5.0-0 d6 6.c3 ♗g4 7.d4 b5 8.♗b3 ♗e7 9.♗e3 0-0 10.♘bd2 ♖e8 11.h3 ♗h5 12.d5 ♘a5 13.♗c2 ♖c8 14.a4 c5 15.a×b5 a×b5 16.g4 ♗g6 17.♘h4 ♘d7?! 18.♘f5?!** Playing on the queenside with 18.♘×g6!? h×g6 19.b4 is more promising because Black will be able to weather the following storms on the kingside. **18...♗×f5 19.g×f5?!** (D)

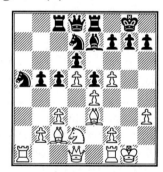

19.e×f5 is more natural, in order to use the e4-square for the knight. **19...♗g5 20.♕e2 c4 21.♔h1 ♖a8 22.♖g1 ♗×e3 23.♕×e3 ♕f6 24.♖g4 ♔h8 25.♖ag1 ♖g8 26.♘f3 ♘b7 27.♖h4 ♖a6** 27...♘bc5!? **28.♕g5 ♘d8 29.♕h5 ♘f8 30.♘h2 g6 31.♕h6 ♕g7 32.♘g4 f6 33.f×g6** 33.♕×g7+!? ♔×g7 34.♘h6 ♖h8 35.f×g6 h×g6 36.♘f5+ ♔g8 37.♘e7+

&#9823;g7 38.&#9816;f5+ forces the draw directly. **33...&#9819;×g6 34.&#9819;e3 &#9819;g5 35.&#10540;h6 &#9819;×e3 36.f×e3 &#9816;d7 37.&#10540;f1** The direct 37.&#9816;×f6!? was the alternative, but Black keeps practical winning chances after 37...&#10540;×g1+ 38.&#9822;×g1 &#10540;a1+ 39.&#9822;f2 &#9816;×f6 40.&#10540;×f6 &#9823;g7 41.&#10540;×d6 &#9816;f7 42.&#10540;c6 &#10540;c1 43.&#9821;a4 b×a4 44.&#10540;×c4 &#10540;c2+ 45.&#9822;g3 &#9816;d6 46.&#10540;×a4 &#10540;×b2 47.&#9822;g4 &#10540;f2. **37...&#10540;a2?!** 37...&#9816;f7 38.&#10540;h5 &#10540;g6 39.&#10540;hf5 &#10540;a2 creates more pressure. **38.&#9816;×f6 &#9816;×f6 39.&#10540;h×f6 &#10540;×b2 40.&#9821;d1?** Far too optimistic. Black's b2-rook should be restricted with 40.&#10540;1f2 &#9816;b7 41.&#10540;f7 &#9816;c5 42.&#10540;a7=. **40...&#10540;gg2?** The rook is already attacking and defending, so the knight should be brought into play with 40...&#9816;b7 41.&#9821;f3 &#9816;c5 −+. **41.&#9821;f3 &#10540;g3?** 41...&#10540;gf2 42.&#10540;×f2 &#10540;×f2 43.&#9822;g1 &#9822;g7 makes better use of Black's activity and superior structure since White's counterattck gives him a draw in the game. **42.&#9821;g4 &#10540;gg2 43.&#10540;a1** Of course not 43.&#10540;f8+? &#9822;g7 44.&#10540;×d8?? &#10540;h2+ 45.&#9822;g1 &#10540;bg2#. **43...&#10540;h2+ 44.&#9822;g1 &#10540;hg2+ 45.&#9822;f1 &#10540;h2 46.&#9822;e1?** (D)

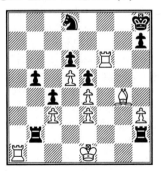

Alekhine wants to win at any price, but this goes too far. He should be satisfied with a draw after 46.&#9822;g1. "This is a blunder. Now Black could get winning chances by playing 46...&#9816;b7 47.&#10540;f7 &#10540;h1+ 48.&#10540;f1 &#10540;×f1+ 49.&#9822;×f1 &#9816;c5" (Alekhine). **46...b4?** Pomar violates the endgame principle "do not rush" and attacks without his knight. It should be activated first, 46...&#9816;b7 −+. **47.c×b4 c3 48.&#10540;c1 h5 49.&#9821;d1 &#9822;g7 50.&#10540;f1 c2 51.&#9821;e2 &#9816;f7 52.&#9822;d2 &#10540;×b4 53.&#10540;×c2 &#9816;g5 54.&#10540;c7+ &#9822;g6 55.&#9822;c3! &#10540;a4** (D)

**56.&#9821;b5?** Alekhine wants too much and miscalculates. He should be satisfied with the draw after 56.&#10540;f8 &#10540;×e2 57.&#10540;g8+. (56.&#9821;d3 &#10540;×h3 57.&#10540;f8 with a draw − Alekhine). **56...&#9816;×e4+ 57.&#9822;b3 &#10540;aa2 58.&#10540;g1+?! &#9822;h6 59.&#10540;b1 &#10540;ad2 60.&#9821;d7 &#10540;×d5 61.&#9822;c4** (D)

**61...&#10540;c2+?** Pomar should not exchange his attacking and winning potential but just play 61...&#10540;dd2 −+. **62.&#9822;×d5 &#10540;×c7 63.&#9822;e4 &#10540;×d7 64.h4 d5+ 65.&#9822;×e5 &#10540;e7+ 66.&#9822;f5 &#10540;×e3 67.&#10540;b6+ &#9822;h7 68.&#10540;d6 &#10540;e4 69.&#10540;d7+ &#9822;h6 70.&#10540;d6+ &#9822;h7 71.&#10540;d7+ &#9822;h6 ½-½**

The third game between Alekhine and Pomar took place in a tournament in Madrid, 1945, where, having chosen the French Defense, the world champion won after forty-nine moves. That same year, in a tournament in Gijon, Alekhine brilliantly defeated Pomar in the eighth round in forty moves (See, Spain). Their last encounter in official competitions occurred in August,1945 in the tournament at Almeria, and was drawn.

Studying and playing with Alekhine were good lessons for the young player. By the following year (1946), fifteen-year-old Pomar became the Spanish champion. It was a title that he would win four more times (1950, 1957, 1962, and 1966). He led the Spanish team in the world chess Olympiads ten times (1958-1976). He also took first and second places in a number of international tournaments, including those at Paris (1949), Hollywood (1952), Gijon (1955), Madrid (1959), Malaga (1964 and 1967), Palma de Mallorca (1965), Malaga (1971), Montilla (1973), Alicante (1975), Ales (1981), and others.

In 1962, Pomar participated in the interzonal tournament at Stockholm, where he shared 11th-12th places with Fridrik Olafsson among twenty-three contestants. Especially memorable for him was his game with the winner of the tournament, Robert Fischer. In it, as Pomar wrote in a letter to Isaak Linder, commenting on the book *The aesthetics of Chess*, "[i]n an endgame that required deep analysis, I managed, in a study-like manner, to achieve a draw" (January 26, 1980). Both the fine play against Fischer and his creed on the art of chess (stated in the aforementioned letter) correspond to the aesthetic views of his famous teacher. "The notion of chess beauty is associated with a huge assumption of risk," the Spanish grandmaster wrote. "It pervades, in most cases, combinative play and attack. But, of course, chess endings may also be beautiful – this is a highly important constituent part of chess."

## The Endgame

While preparing to fight for the world title, Alekhine paid great attention, along with the study of opening theory, to mastering the art of the endgame. The great connoisseur of Alekhine's art, grandmaster Grigory Levenfish, when characterizing the changes in Alekhine's style of play by the time of the 1923 Carlsbad tournament, stressed that "now he is a versatile fighter who has grasped all the subtleties of the Queen's Gambit. Alekhine defeats the best connoisseurs of this opening such as Rubinstein, Grünfeld, and Maróczy by exploiting minimal positional advantages, which requires an exceptionally high technique of handling the endgame phase. Indeed, Alekhine's games testify to a colossal work done to study endings." Alekhine's strategy in the endgame was based on a far-reaching concrete calculation, with an introduction, in full measure, of combinative imagination, and mastering the highest technique of handling the endgame.

Alekhine made valuable analyses, for example, in two rooks versus a rook and a knight. So rare a relation of forces nevertheless occurred four times in Alekhine's tournament praxis: in his games with Lasker (St. Petersburg

1914), Vidmar (Bled 1931), Kashdan (Pasadena 1932), and Bernstein (Zürich 1934). In his *book My Best Games 1924-1937*, Alekhine presented three games won with this ending, supplying the first of them (with Vidmar) with the following introduction:

*Manuals devoted to the endgame... do not give any convincing examples. The materially stronger party should win in the majority of cases, but not without serious technical difficulties. According to the general opinion, I succeeded against Vidmar in finding the shortest and most instructive winning method, and I owe, in great part, this achievement to a practical lesson that I received in the beginning of my career (in St. Petersburg 1914) by the great endgame artist Dr. Lasker. That lesson cost me a full point, for I happened to be the man with the knight! Dr. Lasker, to the general surprise, demonstrated that even with one pawn on each side (and not a passed pawn) the stronger party is able to force the decisive exchange of rooks.*

**(131) Alekhine – Vidmar,Milan Sr.**
Bled 1931
Queen's Gambit Declined [D55]

**1.d4 d5 2.♘f3 ♘f6 3.c4 c6 4.♘c3 e6 5.♗g5 ♗e7 6.e3 0-0 7.♕c2 ♘e4 8.♗×e7 ♕×e7 9.♗d3 ♘×c3 10.b×c3 ♔h8?! 11.c×d5 e×d5 12.0-0 ♗g4?** Too provocative; 12...♘d7 is more natural. **13.♘e5 ♗h5 14.♗×h7 g6 15.g4** The alter-

native 15.♗×g6 leads more or less by force to the endgame: 15...♗×g6 16.♕×g6 f×g6 17.♘×g6+ ♔g7 18.♘×e7 ♔f6 19.♖ab1 b6 20.♘×d5+ c×d5 21.♖fc1 ♖c8 22.c4 d×c4 23.♖b4, which is better for White but not completely clear. **15...♗×g4** (D)

**16.♘×g4** Alekhine opts for the simple solution, which gives him a dangerous, long term attack. 16.♗×g6 is answered by 16...♕e6 with messy complications (but not 16...♗h3? 17.f4 ♗×f1 18.♕d1 ♔g8 19.♗f5 when Black's king is too exposed) **16...♕g5 17.h3 ♔×h7 18.f4 ♕h4 19.♔h2!** This king move is an important part of Alekhine's attacking strategy. **19...♘d7 20.♖ab1 b6 21.♖g1 ♘f6 22.♘e5 ♘e4 23.♖bf1 ♔g7 24.♖g4** (D)

**24...♕h6?!** 24...♕f6!?, in order to lure White into winning the exchange with 25.♘d7? ♕f5 26.♘×f8 ♖×f8, when Black's knight has transformed into an octopus, is met by 25.f5 g5 26.♔g1, and White's attack continues. **25.f5** ♕×e3 Logical. The alternatives also give White a raging attack: 25...♖ae8 26.♖ff4 g5 27.♕g2 ♔h7 28.f6 ♖e6 29.♖×e4 d×e4 30.♕×e4+ ♔h8 31.♘×f7+ ♖×f7 32.♕×e6+−; 25...g5 26.♖×e4 d×e4 27.f6+ ♔h8 28.♕×e4 ♕h7 29.♖f5+−; 25...♘f6!? at least leads to the reduction of attacking potential, but White continues to press after 26.♖g2 g5 27.♖×g5+ ♕×g5 28.♖g1 ♕×g1+ 29.♔×g1 ♖g8 30.♔h2. **26.♕g2 ♕d2?!** 26...♖ae8!? brings more pieces into play and offers better pratical chances, e.g., 27.♖×g6+ (27.f×g6 is met by 27...f6) 27...f×g6 28.♕×g6+ ♔h8 29.♕h5+ ♔g8 30.♖g1+ ♕×g1+ 31.♔×g1 ♖e7 32.♔h2 ♖g7 33.♘g6 ♖h7 34.♕g4. **27.f6+ ♔g8 28.♘×c6 ♕×g2+ 29.♔×g2 ♖fe8 30.♘e7+ ♖×e7 31.f×e7 ♖e8 32.c4** "Without this possibility of obtaining a passed pawn, a win would still be rather dubious" (Alekhine). **32...♖×e7 33.c×d5 ♘c3?** Allowing Alekhine to seize the moment and start an unstoppable initiative in his typical stlye. 33...♔g7, to prepare ...f5, was called for, but White will still win in the long run. **34.d6 ♖d7 35.♖c1 ♘b5 36.♖g5 ♘×d6** 36...♘×d4 37.♖c8+ ♔g7 38.♖d5 ♘e6 39.♔f3 f5 40.h4 ♔f6 41.♔e3+− **37.♖d5** "From this moment there begins the purely technical part of the endgame. With the combined play of all his pieces, White should try to extract the maximum possible advantage from the pinned black knight" (Alekhine). **37...♔f8 38.♖e1** 38.♖c8+ ♔e7 39.♖e5+ ♔f6 40.♖c6 is easier. **38...♖d8?!** It is better to exchange the passive rook with 38...♖e7 39.♖×e7 ♔×e7 40.h4, but White is technically winning. **39.♔f3**

♖d7 40.♔f4 ♔g7?! 41.♖e8 ♔f6 42.h4 ♔g7 43.a4 ♔f6 44.♖c8 ♔e6 45.♖e5+ ♔f6 46.♖c6 ♖d8 47.a5 b5 48.♖×b5 ♔e6 49.♖e5+ ♔f6 50.♖a6 ♖d7 51.♔g4 ♖d8 52.♔f3 ♖d7 53.♔f4 ♖d8 54.h5 g×h5 55.♖×h5 ♖d7 56.♖e5 ♖d8 57.♖×a7 ♘c4 58.♖a6+ ♔g7 59.♖g5+ ♔f8 60.♔e4 ♔e7 61.♖c5 ♘d6+ 62.♔d3 ♔e6 63.♖cc6 ♔d5 64.♖×d6+ ♖×d6 65.♖×d6+ ♔×d6 66.a6 1-0

The above example shows that Alekhine had not only fully assimilated the methods of conducting the endgame from previous theoreticians, but he also tried to work out some general criteria for playing certain complex types of endings.

### (132) Znosko Borovsky,Eugene – Alekhine
St Petersburg 1914 (D)

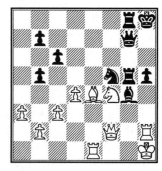

Alekhine probably already had the resulting pawn ending in mind when he played **40...♖e8?!**, but 40...♘d6! 41.♗g2 ♖f5 creates even more pressure. **41.♗×f5?** 41.♗g2 is absolutely forced. **41...♗f3+ 42.♘g2 ♖×e1+ 43.♕×e1 ♖×f5!** 43...♔×g2?? 44.♕e8+ ♕g8 45.♖×h5+ ♗×h5 46.♕×h5+ ♔g7 47.♔×g2+− **44.♔g1 ♖g5 45.♕f2 ♖×g2+ 46.♖×g2**

256

♛×g2+ 47.♔×g2 ♗×g2 48.♔×g2 ♔g7 (D)

49.♔f3?! Surprisingly, Black can also win after 49.b3!? ♔f6 50.a4 b×a4 51.b×a4 because of the shot 51...c5!!, when Black's king is just in time on the queenside: 52.d×c5 ♔e6 53.c6 b6 54.♔g3 ♔d6 55.♔h4 ♔×c6 56.♔×h5 ♔c5 57.♔g4 ♔c4 58.♔f3 ♔×c3 59.♔e2 ♔b4 60.a5 ♔×a5-+ **49...♔f6 50.♔f4 ♔e6 51.b3 ♔d5 52.♔e3 h4 53.a4 h3 0-1**

Occasionally Alekhine was able to draw unfavorable endings because of a profound assessment of the position and exceptional resourcefulness in finding defensive possibilities. Examples of this are his games with Reshevsky from the 1938 AVRO tournament (See, Defense), Foltys at Saltsburg 1943, or, from his "pre-champion" period, the following endgame with Marshall

**(133) Alekhine – Marshall,Frank**
New York 1924
King's Indian Defense [E76]

**1.d4 ♘f6 2.c4 d6 3.♘c3 g6 4.e4 ♗g7 5.f4 0-0 6.♘f3 ♗g4 7.♗e2 ♘c6?!** Probably too provocative. **8.d5 ♘b8 9.0-0 ♘bd7 10.♘g5 ♗×e2 11.♕×e2 h6 12.♘f3 e6 13.e5 d×e5 14.f×e5 ♘g4 15.♗f4 e×d5**

15...♕e7 16.h3 g5 17.♗g3 ♕c5+ 18.♔h1 ♘e3 19.♖fe1 ♘f5 20.♗f2± **16.e6 ♖e8!** The only defense. **17.e×f7+** The alternative 17.c×d5 f×e6 18.d×e6 is probably even stronger because more attacking lines are opened, e.g., 18...♘c5 19.♕c4 ♘×e6 20.♖ad1 ♕e7 21.♘d5 ♕f7 22.♗g3. **17...♔×f7 18.♕d2 ♘df6** (D)

**19.c×d5?!** 19.h3! g5 20.h×g4 g×f4 21.g5 exploits Black's problematic king position more radically. **19...g5 20.♗g3 ♕e7 21.♔h1 ♔g8 22.♖fe1 ♕c5 23.♖e6 ♖ad8 24.♕e2 ♔h8?** The wrong move order: 24...♖×e6 25.♕×e6+ ♔h8=. **25.h3?** Alekhine probably misses Marshall's coming counterblow. He should just activate his sleeping rook with 25.♖e1±. **25...♖×e6 26.d×e6 ♘h5! 27.♘e4** (D)

**27...♕c6?** 27...♕e3 was forced, e.g., 28.♕×e3 ♘×g3+ 29.♘×g3 ♘×e3

30.罝e1 ②d5 31.②f5 罝e8 32.罝d1 c6 33.罝e1 常h7 34.②d6 罝e7 35.②f5=. **28.兔×c7?** Alekhine misses the winning shot: 28.②f×g5 h×g5 29.營×g4 營×e4 30.營×h5++−. **28...營×c7 29.h×g4 ②f4** (D)

**30.營e1?** Too passive. 30.營e3 ②×e6 31.罝c1 營f4 32.營×f4 ②×f4 33.罝c7, and White's activity gives him equality. **30...②×e6** The *zwischenzug* 30...營c2!? was also interesting. At first glance, it looks like White can hardly avoid defeat because his kingside pawns are weak and the major pieces are poorly coordinated. At the same time, the black pieces are very active and threaten to attack the weakened position of the white king. Alekhine makes the only correct decision in this situation: exchange the rooks, sacrifice the pawn on b2, neutralize the threats from the black minor pieces, and activate, as much as possible, his queen and knight, steering the game to the safe haven of a drawn endgame. It is of interest to trace how in the thirty following moves (i.e., the second part of the battle) White manages to carry out his plan. **31.②g3 ②f4 32.罝d1 罝×d1 33.營×d1 兔×b2 34.營a4 兔g7 35.營e8+ 常h7 36.營e4+ ②g6 37.②h5 營c1+ 38.常h2 營c6 39.營d3 營c7+ 40.常h1 兔h8 41.營e4 營c1+ 42.常h2 營c7+**

**43.常h1 營f7 44.營c2 b5 45.營c6 b4 46.②g3 營×a2 46...a5!? 47.營b7+ 兔g7 48.②f5 營a1+ 49.常h2 營f6** (D)

**50.營×a7?** This loses more or less by force. 50.②×g7 營×g7 51.營×b4 offered good practical drawing chances. **50...b3 51.營b7 b2 52.②3d4** (D)

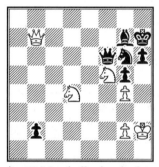

**52...②e5?** Marshall miscalculates and misses 52...營e5+ 53.g3 ②h4 54.②×g7 (54.營×b2 ②×f5 55.g×f5 營×d4−+; 54.②×h4 g×h4 55.營×b2 營g3+ 56.常h1 營e1+ 57.常g2 營e4+ 58.常h3 兔×d4 59.營g2 營e3+ 60.常h2 兔e5+ 61.常h1 h3 62.營f1 營e4+ 63.常g1 h2+−+) 54...營×g7 55.營×b2 ②f3+ 56.常g2 ②×d4 57.營b1+ 常g8 58.營b8+ 營f8−+. **53.營×b2 ②×g4+ 54.常h3 營e5 55.g3** 55.常×g4!? might be even easier, e.g., 55...營e4+ 56.常h3 兔×d4 57.營×d4 營f5+ 58.常h2 營f4+ 59.營×f4 g×f4 60.常h3 h5 61.g4=. **55...營e4 56.營c2 營×c2 56...兔×d4 57.營×e4 ②f2+ 58.常g2

♘xe4 59.♘xd4 g4 should also be drawn because of the reduced winning potential. **57.♘xc2 h5 58.♘ce3 ♘xe3?!** 58...♘f2+ 59.♔g2 ♘e4 was a better practical chance, but the theoretical result is of course still a draw. **59.♘xe3 ♗d4 60.♘f5 ♗c5 61.g4 ♔g6 62.♘h4+ ½-½**

In the process of perfecting his style, the next game bears witness to Alekhine's highest mastery of endgame technique and also the depth of his strategic thinking in the transition from the opening to a promising endgame.

**(134) Alekhine – Spielmann,Rudolf**
New York 1927
French Defense [C14]

**1.e4 e6 2.d4 d5 3.♘c3 ♘f6 4.♗g5 ♗e7 5.exd5 ♘xd5 6.♗xe7 ♕xe7 7.♕d2 ♕b4?!** The resulting endgame is not easy to defend; 7...0-0 is the main line. **8.♘xd5 ♕xd2+ 9.♔xd2 exd5 10.♖e1+ ♗e6 11.♘h3 ♘c6 12.♗b5 ♔d7 13.♘f4 ♖ae8 14.c4 ♔d6 15.c5+ ♔d7 16.♖e5** 16.♖e3!? **16...f6 17.♖xe6 ♖xe6 18.♘xe6 ♔xe6** (D)

**19.♗xc6?!** 19.♖e1+ is more precise, since after 19...♔d7, White does not exchange the bishop. **19...bxc6 20.♖e1+ ♔d7 21.♔c3** 21.♖e3!?

**21...♖b8 22.♖e3 ♖f8 23.♖g3 ♖f7 24.♔b4 ♖e7 25.♔c3 ♖f7 26.♖h3 h6 27.♔d2 ♖e7** (D)

**28.♖a3?!** Alekhine should have tried 28.♖e3!? because the resulting pawn ending is very difficult and tricky for Black. But it seems that he can just hang on by the skin of his teeth: 28...♖xe3! (28...♖e4? 29.♖xe4 dxe4 30.♔e3 f5 31.g4 g6 32.gxf5 gxf5 33.♔f4 ♔e6 34.b4 ♔d5 35.♔xf5 ♔xd4 36.a3+−; 28...♖f7? 29.♖a3 ♖e7 30.♖xa7±) 29.♔xe3 ♔e6 30.♔f4. (D)

*Analysis Diagram*

Now not 30...g6? (but 30...f5, and I have not managed to find a win for White) 31.h4! (31.g4? g5+ 32.♔e3 f5 33.f3 f4+ 34.♔d3 ♔d7 35.♔c3 ♔c8 36.♔b4 ♔b7 37.♔a5 a6 38.b4 ♔a7 39.a3. (D)

Black can generate the spare tempo with the surprising 39...h5!! 40.h3 h4=.) 31...f5 32.♔e3 ♔d7 33.f4 ♔e6

*Analysis Diagram*

34.♔d3 ♔f6 35.♔c3 g5 36.h×g5+ h×g5 37.♔d3 ♔g6 38.♔e3 ♔f6 39.g3 ♔g6 40.f×g5 ♔×g5 41.♔f3 ♔g6 42.♔f4 ♔f6 43.b4 ♔g6 44.♔e5 ♔g5 45.a4 ♔g4 46.b5+−. **28...♖e4! 29.♖a4** 29.♔d3 ♖e1 30.g3 ♖b1 31.b3 ♔c8 32.♖×a7 ♔b8 33.♖a4 g5 should also be tenable for Black. **29...♔c8 30.f3 ♖h4 31.h3 ♔b7 32.♔e3 f5 33.♖b4+ ♔c8 34.a4 g5?** 34...f4+ 35.♔f2 ♖h5 to free the rook, is necessary. **35.a5** (D)

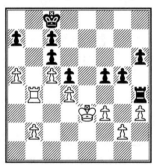

**35...g4?** Freeing the rook is the right idea, but this execution is wrong because it violates the endgame principle of "do not rush." 35...a6 had priority and only after, 36.♖b3 g4!, which was the last chance to fight. But not 36...h5? because Black's rook is imprisoned: 37.♖d3 g4 (37...♔d7 38.♔f2 ♔e7 39.♔g3 ♖f4 40.♔h2 h4 41.♔g1 g4 42.♔f2 +−) 38.♔f2 g×h3 39.g×h3

♖×h3 40.♔g2 ♖h4 41.♖d1 +−. **36.h×g4 f×g4 37.a6!** Securing an important anchor square for White's rook. **37...g×f3 38.g×f3 ♖h1 39.♖b7 ♖e1+ 40.♔f4 ♖d1 41.♔e5 ♖e1+ 42.♔f5 ♖d1 43.♖×a7 ♖×d4 44.♖a8+ ♔d7 45.f4 ♖a4 46.a7 h5 47.b3 ♖a1 48.♔e5 ♖e1+ 49.♔f6 ♖a1 50.♔e5 ♖e1+ 51.♔d4 ♖d1+ 52.♔c3 ♖a1 53.f5 ♔e7 54.♔d4 h4 55.♔e5 ♖e1+ 56.♔f4 ♖a1 57.♔g5 ♖g1+** 57...h3 58.f6+ ♔f7 59.♖h8 ♖×a7 60.♖h7+ +− **58.♔×h4 ♖a1 59.♔g5 ♖g1+ 60.♔f4 ♖a1 61.♔e5 ♖e1+ 62.♔d4 ♖a1** (D)

**63.♔c3!** Alekhine brings his king back to apply the typical winning strategy: **63...♖a3 64.♔b2 ♖a6 65.b4 ♔f7 66.♔b3 ♖a1 67.f6 ♖a6 68.b5 c×b5 69.♔b4**, and Black resigned in view of 69...c6 70.♖h8 ♖×a7 71.♖h7+ +−. **1-0**

This game is justifiably regarded as a classical example of how to play rook endings.

**Aesthetics**

Alekhine "consider[s] chess to be an art and assume[s] all the obligations it imposes on its devotees." His games, vivid combinational ideas, and beautiful mating finales give a tremendous aesthetic satisfaction to all who love chess and who are capable of understanding and feeling its beauty. Many of his games were awarded brilliancy prizes. Here is but one example.

**(135) Alekhine – Wolf,Heinrich**
Bad Pistyan 1922
English Opening [A31]

**1.d4 d5 2.♘f3 c5 3.c4 c×d4 4.c×d5 ♘f6 5.♘×d4 a6?!** This backfires badly in the game. The main line is 5...♘×d5. **6.e4** 6.♕a4+ b5 7.♘×b5 ♗d7 8.♘1c3 from (Browne-Sosonko, Surakarta 1982) is even more ambitious. **6...♘×e4 7.♕a4+ ♗d7 8.♕b3 ♘c5 9.♕e3 g6 10.♘f3** "This win of tempo enables White to prevent 10...♗g7, followed by 11...0-0. As a result, the black king is detained in the center, while White's attack is facilitated as a result of his better development" (Alekhine). **10...♕c7** 10...♘a4!? **11.♕c3 ♖g8 12.♗e3 b6?** Too slow. 12...♗g7 13.♕×c5 ♕×c5 14.♗×c5 ♗×b2 15.♗d4 ♗×a1 16.♗×a1 ♗b5 was a better pratical choice, especially against Alekhine. **13.♘bd2 ♗g7 14.♗d4 ♗×d4 15.♕×d4 ♗b5?! 16.♗×b5+ a×b5 17.0-0 ♖a4?! 18.b4 ♕d8 19.a3 ♘bd7 20.♖fe1 ♔f8 21.d6 ♘e6** (D)

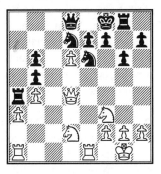

**22.♖×e6!** Alekhine opens lines for his knight and queen. **22...f×e6 23.♘g5 ♕b8** "Or 23...e5 24.♕d5 ♕e8 25.♘d6+ ♔f7 26.♘c7+ e6 27.♕f3+" (Alekhine). **24.♘×e6+ ♔f7** 24...♔e8 does not help, e.g., 25.♘c7+ ♔d8 26.♖c1 ♖×a3 27.♕d5 ♖h8 28.♘e6+ ♔e8 29.♘g5 ♖f8 30.♕e6 ♕d8 31.♖c8+−. **25.♘g5+ ♔f8 26.♕d5 ♖g7 27.♘e6+ ♔g8 28.♘×g7+ ♔×g7 29.d×e7 ♘f6 30.♕×b5 ♖a7 31.♖e1 ♕d6 32.e8♘+** 32.♘f3 ♖×e7 33.♖×e7+ ♕×e7 34.♕b6+− **32...♘×e8 33.♕×e8 ♕×d2 34.♕e5+ ♔f7?!** (D) The king feels a bit safer after 34...♔h6, but White's win is, of course, not in doubt.

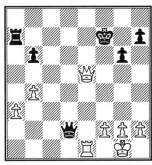

**35.h4!** Alekhine's battering ram moves forward. **35...♖×a3?** Allowing a forced mate, but White's attack also prevails after 35...♕d8 36.h5 ♕f6 37.♕d5+ ♔g7 38.♖e6+−. **36.♕e8+ ♔g7 37.♖e7+ ♔h6 38.♕f8+ ♔h5 39.♖e5+ ♔g4 40.♖g5+ 1-0**

## Chapter 4: Author and Journalist

### Journalist

Alekhine started his journalism career early. In 1912, he began conducting a chess column in the St. Petersburg's newspaper *Novoe Vremya*, in which he published, with his own annotations, games from Russian and international competitions, information about chess events in the world, chess problems, and chess studies.

Until his death, he never stopped appearing in the press, writing on the topical issues of chess life, the struggle for the world championship, theory, and general problems in the art of chess. His articles and commentaries were published in the Moscow magazines *Shakhmatny Vestnik* (1913-1916), *Shakhmaty* (1921-1924), and in the 1920-30s, in the Parisian Russian-language newspaper *Posledniye Novosti*. He also sent correspondence from the 1929 Carlsbad tournament to the *New York Times*. In the early years of World War II, Alekhine collaborated with the Nazi newspaper *Pariser Zeitung*, in which his notorious articles "Jewish and Arian Chess" (1941) were published (See, Epilogue). In the second half of 1943 and in January, 1944, he did the chess column in the Berlin Russian-language newspaper *Novoe Slovo* (New Word).

Of special value in Alekhine's journalistic heritage are, for example, his interview published in the *Wiener Schachzeitung*, the article "How I became a Chess master" published in the *New York Times* (December 11, 1927), letters to Capablanca concerning the forthcoming world championship match and the frustrated return match, the interview "How I Defeated Capablanca," forewords to Lazard's book *My Chess Problems and Studies* (1929), and Kahn's book *The Queen's Indian Defense* (1935), etc.

### Author

Alekhine attained great success as a chess author, analyst, and annotator. His collected best games of 1908-1923 and 1924-1937, his books on the international tournaments in New York (1924 and 1927) and the 1936 Nottingham Tournament initiated the tradition of world champions writing books of predominantly an analytical character. While Lasker and Capablanca authored excellent books of very broad scope that have been reprinted many times and which are considered classics of chess and methodological literature, Alekhine preferred to annotate games played in the major international tournaments in which he participated.

In the annotations to one of the games published in *Shakhmatny Vestnik*, Alekhine wrote that one should not characterize any, even outwardly the most beautiful, sacrifice as "à la Morphy" because the strength and beauty of Morphy's play is that he sees "deeply conceived positional play of a predominantly aggressive character." In his letter to the editor, the St. Petersburg master Eugene Znosko-Borovsky disagreed with this, arguing that Morphy's genius had manifested itself above all in beautiful combinations. In reply, Alekhine published a letter "In Defense of Morphy from his 'Defender,'" his first on an historical chess subject. By constantly improving his playing through analyzing the games of the distant and near past, Alekhine had already comprehended the patterns governing the development of chess thought, and was able to objectively evaluate the contributions made by the greatest creative players to the treasury of chess culture.

Therefore, in response to Znosko-Borovsky, Alekhine argued that the secret of Morphy's phenomenal successes lay in his perfect mastery of the new principles of positional play. Moreover, it was necessary to view anyone's creative heritage within the context of the governing concepts of the time. "Only thus may one judge Morphy and only thus I myself judge him," wrote Alekhine. He further argued that

> *[t]he strength, Morphy's irresistible strength – this is the reason for his success and a pledge of his immortality! And the essence of this strength resides precisely in the fact that Morphy always played as the position required – of course, in the broadest sense of the word. And only owing to this (at that time exceptional) property of his play was he able to defeat in matches such rivals as Harrwitz, Löwenthal, and above all, Anderssen, whose imagination and combinative talent were as great as Morphy's. Let Mr. Znosko-Borovsky review at least these games, even though he will not see anything spectacular in them (with very rare exceptions), but instead he will see the real Morphy, master of all facets*

*of play, stronger than each of his opponents individually, and the strongest of all.*

Let the fervor that characterized Alekhine in this polemic, the defending of his beliefs, and his deep evaluation of phenomena in the historical development of chess thought supplement our idea of his creative potential accumulated by that time.

In 1921, Bernhard Kagan published Alekhine's first German-language book, *Chess Life in Soviet Russia*. The opening pages described the hardships of "chess life in Petrograd and Moscow, which since the outbreak of the war has been insufficiently active, has come to a complete halt directly after the October Revolution." Especially distressing was the situation in Petrograd. Somewhat better was the situation in Moscow, where, despite all the difficulties with playing halls created for them by the "Red authorities," the players not only united but also managed to hold several events, including, with Alekhine's participation, the match-tournament with three of the strongest masters, the Nenarokov-Rabinovich match, etc.

Alekhine reported interesting details about the 1920 All-Russia Chess Olympiad. He presented the final standings of the tournament and characterized the prize winners in detail. He paid special attention to and highly praised the second-prize winner Pyotr Romanovsky, who, by his play at Mannheim in 1914, had generated great hopes and "at the present time is undoubtedly one of the strongest Russian players." According to Alekhine, the

*Alekhine's book on chess life in Soviet Russia.*

success in the organization of the Olympiad under those difficult conditions owed much to the efforts of master Ilyin-Genevsky. It was because of his efforts that the "Red rulers" had rapidly and radically changed their attitude toward the royal game: formerly viewed as bourgeois entertainment, chess became in their eyes "a high and useful art" which developed the mental strength of the younger generation."

In the conclusion of this small book of a mere thirty-two pages of printed text, there were eleven games played by Alekhine during 1917-1920. The book has a short foreword marked by his characteristic humor and sarcasm of Saviely Tartakower: "As did the wild beasts in the myth of Orion, so the Bolshevik rulers succumbed to the

magic of chess. And, the fact that the well-known Berlin publisher succeeded in persuading the Moscow grandmaster and former chess dictator Alexander Alekhine to describe his extraordinary fate and that in editing the German-language edition has supplemented it with the valuable material attached, may be thought of as an especially happy outcome, for which the entire chess world will be extremely obliged to him." Whether joking with Tartakower calling him a dictator or wishing to emphasize his aristocratic origins, Alekhine preceded his name with "von" on the front page of the book

## Tournament Books

Alekhine annotated the games, and commented on the results, of four major international tournaments, two of which were held in the United States and two in England. The first of the books covered the double-round robin tournament at Hastings 1922, which William Watts published the same year, with the annotations by the winner, Alexander Alekhine. Describing the participants, Alekhine especially praised the second-prize winner Akiba Rubinstein for his aggressive play, calling him "a high-caliber player." In 1998, Carl Kersen published the German-language edition.

The next two books dealt with the major New York tournaments of 1924 and 1927. In the first of them, Alekhine annotated all 110 games played in the event and supplemented the annotations with a lengthy article "The Significance of the Tournament at New York for Opening Theory." Alekhine, having received the exclusive right to publish the tournament book from the

Organizing Committee, simultaneously sent the manuscript to American and German publishers, and also to Moscow, to be translated into Russian. Grekov and Nenarokov edited the book and published it in March 1925. In the foreword, they stressed Alekhine's analytical gift and his ability to reveal the true essence – the "soul of the game." They also mentioned the value of his article on opening theory as "the last word of science in the realm of chess."

Just as highly praised was Alekhine's book on the 1927 New York Tournament. Here, too, it was translated into Russian from the German language. Alekhine's annotations of the 60 games of this outstanding event were preceded by his lengthy article "New York Tournament 1927 as Prologue to the Struggle for World Chess Championship at Buenos Aires." It showed to the chess world how deeply and thoroughly Alekhine studied his future rival, how he was preparing for the match, and how strong was his belief in his eventual victory.

Alekhine's high analytical skill, vivid and figurative language, subtle psychological observations, and versatile characterization of Capablanca's playing style all combined to give the book creative interest. In the foreword to the Russian-language edition, Grigoriev wrote that "Alekhine appears to his readers as a player-commentator and player-journalist. However, the main value of Alekhine's annotations lies in the fact that in every game they reveal the crucial moments of the struggle, those critical moments when the game almost imperceptibly becomes from better to even and from even to infe-

rior, etc..." In 1989, both works were combined in a single book titled *International Chess Tournaments at New York 1924 and 1927*, and published in Moscow. Modern "21st-century editions" in English have also recently appeared, released by the American chess publisher Russell Enterprises.

The 1936 Nottingham Tournament book, with games annotated by Alekhine was published in London in 1937 and also enjoyed great success. In that event, the world champion (Euwe), three former champions, and six candidate challengers participated. In 1962, the book was published in Moscow. The editors included Alekhine's most interesting article, which was published shortly before the end of the tournament in the *Manchester Guardian*, as well as an afterword to the Russian-language edition by Salo Flohr, who concluded his reminiscences of the tournament with a panegyric to "the unsurpassed analyst Alexander Alekhine, whose book will be of great benefit to all those who wish to improve in the art of chess."

### My Best Games

Alekhine twice authored books of his best games. The first of them was published in Paris in 1926 and covered the years from 1908 to 1923. It contained one hundred of his best games played in tournaments, matches, and exhibitions, mostly in Russia and from his successes in the two-year period right after he emigrated. The introductory article "The Works of Alexander Alekhine" was written by Tartakower. In 1927, the book was published in Moscow, Leningrad, and London, and in 1929 it came out in Berlin-Leipzig,

The Hague, and Montevideo. Subsequently, it has been repeatedly reprinted in many countries, becoming one of the best-selling book by Alekhine. Thus, in Germany a fifth(!) edition was published by the Beyer Verlag in 1997.

His contemporaries noted the high level of annotations and the desire to reveal the peculiarities of creativity. Introducing the book to the readers, Neishtadt, the editor of the chess column in *Pravda*, believes that "[t]he most objective approach to his own and other's achievements is the distinguishing feature of Alekhine's comments. And then the unusual subtlety of analysis, penetration to the innermost depths and secrets of position, as well as the extraordinary erudition – and all these directed solely to the search for the truth, chess truth – here is what Alekhine is as a commentator. It is no wonder then that even Capablanca admires him."

The next book of Alekhine's best games embraced the period from 1924 to 1937, and it was published in London in 1939. It was a continuation of the previous book and contained 120 games.

# Chapter 5: Impervious to Time

**Epilogue**

Alekhine was in Argentina when World War II erupted. He returned to Europe via Portugal. In Lisbon, he was given a magnificent reception. "Alekhine," the Portuguese champion Francisco Lupi remembered, "gave the impression of a king at the peak of his glory. He was a tall stout man with a noble bearing and very affable. The Portuguese players were charmed with his kindness when he instructed them or offered his advice and when he played his brilliant demonstration games."

In March 1942, Alekhine learned about the death of Capablanca, who had only outlived Emanuel Lasker by a year. The death of the Cuban player shocked Alekhine. He decided to write a book about his great predecessor. The introductory essay about him ended with the words: "Capablanca was too early torn from the chess world. With his death, we lost the greatest chess genius, an equal to whom we will never see..."

While in far-away New York the chess geniuses went into oblivion, the world champion bounced about burning Europe. From Prague, where he was ordered to reside in 1942-43 and where he, by a sheer miracle survived scarlet fever, he moved to the Iberian Peninsula. He no longer was the former Alekhine; the illness had undermined his health, but he still continued winning. From 1941 to 1945 he participated in sixteen tournaments, finishing first in nine of them and sharing first and second in four. In Spain, he won the tournaments at Gijon and Madrid in 1944-1945. The last competition of his

life was a small match played at the Estoril casino in January 1946 with the Portuguese master Francisco Lupi. Alekhine won the match with the score 2½-1½ (+2 -1=1). Alekhine played his last game at the British Embassy in Lisbon on March 9, 1946 against the chess composer F.Anderson (1893-1983).

**(136) Anderson,F – Alekhine**
Lisbon 1946
Semi-Slav Defense [D43]

**1.d4 ♘f6 2.c4 e6 3.♘c3 d5 4.♗g5 c6 5.e3 h6 6.♗×f6 ♕×f6 7.♗d3 ♘d7 8.♘f3 ♗b4?!** 8...d×c4 9.♗×c4 g6 is the main line. **9.0-0 0-0 10.a3 ♗a5 11.e4 d×c4 12.e5 ♕e7 13.♗×c4 ♖d8 14.♕c2 ♘b6 15.♗a2 ♘d5 16.♘e2?!** The direct 16.♗b1 f5 17.e×f6 ♘×f6 (17...g×f6 18.♖e1) 18.♘e4 creates more pressure. **16...♗d7 17.♖ad1 ♖ac8 18.b4 ♗c7 19.♗b1 f5** (D)

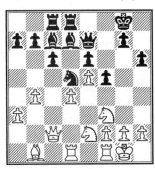

**20.g4?** The weakening of the light squares in White camp is too high a price to pay. Instead, Anderson should weaken Black's light squares with 20.e×f6. **20...♖f8 21.g×f5 e×f5 22.♔h1 g5 23.♖g1 ♔h8 24.♕d2 f4** (D)

267

**25.♘h4?** This bold approach back-fires. Anderson should challenge Alekhine's dominant knight with 25.♘c3 **25...g×h4 26.♖g6 ♕h7?!** 26...♗f5 27.♘×f4 (27.♖×h6+ ♔g7 28.♘×f4 ♔×h6 29.♘×d5+ ♔g5-+) 27...♕h7 28.♗×f5 ♖×f5 29.♘×d5 ♕×g6 30.♘e7 ♕h5 31.♘×f5 ♕f3+ 32.♔g1 ♕×f5 33.♕×h6+ ♔g8-+ is more precise. **27.e6?** Winning the queen with 27.♖f6 was a better practical chance, but Black keeps the upper hand with 27...♘×f6 28.♗×h7 ♘×h7 29.♘×f4 ♗f5. **27...♗e8! 28.♖g4 ♕e7 29.♕d3 h5 30.♖g5 ♘f6 31.d5 c×d5 32.♘d4?! ♘e4 0-1**

Could Alekhine play in tournaments held in Nazi-occupied countries? In fact he did. But, he would not perhaps have been rebuked so much if, like Estonian grandmaster Paul Keres, he had only played in the tournaments. However, Alekhine's reputation suffered because of other episodes when, voluntarily or involuntarily, he had demonstrated his closeness to the Nazi circles, when in the spring of 1941, a series of three articles entitled "Jewish and Aryan Chess" was published in the newspaper *Pariser Zeitung* (March 18-23). These publications had become the saddest page of the last years of his life. In them, the history of chess was treated in the light of the Nazi racial theory and argued that true chess artists were only possible among the Aryans.

Having known about these publications and their content, the chess world was discouraged in the full sense of the word. For they came from the champion, the revered genius, from one who over many years of his sporting and literary career in chess expressed entirely different views both on the historical progress of the chess art and on the role played by Lasker, Réti, Nimzowitsch, Spielmann and other chess luminaries. These were the very same grandmasters and colleagues whose creations he had admired and whose favorable influence on him he repeatedly admitted.

So, how can one explain that Alekhine suddenly decided to publish these "dirty" articles? Possibly, it was a result of his fear of the Nazi regime. Perhaps no small role was played by his depression caused by the outbreak of World War II, the feeling of inner emptiness, the impossibility to change his life. As many other representatives of the intelligentsia, he was shocked by the fact that, almost without resistance, France found itself under the Nazi heel, and Stalin had made a deal with Hitler. The world turned upside down in his mind, challenging his conception of national honor and ways of social development. Too early did he believe in the Apocalypse.

But when the war was over, Alekhine with special acuteness perceived the whole tragedy of his situation. The world community of chessplayers who had inscribed on the banner of the World Chess Federation (FIDE) the motto "Gens una Sumus," turned their backs on him. The invitation to participate in "the tournament of victors" at London that had been sent to him was canceled, because American, Dutch, and some other players were refusing to play in the same tournament with him and demanded that he be deprived of the champion's title.

In January 1946, the *British Chess Magazine* published Alekhine's letter in which he completely denied all charges against him. In it, he pleadingly argues his case:

> *Having devoted all my life to chess, I have never been involved in anything not directly related to my profession. I played chess in Germany and German-occupied countries because it was my only means of subsistence, as well as the price I had to pay for the freedom of my wife.*

> *At that time I was a prisoner of the Nazis, and our only chance was to keep silent. Those years undermined my health and upset my nerves. And I am surprised that I still can play good chess. My devotion to my art, the respect I have always paid to the talent of my colleagues, as well as my whole professional life in the pre-war years should make people realize that the chimeras in the* Pariser Zeitung *were faked.*

Much of what had been said in the letter was true and quite possibly, more than just a little had been added to the articles by the editors of the Nazi newspaper. All this is evident today when it is easier to understand more objectively the circumstances under which those "chimeras" occurred and the overall situation of that time. But, when the war had just ended, chessplayers quite naturally wanted to hear that the man of whom the chess world used to be proud had nothing to do with the notorious articles and that they had been forged by the Nazis from beginning to end. Accordingly, Alekhine's letter in the *British Chess Magazine* was received with a sigh of relief.

Alekhine sent copies of the letter to the American and British chess federations, and the chess world believed him. The first response was a letter from Mikhail Botvinnik, who decided to contest the world title in an honest competition with the champion. His telegram, a challenge for a world championship match, was brief:

> *I regret that the war had prevented our match in 1939. I again challenge you to a world championship match. If you agree, I am waiting for your reply, in which I ask you to give your opinion of the dates and venue of the match.*

> *4 February 1946*
> *Mikhail Botvinnik.*

Soon the British Chess Federation expressed its willingness to host the match. Thus, the return of "the prodigal son" to the bosom of the world chess community was made possible. However, disease and harsh life experiences took their toll: On March 24,

*Alekhine is dead. Estoril, 1946.*

1946, in the Park Hotel of Estoril, near Lisbon, Alexander Alekhine died. In the morning, he was found, asleep forever, at the table upon which stood a chess set and his meal. Alekhine was buried in Portugal. Ten years later his body was reinterred in Montparnasse cemetery in Paris. Speaking at the unveiling of the Alekhine tombstone, grandmaster Vyacheslav Ragozin a vice-president of FIDE, said: "Alekhine's rich creative heritage is studied by the whole chess world. We bow our heads before the ashes of the brilliant creator of chess combinations. We are full of hope, strength and faith in the progress of chess art, to which the great player Alexander Alekhine had devoted his entire life."

[*Editor's note* – On December 26, 1999, a strong windstorm in Paris blew the headstone onto the main gravestone, breaking both the relief of Alekhine and the marble chessboard on the main gravestone. When it was restored, the chessboard, sadly, was placed with a 90° rotation. Instead of approaching Alekhine's grave as though to play the champion, he now observes a game between those on either side of him.]

## World Chess Champions about Alekhine

### Lasker

Alekhine has arisen out of combination; he is in love with it. Everything strategic for him is only preparation, almost a necessary evil. An overwhelming blow, unexpected *pointes* – this is where he is in his element... His imagination is enflamed when he attacks the opponent's king (1926).

I greet the brilliant victory of Alekhine who realized the cherished dream of Chigorin, whose direct heir he is, both in his passionate genius and in the temperament of his playing (1927).

270

## Capablanca

Nowadays, perhaps none of the masters has such completeness in all phases of the game, as does Alekhine (Feb 19, 1927).

Alekhine played in this match better than I did and, therefore, deserves the success he has achieved (December, 1927).

## Euwe

The outcome of the match just finished has given an exhaustively clear answer: Alekhine is not only very strong, but he also should be considered the world's best player... Alekhine played amazingly well, and I am definitely not ashamed to be defeated by such an opponent (1937).

*Alekhine's tombstone in Montparnasse cemetery.*

## Botvinnik

Alekhine is mainly dear to the chess world as an artist. The depth of plans, far-reaching calculations, and inexhaustible inventions are typical of Alekhine. However, his main strength – developing from year to year – was his combinative "sight": he "saw" combinations and calculated forced variations with sacrifices both very easily and accurately... That is why Alekhine's combinations possessed such a shattering force and crushed the resistance... Yes, that was a truly wonderful gift (1956)!

Deep and far-seeing at the chessboard, in his life he repeatedly demonstrated his political short-sightedness. But, let us speak the truth: when faced with the choice between chess and politics, Alekhine unequivocally sided with chess. He sought to meet Soviet chessplayers over the board, and he welcomed their successes (1992).

## Smyslov

Alekhine's name shines with the brilliance of his chess combinations. Alekhine had an exceptionally rich imagination; his skill in creating combinational complications has no equal. It is necessary to mention here that Alekhine's technique was perfect and combinations were not for him an end in itself, but a logical outcome of what the position required (1962).

## Tal

Alexander Alekhine regarded chess as an art, and he wrote that chess should be treated as an art. We are fascinated by his exceptional combinational talent and his selfless love of chess (1960).

**Spassky**
I consider Alexander Alekhine to be the greatest chessplayer ever – perhaps because for me and for many others he remains a mystery (1967).

Alekhine! He, by the way, believed that chess was closest to art and was able to prove it with his optimistic, ever-young creativity. That is the reason why the games of the great fanatic of chess are played over again and again with such great pleasure by both masters and amateurs (1969).

In my fairy-tale world of chess, Alekhine was first to come, and filled it completely. I have been in love with him since my early years, attracted by the purity of his chess thought, the absence of gratuitous comments – everything was clear and accurate, with the live spirit of imagination and invention always present. Especially attractive were his combinations. I have been interested in Alekhine all my life, closely following all publications on his biography. In my childhood years, I found his games in annuals.

I was so fascinated by Alekhine's art that I tried to imitate him. I willingly sacrificed pawns, trying to seize the initiative just as patiently. For Alekhine was the strategist of attack. I have a few such games, and it seems to me I played them not at all badly, in Alekhine's style. I am proud of them, and I consider Alekhine as my inspiration (2005).

**Fischer**
In his games, Alekhine produced colossal concepts, full of violent and unprecedented ideas... As far as the depth of positional penetration is concerned, he had no equals in the whole history of chess (1964).

**Karpov**
Both Lasker and Alekhine deserve the same attention (as Capablanca). The changes that came next (after Steinitz) were broadly outlined by Alekhine, but were introduced and further developed by Botvinnik – I am talking about the scientific approach to chess.

Alekhine did much homework. Quite a number of well-known games he won by taking the opponent into his home-prepared vise. And his grip was strong: once he had someone in his grip, he never let his victim out (1979).

**Kasparov**
Alekhine's games and writings have had a great influence on me from the early years. I tried to imitate the dynamic style of the great Russian champion, who was able to wrest the chess crown from the hands of Capablanca in 1927. I was captivated by the intricacy of his ideas generated over the chessboard. Alekhine's attacks appeared as a devastating bolt from the blue.

Alekhine's style is that of a psychological aggression: huge preparatory work, an explosion of energy on the board, the maniacal desire to finish the opponent off in conjunction with rich combinative fantasy (1999).

**Kramnik**
Of course, Alekhine was an outstanding world champion. While possessing an amazing strategic talent, he was the first who felt very delicately the dynamics of play. He showed that it was

possible while (naturally) observing the main positional principles to put the game completely on the rails of dynamics. Not to seek long-term advantages, but start from the very first moves weaving a peculiar net to catch the opponent, to mount threats with every move, to attack. In such peerless skill of deploying dynamic game, Alekhine was probably the trailblazer (2004).

## Literature on Alekhine

The first thorough book about the fourth world champion, *Chess Genius Alekhine. The Man and His Works* by Hans Müller (an Austrian master) and Adolf Pawelczak (a German player), appeared in Berlin in 1953. Both authors were not only personally acquainted with Alekhine but also had been his friends over many years. It makes their work on the life of Alekhine especially interesting and explains why a number of extremely rare pictures made their first appearance there. The book contains one hundred of Alekhine's best games and crosstables from the most important competitions in which he participated.

At about the same time, anthologies of Alekhine's games appeared. In 1949, *Alekhine's Best Games of Chess 1938-1945* by C.H. O'D. Alexander was published in London, thus becoming the conclusive finale of the previous collections (1908-23 and 1924-1937). In 1954, *Alekhine's 300 Best Games with His Annotations*, compiled by V.N.Panov, was published in Moscow. Grandmaster Alexander Kotov (1913-1981) devoted many years to the study of Alekhine. His two-volume work, *Alekhine's Chess Heritage*, was published in two editions (the second, in 1982). The author had analyzed the most important aspects of Alekhine's chess praxis and theoretical discoveries. Kotov also penned a novel about Alekhine's life, entitled *White and Black* (1965) and a play of the same name, as well as a film script *The White Snow of Russia*, both based on that novel. In the early 1970s, the play was produced and directed by Boris Golubovsky at the Moscow Drama Theater named after Gogol. The role of Alekhine was performed by L. Kulagin.

Spanish master Pablo Moran's *A. Alekhine. The Agony of a Chess Genius*, which was devoted to Alekhine's life and activities during World War II, was published in Spain in 1972, and its English-language edition, with significant additions and commentaries by Frank Mur, in the United States. In the American edition, the findings of well-known chess American historians Dale Brandreth and Fred Reinfeld, Ken Whyld (England), and others were used. Many new facts of Alekhine's life and career were published in the postwar years: documents pertaining to his parents and ancestors, notebooks of the young Alekhine, his letters from the last period of his life, as well as reminiscences of his contemporaries – Romanovsky, Levenfish, Znosko-Borovsky, Duz-Khotimirsky, Ilyin-Genevsky, Shishko, Lyubimov, Botvinnik, Euwe, Flohr, the studies of Kotov, Keres, Konstantinopolsky, I. Linder, Panov, Romanov, Krogius, Goldin, Averbakh, Suetin, Lazebnik, Charushin, Shaburov...

New publications devoted to the life and works of Alekhine were released in the early 1990s to commemorate his centenary. The first of them was a one-volume collection of his best games, compiled from the books by Alekhine himself and the book by Alexander. It was published in London in 1990, and Garry Kasparov penned the foreword.

Czech authors Jan Kalendovsky and Vlastimil Fiala prepared a four-volume collection of Alekhine's games for the centenary celebration. The first volume was published in 1992. The same year two books, *Alekhine in America* and *Alekhine in Europe and Asia*, were published in the United States. They contain about 700 games collected by well-known American grandmaster Yasser Seirawan and masters John Donaldson and Niklay Minev. The book by Isaak and Vladimir Linder containing the authors' reflections on the main trends in the creative career of the fourth world champion came out in both Moscow and Berlin. The Moscow chess author Yu.N. Shaburov (1926-2001) published some previously unknown archival materials pertaining to the period before Alekhine's emigration and also the period of his life in Paris in his two books: *Alexander Alekhine – Undefeated Champion* (Moscow, 1992) and *Alekhine* (2001, Zh ZL – series-zhizn' zamechatel'nykh lyudei). V.A. Charushin's *At the Point of No Return* presented 179 games of Alekhine played in 1939-1946 and was published in Nizhni Novgorod in 1996.

At the turn of the century, there appeared several monographs concerned with the various aspects of the life and career of the fourth world champion, such as W. Haas's *Alexander Alekhine – Genius of Combinations* (1993),

Raetsky and Chetverik's *Alexander Alekhine –Master of Attack* (2004), Krizsany and Videkis's *Alekhine Defense* (1999), and Soloviev's two-volume collection of Alekhine's games played during 1902-1922 published in the *Chess Star* series (2002).

The third edition of the book by well-known English historian Kenneth Whyld, concerned with analysis of the notorious publications by Alekhine originally made in the newspaper *Pariser Zeitung* (March, 1941), was published by Olomouc (the Czech Republic) in 2002.

The second edition of the excellent work by German grandmaster Robert Hübner, *World Champion Alekhine*, was published in Hamburg in the CD-ROM series by ChessBase. It contains 2,129 games, 500 of which are annotated by different analysts, including Tarrasch, Kotov, and Hübner. There are also various articles about Alekhine, anecdotes, interviews and other materials dealing with the personality of the great player. A computer diagnostic of Alekhine's games was first performed by Garry Kasparov, and the results were published in the first volume of his work (coauthored by Plisetsky) *My Great Predecessors* (Moscow, 2003).

**Memorials**

International tournaments to commemorate Alexander Alekhine have been held in Moscow since 1956. The first such tournament of sixteen players was held at the Chaikovsky Concert Hall. Botvinnik and Smyslov tied for first ahead of the world championship candidates Taimanov, Gligoric, Bronstein, and Najdorf. In 1971, the

*Program of the first Alekhine Memorial. Moscow, 1956.*

Timman 8th. Anatoly Karpov was awarded the prize for his Alekhine-style play against Kamsky.

The international correspondence tournament dedicated to Alekhine lasted for five years. Among the participators were thirteen grandmasters from Russia, Poland, Latvia, England, Finland, Yugoslavia, Germany, Israel, Bosnia, and Herzegovina. The tournament started on the eve of the centenary celebration, March 31, 1991, and ended in 1996. The winner of this so called "Star Tournament" was Latvian grandmaster Gipslis (8 points out of 12), ahead of the Russian former world correspondence chess champion Sanakoyev.

Alekhine Memorial tournaments were also held in other countries. For example, in April 1979, such an event took place in Calcutta, with the participation of twelve players (from India, the USSR, Bangladesh, Pakistan, and Sri Lanka). Grandmaster Aivar Gipslis of Riga won. Also, among the prize winners was the Indian champion Paramesvaranti. In 1996, an Alekhine Memorial was held in Portugal. Bagirov (USSR) won, scoring 7 points out of 10; second and third places were shared by Mikhalchishin and Davies, with Bellon and Froysh sharing 4th-5th places.

### "Planet Alekhine"
One autumn night in 1978, a member of the Board of the Central Chess Club of the USSR, grandmaster Alexander Kotov, received, in the presence of many guests, a certificate stating that one newly discovered small planet had been named after Alexander Alekhine.

second Alekhine Memorial, with eighteen participants, was held. Karpov and Stein tied for first, ahead of Smyslov, Petrosian, Tukmakov, Spassky, and Tal.

In 1975, the Alekhine Memorial gathered sixteen participants. Geller won. Boris Spassky finished second, ahead of Vaganian, Kortschnoi, and Kholmov, who shared 3rd-5th places. In 1992, an international festival was held to commemorate Alekhine's centenary. Tiviakov won a Swiss-system tournament with a field of no less than sixty grandmasters, while Anand and Gelfand shared 1st-2nd places in a super-tournament of eighteen. Kamsky was third, with Karpov, Salov and Yusupov sharing 4th-6th places. Shirov was 7th and

It read: "Below is the text of the official statement concerning the approval by the Center for Small Planets (Cincinnati, United States) of the name 1909 ALEKHINE 1972 PB2 of the small planet discovered September 4, 1972 by L. Zhuravleva at the Crimean Astronomical Observatory. It is so named in honor of Alexander Aleksandrovich Alekhine (1892-1946), an outstanding Russian chessplayer, world champion 1927-1935 and 1937-1946."

### *White Snow of Russia* (movie)

In 1981, the Mosfilm studio finished shooting the film *White Snow of Russia* about the life of the great Russian player Alexander Alekhine. The screenplay was written by grandmaster Alexander Kotov. The film was directed by Yuri Vyshinsky. The leading roles were played by Alexander Mikhailov (as Alekhine), Natalia Gundareva (as Alekhine's wife Nadezhda), Vladimir Samoilov (as Kuprin, a famous Russian writer), Vsevolod Yakut (as Lasker), Kristina Mikolaevska (as Grace Wishart, Alekhine's last wife) and others. It was based on the novel by Alexander Kotov, *White and Black*.

Twenty-five years of Alekhine's émigré life (1921-1946) fly by like a flash. The viewer becomes a witness of the matches against Capablanca in Buenos Aires, Euwe in Holland, the global cir-

*A frame from the movie* White Snow of Russia *with Alexander Mikhailov as Alekhine.*

cumnavigation with the favorite cat named "Chess," a blindfold exhibition given to Wehrmacht officers... Thanks to the brilliant acting, the intertwining fates, love and separation, friendship and betrayal – all that Alekhine had experienced during those years – hold the viewer from the first to the last moment.

One of the most partial judges at the debut was Mikhail Botvinnik, who pronounced: "An interesting film, unlike any other, deeply patriotic... Alekhine was slightly shorter, but the actor looks like him, and his hands move very naturally over the board. Thank you!"

# Significant Dates in the Life and Work of Alexander Alekhine

**1892, October 31**. Alexander Alexandrovich Alekhine was born in Moscow.

**1899**. His mother acquaints him with the rules of chess.

**1901**. He enters the L.I.Polivanov Classical Gymnasium in the Prechistenka Street, a privileged school for the children of merchants and nobility.

**1902**. Together with his elder brother Alexei, he starts playing by correspondence.

**1905**. He makes his debut in the 16th (gambit) correspondence tournament organized by the magazine *Shakhmatnoe obozrenye*, and he takes the first prize. The participants are unaware of his age, and Prince Shakhovskoi, sending the opponent his move, addresses as Mr. Alekhine, Esq.

**1907**. In the autumn, for the first time, he participates in the over-the board tournament, organized by the Moscow Chess Circle, becoming a member.

**1908**. His first appearance abroad, in the amateur tournament of the German Chess Congress in Düsseldorf, where he shares 4th-5th places (+8 -3 =2).

**1908**. He wins matches with masters Bardeleben (Germany) and Blumenfeld (Moscow) by the same score (4½-½).

**1909, February**. Sixteen-year old Alekhine wins the All-Russia Mikhail Chigorin Memorial Tournament in St. Petersburg and is awarded the master title.

**1910, Spring**. Alexander graduates from the Polivanov Gymnasium.

**1911, August-September**. In the international tournament (with 26 participants) in Carlsbad (now Karlovy Vary) he shares 8th-11th places, defeating such well-known masters as Vidmar, Duras, and S. Tartakower.

**1911, Autumn**. He moves from Moscow to St. Petersburg, entering the Imperial School of Law.

**1912, April**. He starts as a columnist in the newspaper *Novoe Vremya*.

**1912, Summer**. Alekhine wins the Championship of Northern Countries in Stockholm.

**1912, August-September**. In the double round-robin tournament of ten masters in Vilno (now Vilnius), he suffers a failure, sharing 5th-6th places, losing both games to the tournament winner Akiba Rubinstein and the third-prize winner Levitzky.

**1913, February-March**. In St. Petersburg, he defeats one of the strongest Russian masters Levitzky in a hard-fought match (+7 -3 =0).

**1913, July-August**. He wins first prize in the international tournament in Scheveningen (The Netherlands), then tours Berlin and Paris.

**1913, November-December**. For the first time, he plays the Cuban master Capablanca in a training match, losing both games. Friendly relations are established between them.

**1913, December-1914, January**. He shares first and second places with Aron Nimzowitsch in the All-Russia Masters Tournament. After their drawn two-game match (+1 -1), both are admitted to the "Champions Tournament" in St. Petersburg.

**1913, December 15**. The St. Petersburg painter baroness Anna von Severgin gives birth to an illegitimate child (a daughter named Valentine) by Alexander Alekhine.

**1914, January 15**. His polemical article "In Defense of Morphy from His 'Defender,'" directed against Eugene Znosko-Borovsky, is published in the Moscow journal *Shakhmatny Vestnik*.

**1914, April-May**. St. Petersburg. Finishing third (after world champion Emanuel Lasker and José Raúl Capablanca) in the major international chess tournament ("Champions Tournament"), he becomes one of the candidates to compete for the world title.

**1914, May 16**. Alekhine graduates from the Imperial Law School attaining the tenth rank title of titular council, and is assigned to the Ministry of Justice.

**1914, July 18**. A strong international masters tournament, organized by the German Chess Congress, starts in Mannheim. Alekhine takes the lead. However, on August 1st, World War I erupts, putting an end to all competitions, Alekhine being declared the winner. Alekhine, Bogoljubow, Romanovsky, Selezniev, Bogatyrchuk, and I.Rabinovich are interned. Deemed unfit for military service by the German authorities, Alekhine is released. He goes to Switzerland, via Italy and Sweden, to return to Russia.

**1914**. He gives charitable exhibitions for the benefit of the Russian players interned in Germany.

**1915, December 28**. In Basel (Switzerland), his mother Anisia Ivanovna Alekhine (née Prokhorova, b. April 5, 1861) dies.

**1916, April**. His Odessa tours are widely covered by the newspaper *Odessky Novosti*.

**1916, May**. At the Kiev Chess Society, Alekhine gives a blindfold simultaneous exhibition and wins a match against master A. Evenson (+2 -1 =0).

**1916, Summer**. He volunteers to go to the Galicia front and is appointed the Head of a Red Cross detachment. For rescuing the wounded at the battle field, he is decorated with two St. George medals and the Order of St. Stanislaus with swords. Suffering contusions, he is taken to the hospital in Ternopol, where he gives blindfold simultaneous exhibitions to local chessplayers, winning the famous game against Feldt.

**1917, May 28**. His father Alexander Ivanovich Alekhine (b. November 18, 1856), a member of the 4th State Duma and Marshall of Nobility in the Voronezh governorate, dies.

**1918, April-May**. Moscow. He wins a match-tournament with the participation of masters Nenarokov and A. Rabinovich.

**1919, Summer**. Odessa. Alekhine is arrested and imprisoned on a charge of being a member of the nobility and for involvement in anti-Soviet activities. He is sentenced to execution by firing squad. Two hours before the execution, owing to a sudden intervention of a leading revolutionary, he is released from prison.

**1919, August**. Moscow. Having decided to give up chess, Alekhine enters the State Studio of Cinematographic Art, directed by Gardin.

**1920, May 13**. Alekhine leaves the Studio to join the Moscow Criminal Investigation Department as an interrogator at the Chief Directorate of Militia.

**1920, October 4-20**. He comes out victorious (+9 -0 =6) in the All-Russia Chess Olympiad, organized by the Chief Administration of the Vseobuch (the Education-for-All Organization). In fact, this was the first chess championship of Soviet Russia.

**1920, November**. He joins the Russian Communist Party of Bolsheviks (RCPB) as a member candidate, becoming an official interpreter with the Comintern.

**1921, March 15**. He marries Anneliese Ruegg, a member of the Swiss Social Democratic Party. She was born in 1879 and died May 2, 1934 in Lausanne, their son Alexander then living in Zürich.

**1921, April**. Together with his wife, he leaves Russia, heading for France via Riga and Berlin. He stops over in Berlin for a while, where he plays short matches with the German masters Sämisch and Teichmann.

**1921, Summer**. In Berlin, the Kagan Publishing House puts out Alekhine's first book (in German), *Chess Life in Soviet Russia*.

**1921**. Having taken first prizes in tournaments in Triberg, Budapest, and The Hague, he challenges Capablanca to a match.

**1921**. In a consultation game played in Zürich (in August) and a month later in a game with E. Steiner in the Budapest Tournament, he adopts for the first time, the opening subsequently named "Alekhine's Defense" (1.e4 ♘f6).

**1922**. He participates in international tournaments in Piestany, London, Hastings, and Vienna. In London, he signs the agreement, proposed by Capablanca, about the regulations for world championship matches. In Hastings, against Efim Bogoljubow, he plays one of his most famous games.

**1923, April-May**. He shares 1st-3rd places with Bogoljubow and Maróczy at Carlsbad.

**1923, November 8**. Alekhine repeats his challenge to Capablanca.

**1923, November-1924, January**. He tours Canada and the United States.

**1924, March-April**. He plays in the international tournament at New York (with eleven masters participating). The outcome of the St. Petersburg tournament held ten years previously is repeated: Lasker finishes first, Capablanca second, Alekhine third.

**1924, April 28**. A record blindfold exhibition in New York: in twelve hours, twenty-six games are played with Alekhine scoring +16 -5 =5.

**1924**. Upon returning to Paris, he works on two books, *The New York Tournament of 1924* and *My Best Games (1908-1923)*.

**1925, February**. A new record is set in blindfold play in Paris against twenty-seven opponents (+22 -3 =2). He wins the Paris tournament.

**1925, April 14-May 13**. He wins the major international tournament in Baden-Baden, scoring 16 points out of 20. Among his best creative achievements is the game against Réti. "I consider this game and my game with Bogoljubow (1922) the most brilliant games in my chess career," he said.

**1925**. Civil marriage with Nadezhda Semoynovna Vassiliev (née Fabritskaya, b. March 19, 1884, in Odessa), the widow of a Russian general-émigré. He made her acquaintance at a ball in Paris in 1924.

**1925, second half**. He prepares and defends his dissertation, "The Penitentiary System in China," for which the Sorbonne awards him the degree of Doctor of Law.

**1926**. He takes part in six international tournaments, which he regards as preparatory for his world championship match, winning three of them (Hastings, Scarborough, and Birmingham) and placing second in two (Semmering, after Spielmann, and Dresden, after Nimzowitsch).

**1926, August**. He visits Buenos Aires. The government of Argentina undertakes to fulfill all financial obligations according to the 1922 London Agreement to back the world championship match between Capablanca and Alekhine.

**1926, October-November**. He tours Uruguay and Brazil. "Everywhere I was given an excellent welcome, the people showing an enormous interest in the forthcoming match."

**1926, December-1927, January**. He is back in Europe, where his training match against Max Euwe ends with the score +3 -2 =5 in favor of Alekhine.

**1927, February 19-March 25**. In the major quadruple round-robin, six-player tournament in New York, he places second after Capablanca, but ahead of Nimzowitsch, Vidmar, Spielmann, and Marshall. The tournament offered him the opportunity, before the decisive battle, to study even more deeply the style of Capablanca's play and "to test, against a number of new examples of Capablanca's play, observations of the previous years, thus making it possible to come to the correct conclusions."

**1927, June 15-July 14**. He wins the international tournament at Kecskemet (Hungary). There, not long before his match with Capablanca, he becomes assured that he "plays quite confidently and with the same clarity and ease as in Baden-Baden."

**1927, September 16-November 29**. The match with Capablanca ends with Alekhine's victory (+6 -3 =25) and the world championship title. "At last the dream of my life has come true, and I have been able to reap the fruits of my long labors and efforts… A new epoch of my chess activity has dawned, an epoch of new objectives and a new responsibility." Describing the main distinguishing feature of the new world champion, grandmaster Rudolf Spielmann wrote that it is "a purposeful scientific activity, spurred on by the ever-burning ambition and overflowing strength."

**1927, December 8**. Buenos Aires. Alekhine is awarded with a gold medal of a world chess champion, the fourth in chess history.

**1928, January**. The world champion returns to Paris where he is much lionized in clubs frequented by chessplayers ("Palais Royale," "Rotonda," "Café de la Régence," and the Russian Club). He starts working on the 1927 New York tournament book, writing the introduction, entitled "The New York Tournament of 1927 as Prologue to the World Championship Match in Buenos Aires."

**1928**. His article "Two Kinds of Chess Art" is published in *Collected Chess Problems and Studies* by the French chess composer F. Lazard (Paris). In it, Alekhine writes that, in the process of chess struggle, a hidden drama is played out in the mind of a chess master, a drama "which is characterized by the continual collision between creative ideas, tending to infinity, and the striving of the opponent to refute it."

**1928, February 29**. In connection with Capablanca's letter to FIDE President A. Rueb, proposing to change the regulations for world championship matches by reducing the number of the games to sixteen, Alekhine sends his reply to the former champion, in which he emphasizes his principled stand: to play the return match on the same conditions as their previous match.

**1928, August**. He participates in the work of the 5th FIDE Congress in The Hague.

**1928, September**. He accepts Efim's Bogoljubow's challenge to a world championship match.

**1928, October 8**. Capablanca challenges Alekhine to the return match to be played according to the London Agreement Regulations. On October 12, Alekhine replies that he has already accepted Bogoljubow's challenge.

**1929, Spring**. Alekhine tours the United States.

**1929, July 30-August 27**. He attends the major international tournament in Carlsbad as a *New York Times* correspondent, publishing articles of a problematic character on the ways of development of contemporary chess art, on the creativity of the prize winners of the tournament (Nimzowitsch, Capablanca, Spielmann, and Rubinstein), summing up the results of the tournament.

**1929, September 6-November 12**. In several German and Dutch cities, the Alekhine -Bogoljubow world championship match is held, and it is decided before the 30-game limit is reached. Already after twenty-five games, the score becomes 15½-9½ in favor of Alekhine (+11 -5 =9).

**1929, November 28**. In reply to the challenge sent by Capablanca from Barcelona on October 1, Alekhine agrees to play a return match at the end of 1930.

**1930, January 16- February 5**. Alekhine wins the major international tournament in San Remo (Italy) impressively, scoring 14 points out of a possible 15, conceding only two draws and leaving second-prize winner Nimzowitsch 3½ points behind.

**1930, July 13-27**, Hamburg. He, for the first time, participates in a world chess Olympiad – "The Tournament of Nations." Leading the French team, Alekhine wins all nine games he plays.

**1931, July 11-26**. Prague. Playing on first board for France in the fourth world chess Olympiad, he has the best result (+10 -2 =7).

**1931, August 23-September 28**. At the major international tournament in Bled (Yugoslavia), he sets a record, scoring 20½ points out of 26, a full 5½ points ahead of second-prize winner Bogoljubow.

**1932, January**. He wins the international tournament in London (+7 -0 =4), a point ahead of Salo Flohr.

**1932, June 16-30**. He takes first prize in the open Swiss championship (+11 -2 =3), a point ahead of Flohr and Euwe, who shared 2nd-3rd places.

**1932, August 3**. His "circumnavigation tours" begin, which will last until May 11, 1933.

**1932, August-December**. He tours the United States, Mexico, and Cuba. During the Pasadena tournament, he meets Grace Wishart, widow of British captain Archibald Freeman; two years later she becomes Alekhine's wife.

**1932, November-May**. He visits Hawaii, Japan, Shanghai, Hong Kong, the Philippines, Singapore, Sumatra, Java, New Zealand, Ceylon, Alexandria, Jerusalem, and Genoa, and then he returns home.

During these travels, Alekhine played 1,320 games in simultaneous exhibitions, winning 1,161 and losing 65. The "Chess Magellan" also took interest in local customs and national games of the various countries and peoples. Thus, in Japan, he becomes acquainted with Japanese chess: "I got down to studying it, which I continued all the time while traveling, also adding to it Chinese chess. I sought out a whole library devoted to these varieties of chess."

**1933, June 12-23**. He participates in the 5th world chess Olympiad in Folkstone (England). He has the best result on first board, 9½ points out of 12.

**1933, July 25**. A record blindfold exhibition on thirty-two boards (+19 -4 =9) at the World Exhibition "An Age of Progress" in Chicago.

**1934, March 26**. His wedding to Grace Wishart (b. New Jersey, October 26, 1876) is held on the French Riviera.

**1934, April 1-June 14**. Alekhine wins the second world championship match with Bogoljubow, again before the game limit, after game 26 (+8 -3 =15). The match was held in twelve German cities, starting in Baden-Baden and finishing in Berlin.

**1934, July 14-28**. He wins the international tournament in Zürich (Switzerland), scoring 13 points out of 15 (+12 -1 =2), a full point ahead of Flohr and Euwe, who shared 2nd-3rd places. For the first time, Alekhine wins a game against Emanuel Lasker. At the closing ceremony he says that "Lasker was [his] teacher and without him [he] would not be able to become what [he is] now." Soon after, Euwe sends Alekhine a letter in which he challenges him to a world championship match of thirty games. Alekhine agrees.

**1935, May**. The agreement concerning the Alekhine-Euwe match is signed. One of the clauses is that in case the champion loses the match, he is entitled to a return match within the next two years.

**1935, October 3**. At the Carlton Hotel in Amsterdam, the world chess championship match between Alekhine and Euwe begins. It is to be played in thirteen cities of The Netherlands.

**1935, December 15**. After the thirtieth game, played in "Belle Vue," the largest hall in Amsterdam, the match ends with a victory for Euwe, 15½-14½ (+9 -8 =13). Alekhine extends his hand to him and exclaims (in French): "Long live world chess champion Max Euwe! Long live Chess Holland!" Leaving The Netherlands, Alekhine said that "[n]othing terrible has happened. Let us assume that I have lent the title for... two years!"

**1936**. Of the nine major competitions held in Europe at the time, Alekhine participates in six, viewing them as preparation for the return match. Among them are the tournaments at Bad Nauheim (May, 1st-2nd with Paul Keres), Dresden

(June, 1st), Podebrady (October, 3rd behind Euwe and Fine), Hastings (December-January 1937, 1st).

**1936.** Conversing with the president of the world correspondence chess federation K. Abonyi, Alekhine puts forth the idea of also holding world correspondence championships. According to him, correspondence chess and over-the-board chess "complement one another."

**1936, August 10-28.** Nottingham (England). In this major event, where the world champion and three former world champions (including himself), as well as four young challengers participated, Alekhine scores 9 points out of 14, i.e., a point behind the winners of the tournament, Mikhail Botvinnik and José Raúl Capablanca, and only takes 6th place.

**1936.** He works on the book on the Nottingham Tournament, and intensively prepares for the return match with Euwe.

**1937, October 5-December 7.** In Holland, the world championship return match is held. It ends after the 25th game, 15½-9½ in favor of Alekhine. For the first time, a former champion wins a return match and regains the world title. In his article "Obituary," Euwe admits that "Alekhine's play was amazing, and I am definitely not ashamed to be defeated by such a rival."

**1938, first half.** He wins the international tournaments in Montevideo and in two English cities, Margate and Plymouth.

**1938, May.** Prague. An agreement is signed for the world championship match with grandmaster Salo Flohr. The match is to be held in Czechoslovakia in the autumn of 1939 on the same terms as the Alekhine-Euwe match was held.

**1938, November 2-27.** He participates in the double round-robin AVRO tournament of the eight strongest players in the world, which is held in different Dutch cities. He shares 4th-6th places with Euwe and Reshevsky, behind Fine and Keres (1st-2nd) and Botvinnik (3rd). The negotiations on his match for the world title with Mikhail Botvinnik begins.

**1939.** Alekhine's book *My Best Games, 1924-1937* is published in London.

**1939, August.** Alekhine's elder brother Alexei Alexandrovich (born in 1888) dies in Kharkov (Ukraine).

**1939, August 24-September 19.** Buenos Aires. He participates in the 8th world chess Olympiad, playing on first board for France.

**1939, Autumn**. He tours South America, winning, in particular, tournaments in Montevideo and Caracas. The negotiations with Capablanca about a return match come to nothing.

**1940, January**. He returns to Europe. He is given a gala reception in Portugal. He comes to Paris and joins the French Army as an interpreter.

**1940, June**. After the defeat of the French Army, he stays in Europe, playing in international tournaments and working as a journalist.

**1941, March 18-23**. His articles "Jewish and Aryan Chess" are published in *Pariser Zeitung*. Soon after that, they are reprinted in The Netherlands (*Deutsche Zeitung*, March-April) and in Germany (*Deutsche Schachzeitung*, April-June).

**1941, April**. He arrives in Lisbon. Portuguese champion Francesco Lupi notices a great change in his outward appearance compared to what it was in January 1940, saying that "[h]e looked much older and there had not been either the former majestic bearing or the piercing sight." The same year (August, October) and the next, Alekhine's articles from *Pariser Zeitung* are reprinted in the British magazine *Chess* with the following comment: "If these articles were indeed written by Dr. Alekhine, we have no doubt that he had found himself under cruel circumstances. They are omens of a sad time."

**1941, Summer**. He plays in the European Championship tournaments in Munich (a tie for 2nd-3rd places with Lundin, behind Stoltz) and in Krakow (tied for 1st-2nd with Schmidt).

**1941, September**. He stays in Madrid and Lisbon. In an interview given to correspondents of the Madrid newspapers *Informaciones* and *El Alcazar*, he confirms his authorship of the articles published in *Parisier Zeitung*.

**1941, December**. He wins a tournament in Madrid.

**1942**. He wins tournaments in Salzburg (Austria), Munich, Warsaw/Krakow and Prague.

**1942, December 24**. He is hospitalized in Prague for scarlet fever.

**1943, March-April**. He participates in tournaments in Salzburg (tied for 1st-2nd with Keres) and Prague (1st-2nd places with Junge).

**1943, October**. At the invitation of the Spanish Chess Federation, he moves to Spain. The Gestapo grants him a visa, but refuses his wife permission to accompany him. Alekhine starts working on a book about Capablanca.

**1944**. He takes first prize in a tournament at Gijon.

**1945**. He wins a number of Spanish tournaments in Madrid, Sabadell, and Melilla. He gives chess lessons to fourteen-year-old Arturo Pomar, who would later become an international grandmaster.

**1945, November**. The last tournament in which he participated is held at Caceres. He takes second prize, behind Lupi. Since Fine and some other players refuse to play Alekhine, the invitations to participate in the international tournaments in London and Hastings are revoked.

**1946, January**. Alekhine's long letter is published in *British Chess Magazine*. Concerning the 1941 articles, he states that "[t]he chimeras published in *Parisier Zeitung* were false." He sends copies of the letter to the American and British chess federations.

**1946, January**. In Estoril (Portugal) he plays a small friendly match with Lupi, winning it by the score 2½-1½.

**1946, Early March**. He receives a telegram from the Soviet champion, Mikhail Botvinnik, challenging him to a world championship match. The British Chess Federation agrees to hold the match under its auspices in England.

**1946, March 9**. At the British Embassy in Lisbon, Alekhine plays his last game ever against the chess composer and foreign office official F. Anderson. He wins it with Black.

**1946, March 24**. At the Park Hotel of Estoril, near Lisbon, Alekhine dies at the age of 53. It is the first time a world champion has died while holding the title. He is buried in Estoril.

**1956, March 25**. His body is reinterred in Montparnasse cemetery (Paris), and the inscription on his tombstone reads, "To the Chess Genius of Russia and France."

# Alexander Alekhine: Fourth World Chess Champion

## Summary of Career Results

Given below are all of Alekhine's serious over-the-board tournaments and matches for which at least his place and score are known, derived from Skinner and Verhoeven's *Alexander Alekhine's Chess Games, 1902-1946*. Not included are several early events in Russia Alekhine is known to have taken part in, but for which no records of scores or standings have survived, and perhaps some minor events from late in his career.

Note that although originally scheduled for 17 rounds, Mannheim 1914 was truncated by the outbreak of World War I. Results given here are from the 11 rounds actually played. The last few tournaments, held in Spain, were "international" mainly by virtue of Alekhine's participation, otherwise being composed almost entirely of players of only local renown. Finally, totals include estimated scores, with fewest possible draws, for the three tournaments where W-L-D numbers are not known.

### Alekhine's Tournament Record

| Date | Venue and Event | Place | # gms | W-L-D | Score |
|------|-----------------|-------|-------|-------|-------|
| 1907-8 | Moscow Chess Club Autumn Tournament | =11-13 | 14 | +4 -9 =1 | 4½-9½ |
| 1908 | Düsseldorf, 6th German Federation Congress | =4-5 | 13 | +8 -3 =2 | 9-4 |
| 1908-9 | Moscow Chess Club Autumn Tournament | 1st | 9 | +5 -1 =3 | 6½-2½ |
| 1909 | St. Petersburg All-Russian Amateur Tournament | 1st | 16 | +12 -2 =2 | 13-3 |
| 1909 | Moscow Chess Club Spring Tournament | 5th | 10 | +6 -3 =1 | 6½-3½ |
| 1909-10 | Moscow Chess Club Autumn Tournament | 1st | 7 | +6 -0 =1 | 6½-½ |
| 1909-10 | Moscow Chess Club Winter Tournament | 1st | 8 | +7 -1 =0 | 7-1 |
| 1910 | Hamburg, 7th German Federation Congress | =7-8 | 16 | +5 -4 =7 | 8½-7½ |
| 1910-11 | Moscow Chess Club 2nd Handicap Tournament | =2-4 | 14 | unknown | 10-4 |
| 1911 | Moscow Chess Club 3rd Handicap Tournament | 1st | 11 | unknown | 9½-1½ |
| 1911 | Carlsbad International Tournament | =8-11 | 25 | +11 -9 =5 | 13½-11½ |
| 1912 | St. Petersburg Chess Club Winter Tournament | =1-2 | 9 | unknown | 8-1 |
| 1912 | St. Petersburg First Category Tournament | 1st | 9 | +6 -1 =2 | 7-2 |
| 1912 | Stockholm Nordic Masters Congress | 1st | 10 | +8 -1 =1 | 8½-1½ |
| 1912 | Vilna All-Russian Masters Tournament | =6-7 | 18 | +7 -8 =3 | 8½-9½ |
| 1913 | St. Petersburg Masters Quadrangular | =1-2 | 3 | +2 -1 =0 | 2-1 |
| 1913 | Scheveningen International Tournament | 1st | 13 | +11 -1 =1 | 11½-1½ |
| 1914 | St. Petersburg All-Russian Masters Tournament | =1-2 | 17 | +13 -3 =1 | 13½-3½ |
| 1914 | St. Petersburg International Tournament | 3rd | 18 | +6 -4 =8 | 10-8 |
| 1914 | Paris Café Continental International Tournament | =1-2 | 3 | +2 -0 =1 | 2½-½ |
| 1914 | Mannheim International Tournament | 1st | 11 | +9 -1 =1 | 9½-1½* |
| 1915 | Moscow Chess Club | 1st | 10 | +9 -0 =1 | 9½-½ |
| 1918 | Moscow Triangular | 1st | 6 | +3 -0 =3 | 4½-1½ |
| 1919-20 | Moscow City Championship | 1st | 11 | +11 -0 =0 | 11-0 |
| 1920 | Moscow All-Russian Olympiad (1st Soviet Ch) | 1st | 15 | +9 -0 =6 | 12-3 |
| 1921 | Triberg International Tournament | 1st | 8 | +6 -0 =2 | 7-1 |
| 1921 | Budapest International Tournament | 1st | 11 | +6 -0 =5 | 8½-2½ |
| 1921 | The Hague International Tournament | 1st | 9 | +7 -0 =2 | 8-1 |
| 1922 | Pistyan International Tournament | =2-3 | 18 | +12 -1 =5 | 14½-3½ |
| 1922 | London International Tournament | 2nd | 15 | +8 -0 =7 | 11½-3½ |
| 1922 | Hastings International Tournament | 1st | 10 | +6 -1 =3 | 7½-2½ |
| 1922 | Vienna International Tournament | =4-6 | 14 | +7 -3 =4 | 9-5 |
| 1923 | Margate International Tournament | =2-5 | 7 | +3 -1 =3 | 4½-2½ |
| 1923 | Carlsbad International Tournament | =1-3 | 17 | +9 -3 =5 | 11½-5½ |
| 1923 | Portsmouth BCF Congress Major Open | 1st | 11 | +10 -0 =1 | 10½-½ |
| 1924 | New York International Tournament | 3rd | 20 | +6 -2 =12 | 12-8 |
| 1925 | Paris Palais Royal Five Masters Tournament | 1st | 8 | +5 -0 =3 | 6½-1½ |
| 1925 | Bern Four Masters Tournament | 1st | 6 | +3 -1 =2 | 4-2 |
| 1925 | Baden-Baden International Tournament | 1st | 20 | +12 -0 =8 | 16-4 |
| 1925-6 | Hastings International Tournament | =1-2 | 9 | +8 -0 =1 | 8½-½ |
| 1926 | Semmering International Tournament | 2nd | 17 | +11 -3 =3 | 12½-4½ |
| 1926 | Dresden International Tournament | 2nd | 9 | +5 -0 =4 | 7-2 |
| 1926 | Scarborough Masters Tournament, Section A | 1st | 6 | +5 -0 =1 | 5½-½ |
| | Playoff with Section B winner, Colle | | 2 | +2 -0 =0 | 2-0 |
| 1926 | Birmingham Club Tournament | 1st | 5 | +5 -0 =0 | 5-0 |
| 1926 | Buenos Aires Club Argentino | 1st | 10 | +10 -0 =0 | 10-0 |
| 1927 | New York International Tournament | 2nd | 20 | +5 -2 =13 | 11½-8½ |

| 1927 | Kecskemet International Tournament | 1st | 16 | +8 -0 =8 | 12-4 |
|------|-----------------------------------|-----|----|---------|------|
| 1929 | Bradley Beach International Tournament | 1st | 9 | +8 -0 =1 | 8½-½ |
| 1930 | San Remo International Tournament | 1st | 15 | +13 -0 =2 | 14-1 |
| 1930 | Hamburg, 3rd FIDE Olympiad (board 1, France) | n/a | 9 | +9 -0 =0 | 9-0 |
| 1931 | Prague, 4th FIDE Olympiad (board 1, France) | n/a | 18 | +10 -1 =7 | 13½-3½ |
| 1931 | Bled International Tournament | 1st | 26 | +15 -0 =11 | 20½-5½ |
| 1932 | London International Tournament | 1st | 11 | +7 -0 =4 | 9-2 |
| 1932 | Bern Training Tournament | =1-3 | 3 | +2 -1 =0 | 2-1 |
| 1932 | Bern International Tournament | 1st | 15 | +11 -1 =3 | 12½-2½ |
| 1932 | Pasadena International Tournament | 1st | 11 | +7 -1 =3 | 8½-2½ |
| 1932 | Mexico City International Tournament | =1-2 | 9 | +8 -0 =1 | 8½-½ |
| 1933 | Folkestone, 5th FIDE Olympiad (board 1, France) | n/a | 12 | +8 -1 =3 | 9½-2½ |
| 1933 | Paris International Tournament | 1st | 9 | +7 -0 =2 | 8-1 |
| 1933-4 | Hastings International Tournament | =2-3 | 9 | +4 -0 =5 | 6½-2½ |
| 1934 | Rotterdam Chess Club | 1st | 3 | +3 -0 =0 | 3-0 |
| 1934 | Zurich International Tournament | 1st | 15 | +12 -1 =2 | 13-2 |
| 1935 | Örebro International Tournament | 1st | 9 | +8 -0 =1 | 8½-½ |
| 1935 | Warsaw, 6th FIDE Olympiad (board 1, France) | n/a | 17 | +7 -0 =10 | 12-5 |
| 1936 | Bad Nauheim Olympiad Training Tournament | =1-2 | 9 | +4 -0 =5 | 6½-2½ |
| 1936 | Dresden Olympiad Training Tournament | 1st | 9 | +5 -1 =3 | 6½-2½ |
| 1936 | Podebrady International Tournament | 2nd | 17 | +8 -0 =9 | 12½-4½ |
| 1936 | Nottingham International Tournament | 6th | 14 | +6 -2 =6 | 9-5 |
| 1936 | Amsterdam Chess Club Jubilee, group 1 | =1-2 | 3 | +2 -0 =1 | 2½-½ |
| 1936 | Amsterdam International Tournament | 3rd | 7 | +3 -1 =3 | 4½-2½ |
| 1936-7 | Hastings International Tournament | 1st | 9 | +7 -0 =2 | 8-1 |
| 1937 | Nice Club Tournament | 1st | 3 | +2 -0 =1 | 2½-½ |
| 1937 | Margate International Tournament | 3rd | 9 | +6 -3 =0 | 6-3 |
| 1937 | Kemeri International Tournament | =4-5 | 17 | +7 -1 =9 | 11½-5½ |
| 1937 | Bad Nauheim Four Masters Tournament | =2-3 | 6 | +3 -2 =1 | 3½-2½ |
| 1938 | Montevideo International Tournament | 1st | 15 | +11 -0 =4 | 13-2 |
| 1938 | Margate International Tournament | 1st | 9 | +6 -1 =2 | 6-3 |
| 1938 | Plymouth Chess Club Jubilee, Premier Tournament | =1-2 | 7 | +5 -0 =2 | 6-1 |
| 1938 | Holland, AVRO International Tournament | =4-6 | 14 | +3 -3 =8 | 7-7 |
| 1939 | Caracas Olympiad Training Tournament | 1st | 10 | +10 -0 =0 | 10-0 |
| 1939 | Buenos Aires, 8th FIDE Olympiad (board 1, France) | n/a | 16 | +9 -0 =7 | 12½-3½ |
| 1939 | Montevideo, Millington Drake Tournament | 1st | 7 | +7 -0 =0 | 7-0 |
| 1941 | Munich, 2nd Europa Tournament | =2-3 | 15 | +8 -2 =5 | 10½-4½ |
| 1941 | Cracow/Warsaw, 2nd General Govt. Championship | =1-2 | 11 | +6 -0 =5 | 8½-2½ |
| 1941 | Madrid Club Tournament | 1st | 5 | +5 -0 =0 | 5-0 |
| 1942 | Salzburg International Tournament | 1st | 10 | +7 -2 =1 | 7½-2½ |
| 1942 | Munich, Europaschachbund Championship | 1st | 11 | +7 -1 =3 | 8½-2½ |
| 1942 | Warsaw/Lublin/Cracow, 3rd General Govt. Ch. | 1st | 10 | +6 -1 =3 | 7½-2½ |
| 1942 | Prague International Tournament | =1-2 | 11 | +6 -0 =5 | 8½-2½ |
| 1943 | Prague International Tournament | 1st | 19 | +15 -0 =4 | 17-2 |
| 1943 | Salzburg International Tournament | =1-2 | 10 | +5 -0 =5 | 7½-2½ |
| 1944 | Gijón International Tournament* | 1st | 8 | +7 -0 =1 | 7½-½ |
| 1945 | Madrid Training Tournament | 1st | 9 | +8 -0 =1 | 8½-½ |
| 1945 | Gijón International Tournament | =2-3 | 9 | +6 -2 =1 | 6½-2½ |
| 1945 | Sabadell International Tournament | 1st | 9 | +6 -0 =3 | 7½-1½ |
| 1945 | Almería International Tournament | =1-2 | 8 | +4 -1 =3 | 5½-2½ |
| 1945 | Melilla International Tournament | 1st | 7 | +6 -0 =1 | 6½-½ |
| 1945 | Cáceres Consultation Tournament | 2nd | 5 | +3 -1 =1 | 3½-1½ |

Tournament Totals: 1102 games, +694 -105 =303, 845½-256½, 76.72%

## Matches

| Date | Venue | Opponent | # gms | W-L-D Score |
|------|-------|----------|-------|-------------|
| 1908 | Düsseldorf | C. von Bardeleben | 5 | +4 -0 =1 4½-½ |
| 1908 | Munich | H. Fahrni | 3 | +1 -1 =1 1½-1½ |
| 1908 | Moscow | B. Blumenfeld | 5 | +4 -0 =1 4½-½ |
| 1908 | Moscow | V. Nenarokov | 3 | +0 -3 =0 0-3 |
| 1913 | St. Petersburg | S. Levitsky | 10 | +7 -3 =0 7-3 |
| 1913 | Paris/London | Edward Lasker | 3 | +3 -0 =0 3-0 |
| 1914 | St. Petersburg | A. Nimzovitch | 2 | +1 -1 =0 1-1 |
| 1916 | Kiev | A. Evenssohn | 3 | +2 -1 =0 2-1 |
| 1921 | Moscow | N. Grigoriev | 7 | +2 -0 =5 4½-2½ |
| 1921 | Berlin | R. Teichmann | 6 | +2 -2 =2 3-3 |
| 1921 | Berlin | F. Sämisch | 2 | +2 -0 =0 2-0 |
| 1921 | Triberg | E. Bogoljubow | 4 | +1 -1 =2 2-2 |
| 1922 | Paris | O. Bernstein | 2 | +1 -0 =1 1½-½ |
| 1922 | Paris | A. Aurbach | 2 | +1 -0 =1 1½-½ |
| 1926-7 | Holland | M. Euwe (training match) | 10 | +3 -2 =5 5½-4½ |
| 1927 | Buenos Aires | J.R. Capablanca (world championship) | 34 | +6 -3 =25 18½-15½ |
| 1929 | Germany/Holland | E. Bogoljubow (world championship) | 25 | +11 -5 =9 15½-9½ |
| 1933 | Paris | O. Bernstein | 4 | +1 -1 =2 2-2 |
| 1934 | Germany | E. Bogoljubow (world championship) | 26 | +8 -3 =15 15½-10½ |
| 1935 | Holland | M. Euwe (world championship) | 30 | +8 -9 =13 14½-15½ |
| 1937 | Holland | M. Euwe (world championship) | 25 | +10 -4 =11 15½-9½ |
| 1937 | Holland | M. Euwe (exhibition match) | 5 | +1 -2 =2 2-3 |
| 1944 | Zaragoza | R. Rey Ardid | 4 | +1 -0 =3 2½-1½ |
| 1946 | Estoril | F. Lupi | 4 | +2 -1 =1 2½-1½ |

Match Totals: 224 games, +82 -42 =100, 132-92, 58.93%

# Opening Index

## Player Index

Numbers Refer to Game Numbers. Bold indicates the player had White.
(f) = Game fragment

**Russell Enterprises, Inc.** is one of the world's major publishers of fine chess books. For complete descriptions of all our books, we invite you to visit our website:

www.Russell-Enterprises.com

The following Russell Enterprises titles are also available as eBooks (Kindle, iPad, etc.):

*212 Surprising Checkmates* by Bruce Alberston & Fred Wilson
*Alexander Alekhine: Fourth World Chess Champion* by Isaak & Vladimir Linder
*Art of Bisguier* by Arthur Bisguier & Newton Berry
*Back to Basics: Fundamentals* by Branislav Francuski
*Back to Basics: Openings* by Carsten Hansen
*Back to Basics: Strategy* by Valeri Beim
*Back to Basics: Tactics* by Dan Heisman
*Basic Chess Tactics for Younger Chessplayers* by Bruce Alberston
*Bobby Fischer: The Career and Complete Games of the American World Chess Champion* by Karsten Müller
*Bullet Chess* by Hikaru Nakamura & Bruce Harper
*Chess Analytics: Training with a Grandmaster* by Efstratios Grivas
*ChessCafe Puzzle Book 1* by Karsten Müller
*ChessCafe Puzzle Book 2* by Karsten Müller
*ChessCafe Puzzle Book 3* by Karsten Müller & Merijn van Delft
*ChessCafe Puzzle Book Sampler* by Karsten Müller (free!)
*Chess Puzzle Book 4* by Karsten Müller & Alex Markgraf
*Chess Juggler* by Dr. James Magner
*Chess Mazes 1* by Bruce Alberston
*Chess Mazes 2* by Bruce Alberston
*Chess Movies 1* by Bruce Pandolfini
*Chess Movies 2* by Bruce Pandolfini
*Chess Words of Wisdom* by Mike Henebry
*Common Sense in Chess* by Emanuel Lasker
*Dvoretsky's Endgame Manual* by Mark Dvoretsky
*Elements of Positional Evaluation: How the Pieces Get Their Power* by Dan Heisman
*Emanuel Lasker: Second World Chess Champion* by Isaak & Vladimir Linder
*Endgame Workshop* by Bruce Pandolfini
*A History of Chess: From Chaturanga to the Present Day* by Yuri Averbakh
*How to Beat Your Kids at Chess* by David MacEnulty
*How to Think in Chess* by Jan Przwoznik & Marek Soszynski
*José Raúl Capablanca: Third World Chess Champion* by Isaak & Vladimir Linder

*The KGB Plays Chess* by Gulko, Felshtinsky, Popov & Kortschnoi
*Kramnik-Kasparov 2000* by Karsten Müller
*Lasker's Manual of Chess* by Emanuel Lasker
*Legend on the Road* by John Donaldson
*Let's Play Chess* by Bruce Pandolfini
*The Life & Games of Carlos Torre* by Gabriel Velasco
*London 1922* by Geza Maróczy
*Looking for Trouble* by Dan Heisman
*Masters of the Chessboard* by Richard Réti
*Max Euwe: Fifth World Chess Champion* by Isaak & Vladimir Linder
*Modern Ideas in Chess* by Richard Réti
*Modern Morra Gambit* (2nd. ed.) by Hannes Langrock
*New York 1924* by Alexander Alekhine
*New York 1927* by Alexander Alekhine
*Nottingham 1936* by Alexander Alekhine
*Paul Morphy: A Modern Perspective* by Valeri Beim
*A Practical Guide to Rook Endgames* by Nikolay Minev
*Profession: Chessplayer – Grandmaster at Work* by Vladimir Tukmakov
*The Rules of Chess* by Bruce Pandolfini (free!)
*St. Petersburg 1909* by Emanuel Lasker
*Strategic Opening Repertoire* by John Donaldson & Carsten Hansen
*Studies for Practical Players* by Mark Dvoretsky & Oleg Pervakov
*Tal-Botvinnik 1960* by Mikhail Tal
*Topalov-Kramnik 2006* by Veselin Topalov with Zhivko Ginchev
*Tragicomedy in the Endgame* by Mark Dvoretsky
*Vienna 1922* by Larry Evans
*Zürich 1953* by Miguel Najdorf